RADIO AND TELEVISION BROADCASTING
ON THE EUROPEAN CONTINENT

◄◄ RADIO AND TELEVISION BROADCASTING on the EUROPEAN CONTINENT

by Burton Paulu

97401

UNIVERSITY OF MINNESOTA PRESS *Minneapolis*

Library of Congress Catalog Card Number: 67-27097

Second printing 1968

PUBLISHED IN GREAT BRITAIN, INDIA, AND PAKISTAN BY THE OXFORD
UNIVERSITY PRESS, LONDON, BOMBAY, AND KARACHI, AND IN CANADA
BY THE COPP CLARK PUBLISHING CO. LIMITED, TORONTO

Preface and Acknowledgments

This book is a description and appraisal of radio and television broadcasting on the European continent. To some extent, therefore, it follows from my two previous volumes on British broadcasting, although it deals almost entirely with the continental countries, referring to the United Kingdom only for illustrations.

In a sense this research began in 1944–45, when I went to the United Kingdom and Luxembourg for the United States Office of War Information, and continued when Fulbright and Ford grants made possible studies of British broadcasting in 1953–54 and 1958–59. But the basic work for this volume was done in Geneva in 1964–65, when on sabbatical leave from the University of Minnesota, assisted by another grant from the Ford Foundation. Two short trips, one to Eastern Europe in the summer of 1965 and the other to eight countries during the fall of 1966, were supported by the small grants program of the Office of International Programs of the University of Minnesota, and the actual writing was aided by grants from the Graduate School of the University.

In Geneva I benefited tremendously from the help of the European Broadcasting Union, which literally gave me the key to its offices plus a desk in its library, and facilitated attendance at a number of its meetings. A list of all the EBU employees who helped would be almost equivalent to the entire staff roster, but special mention should be made of the following: Henrik Hahr, Director of the Administrative Office; Dr. George Straschnov, Director of Legal Affairs; Anthony Dean, Head of Radio, who was my daily consultant and expediter; M. Vilcek, Head of Television; Mrs. George Straschnov and James Magee, Editor and Assistant Editor, respectively, of the *EBU Review*; and J. Treeby Dickinson, Chief Engineer of the Technical Center in Brussels. In Geneva, Colin Mackenzie, Public Relations Officer of the International Telecommunication Union, also played host and arranged access to the ITU's excellent library.

The research for this book involved visits to the broadcasting organizations of twenty European countries, after which I sent manuscript to people in most of those countries for critical reactions. A partial list of those who served as hosts and advisers includes the following, arranged alphabetically by country of residence. Needless to say, none of them bears any responsibility whatsoever for what is said here. (Positions held are in the broadcasting systems of the countries concerned, unless otherwise indicated.)

Andorra
Claude Delépine, ASSOCIATE DIRECTOR, RADIO DES VALLEES.

Austria
Gerhard Freund, DIRECTOR OF TELEVISION. Erika Prager, EUROVISION COORDINATOR.

Belgium
L. P. Kammans, PROGRAM DIRECTOR, FRENCH TELEVISION PROGRAMS. L. Wallenborn, DIRECTOR FOREIGN RELATIONS. Robert Wangermée, DIRECTOR GENERAL FRENCH PROGRAMS.

Czechoslovakia
Jaromir Hrebík, SECRETARY GENERAL OIRT. Lubomir Kubiček, DIRECTOR INTERNATIONAL RELATIONS, CZECHOSLOVAK TELEVISION. Karol Reif, HEAD FOREIGN RELATIONS, CZECHOSLOVAK RADIO. Ales Suchy, HEAD INTERVISION, PROGRAM CENTER OIRT. Sona Vávrová, INTERNATIONAL RELATIONS, CZECHOSLOVAK TELEVISION.

France
Henri Dieuzeide, DIRECTOR SCHOOL PROGRAMS, NATIONAL PEDAGOGICAL INSTITUTE. Jacques-Bernard Dupont, DIRECTOR GENERAL. J. R. Parturier, SALES MANAGER, EUROPE 1 AND TELE-MONTE-CARLO. Eugène Pons, HEAD OF FINANCE DEPARTMENT. Georges Riou, DIRECTOR GENERAL ADMINISTRATION.

Germany (German Democratic Republic)
Ernst Zaph, INTERNATIONAL RELATIONS.

Germany (German Federal Republic)
Horst Bode, ARD TAGESSCHAU. Richard Dill, ARD TELEVISION COORDINATION, BAYERISCHER RUNDFUNK. Bernd C. Hesslein, NORDDEUTSCHER RUNDFUNK. Claus Janus, NORDDEUTSCHES WERBEFERNSEHEN. Haynes R. Ma-

honey, DEPUTY DIRECTOR RIAS. Helmuth Petrick, FOREIGN RELATIONS, SENDER FREIES BERLIN. Hans-Joachim Reiche, DIRECTOR TAGESSCHAU. Franz Reinholz, NORDDEUTSCHER RUNDFUNK. Gerhard Schulz, FINANCE DIRECTOR, NORDDEUTSCHER RUNDFUNK. Egon Wagner, LEGAL ADVISOR, SUD-WESTFUNK. Henning Wicht, RADIO PROGRAM DIRECTOR, HESSISCHER RUND-FUNK.

Italy

Fabio Borrelli, FOREIGN RELATIONS. Paolo Grilli, DIRECTOR SACIS. Italo Neri, DIRECTOR TELESCUOLA. Maurizio Pardi, FOREIGN RELATIONS RADIO. Gian Franco Zaffrani, DIRECTOR FOREIGN RELATIONS.

Luxembourg

Metty Felten, DIRECTOR GENERAL. Loll Maach, CHIEF ENGINEER.

The Netherlands

J. B. Broeksz, NEDERLANDSCHE RADIO-UNIE. P. J. Koop, PRESS OFFICER.

Rumania

Mrs. Clarisse Marcovic, FOREIGN RELATIONS. D. Natu, HEAD FOREIGN RE-LATIONS. Victor Popa, DIRECTOR CHILDREN'S PROGRAMS.

Soviet Union

John A. Armitage, COUNSELOR FOR CULTURAL AFFAIRS, AMERICAN EM-BASSY. M. Monusov, HEAD INTERNATIONAL RELATIONS DEPARTMENT, STATE COMMITTEE FOR BROADCASTING AND TELEVISION. Ernest G. Wiener, COUN-SELOR FOR CULTURAL AFFAIRS, AMERICAN EMBASSY.

Spain

Joaquin de Aguilera, TELEVISION ESPANOLA. Enrique Pascual Souto, CHIEF OF PUBLIC RELATIONS.

Sweden

Olof Rydbeck, DIRECTOR GENERAL. Nils-Olof Franzén, DIRECTOR OF SOUND BROADCASTING.

Switzerland

Jacques Bourquin, PRESIDENT INTERNATIONAL ASSOCIATION, MASS COM-MUNICATION RESEARCH. M. T. Drack, HEAD PRESS AND DOCUMENTATION.

Vatican City

Father Lynch, VATICAN RADIO.

Yugoslavia

Mrs. Olivera Voyvodic, DIRECTOR FOREIGN RELATIONS. Ivko Pustisek, GEN-ERAL SECRETARY.

My dependable and hard-working research and typing team included graduate assistants Vida Ditter and Susan Hood, and secretary La-Vonne Thomsen.

Finally, there were those at home who had to sacrifice some social life and forgo my limited talents as home handyman while the manuscript was being completed: wife, Frances; children, Sarah, Nancy, and Thomas; Bedlington, Lancelot.

BURTON PAULU, *Director*
Department of Radio and Television

University of Minnesota
October 1967

Table of Contents

List of Tables

RADIO AND TELEVISION BROADCASTING
ON THE EUROPEAN CONTINENT

CHAPTER I

Introduction

Every historian of the twentieth century must recognize the important role of radio and television. At home and abroad, broadcasting has proved to be a dramatic means both to unite and to divide peoples and countries.*

Radio developed in the industrially advanced countries during the early 1920's when technological developments, stimulated by World War I, made sound broadcasting possible. By the middle 1930's radio broadcasting was well established. In the United States, programs from the predominant privately owned commercial stations were supplemented by service from some noncommercial educational stations. In Europe, the usual pattern was a state-chartered corporation supported mainly by license fees. Programs everywhere ran the gamut from information and education to light entertainment. The European networks, however, because of their organization and economic structure, emphasized serious materials more than the networks in the United States, where there was an increasing trend toward programs for entertainment and escape.

The most dramatic uses of radio were related to the political catastrophes of the 1930's. Europe's dictators—Mussolini, Hitler, and Stalin, particularly—controlled and censored broadcasting to organize support for their policies. Hitler successfully used radio to involve his entire nation in the great mass meetings of the Nazi party. But the democratic countries, too, produced master broadcasters. Who can forget the tremendous influence achieved by Winston Churchill? Or the effectiveness of Franklin Delano Roosevelt in his fireside chats?

* As used here "broadcasting" includes the two media called "radio" and "television" in the United States, and "sound radio" and "television" in Europe. Although the term "broadcasting" is sometimes limited to sound radio it is used here in its more inclusive sense.

International broadcasting grew as the totalitarian countries began to propagandize their neighbors—frequently with the ultimate objective of conquering them—and the democratic countries began international services in response to the dictators' broadcasts. During World War II, the propaganda services of the German Reich and the British Broadcasting Corporation competed for acceptance in Europe and throughout the world. The BBC probably gained more prestige from its victory in this contest than has any other broadcasting organization from any single project in which it ever engaged.

Just as World War I stimulated the development of radio, so the electronic advances of World War II contributed to the emergence of television which soon became the dominant electronic medium. The transition from radio to television was difficult enough in the United States, because of the problems of setting technical standards and allocating stations, but it was even harder in Europe where extensive war damage retarded development until the basic necessities of life had been provided.

Most European countries now have television and offer two and in some cases three services. However, with this growth came major problems which were the direct result of television's power. Because of its political significance, the parties in most democratic countries have agreed to share television equally, while the totalitarian countries have carefully limited its availability to the recognized party. In France, a special situation evolved because the strong-willed president, Charles de Gaulle, found broadcasting so important that an extended battle was waged before his political opponents could wrest control from his grasp. At the same time, the need for additional financial support, together with television's value as an advertising medium, led to bitter contests in several countries, such as the United Kingdom and West Germany, over the nature and extent of its commercialization.

The social importance of broadcasting is universally recognized. This is the reason all countries—European and American—impose certain minimum program standards. It also is the basis for the concern in many European countries over the broadcasting of television programs of foreign origin, particularly American telefilms. Pressure against their widespread use comes not only from unions interested in obtaining work for their members, and national treasuries concerned with foreign

4

exchange, but also from serious-minded citizens who fear that such programs may undermine national cultures and ideals.

The desire of the various national services for programs from abroad, especially sports and news, plus the need to share programs in order to conserve financial resources, led first to regional and then to continental exchange projects. West Europe's Eurovision and East Europe's Intervision contributed initially to the political and social hegemony of their respective areas, and then developed exchanges that might conceivably make long-term contributions to international understanding.

This description and appraisal of continental broadcasting is based on the assumption that radio and television are integral parts of the countries they serve. Like all important national activities, they grow out of and contribute to their environments. A thorough study of any country's broadcasting, therefore, must take account of its political, economic, social, religious, and cultural life. But since it is impractical to publish a twenty-four-volume study of European broadcasting, one can deal only with those factors which are most basic to its existence and operation.

The initial—and most unalterable—factor is geography, with special reference to size, shape, and terrain of national territories. A very large country like the Soviet Union needs more transmitters than does small Belgium. Long and slender Portugal, Italy, and Sweden require different coverage patterns than more or less rectangular France. Mountainous Switzerland encounters propagation problems not faced by the flat Netherlands. But geography alone is not the sole determinant of transmitter needs. The small countries of Luxembourg, Monaco, and Andorra could be served by a few low-power stations covering their own populations. Instead they have installed high-power facilities in order to direct commercial broadcasts to their neighbors.

History and politics also are important. A country with traditions of press freedom, like the United Kingdom, may be expected to develop a free system of broadcasting, while one with Communist ideology, such as the German Democratic Republic or the Soviet Union, will almost certainly censor broadcasting along with all other information media. Even in a democratic country the presence of an aggressive leader, like De Gaulle, who is willing to manipulate organs of communication to advance his political objectives, may lead to some control

5

of broadcasting content. A country with a highly centralized government, like France, is apt to have a unified broadcasting organization; one with a federal system, such as the German Federal Republic, Switzerland, or Yugoslavia, may develop decentralized broadcasting.

Religious traditions are another consideration. Countries with one strong dominant religion, such as Portugal, Spain, Greece, and Turkey, often forbid or seriously curtail broadcasts by minority faiths. The Eastern countries, for the most part anti-religious, severely limit and in most cases prohibit religious programs. But France, West Germany, and Sweden are countries in which religious freedom is practiced on the air as well as in the churches.

Educational and cultural status also is a factor. A country's literacy level affects its program needs; and since illiteracy is often accompanied by economic deficiencies, countries with a low literacy level often have limited program resources. But when a country with educational deficiencies, like Italy, tries hard to catch up, the result may be imaginative broadcasting on the order of Telescuola for elementary schools during the daytime and "Non è mai troppo tardi" for adult illiterates in the evening. The extent of such broadcast-related activities as theater, music, ballet, films, newsgathering, and publishing determines to some degree the materials with which broadcasters may work.

Language is always a basic factor. Switzerland has three languages and three virtually independent broadcasting systems, but since these three groups are politically compatible, centralized control is maintained without major intercultural problems. For its two language groups Belgium maintains two services; because the French and Flemish portions of the country are antagonistic, the two systems are separate, although unified at the top. On the basis of language the USSR is strictly in a class by itself, with domestic radio broadcasts in sixty languages!

Many European countries have cultural enclaves which speak foreign languages. For this reason Finland broadcasts in Swedish for its Swedish-speaking residents; Czechoslovakia broadcasts in Bulgarian, German, Hungarian, Polish, and Ukrainian as well as in Czech and Slovak (its two major languages); and Yugoslavia broadcasts in Albanian, Hungarian, Italian, Rumanian, Slovak, and Turkish in addition to Macedonian and Serbo-Croatian. Even the United Kingdom presents a few programs in Welsh for listeners in Wales. Adjacent countries with common or similar languages usually exchange programs. Nord-vision is the name of the television program exchange in Scandinavia; the French-speaking countries have exchanges among themselves as well as with French Canada; and German-speaking Switzerland, West Germany, and Austria have regular exchanges.

National economic standards also affect broadcasting. A wealthy country with extensive manufacturing can build its own transmitters and receivers rather than have to import equipment, with consequent lower costs. When advertising emerges as a supplementary—or pri-mary—source of television revenue, competitive enterprise status be-comes more important. For highly industrialized countries with a large output of consumer goods, such as West Germany, Switzerland, and Italy, advertising is a more promising source of broadcasting funds than in Communist states with noncompetitive socialized industries of limited capacity. Furthermore, countries with large and highly com-petitive industries find themselves under pressure from advertisers to introduce commercial television, at the same time that the broadcasters themselves often look to advertising for additional money. But whether broadcasting is supported by taxes on sets, advertising, or both, wealth-ier countries have more funds and hence can broadcast longer hours and produce better programs.

Relations between neighboring countries also influence broadcasting. Small democratic countries with powerful Communist neighbors, such as Finland and Austria, may be tempted to be neutral in programs with political implications. Commercial programs in one country may induce commercial broadcasting in another. Thus, the viewing of Italian and German commercial programs in Switzerland and of German programs in the Netherlands hastened the emergence of commercial broadcast-ing in Switzerland and the Netherlands. Then there is the whole field of international broadcasting. Many countries present programs for their own nationals, knowing—or hoping—that they will be received in neighboring countries. East and West Germany are the best exam-ples of this. But almost all European countries do some programming for audiences abroad, either on the short-wave band for distant listen-ers or on the regular broadcast band for listeners next door.

In the chapters that follow continental broadcasting will be dis-cussed with reference to all the factors mentioned above and it always will be examined in its national setting. This is not, however, a handbook presenting facts and figures about each country in turn although such a compilation might be extremely useful. Rather it deals comprehensively with basic issues, problems, and functions. Technical, organizational, financial, and program matters will be discussed in turn.*

* This book deals mainly with radio and television on the continent of Europe, and hence makes only occasional references to the United Kingdom. Because of its influence on many aspects of continental broadcasting, the British example often is cited, but the emphasis always is on continental activities.

CHAPTER II

The Facilities for Continental Broadcasting

THE facilities for broadcasting are important as instruments of communication and not as ends in themselves. Nevertheless, some knowledge of them is essential for understanding the organization and programming of radio and television. Because radio waves ignore boundaries, international agreements on broadcasting facilities are necessary: There must be global agreements on spectrum use supplemented by regional allocations of frequencies and channels. Futhermore, there must be standardization of systems if microphones or cameras in one place are to originate signals that can be reproduced in another.

International Telecommunication Union

Since 1947 the International Telecommunication Union has been the specialized agency of the United Nations dealing with telecommunications. The ITU was established in 1865 as the International Telegraph Union and had twenty members. The invention of the telephone and radio took the ITU into those fields too, and it subsequently became involved in television and satellite communications. In recognition of these expanded activities the agency's name was changed in 1932 to the International Telecommunication Union, and its headquarters were transferred in 1948 from Berne to Geneva. At the end of 1965 it had 129 members—more than the United Nations itself.

LEGAL BASIS FOR THE ITU

The International Telecommunication Union is a corporate entity in international law, deriving its authority from the International Telecommunication Convention signed in Montreux on November 12, 1965. The convention defines the purposes of the union as follows: "to maintain and extend international cooperation for the improvement and rational use of telecommunication of all kinds; to promote the development of technical facilities and their most efficient operation with a view to improving the efficiency of telecommunication services, increasing their usefulness and making them, so far as possible, generally available to the public; [and] to harmonize the actions of nations in the attainment of those common ends."[1] To attain these objectives, the union is, among other things, to "effect allocation of the radio frequency spectrum and registration of radio frequency assignments in order to avoid harmful interference between radio stations of different countries" and to "coordinate efforts to eliminate harmful interference between radio stations of different countries and to improve the use made of the radio frequency spectrum."[2]

As defined in the convention, "telecommunication" includes "Any transmission, emission or reception of signs, signals, writing, images and sounds or intelligence of any nature by wire, radio, optical or other electromagnetic systems."[3] "Broadcasting" is "A radiocommunication service in which the transmissions are intended for direct reception by the general public. This service may include sound transmissions, television transmissions or other types of transmission."[*] It is important to notice that broadcasting includes only programs for reception by the general public and not such point-to-point services as ship-to-shore, amateur, or police radio interchanges.

Several other sections from the convention should also be noted. The contracting states pledge themselves to abide by and secure the observance of the agreement's provisions by all persons or groups engaged in telecommunication activities within their respective jurisdictions, if those services might otherwise cause harmful interference with the services of other countries.[4] Transmitting stations must have licenses from countries to which they are subject,[5] and the Radio Regulations prohibit the establishment and operation of radio or television broadcasting stations on ships, aircraft, and floating or airborne objects outside national territories.[6]

The ITU's already difficult regulatory problems have been further complicated because a number of major as well as minor powers have

---

[*] *Montreux Convention 1965*, Annex 2, para. 417. The corresponding passage in the Communications Act of 1934, the legal basis for the regulation of broadcasting in the United States, reads: " 'Broadcasting' means the dissemination of radio communications intended to be received by the public, directly or by the intermediary of relay stations." (*Communications Act of 1934*, Sec. 3 (o).)

signed its conventions with reservations. The 1959 convention was signed by eighty-four countries but the United States did not "accept any obligation in respect of the Telephone Regulations or the additional Radio Regulations"; Albania, Bulgaria, Czechoslovakia, Hungary, Poland, and Rumania reserved "the right to accept or not to accept the Radio Regulations in whole or in part"; while the USSR, in addition to stipulating the foregoing reservation, left open the question of compliance with the actions of the International Frequency Registration Board.[7] With regard to the Montreux Convention in 1965, reservations were also made about the Telephone, Telegraph, or Radio Regulations by Austria, Belgium, Bulgaria, Czechoslovakia, Denmark, Finland, the German Federal Republic, Hungary, Iceland, Liechtenstein, Luxembourg, the Netherlands, Norway, Poland, Rumania, the Soviet Union, Sweden, Switzerland, and the United States.

The milestones in the hundred-year history of the ITU have been its periodic international conferences.[8] The first one met in Paris in 1865. At the first International Radio Conference, held in Berlin in 1906 with twenty-seven states present, the first radio convention and regulations were drawn up. Other conferences were held in Washington in 1927 (which set up the International Radio Consultative Committee); in Madrid in 1932 (which changed the name to International Telecommunication Union); in Atlantic City in 1947 (which created the International Frequency Registration Board); in Buenos Aires in 1952; in Geneva in 1959; and in Montreux in 1965.

These plenipotentiary conferences, held approximately every five years, constitute the ITU's "parliament." In Montreux, for example, a new convention, not fundamentally different from the 1959 Geneva convention, was signed by the delegations of 118 countries, and became effective on January 1, 1967. In addition, there are frequent administrative conferences to revise regulations annexed to the convention, to plan the use of various parts of the radio frequency spectrum or, if necessary, to meet emergencies. In this connection, mention should be made of the Space Radiocommunication Conference held in Geneva in 1963.

An administrative council of twenty-nine members convenes for one month each year in Geneva. The two permanent organs concerned with broadcasting, among other matters, are the International Frequency Registration Board (IFRB), and the International Radio Consultative

11

Committee (known by the initials CCIR for its French name, Comité Consultatif International Technique des Communications Radioélectriques). Most of the ITU's permanent staff of 406 members are housed in a fine new building in Geneva.[9]

WORK OF THE ITU

One of the ITU's fundamental tasks is to divide the radio spectrum among the many services seeking to use it. Although the world is most familiar with radio and television broadcasting directed to the general public, the ITU recognizes some twenty different telecommunication services.* Competition among these for spectrum space is just as bitter as among applicants for individual broadcast facilities. Since the number of requests always greatly exceeds the amount of space available in a ratio of about five to one, no allocation can be made that will satisfy all groups.

Whereas in 1906 it was sufficient to assign only a few radio bands, leaving users to choose the frequencies they wanted, by the time of the Washington Conference in 1927 the allocation table ranged from 10 kilocycles to 60 megacycles. At the 1947 Atlantic City Conference, it extended from 10 kilocycles up to 10,000 megacycles; and it subsequently was pushed up to 40,000 megacycles at the 1959 Geneva Conference.[10]

In allocating broadcasting bands, the Geneva Radio Conference divided the world into three regions reflecting the various propagation characteristics and spectrum needs of the several continents: Europe, USSR, Asia, and Africa; North and South America and the Northeast Pacific; and Asia (excluding the USSR), Australia, New Zealand, and part of the Pacific. In Europe, but not the Americas, radio broadcasting is allocated the frequency band between 150 and 285 kilocycles (the long-wave band) and in both Europe and the Americas, the band between 525 and 1605 kilocycles (the medium-wave or standard broadcast band.)

Television allocations extend from 41 to 68 megacycles (Band I) and from 174 to 216 megacycles (Band III) in Europe; and from 54

* These services include among others Aeronautical Fixed; Broadcasting; Mobile; Aeronautical Mobile; Maritime Mobile; Land Mobile; Radiodetermination; Radionavigation; Aeronautical Radionavigation; Radiolocation; Radar; Safety; Space; Earth-Space; Meteorological Aids; Amateur; Standard Frequency; Time Signals; and Special. (*Radio Regulations,* Art. 1, paras. 24–84.)

12

to 88 megacycles and from 174 to 216 megacycles (the very-high-frequency band) in the Americas. Television also has the band between 470 and 960 megacycles (Bands IV and V) in Europe, and between 470 and 890 megacycles (the ultra-high-frequency band) in the United States. FM radio has allocations in the very-high-frequency band; that is, between 66 and 73 megacycles in Eastern Europe; between 87.5 and 100 megacycles in Western Europe (Band II); and between 88 and 108 megacycles in the Americas. In addition, a number of bands are assigned to short-wave broadcasting, these being much higher frequencies—or shorter waves—than the domestic service bands mentioned above.*

Once the spectrum is divided among the different types of services on a global basis it is necessary to assign definite frequencies and channels to the countries in each area.[11] In Europe there were attempts at voluntary cooperation under the Geneva Plan of 1926 followed by the official Prague Plan of 1929 and the Lucerne Plan of 1933. Next came the Montreux Plan of 1939 which was never put into effect. After World War II there were conferences in Copenhagen on medium- and

* Radio waves are mainly of three types: ground waves, which travel along the surface of the earth; sky waves, which travel up to the ionized layers in the upper atmosphere, and then are reflected back to earth; and direct waves, which travel on line-of-sight. The frequencies between 150 and 285 kilocycles, with excellent ground-wave propagation, provide good coverage over wide areas (George A. Codding, *Broadcasting Without Barriers,* pp. 77–78, hereafter cited as Codding), and are highly prized in Europe, where most countries wish to cover large areas with strong signals; however, they are not used for broadcasting in the United States. (In the United States they are assigned to maritime, aeronautical, and other point-to-point services.) A large country with much spectrum space may wish to emphasize local and regional services, depending upon networks of medium-power transmitters for national coverage. But many European stations on the long-wave band utilize 200 kilowatts or more; Radio Luxembourg, for example, has 600 kilowatts.

The medium-wave or standard broadcast band, extending from 525 to 1605 kilocycles, is the part of the spectrum to which are assigned most domestic broadcasting stations in Europe and the Americas. This band, with both ground-wave and sky-wave propagation, can provide good reception over a radius of at least forty or fifty miles day and night. European medium-wave stations often use very high power, although in the United States no domestic station has more than fifty kilowatts.

The high-frequency or short-wave bands, because of their predominately sky-wave propagation, are especially good for long-distance communication, and hence are used to reach listeners hundreds or thousands of miles away. Such overseas services as the Voice of America, the BBC, and Radio Moscow make extensive use of these bands. Countries like the Soviet Union and Australia, with large, lightly populated areas, do some short-wave broadcasting for domestic reception, too.

In amplitude modulation, or AM broadcasting, the most widely used method of broadcasting, the amplitude or strength of the transmission is varied by the volume long-wave allocations in 1948, and in Stockholm on television and FM allocations in 1952 and 1961. From these conferences came assignment tables for European stations. Similar agreements have been made in other parts of the world too, such as the North American Regional Broadcasting Treaty of 1950, signed by the Bahama Islands, Jamaica, Canada, Cuba, the Dominican Republic, and the United States.*

Although these various plans have marked successive advances in the systematic assignment of frequencies and channels, none of them has been entirely successful. In the first place, not all countries adhere to the conventions. Thus, even as late as 1964 seventeen countries had not signed and ratified the Copenhagen Convention of 1948.† The USSR and other countries have boycotted some meetings. The United States contributed to Europe's problems by operating high-power stations for the American forces and for international propaganda services in Germany after World War II.‡ Finally, the ITU does not have absolute control over station assignments so each country is free to broadcast as it wishes. The deterioration of international politics has affected the willingness, particularly of the Eastern countries, to take part in and abide by international radio conventions.§

Luxembourg is a good example of a country which has exceeded its frequency assignments. With only 999 square miles of territory and

of sound. Therefore, the louder the sound, the greater the fluctuation in the strength of the radio wave. In frequency modulation, or FM, it is the frequency rather than the strength or amplitude of the transmission that is modulated. AM broadcasting has the advantage of potentially greater coverage, with FM limited mainly to reception within line-of-sight distance from the transmitter. But FM transmissions are almost static-free; they have a potentially wider frequency range; and mutual interference is less troublesome since an FM receiver tends to receive only the strongest signal on the frequency to which it is tuned. An FM transmitter also can transmit two or more signals at a time, thus facilitating stereophonic and multiplex broadcasting.

* *United States Treaties and Other International Agreements, North American Regional Broadcasting Agreement.* The United States did not sign the treaty until 1960 and Mexico has not signed it at all.

† Nonsignatories included Luxembourg, Portugal, Spain, Sweden, and Turkey. (*EBU Review,* 84A:66 (April 1964).)

‡ For example, from August 19, 1953, to February 2, 1964, the United States operated in Munich a 1000 kilowatt station, the most powerful in Europe, on 173 kilocycles, a frequency assigned by the Copenhagen Plan exclusively to Moscow with maximum power of 500 kilowatts. (*EBU Review,* 83A:24 (February 1964).)

§ An interesting exception to the general rule was the Stockholm Conference of 1952, which drew up allocations for FM radio and television. Since there were few FM and television stations on the air the delegates had a relatively easy task, whereas most conferees are faced with the impossible assignment of changing the frequencies and reducing the power of long-established stations. (Codding, pp. 97–98.)

little more than 300,000 people, Luxembourg refused to accept either the Madrid agreement of 1932 or the Copenhagen agreement of 1948, because it wanted to broadcast commercial programs to listeners in neighboring countries.[12] Luxembourg now operates one 600 kilowatt transmitter on 233 kilocycles in the long-wave band; a 350 kilowatt transmitter on 1439 kilocycles on the medium-wave or standard broadcast band; two FM stations, with 50 and 100 kilowatts of power respectively; and two short-wave transmitters, using respectively 5 and 50 kilowatts of power. It also operates a television station. Among them, in addition to domestic programs in the Luxembourg dialect for the home audience, these various services broadcast commercial radio and television programs in French, Dutch, German, and English to a number of countries. Clearly, here is a very small country which uses far more spectrum space than its size or population warrant.*

Because of the shortage of spectrum space, frequency jumping, and power increases in violation of international assignments the quality of reception on the medium-wave band in Europe has steadily declined. A vicious circle has developed: More powerful transmitters are installed to overcome the interference resulting from the fact that there already are too many high-powered stations in use.† Therefore, FM broadcasting developed widely in Europe after World War II in order to supplement the inadequate AM radio service.

ITU BROADCASTING COMMITTEES

The two divisions of the ITU concerned with broadcasting are the International Frequency Registration Board and the International Radio Consultative Committee. Other organizations concerned with utilization of the radio spectrum are the European Broadcasting Union (EBU); the International Radio and Television Organization (OIRT from the initials of its French name, Organisation Internationale de

---

* In its earlier years Radio Luxembourg was widely criticized for its illegal use of usurped frequencies for commercial operations. But in 1962, the station having achieved acceptance by its European Broadcasting Union colleagues, its sponsoring country, the Grand Duchy of Luxembourg, was among the signatories of the European Agreement for the Prevention of Broadcasts Transmitted from Stations Outside National Territories, which had the purpose of outlawing unauthorized commercial stations transmitting from the high seas outside national territories.

† The EBU periodically publishes charts listing the stations in the long- and medium-wave bands. On May 1, 1967, for example, on the 15 long-wave channels used in the European area, 17 stations were operating in accordance with the Copenhagen Plan, and 9 outside the plan. On the 119 medium-wave channels to which

Radiodiffusion et Television), the Eastern organization similar to the EBU; the International Chamber of Shipping; the International Scientific Radio Union; the International Special Committee on Radio Interference; and the World Meteorological Organization.*

The International Frequency Registration Board (IFRB), set up following the Atlantic City Conference of 1947, consists of eleven experts working full time in Geneva. In 1928 the International Telegraph Union (now the ITU) began to publish cumulative lists of the frequencies used by all countries. The theory was that by consulting this list any country could choose a frequency with fair prospect that no interference would result. The first such list, published in December 1928, contained about 2,000 entries; by the outbreak of World War II, nine editions had been published. But this informal procedure broke down with the widespread increase of broadcasting after World War II.

At the 1947 Atlantic City Conference, therefore, it was decided to set up a special radio registration board.[13] Any signatory country intending to establish a new radio station that might cause foreign interference is required to report its plans to the IFRB, which then examines the application to determine if the proposed station would cause interference. If so, the board requests the applicant to seek another frequency or make other changes. When the board's finding is favorable the frequency is recorded in the huge international frequency register. An average of more than 1,700 assignment notices arrive at the IFRB each week, and the complete master list contains over half a million entries that give, in coded form, each station's name, location, points of reception, transmitter power, antenna characteristics, hours of operation, and purpose of service. The board also has the responsibility of issuing seasonal schedules of high-frequency (short-wave) broadcasting assignments.

The system, of course, does not work perfectly, but at least it does provide an international body to evaluate, make recommendations, and pass judgment on the use of radio frequencies throughout the world. It should be emphasized again, though, that the IFRB, like all of the

stations were allocated, the 206 stations operating within the plan were joined by 315 unauthorized stations. (*EBU Review,* 103A:132 (June 1967).)

* The EBU maintains several committees of technical experts; conducts investigations into technical problems of all sorts; operates a Technical Center in Brussels, which among other things, monitors and measures transmissions from all parts of Europe; and publishes a technical periodical as well as many monographs.

ITU, has no legal authority to enforce its decisions. In fact, the problem of policing the wave lengths is so complex that it has been seriously suggested that the IFRB's function be limited to the 1928 practice of merely recording spectrum utilization.*

The International Radio Consultative Committee (the Comité Consultatif International Technique des Communications Radioélectriques or CCIR) was set up at the Washington Conference in 1927.[14] It is meant to "study technical and operating questions relating specifically to radio-communication and issue recommendations on them." All member countries, as well as certain international organizations and private telecommunication companies, may participate in its work. The CCIR has fourteen groups studying subjects such as transmitters, receivers, radio astronomy, signal propagation, and radio and television broadcasting. It has attempted through working parties to develop international standards for FM radio and television, and recently tried unsuccessfully to secure agreement on a single color television system for Europe.

Jamming

Because broadcasting is the only method of communication that freely crosses international boundaries, many countries have used it to propagandize their neighbors.† This has led at times to the systematic jamming of radio signals.‡ Therefore, one may ask two questions: Is it morally and legally correct for one country to broadcast to another programs which the government of the latter believes may constitute a "clear and present danger" to its tranquillity and stability?§

* There is no plan for assigning definite frequencies to individual short-wave stations. There was agreement in Atlantic City in 1947 on which bands should be used; but attempts at Mexico City in 1949, Florence and Rapallo in 1950, and Geneva in 1951 to assign definite frequencies, as was done with the long-wave and medium-wave bands, were not successful. Short-wave frequencies, therefore, are merely registered with the IFRB when initially used, rights being based on priority of registration. Any short-wave frequency may legally be used by a country provided an earlier registrant is not using it.

† The word "propagandize" need not have a bad connotation. "Propaganda" is defined by the Funk and Wagnalls *New Standard Dictionary* as "any institution or systematic scheme for propagating a doctrine or system." Webster's *New International Dictionary* defines it as "any organized or concerted group, effort, or movement to spread a particular doctrine or system of doctrines or principles."

‡ "Jamming" consists of broadcasting noise on or near the frequency of the station whose programs it is desired to exclude.

§ For a discussion of the "clear and present danger" concept as applied to broadcasting, see pp. 48–51 below.

And, if so, is it all right for the receiving country to jam the programs to prevent their being heard?

In the 1920's and 1930's the signatories of various international agreements pledged not to broadcast programs that might cause political difficulties for their neighbors. In September 1936 a League of Nations conference in Geneva, attended by delegates from thirty-seven countries, drew up an International Convention Concerning the Use of Broadcasting in the Cause of Peace, which among other things required the contracting states to prohibit broadcasts calculated "to incite the population of any territory to acts incompatible with internal order or . . . security"; to ensure that their domestic transmissions did "not constitute incitement either to war . . . or to acts likely to lead thereto"; and, not knowingly to broadcast incorrect information which might lead to international misunderstanding.[*] Following World War II this convention was revived in 1954 by action of the General Assembly of the United Nations.[15]

Such agreements illustrate the positive approach that broadcasting should advance international understanding rather than create dissension. But it is common knowledge that many countries broadcast programs to foreign audiences criticizing the policies of the latter's governments and that this sometimes leads to jamming of the offending programs. The first jamming occurred in 1933 when the Dollfuss government in Austria jammed Nazi radio attacks from Germany.[16] The next year Germany began jamming Moscow. From then until the fall of Hitler there was hardly a time when jamming did not occur somewhere in the world. After 1945 jamming ceased for about twelve months, but then a jamming war broke out between Moscow and Madrid, after which there was much jamming, particularly by the USSR of Western programs directed to Soviet Russia and the satellite countries.

During World War II the Allies (with the exception of Russia) did not jam enemy broadcasts, and the United States has never jammed broadcasts from any source. But for a period in 1956 the British government did jam broadcasts from Athens to Cyprus on the grounds that the programs spread false anti-British propaganda that caused "irresponsible Greek Cypriot youths" to riot and kill British soldiers

[*] League of Nations, *Treaty Series*, 4301–4327, 186:303–317 (1938). Signatories included the USSR but not the United States.

18

and policemen.[17] In 1966 Rhodesia jammed a station in Francistown, Bechuanaland, when it was relaying BBC programs about Rhodesia which could be heard in that country. Programs on other subjects were not interfered with.[18]

In recent years, however, most of the jamming has been done by the East European countries. The USSR and its neighbors have jammed the BBC, the Voice of America, Radio Liberty, Radio Free Europe, and Vatican Radio and have concentrated in particular on programs in East European languages, English-language transmissions often going unchallenged. But as these countries have become stronger and more confident, and as they have relaxed internal controls on freedom of speech, they also have discontinued jamming. At present there is hardly any jamming on the European continent, although East Germany jams RIAS, the American station in West Berlin, and the Soviet Union jams some broadcasts directed to its territory by Red China. But a severe international crisis might bring about a general resumption of jamming at any time.

All this jamming has taken place despite the fact that under international law it is illegal. On December 10, 1948, in Article XIX of the Universal Declaration of Human Rights, the General Assembly of the United Nations stated that "everyone has the right to freedom of opinion and expression," this to include the right to "seek, receive and impart information and ideas through any media and regardless of frontiers."[19] At about the same time, the General Assembly of UNESCO in its first session in Beirut recommended that member states "recognize the right of citizens to listen freely to broadcasts from other countries."

On December 14, 1950, by a vote of forty-nine to five, the United Nations General Assembly pointed out that "freedom to listen to radio broadcasts regardless of source is embodied in Article XIX of the Universal Declaration of Human Rights," and reminded members that Article 44 of the 1947 International Telecommunication Convention at Atlantic City required that all stations "be established and operated in such a manner as not to result in harmful interference to the radio service or communications of other members."[20] Since jamming constituted "a violation of the accepted principles of freedom of information," the General Assembly therefore invited "the governments of all Member States to refrain from such interference with the right of their peoples to freedom of information."

A country which really believes in freedom of information, and does not fear the consequences of a free press, will seldom if ever jam foreign broadcasts even if it dislikes them. On the other hand, countries which feel the need for a controlled press often jam programs which they consider objectionable. Eastern countries have justified jamming as a defense against incitements to disorder and revolution, contending that a country has the same right to defend itself against subversive propaganda as against the smuggling of drugs or the sale of pornographic literature. The representative of the Soviet Union at the December meeting of the United Nations cited above, asserted that the anti-jamming resolution had been introduced by countries wishing to "take advantage of the United Nations and its proclaimed principles of freedom of information in order to conduct unlimited 'psychological warfare.'" Such warfare, he said, had been undertaken by the ruling circles of the United States and the United Kingdom against a number of states, including the USSR, the People's Democracies, and the Chinese People's Republic.

"It was only to be expected," he continued, "that the countries against which such 'psychological warfare' was conducted should take measures to counteract it in order to paralyze the aggressor, to defend their peoples from the consequences of that type of attack, and to nullify and render ineffective a weapon of aggression which was formerly used only in the time of war. The States against which psychological warfare has been directed have, in fact, taken measures to counteract that type of aggression. There can be no doubt regarding the legality and justice of those counter-measures against aggression by radio."

The spokesman from Czechoslovakia supported the USSR, stating that his country also voted against the resolution because "the intention of its sponsors was primarily to divert the attention of the Assembly from an organized campaign of radio propaganda which constitutes a direct threat to peace, is based on this interpretation, misinformation and distortion of facts, and is beamed daily for ten full hours to my country." This, of course, is essentially the same argument the British government used to justify its jamming during the Cyprus crisis of 1956.

It is reasonable to assume that, despite the resolutions of the United Nations, the International Telecommunication Union, and other international bodies, whenever a country with a controlled press becomes concerned about the effects of foreign broadcasts on its domestic affairs it probably will resort to jamming.

Pirate Stations

The expectation of profits from commercial programs directed to countries without broadcast advertising has led to the establishment of so-called "pirate" broadcasting stations on ships or artificial islands located outside territorial waters.* Financial backing is provided by adventuresome entrepreneurs from Britain, Canada, Switzerland, and the United States, with money from Texas very much in evidence. The ships used are largely of Panamanian or Liberian registry.

The pirate stations have built very considerable audiences with their programs of popular music in the American disc jockey style. Some surveys indicated that in the spring of 1966 certain British stations had audiences ranging from 2,400,000 to 10,500,000 listeners per week, while the National Opinion Poll gave Radio London a weekly audience of 10,330,000. But BBC figures released a few months later claimed that its Light Programme was heard each day by more than four times as many people as listened to all the pirates combined, and the Home Service was heard by more than twice as many.[21] Construction costs for pirate stations broadcasting to the United Kingdom average about £200,000 ($560,000), while profits may be as high as £80,000 per month ($224,000). Big advertisers, such as Unilever, Beecham, and Imperial Tobacco, as well as many smaller groups, use the stations. Since they do not pay record or copyright royalties, these stations avoid some of the expenses incurred by regularly licensed broadcasters.[22]

The first pirate station, set up in 1958 on a vessel anchored on the high seas between Sweden and Denmark, broadcast to listeners in Copenhagen. In 1961, another pirate began broadcasting to Denmark, Radio Nord on a vessel near Stockholm aimed programs at Sweden, and other vessels began broadcasting to the Netherlands. But the most popular target was the United Kingdom where stations operated from vessels and abandoned forts in the Thames estuary. For a time there also was a pirate television station serving the Netherlands. The number of pirate stations on the air varies from time to time depending

* There are precedents for pirate broadcasting stations in the gambling ships off the American coast and the drinking ships anchored off countries with strict liquor laws.

on their financial success and the steps taken to confiscate them. As of April 15, 1967, eleven stations were broadcasting with power ranging from 10 to 75 kilowatts. However, stations, frequency, and power change so often that no published list is correct for long.* Although the pirate stations attempt to select frequencies that will not interfere with regularly licensed transmitters, the crowded radio spectrum makes this difficult. For example, the American radio ship *Olga Patricia,* moored off Harwich, Essex, even went so far as to reduce its power because of interference with a station in Rome.[23]

The pirate stations pose several problems for the countries concerned. They threaten the national broadcasting monopolies; they introduce commercial broadcasting to countries that have decided against it; and, by operating on frequencies not assigned by a responsible international agency, they often interfere with authorized maritime, aircraft, and broadcasting services. In addition, they offer unfair competition to legitimate land-based operations because they do not comply with those sections of the copyright and performance rights laws which in most European countries require payments not only to holders of music copyrights, but also to record manufacturers for the use of recordings on the air. For this reason, the United Kingdom's record manufacturers have been against the pirate broadcasters even more than has the BBC.

Various international agreements, of course, prohibit such operations. The Montreux Convention of 1965, repeating the ruling of previous international telecommunication conventions, declared that stations should not cause "harmful interference to the radio services or communications of other Members," while the radio regulations prohibit the establishment or operation of broadcasting stations "on board ships, aircraft or any other floating or airborne objects outside national territories."† "The Convention on the High Seas" holds each country responsible for all ships registered under its laws.[24] However, most of these

---

* Of these eleven stations, one was located off the Netherlands, one off southwest Scotland, one off the Isle of Man, and eight east of Britain. The frequencies used included 845, 1034, 1115, 1133, 1169, 1187, 1295, 1322, 1349, and 1362 kilocycles. (*WRTH 1967,* p. 301.) Each issue of the technical section of the *EBU Review* reports on the current situation under the heading "On the High Seas."

† *Montreux Convention 1965,* Art. 48, para. 303; *Radio Regulations,* Art. 7, para. 422; Art. 28, para. 962. This regulation applies only to "broadcasting stations," that is, to stations serving the general public; there is, of course, no prohibition against ships and aircraft using radio for point-to-point communication.

boats fly flags of convenience, and even though Panama and Liberia signed the 1965 Montreux convention they are not very strict about enforcing it. Furthermore, some of these stations are located on abandoned forts or towers on the continental shelf and the law is unclear in these cases. But even where the law does clearly and unequivocally forbid such stations there is no international legislation authorizing any country to seize them.

Nevertheless, Sweden, Denmark, Finland, Norway, the Netherlands, and Belgium have passed laws providing penalties for the establishment, operation, or servicing of pirate stations, and some of them have been seized by authorities from those countries.* The Council of Europe in 1965, acting upon a suggestion of the Legal Committee of the European Broadcasting Union, requested its members to prohibit the establishment or operation of such stations and to punish anyone who provided them with supplies, transportation, or advertisements.[25]

No legal steps were taken against the pirate stations in the United Kingdom until a bill was introduced into the House of Commons on July 28, 1966. There never was any doubt about the authority of the government to prosecute stations operating illegally inside territorial waters—although there were disputes as to what constituted "territorial waters"—but there were many delays in providing the legislation necessary to close down the pirates broadcasting to Britain from the high seas.[26] In addition to defying the government the British operators engaged in some widely publicized highjacking of each other's installations. This activity was brought to a climax on the evening of June 20, 1965, when eleven men forcibly seized Radio City, which was located on an old gun site off the east coast. The following day the leader of the ousted group killed the head of the rival faction; he subsequently was acquitted of the manslaughter charge brought against him on the grounds that it was self-defense.[27]

Britain has commercial television but does not have commercial radio. An influential wing of the Conservative party was in favor of it and various MPs—Labourites as well as Conservatives—felt that many of their constituents wanted these pirate stations to continue.[28] The prob-

* A Danish law of June 22, 1962, holds that such transmissions fall under Danish jurisdiction if the station either broadcasts to Denmark or interferes with Danish radio reception. (*EBU Review*, 78B:55–56 (March 1963). See also Gunnar Hansson, "Revision of the Swedish Law on Pirate Broadcasting Stations," *EBU Review*, 101B: 52–53 (January 1967).)

lem was complicated by the need to provide a substitute service after the pirates had been eliminated, and this had to be a day-long popular music program based largely on recordings.[29] Neither the BBC nor anyone else could provide this without securing "needle time" from the record companies. But the companies believed that sales would fall if records were broadcast too frequently and so were unwilling to increase the allowance of record playing time sold to the BBC (seventy-five hours a week plus a little extra for each region), unless they received additional payments. The musicians union also opposed more broadcasting of records, fearing it might cause unemployment for its members.

Nevertheless, the bill was passed in July 1967, and took effect the following month. It followed the suggestion of the Council of Europe and the Scandinavian precedent and made it illegal for British subjects to own, operate, supply, or advertise on pirate stations or to induce anyone else to do so.[30] In December 1966, a government White Paper had supplemented the bill by announcing that the BBC was authorized to develop a continuous popular music program on one of the frequencies previously used for its Light Programme. This service, called Radio 247, which began September 30, 1967, broadcasts popular music weekdays from 5:30 A.M. to 7:30 P.M. and from 10:00 P.M. to 2:00 A.M., as well as on most of Sunday. Over six hours of this time are from phonograph records and the remainder either live broadcasts or BBC recordings made especially for this purpose.

The first pirate television station, TV Noordsee, began its broadcasting to the Netherlands in September 1964.[31] In the same month the Dutch Parliament by an overwhelming vote authorized the confiscation of the station, which was located on an artificial island on the continental shelf near shore. The law said that "in order to protect legitimate interests," it was necessary "to take steps in respect of [broadcasting] installations" on "the Continental Shelf assigned to the Netherlands, pending the enactment of international regulations on this subject." Therefore, "The provisions of Dutch criminal law are applicable to any person committing an infringement on an installation erected at sea," and "the public authorities" may "specify the Dutch legal provisions applicable to installations at sea." Netherlands officials landed on the island and closed down the operation.

There are two points of view on whether the actions taken to confiscate these pirate stations are legally defensible under international law. On the one hand, it has been argued that the rights of states over those portions of the continental shelf adjacent to their territories are restricted to the exploitation of natural resources, and do not include jurisdiction over broadcast stations operating there. As one expert put it: "The regulations covering the Continental Shelf are . . . not applicable to installations used as a base for a television station. An installation of this type constitutes a new form of use of the high seas, for which no provision is made in the conventions on the use of the high seas." He comes to the conclusion that the final solution will have to be an international conference to create legislation. But, recognizing that it might take years to accomplish this and that broadcasting chaos could develop in the interim, he concludes that confiscation is a defensible expedient.[32] On the other hand, another expert wrote: "The installation of a 'television island' in the North Sea would be in contravention of international law, and it would, in the first instance, be the responsibility of the coastal state maintaining the closest relations with the enterprise in question, by virtue of the nationality of the persons concerned, of its exclusive rights over the adjacent continental shelf, and the repercussions of such broadcasts on its national territory, to oppose the erection of such installations."[33]

Radio Facilities

Every European country except San Marino and Liechtenstein has a radio broadcasting service; since these two countries receive programs from their neighbors, in effect all of Europe has access to radio. Through a combination of AM and FM most countries provide nearly complete coverage of their populations, usually with two if not three networks. Transmitters are linked by wire lines or microwave relays for nationwide coverage, in addition to international connections which are arranged with little more difficulty than interstate exchanges in the United States.*

* It should be noted that in many European countries responsibility for technical facilities is divided between the broadcasting and the postal, telephone, and telegraph authorities. Although studio equipment almost always is under the jurisdiction of the broadcasting organization, more often than not the transmitters, studio-transmitter links, and national network lines are the responsibility of the postal, telephone, and telegraph agency. Examples include Switzerland, Sweden, Hungary, Poland, and the Netherlands. (Albert Namurois, *Problems of Structure and Organization of Broadcasting in the Framework of Radiocommunications*, pp. 53–54.) In the United States all stations, in addition to operating their own studio equipment, run

Belgium, Italy, and the Soviet Union are examples of countries of different size with two or more radio services.[34] Belgium is required by law to provide separately for its two culture groups. In 1967, therefore, it operated seven AM transmitters, varying in power from 500 watts to 150 kilowatts, which carried both national and regional programs in one or the other of its two languages. These were supplemented by fifteen FM transmitters duplicating the AM transmissions. Belgium also operated one FM station with programs in German for its German-speaking population, as well as a short-wave international service designed primarily for nationals abroad or at sea. The principal radio studios were located in the capital city of Brussels, but there also were studios in seven other towns: Antwerp, Ghent, Courtrai, and Hasselt in the Flemish part of the country and Liège, Namur, and Mons in the French part.*

Italy faces a radio propagation problem very different from that of Belgium. Whereas Belgium is compact with predominantly flat terrain, Italy, often hilly and in places mountainous, stretches 725 miles from north to south, and varies from 80 to 135 miles in width. Italy's three national radio program services are carried simultaneously on AM and FM.[35] For Sicily, and for Italian-speaking listeners in Libya, Tunisia, Algiers, Egypt, and elsewhere in the Mediterranean region, some domestic AM programs are broadcast simultaneously on short wave. Italy also has an FM service for its German-speaking population in the Italian Alps and some Slovenian programs for listeners near the Yugoslav border. In 1965, Italy operated 127 medium-wave transmitters ranging in power from 100 watts to 150 kilowatts, plus more than 1,470 FM transmitters, and these facilities brought radio to almost every part of the country. Italy also has an extensive foreign short-wave service.

The Soviet Union, a country of great size with many nationality groups and eleven time zones, requires an enormous broadcasting installation.† From Moscow the USSR operates five radio network services: two for

their own transmitters, although they usually rent from a telephone company the links between studios and transmitters.

* Although in the United States there normally is one studio installation for each transmitter, in Europe studios usually are located only in cities where program originations are desired. Customarily, then, each studio center serves a number of transmitters, and one center may provide programs for a large region or even an entire country.

† Information about Soviet broadcasting was supplied by the International Relations Department of the State Committee for Broadcasting and Television. For programing details, see pp. 127–128, 131 below.

the entire Soviet Union, one of which is the around-the-clock "Majak"; a third which is on the air six hours a day in European Russia only; a fourth for eastern and western Siberia and the Far East; and a fifth for western Siberia, Soviet citizens abroad, merchant seamen, and fishermen. Seventeen regional centers, whose boundaries approximate those of the fifteen Soviet republics, originate one or more programs of their own in addition to relaying the national services from Moscow.

The Soviet Union operates over 600 medium- and short-wave transmitters plus a number of FM stations. It also broadcasts many domestic programs by short wave for listeners in distant parts of the country not reached by standard broadcast or FM stations. There are studios in Moscow as well as in the seventeen regional centers including, among others, such major cities as Alma-Ata, Kiev, Leningrad, Minsk, Riga, Tashkent, and Tbilisi. The Soviet Union also operates an extensive broadcasting service for listeners abroad, utilizing a great many short-wave as well as some medium- and long-wave transmitters.

FM BROADCASTING

As mentioned before, Europe even more than the United States had good reason to develop extensive frequency modulation services in the very-high-frequency band because of the progressive deterioration of reception in the AM band.*

West Germany, for example, was greatly affected by the changes in the long- and medium-wave assignments made at the European Broadcasting Conference in Copenhagen in 1948.[36] One of the problems was the use of AM frequencies by the various Allied troop and propaganda services established after the war. Even as late as 1967, the United States Armed Forces Network was operating thirty AM stations on nine different frequencies; the United States Information Agency used four frequencies on the standard broadcast band for RIAS; while a number of FM and short-wave channels were used by these as well as by Radio Free Europe, which beamed programs toward the satellite countries,

* "VHF Sound Broadcasting in Europe," EBU Bulletin, VI (No. 33):593–611 (November–December 1955); EBU Bulletin, VI (No. 35):29–48 (January–February 1956). In Europe the expression "VHF," referring to the frequencies employed, is used rather than the American term "FM," which refers to the type of modulation. Both continents use the same band for this purpose, however: Western Europe, 87.5 to 100 megacycles; Eastern Europe, 66 to 73 megacycles; and the United States, 88 to 108 megacycles.

and Radio Liberty, serving listeners in the USSR.[37] Furthermore, because Germany was divided, it needed more frequencies than would have been necessary had it been under one government. Accordingly, West Germany began to experiment with FM broadcasting in 1949.[38] By the middle of 1954 it had more than 100 stations on the air serving 50 per cent of its population and by 1967 this had grown to over 200. These FM stations bring the basic West German radio services to the entire country. Almost anywhere in West Germany at least two FM stations are available and more than 50 per cent of the population can hear four or more.

The BBC began in 1955 to construct a nationwide chain of FM stations to improve reception for its domestic programs. It now has 186 FM transmitters in 61 locations, bringing the Home, Light, and Third Programmes to 99.75 per cent of the population of the United Kingdom.[39] Spain too is moving to FM to solve its coverage problems. In December 1964 the government announced that it would replace almost all medium-wave transmitters with FM stations.[40] Switzerland operates six regional networks, two in each of its three language areas. For each language one service is broadcast simultaneously on AM and FM, and the second on FM only. Most European countries are proceeding rapidly to develop FM services, not so much to provide more program choices as to assure better reception.

Europe is developing stereophonic broadcasting along with FM. Although less highly publicized than in the case of television, stereophony also poses problems of international standardization.[41] Three standards for stereophony were proposed at the CCIR meeting held in Norway in the summer of 1966 (at which color television was the principal agenda item). The American pilot-tone system, adopted by the Federal Communications Commission in 1961, had been discussed by the CCIR in January 1963, and in April of that year the Technical Committee of the European Broadcasting Union recommended it for Europe. Accordingly a number of countries adopted it. But the Oslo meeting also considered a compression-expansion standard proposed by Sweden, along with the USSR polar-modulation system. Although there was no formal agreement, the pilot-tone system emerged as the unofficial European standard. In 1967 there were regular stereophonic broadcasts in Austria, France, West Germany, Italy, the Netherlands, and the United Kingdom with others soon to follow, while Rumania, East Germany, and the Soviet Union were among the Eastern countries experimenting with stereophony. In view of the great emphasis on good music, continued expansion may be expected in this area.*

WIRED DISTRIBUTION

To supplement radio broadcasts many European countries also distribute programs directly to homes, offices, hotel rooms, and places of business by telephone line. In 1960 a dozen continental countries had services of this kind, their subscribers frequently constituting a high percentage of the total number of radio license holders.[42] At that time the Soviet Union was first with 30,500,000 sets, and Poland second with 1,331,000. By 1965 Western Europe, in addition to 116,500,000 off-the-air receivers, had 2,500,000 wired receivers and in the Eastern countries there were 59,700,000 off-the-air receivers and 43,400,000 wired receivers. Incomplete 1966 figures indicated that the leaders included Poland with 1,073,501 wired receivers, Bulgaria with 675,152, Czechoslovakia 649,814, Switzerland 463,848, Sweden 399,175, and the Netherlands 383,-500.[43]

The prevalence of wired services in Eastern Europe might suggest that wired distribution is especially attractive to totalitarian countries wishing to reduce the reception of foreign programs. This undoubtedly

* Experiments with stereophonic tape recording were begun in Berlin in 1941, and by the autumn of 1944 some 240 dual-track tapes had been recorded, of which a few still survive in the archives. These early stereo broadcasts were radiated on two FM frequencies, a practice continued when stereophonic broadcasting was resumed at Christmas time in 1958 by Sender Freies Berlin. Not until 1963 was this system replaced with one resembling the American multiplex process, with two channels on a single frequency, the method now used by almost all countries. At present all Sender Freies Berlin symphonic recordings for broadcasting are made in stereo in the belief that symphonic production is more easily done that way, whether or not the actual broadcast is stereo or monaural. The increase in the number of stereophonic receivers is astonishing: in 1966 there were some 1,000,000 such receivers in Europe, of which 900,000 were in West Germany; by the middle of 1967, the number of stereo sets in West Germany had doubled. (Sender Freies Berlin, "Stereophony in Radio," *Informations*; Wolfgang Geiseler, "Stereophonic Radio in Germany. A Decisive Innovation in the Television Age." *EBU Review*, 103B:49–51 (May 1967).) Studies of stereophonic broadcasting in Eastern Europe include G. Steinke, "Effects of Stereophony on Broadcasting Studio Techniques," *Radio and Television Review of the International Radio and Television Organization*, No. 1:24–35 (1962), hereafter cited as *OIRT*; "Investigation into the Perceptibility of Distortion in a Two-Channel Stereophonic System," *OIRT*, No. 5:32–38 (1962); Marian Rajewski, "Contribution to the Analysis of Stereophonic Broadcasting Transmission Methods," *OIRT*, No. 1:23–32 (1963); *OIRT Information*, No. 3:2–3 (1965); Liviu Zanescu, "Listening Room for High-Quality Stereo Replay," *OIRT*, No. 5:33–38 (1965).

is true, but its extensive development in Western countries clearly indicates that other important conditions are involved. Wired services of various types grew up in many European countries in the 1920's.* Originally they had the attraction of requiring little or no capital outlay from the subscribers, they were cheaper to maintain, and they provided static-free reception, particularly of distant stations. More recently, wired distribution has offered clear reception despite the deterioration of the AM band, a wider choice of programs, particularly from foreign countries, and high fidelity plus stereo.

Switzerland's six-channel telediffusion, operated by the postal authorities, is a good example of wired services. At a very low cost a subscriber may have a loudspeaker installed (an elaborate one, if he pays extra for it) with a selector switch giving him a choice of the three basic Swiss programs in French, German, and Italian on three different channels; a fourth channel for the second program in his region; and assorted features on the other two channels from Austria, Germany, France, Italy, the United Kingdom, and the Swiss short-wave service, altogether totaling about 130 hours of programing per day. The weekly Swiss radio program journals provide detailed information about this wired service so that subscribers know in advance exactly what is available.

In twelve major cities Italy offers *filodiffusione*, a program service by telephone wire, which has been operated by the broadcasting authorities since December 1, 1958. Originally service was available in four major cities but eight others have since been added.† Filodiffusione provides three Italian radio services and a wide range of light and serious music, plus special stereophonic musical programs.

It is the USSR that really makes extensive use of wired distribution.

---

* In Britain, the development of relay exchanges, as these are called in the United Kingdom, was complicated by the attempts of the BBC in the 1920's to take over the exchanges, the Corporation being motivated partly by concern lest they "have power, by replacing selected items of the Corporation's programmes with transmissions from abroad, to alter entirely the general drift of the BBC's programme policy." However, the British government finally decided that the relay companies should be continued, but only on condition that, in addition to offering two or more BBC programs, they originate no programs of their own. They also were prohibited from relaying from abroad English-language programs containing political, social, or religious propaganda, or from receiving any payments for the distribution of programs. (Paulu, *British Broadcasting: Radio and Television in the United Kingdom*, pp. 26–29, hereafter cited as Paulu, *British Broadcasting*.)

† *EBU Review*, 52B:19–20 (December 1958); *Annuario RAI 1966*, pp. 25–26. Originally the service was available in Rome, Milan, Naples, and Turin, with Genoa, Bologna, Bari, Venice, Florence, Palermo, Cagliari, and Trieste being added later.

The Soviet Union first introduced wired broadcasting in 1924 and by 1959 had over 40,000 radio relay centers in industrial plants, collective farms, and cities. Subscribers usually have a choice of several Moscow as well as local programs; in addition, in many outlying areas, the redistribution systems themselves originate programs. Latest figures indicate that the USSR has as many wired receivers as off-the-air sets—about 40,000,000 in each case.[44]

RADIO STUDIOS

European radio studios vary greatly from country to country. There usually are extensive installations in the capitals, and often in regional centers too, supplemented by limited studios for talks and interviews in smaller cities. The Broadcasting House in Brussels, completed before World War II, is surprisingly elaborate, considering that the entire country for which it provides programs is about equal in population to New York City. At present a part of this building is assigned to television but when the projected new television studios are completed, it will be devoted to radio. This building has facilities for programs ranging from talks and interviews to drama, besides a superb symphony orchestra studio with a fine pipe organ and seating for an audience of 500. Because of Belgium's two languages, all the studios except the one for concerts were constructed in duplicate. Other countries, too, have radio concert halls with fine audience accommodations. This is true of the radio houses in Frankfurt, Hamburg, and Bucharest.[45] In Copenhagen, although construction of the Radio House began in 1938, the concert studio was completed only in 1945. This very beautiful hall, like that in Brussels, includes a fine pipe organ, and has seats for 1,200 people.

Italy has a total of 145 sound broadcasting studios. Major installations are in Rome, as well as in fourteen regional centers, such as Milan, Turin, Florence, and Naples.[46] The studio in Naples, officially opened in March 1963, is a radio and television center. In addition to administrative offices it contains an auditorium suitable for both radio and television productions, with a large concert organ, seating for 1,000 people, and seats arranged on steps which can be adjusted to different angles. All told, Italy's radio technical equipment in 1965 included 31 motor vehicles carrying FM transmitters used as mobile radio links, 62 mobile vehicles for remote pickups, and 900 tape recorders of which 526 were portable.

The new Broadcasting House in Paris, devoted principally to radio, is probably the most elaborate building of its kind in the world.[47] A French promotion sheet, in fact, says that this $40,000,000 radio center "probably is the largest building in Europe and the world's most modern radio center."[48] Completed in 1964, and occupying a large site on the banks of the Seine not far from the Eiffel Tower, it was designed to bring together the radio offices and studios which for some years had been divided among twenty-three buildings all over Paris, as well as to serve as headquarters for the entire ORTF (Office de Radiodiffusion-Télévision Française).

The building contains 1,200 offices and 60 studios, ranging from small to very large, besides an enormous amount of electronic equipment. There are 12 studios for news, 8 for music, 6 for drama, 7 for variety, 11 for small dramatic productions, and 11 for short-wave programs. Six are audience studios with seating capacities ranging from 25 up to 1,000. Several of the larger studios are equipped for television as well although radio is the principal purpose of the building. The Paris Broadcasting House can provide 500 hours of programs every week for domestic distribution by the three nationwide French networks and some regional transmitters; 200 hours a week of short-wave transmissions; and various types of recordings for overseas use. In addition to this building and two large television production centers in Paris the ORTF has a number of regional centers for the origination of local radio programs as well as for contributions to the national service.*

Most of the equipment in European radio centers is of European manufacture and of high quality: In fact, much of it has earned a position of honor in American broadcasting too. Among the better known manufacturers are Philips in the Netherlands, Marconi in England, Telefunken in Germany, AKG in Austria, and Brown Boveri in Switzerland. As might be expected, Eastern Europe prefers to manufacture its own equipment but since a wider range often is available from the highly industrialized West, there is much Western—especially West German—

* The BBC is another organization with excellent radio facilities. The London headquarters office and studio building, Broadcasting House, was opened in 1932, and has had extensive additions since then. At present there are 57 attended and 9 unattended radio studios in London, plus 71 attended and 28 unattended in the regions, for a total of 165 radio studios for domestic programs in the United Kingdom. Thirty-eight more London studios for broadcasts to foreign audiences raise the total to 203. Since the BBC also maintains 7 studios abroad for its external services, the grand sum of its sound studios is 210. (*BBC Handbook 1967*, p. 137.)

equipment in the East. When a major technical assignment is involved, as with the 1964 Winter Olympics in Austria, for example, the European broadcasting organizations can provide technical installations just as elaborate and efficient as any American network.[49]

Television Facilities

Television like radio requires international agreements on standards, spectrum space, and channels. Spectrum space was allocated and channels were assigned before television was widespread so agreement here was easily reached (Codding, pp. 97–98). But despite attempts by the International Radio Consultative Committee (CCIR) of the International Telecommunication Union to establish uniform standards, Europe uses four basically different and incompatible black-and-white systems and seems headed toward two different and incompatible color systems as well.*

STANDARDIZATION

The different television systems usually are identified by the number of horizontal lines in their pictures: 405, 525, 625, or 819. Actually, besides the number of lines there are many other variables which must be determined in establishing a television system, including agreement on the frequency limits of each channel.†

When the British went on the air in 1936 with the world's first regular television program service, their 405 lines represented very high definition. But the American standard was set at 525 lines in 1941, and the French, striving for extremely fine picture detail, chose 819 lines in 1949 (after having previously operated on 441 lines, which was the standard originally proposed by some American manufacturers). Monaco and Luxembourg also use the French 819-line system, as did Belgium for one of its networks until 1965, though with some changes in the case of the latter two countries.‡ The CCIR had discussed a 625-line standard as

---

* In this sense "incompatible" means that a camera, recorder, transmitter, receiver, or other instrument designed for one system will not work on another one. A given color and black-and-white system are said to be "compatible" when signals from the color system can be reproduced in monochrome by the black-and-white system.

† The Appendix on pp. 249–252 provides details about Europe's several television systems.

‡ The Belgians also modified the 625-line standard. (*EBU Review*, 88A:272 (December 1964).)

early as 1950, and this was adopted by most West European countries.*
Europe uses both the VHF and UHF bands. In most cases the first stations operated in the VHF band—equivalent to America's channels 2
through 13—but as more stations were added there also was wide use
of the UHF band—America's channels 14 through 82.

The East European or OIRT 625-line standard, adopted in 1957, differs mainly from the Western 625-line standard in band width details.[50]
OIRT spokesmen claim that their standard provides better picture
definition and also facilitates the development of high quality color television. The OIRT system is used by all the Eastern countries except
East Germany, which uses the Western standard (as, of course, does
West Germany). There now is a tendency for all countries to move
toward 625 lines. Thus, the second BBC network, broadcast on UHF
since April 20, 1964, and the second French system, also on UHF and
inaugurated on April 18, 1964, use the 625-line system, while Belgium
now has discontinued 819-line broadcasts and operates only on 625
lines.†

This lack of standardization leads to many complications. Because
receivers designed to operate on one standard usually will not work on
another, elaborate conversion systems must be used when programs are
to be exchanged by countries using different standards. Then there are
the problems of receiving programs from transmitters in neighboring
countries using different standards. For example, from 1952 until early
1965 Belgium used an 819-line system for its French- and a 625-line system for its Dutch-language programs, following in the first instance the
French and in the second the Netherlands pattern. Consequently, all
receivers sold in Belgium were designed to work on both standards.

Switzerland and its neighbors are a special problem. All of Switzerland uses the Western 625-line standard as does West Germany to the
north. But France's first network operated on 819 lines, although its
second is being developed on the 625-line standard. Italy, to the south,
uses the same 625-line system as does Switzerland but with a different
arrangement of channels.[51] Accordingly, people in Switzerland, France,
or Italy wishing to view programs broadcast on two standards must buy

* The West European standard often is identified as the "CCIR standard," although the CCIR never officially endorsed any standard.
  † It was the French decision to introduce 625 lines for their second television network that led the Belgians to standardize on the 625-line system. (*BBC Handbook
1967*, p. 224; *EBU Review*, 85A:121–122 (June 1964).)

sets equipped to receive both systems, although both purchase and maintenance costs are thereby increased and performance quality is lowered.

Because the OIRT and Western 625-line systems are much alike it is possible for receivers operating on one standard to be modified to receive programs broadcast on the other one. But since this requires considerable technical skill, the odds are against viewers in the Communist countries—except East Germany which uses the Western standard—watching programs from the West. However, there is no problem in exchanging programs by cable or microwave relay since the same scanning methods are used by both systems.

European television now faces the almost certain prospect of having two incompatible standards for color television. Originally three systems were under consideration: the American NTSC (National Television System Committee); the French SECAM (Sequential and Memory); and the German PAL (Phase Alternating Line), all three being adaptations to European conditions of the system used in the United States.[52] In most respects these systems are similar; in fact, 95 per cent of their components are the same. Nevertheless, a set designed to work on one will not necessarily reproduce signals broadcast by another. Throughout all the discussions the proponents of each strongly urged its adoption, although the average viewer found little difference among them. Whichever would be best, its superiority would be slight in view of the tremendous advantage of continent-wide agreement on one standard.*

Unfortunately, at a CCIR meeting about color television standards held in Vienna from March 25 to April 7, 1965, there was a three-way disagreement. Twenty-two nations voted for the French SECAM system; eleven for the German PAL; and six for the American NTSC.† Poli-

---

* The director of the technical center of the European Broadcasting Union believed that the NTSC system had the advantage of a ten-year test in the United States as well as of lower receiver cost. Furthermore, NTSC black-and-white reception would be better than PAL or SECAM. But the PAL and SECAM systems would be less sensitive to differential-phase distortion, and could make exchanges more easily, while long-distance transmissions would be easier by either PAL or SECAM (Georges Hansen, "Colour-Television Standards for Europe," *WRTH 1965*, p. 28). Britain's *Financial Times* (April 8, 1965) wrote: "The foremost television experts stated here time and time again that on objective technical grounds there was no doubt that NTSC was the best system although PAL was perhaps better suited to Europe. No one here doubts that SECAM is the worst of the three systems."

† SECAM was supported by all the Communist countries except Yugoslavia

tics, economics, and prestige, much more than electronic theory, brought about this impasse. Just before the Vienna meeting, France and the Soviet Union agreed privately to support SECAM, a decision widely interpreted as a result of the current political rapprochement between De Gaulle and the USSR.[53] The USSR opposed the NTSC system partly because of its American origin; West Germany, as would be expected, pressed the case for its own PAL; while only the British, with assistance from the Netherlands, favored NTSC. In view of the similarity of the American NTSC and German PAL systems it was hoped for a time that they could be merged for adoption by most West European countries, the system to be called QUAM for "Quadrature Amplitude Modulation."* But this was not to happen.

The matter was discussed exhaustively by the 650 delegates from sixty-nine countries who attended the 11th Plenary Assembly of the CCIR in Oslo from June 22 to July 22, 1966.[54] Serious consideration was given to two developments of SECAM, SECAM III and SECAM IV, as well as to PAL. The NTSC system was out of the running because those countries previously in favor of it had switched their support to the West German PAL. In the end, PAL was supported by all the West European countries except France, while SECAM III was favored by France, the Soviet Union, and all the other Eastern countries.

Although they were not prepared to recede from their position, Eastern as well as Western spokesmen regretted the breakdown. Following the failure to reach agreement in Vienna in 1965, the OIRT bulletin had commented that "the failure to select a single colour television

(which did not vote); by Algeria, Greece, Luxembourg, and Monaco (the last two use the French 819-line standard); and by Spain, Tunisia, Argentina, and some African countries. PAL was supported by Austria, Denmark, West Germany, Finland, Iceland, Ireland, Italy, Norway, Sweden, Switzerland, and New Zealand. NTSC was supported only by Britain and the Netherlands from the European area, plus Brazil, Canada, Japan, South Africa, and the USA. Belgium, Pakistan, and Turkey, as well as Yugoslavia, did not vote. (*OIRT*, No. 4:40–41 (1965).)

* *New York Times*, April 9, 1965, p. 3. There was a long and bitter controversy in the United States before agreement was reached on the present NTSC standard. In 1946, the Columbia Broadcasting System asked the Federal Communications Commission to authorize commercial operation with its system. The FCC first refused but then accepted the CBS standard in 1960. Because CBS color could not be received on black-and-white sets, this decision was widely criticized. After a series of legal actions brought by RCA, which among other things had the objective of delaying the final decision, and after the suspension of television receiver manufacturing because of the Korean War in 1952–53, the present compatible NTSC system was adopted by the FCC in December 1953. Accordingly, the United States, along with the rest of the North American continent, has a single color standard.

system will considerably complicate further international exchange of colour television programmes."[55] Britain, West Germany, France, and the Soviet Union are scheduled to start color television in 1967 with other countries, East and West, to follow in a few years, so it appears that the last opportunity to reach agreement has been missed. This of course does not mean that programs cannot be exchanged since methods of transcoding already are being developed. However, because of these dual standards program costs will be raised, the exchange of programs complicated, technical quality lowered, and receiver costs increased particularly for those viewers living on PAL-SECAM frontiers where sets capable of receiving programs from both systems will be in demand.

TELEVISION STATIONS

All European countries except Andorra, Liechtenstein, San Marino, and Vatican City have regular television services. But since all of these receive programs from their neighbors it can be said that the entire European continent has television. In 1964 there were 2,321 television transmitters in Western Europe (including the United Kingdom), an increase of 518 over the previous year, while Eastern Europe had 1,169, of which 291 were new. That gave Europe a total of 3,490 television transmitters in 1964 compared to about 700 in the United States.[56]

The United Kingdom was the first country to begin a regular television service. It went on the air on November 2, 1936, but signed off on September 1, 1939, for World War II. There also were prewar operations in France, Germany, and the USSR.[57] On June 7, 1946, Great Britain was the first European country to resume broadcasting. Because the transmitters and receivers already existed the British decided to continue their 405-line system, although in retrospect it might have been better if they had waited until they could convert to the 625-line system that was to emerge as the European standard. But in order to maintain their leadership, and also to stimulate their electronics industry, they decided to resume service at the earliest possible date.* By the middle 1950's most countries had at least one television service. In

---

* Other countries began regular transmissions in the following years: 1951, the Netherlands; 1952, Poland; 1953, Belgium and Switzerland; 1954, Czechoslovakia, Denmark, East Germany, and Italy; 1955, Luxembourg; 1956, Austria, Portugal, Spain, and Sweden; 1957, Rumania; 1958, Hungary; 1959, Bulgaria; 1960, Finland and Norway. (UNESCO, *Television: A World Survey*, pp. 12–14; UNESCO, *World Communications: Press, Radio, Television, Film, passim.*)

early 1967, three countries had three television services: the United Kingdom (two BBC, one ITA); USSR (the third channel in Leningrad and Moscow only); and West Germany (the third on forty-one transmitters serving portions of five or six *Länder*).[58] There were two services in Austria, Belgium, Finland, France, Italy, the Netherlands, and Spain. All the remaining countries had one network only, including the entire Eastern area excepting the Soviet Union. In one sense, Switzerland has three networks, broadcasting in German, French, and Italian, but since each covers the section of the country using that language they should be regarded as three regional services which occasionally are combined into one national network.

A typical European television service will have a combination of high-power transmitters, each covering a large population center, with low-power stations or repeaters, known also as transposers, for concentrations of population which because of location or terrain do not have good reception from the main transmitters.* In 1966, for example, Belgium had three stations for its French-language programs, two for its Dutch, plus five satellite transmitters for the former and two for the latter service.[59] Italy at the end of 1965 used 32 high-power transmitters and 637 repeaters for its first television network, and 32 transmitters and 87 repeaters for its second. Like all European countries, however, it had only a few studio centers. As mentioned before, there were elaborate installations in Rome, Milan, Turin, and Naples.

The Soviet Union, like the other Eastern countries, lags behind the West in television development. Moscow and Leningrad have three channels each, and much of the USSR west of the Urals can receive two services; but in the eastern portions of the country there is only one service if any at all. Programs from the first Moscow channel are fed to 500 transmitters serving 120 cities which are all interconnected by cables or microwave relay. There are origination facilities for 120 of these transmitters. In the eastern part of the Soviet Union, where no stations are linked for live simultaneous broadcasting, programs usually

---

* Normally, these repeaters are located in the country being served, but an interesting exception is a 50-watt transmitter located near the Austro-German frontier on Austrian territory which tunes in programs off-the-air from a Bavarian station and rebroadcasts them on UHF to a valley which otherwise would be without television service. (*EBU Review*, 83A:23 (February 1964).) Monaco, whose transmitter is located on French military property in France, is probably the only country whose entire television transmitting facilities are located abroad. (François Pigé, *La Télévision dans le Monde*, p. 82, hereafter cited as Pigé.)

are exchanged by film or videotape recording. The third, educational channels in Moscow and Leningrad are not interconnected nor will be the other third channels as they come into service in various large cities.

Most television transmitters within a country are linked by microwave and sometimes by cable, as are the systems of adjacent countries.* It was inevitable, therefore, that Europe like the United States would develop continental networks as soon as technical developments permitted. Western Europe set up Eurovision in 1954 and Eastern Europe has had Intervision since 1960. The two exchange programs regularly.

The European Television Community, known as Eurovision, is one of the proudest achievements of the European Broadcasting Union.[60] The first international television relay connected Calais and London in August 1950, though the problems of standards conversion was not involved since only the BBC carried the programs. By 1952, however, the French and British had succeeded in converting signals from one standard to the other and in July of that year eighteen programs originated in Paris were sent to London for simultaneous broadcast in both countries. Services on the continent were very anxious to televise the Coronation of Queen Elizabeth in June 1953, so the Coronation broadcasts were carried by twelve transmitters in France, the Netherlands, and Western Germany. In addition, during the weeks immediately before and after the Coronation, twenty other BBC programs were broadcast in those countries.[61] Even before the inauguration of regular live network connections, however, there were exchanges of films among European broadcasting organizations, along with some cooperative production of programs. There also were exchanges of short filmed items for insertion into longer programs.

Live Eurovision began officially on June 6, 1954, with experimental transmissions over a temporary network linking Belgium, Denmark, France, West Germany, Italy, the Netherlands, Switzerland, and the

---

* The radio and television stations of West Berlin are tied into the West German system by a single microwave link to the West German border, as are its telephone services, because the East German authorities do not permit West German installations on their territory. (*EBU Review*, 87A:224 (October 1964).) However, RIAS, the American radio station in Berlin, does have land-line telephone relays over East German territory in accordance with treaty commitments made by the USSR following World War II.

United Kingdom. A temporary technical center at Lille, France, supervised the experiment and signals were converted to the 405-, 625-, and 819-line standards as required. Enthusiastic public and press response to these programs led to the establishment of a permanent coordination center in Brussels at the end of 1955.

Thereafter, the technical facilities for Eurovision gradually expanded until they now include all the countries of Western Europe, plus Yugoslavia.[62] During the first months the shortage of television circuits made it impossible to relay a program through a country unless the transmitters of that country either carried the program themselves or dispensed with network service while it was on the air. As an example, Italy for a time could not get a program from Denmark unless both Switzerland and Germany carried it. But by the end of 1955 there were enough duplicate circuits to eliminate this problem. By 1962 the EBU had acquired permanent audio circuits connecting the principal participants, but vision circuits still have to be ordered separately for each occasion, and for several daily transmissions considerable advance scheduling is involved. For example, currently there are regular daily hookups during which members feed each other film and video tape recordings for use in news broadcasts.

Eurovision's technical statistics now are very impressive.* As of January 1, 1965, twenty-one television services in sixteen European countries took part. The total length of vision circuits exceeded 100,000 kilometers (62,100 miles), consisting of about 12,000 kilometers (7,452 miles) of cable and 90,000 kilometers (55,890 miles) of microwave relay. The total network included over 2,382 television transmitters serving more than 45,000,000 receivers, representing a maximum audience of about 200,000,000 people. Standards converters are in widespread use, being located in most countries. Supplementing Eurovision are many exchanges among neighbors, particularly among countries with the same or similar languages, such as the French-language community (France, Belgium, Luxembourg, Monaco, and western Switzerland); the Dutch-language area (Belgium and the Netherlands); the German-language group (Germany, Austria, and northern Switzerland); and the Scandinavian countries (Nordvision).

In Eastern Europe, too, television exchanges began on an *ad hoc*

* *This Is the EBU*, p. 38. The program aspects of Eurovision and Intervision are discussed on pp. 137–142 below.

and bilateral basis.[63] Early in 1956 some stations in East Germany and Czechoslovakia broadcast part of the Eurovision coverage of the Olympic hockey matches relayed from Italy, and in 1957 interconnections also were extended to Poland. In January 1960 the OIRT Administrative Council decided to create Intervision, and formal inauguration came on September 5, 1960, with participation by Hungary, East Germany, Poland, and Czechoslovakia. When links became available the Soviet Union joined in 1962.

By 1966 Intervision had thirteen members including all the Communist countries except Albania, which had only experimental television, and Yugoslavia, which received Eurovision programs as an EBU member and took some Intervision programs as well, though it was not formally an Intervision member. Finland belonged to both Eurovision and Intervision.[64] Negotiations between OIRT and EBU for program exchange began in February 1960, and there now are connections between Eurovision and Intervision on the frontiers of the two Germanys, as well as at the Austrian-Czechoslovak and Austrian-Hungarian borders. With East as West there also are frequent exchanges among neighboring countries, although until tape recorders are more widely available in the East European countries the use of material on a delayed basis will be complicated for them.

The development of European television studios followed the pattern previously observed in the United States. Originally programs were produced in poorly equipped studios, often improvised from radio studios, theaters, and auditoriums.[65] In Prague the advent of state socialism made available an old grain exchange as one studio center. In 1966 Czech television had three studios in Prague and five elsewhere, the Prague staff being housed in fifty-three different buildings, although there were plans dating from 1957 for an elaborate new building with extensive facilities for both radio and television. Western countries, too, often improvise studios. Belgium, for example, crowded television production into its prewar Broadcasting House in Brussels, with some overflow facilities, while building a large-scale production center in the suburb of Schaarbeck. Although this will take twelve years to complete, by 1967, three new studios for each of the French and Dutch services are scheduled for use.

Hamburg has a studio especially designed for the production of news programs for the first German television network.[66] Poland is among the Eastern countries with big plans, although facilities are very crowded at present. Blueprints were begun, however, in 1960, and it is hoped that the new broadcasting center—the largest capital construction ever undertaken in that country—will be completed by 1970. The building will include fifteen studios, five for television and ten for radio.[67]

Moscow also struggles along with temporary accommodations but is building a television center on the outskirts of the city which Soviet spokesmen predict will outdo all other television centers, together with a tower 1,722 feet high.* Specifications for television studios are apt to be outmoded as soon as they are drawn up, but the new European studios equal in size and equipment those found anywhere else in the world. There now are many impressive television centers throughout Western Europe, notably in the United Kingdom (both BBC and ITA), France, Ireland, Italy, West Germany, Denmark, Finland, and Sweden.[68]

Most Western studio centers have video tape recorders, usually American-made Ampex or RCA. Other equipment is largely European, such as Siemens, Telefunken, and Fernseh from Germany; Marconi, Pye, and EMI from Great Britain; Philips from the Netherlands; Thomson-Houston from France; and Brown Boveri from Switzerland. Japanese equipment also is beginning to appear. Eastern countries use much Western equipment: For example, the USSR has Marconi and Pye, as well as equipment of its own.

Because the United States for security reasons refuses to sell video tape recorders to East European countries and persuaded Japan also to withhold equipment, the Eastern countries had relatively few video tape recorders even as late as 1967, and not all of these were of compatible design. The first experimental video tape recorders in the Soviet Union were tested in 1961. East Germany first reported developments in 1964, and by 1967 had five video tape recorders of its own manufacture.[69] The number of video tape recorders in Eastern Europe is growing, however, and in time that part of the continent will be well sup-

---

* I visited Moscow during the summer of 1965 when Viet Nam was a source of Russian-American differences. A member of the Russian broadcasting staff remarked: "After we finish our new tower, we can stand on top of it and look down to see what you are doing in Viet Nam." Actually, the Moscow television tower is exceeded in height by several in the United States, including KTHI-TV, Fargo, North Dakota, 2,069 feet; KSLA-TV, Shreveport, Louisiana, 1,791 feet; WRBL-TV, Columbus, Georgia, and WBIR-TV, Knoxville, Tennessee, 1,749 feet. (*Television Factbook*, No. 36, 1966.)

plied. But in the meanwhile, the exchange of programs among Eastern countries as well as between East and West is complicated, since tapes from a limited number of incompatible video tape recorders must be supplemented with film recordings made by the older and less effective kinescope method.

For such special events as the Olympic Games, members of the European Broadcasting Union pool their resources with impressive results.[70] Thus, during the Winter Olympic Games held in January and February of 1964 at Innsbruck, 59 events were transmitted for television and 93 for radio, to 32 radio and 29 television services. The technical staff totaled 485 persons, of whom 104 worked on radio, 242 on television, 98 on film, and 41 on related activities, and 112 motor vehicles were involved, including 15 remote outside broadcast units. This extensive installation was necessary to provide the intricate picture and sound pickups required for the many events, as well as for commentaries and interviews in all the languages involved. EBU committees of legal experts, engineers, and production personnel went to Mexico City in 1966 to lay plans for the 1968 Olympic Games. From their discussions came proposals for a pooled pickup to serve some 47 countries, including OIRT members. Satellite transmissions will be supplemented by the air shipment of tapes, and there will be direct radio circuits to all parts of Europe.*

SATELLITES

Satellites are important both to Europe and America for international program exchange as well as for long-distance domestic transmissions.[71] From October 30 to November 8, 1963, an administrative conference devoted to space communications met in Geneva under the auspices

---

* The rapid expansion of television in Europe has led to the development of central antenna distribution systems to eliminate unsightly jungles of crossbars as well as to improve reception. A German writer even reported that it "is becoming obsolete to have an individual antenna for each receiving set." (Karl Neufischer, "The Definition and the Meaning of the Expressions 'Collective Antenna' and 'Central Antenna,'" EBU Review, 96B:47–59 (March 1966).) In The Hague the Postal and Telegraph Service experimented with connecting 6,000 homes to a central system which provided twelve FM and three television signals, not only from the Netherlands but also from Belgium, Germany, Britain, and France. (Televisie Nieuws, No. 8:1 (1963).) In Amsterdam, where there were more than 10,000 central antenna connections by 1964, this was regarded as a great improvement for everyone except the pigeons: "For when the jungle of masts and crossbars has been swept from the city scene the famous Amsterdam pigeons will be left . . . perchless!" (Televisie Nieuws, No. 15:5 (1964).) Other Western countries experimenting with

of the International Telecommunication Union. The final agreement, signed by over seventy nations, allocated frequencies for the first time to space communications, effective January 1, 1965. Forty-eight frequency bands were assigned for such purposes as space research, space vehicles, the rescue of astronauts, and meteorological satellites. A recommendation was adopted "that the utilization and exploitation of the frequency spectrum for space communication be subject to international agreements based on principles of justice and equity permitting the use and sharing of allocated frequency bands in the mutual interest of all nations."[72]

Satellites can be classified in several ways. There are passive and active satellites, the former merely reflecting radio waves while the latter, far more complex, amplify signals received from earth before retransmitting them. Another important difference is the nature of the orbit. Nonsynchronous satellites do not maintain a constant position relative to the earth's rotation, and hence can be used to relay signals only during those limited periods when they are within sight of both the transmission and reception points. From the standpoint of television, therefore, the synchronous orbit satellite is much more desirable since its speed and altitude keep it constantly over one spot.

The first satellite practical for American-European exchanges was Telstar, launched from Cape Canaveral, Florida, on July 10, 1962. The very next day an experimental program transmitted from Paris to the United States was carried by all three American networks.* This transmission was followed by programs beamed from America to Europe and Europe to America on July 23.[73] Though attracting wide attention, these were limited to about twenty minutes each because of the scheduling problems caused by the different time zones of the two continents and the thirty minutes or less during which the satellite was simultaneously visible from both sides of the Atlantic.

In 1964, satellites were used to relay television programs between the

central distribution systems include Austria, Belgium, and West Germany, while Czechoslovakia and the USSR are among the Eastern countries anticipating similar developments. (Milan Cesky, "Central Antenna Arrays," OIRT, No. 5:39–48 (1962).) There are some parallels to all this in the satellite and translator systems used in the United States, although good reception rather than improved appearance seems to have been the major motivation in the United States.

* This caused considerable dispute between the French and other European television organizations, since the latter contended that the broadcast violated an agreement for a joint inaugural transmission. (New York Times, July 12, 1962.)

United States and Europe on over one hundred occasions. The launching of Syncom 3 on August 19, 1964, in a stationary synchronous orbit over the Pacific Ocean, made possible live transmission of the Japanese Olympic Games to North America and to Europe. Signals were sent by satellite from Japan to California and then by land-line to Montreal, where video tape recordings were made and airlifted to Europe for Eurovision. Signals also were transmitted by microwave relay from Montreal to Andover, Maine, and then via the satellite Relay 1 to Europe.

Synchronous satellites such as the Early Bird, launched on April 6, 1965, are of course the most useful for American-European exchanges. In a stationary orbit some 22,300 miles above the Atlantic Ocean, this satellite can relay signals in either direction between Europe and the United States virtually on a twenty-four-hour basis. Early Bird has a capacity of 240 circuits although later satellites probably will carry at least 1,000. Since a television signal requires the equivalent of about 180 circuits, the telephone and telegraph capacity is reduced to 60 circuits whenever the satellite is used for television. Already this has led to disputes over use priorities which have been complicated because the income potentiality is greater for telephone and telegraph than for television use. Also, European broadcasters complained that the charges for Early Bird were too high, and this produced a year-long boycott of the satellite which ended in the summer of 1966.[74] Synchronous satellites will not eliminate shipping of some video tapes by air, since European-American time differences cancel out the advantages of the expensive satellite transmissions during certain hours. Nevertheless, the intercontinental exchange of television programs by satellite surely will increase in future years.[75]

Of course Europe, too, will have its satellites. The Russians were first with Molnya 1, on April 23, 1965, which began at once to relay programs within the Soviet Union, as well as between Moscow and Paris.[76] By May 1967, five Molnya satellites were in use, providing long-distance telephone, telegraph, and other electronic connections between Moscow and Vladivostok, a distance of some 4,500 miles, and capable of exchanging signals with North America as well. In the future, satellites launched by both East and West will facilitate the exchange of programs among European countries as well as between continents.

CHAPTER III

The Structure and Organization of Continental Broadcasting

A COUNTRY with radio and television broadcasting must assign technical facilities to stations. It must set policies for the regulation of programs and decide on methods of finance. Finally, it must determine the nature of the organization that is to do the broadcasting. Inevitably, government is involved in these processes. There is much debate about its proper role, but government must at least participate in allocating technical facilities and in selecting the broadcasting instrument. Should a government decide to do the broadcasting itself, its role becomes a major one, but even in the United States, the traditional preserve of free enterprise, there must be many pages of laws and hundreds more of regulations before broadcasting can proceed.[1]

At the outset each government must assign technical facilities. The radio regulations accompanying the 1959 Geneva convention stipulate that every station must be licensed by its government,[2] and all countries agree that there must be an orderly assignment of facilities in order to avoid electronic chaos. But no government stops with that. There usually are elaborate procedures for the creation, selection, and regulation of the broadcasting organization.

The fact that broadcasting was the technological successor to postal, telegraph, and telephone services, all of which were mainly government-operated monopolies in Europe, predisposed many countries to government operation of broadcasting too. But the main reason for government involvement is recognition of the importance of broadcasting as a means of communication. Broadcasting has a great potential for good and if possible this should be realized. Radio and television, therefore, usually are expected to meet certain public service standards,

46

and the laws require broadcasters to provide information, education, and culture as well as entertainment. In the United States, for example, Congress decreed that station licenses should be granted only when the Federal Communications Commission found that "public convenience, interest, or necessity will be served thereby."[3]

Broadcasting's potential harm is another reason for regulation. The fact that broadcasts, unlike books and films, can be received in the home without previewing may justify requirements for high moral tone, together with prohibitions against obscenity and profanity. The effects of programs on law and order also are a factor: In January 1926, for example, British listeners were upset by an imaginary BBC news bulletin reporting street riots, while America had its *War of the Worlds* scare in 1938.[4] Almost thirty years later, in 1967, an hour-long April fool broadcast over the German-language radio network in Switzerland, which was a simulated actuality report like its predecessor put on by Orson Welles, convinced thousands that American spacemen had landed on the moon and led many people to the hills to watch for the return of the spaceship. Then there is concern about the influence of broadcasts on international relations: Most European licensees are pledged not to present programs that might imperil the neutrality of the country and programs for foreign audiences are almost always under direct government control.

In most countries, therefore, requirements for public service are more stringent for broadcasters than for the printed press. Because of a shortage of channels, assurances of program excellence sometimes are used as the basis for selection among competing applicants.[5] Channel shortages, and the impossibility of quickly erecting stations to carry statements from "out" groups, probably underlie the frequent requirement that diverse points of view and all recognized political parties be given access to the air—assuming, of course, that conflicting opinions are allowed at all. On the other hand, those countries fearful that hostile political groups may seize broadcasting, or employ it to the detriment of the party in power, may regulate it so as to exclude all minority viewpoints. However, as previously mentioned, countries with a tradition of free speech often prohibit censorship entirely. The importance of radio and television in times of disaster has led to the nearly universal requirement that broadcasters must, upon request from the proper authorities, present certain types of information and announcements. Finally, government almost invariably has the prerogative of taking over broadcasting in time of dire emergency or war.

The Two Basic Theories

Broadcasting grows out of, reflects, and contributes to its environment. Government attitudes toward broadcasting, therefore, are just one aspect of their prevailing theories about information media in general. Where the basic philosophy favors freedom of expression, there probably will be freedom for all means of communication including both printed and electronic media. On the other hand, governments which control information as a general principle probably will control all communication media. Most West European countries follow a free press policy, while those in the Communist East have government-controlled systems. Although this is not a study of political theory, a brief review of these two basic approaches will provide an introduction to the description of broadcasting organizations which follows.[6]

In his *Areopagitica: A Speech for the Liberty of Unlicensed Printing to the Parliament of England,* John Milton in 1644 outlined the issues so clearly that most subsequent treatises on the subject have been indebted to him. Milton declared: "Give me the liberty to know, to utter, and to argue freely according to conscience, above all liberties." If truth and falsehood should be in contest, he continued, "who ever knew Truth put to the worse, in a free and open encounter?"[7]

Another famous statement was provided by John Stuart Mill in his essay *On Liberty*: "If all mankind minus one, were of one opinion, and only one person were of the contrary opinion, mankind would be no more justified in silencing that one person, than he, if he had the power, would be justified in silencing mankind. Were an opinion a personal possession of no value except to the owner; if to be obstructed in the enjoyment of it were simply a private injury, it would make some difference whether the injury was inflicted only on a few persons or on many. But the peculiar evil of silencing the expression of an opinion is, that it is robbing the human race; posterity as well as the existing generation; those who dissent from the opinion, still more than those who hold it. If the opinion is right, they are deprived of the opportunity of exchanging error for truth; if wrong, they lose, what is almost as great a benefit, the clearer perception and livelier impression of truth, produced by its collision with error."[8]

The distinguished American historian Carl Becker summarized the issues very well in 1944: "The democratic doctrine of freedom of speech and of the press, whether we regard it as a natural and inalienable right or not, rests upon certain assumptions. One of these is that men desire to know the truth and will be disposed to be guided by it. Another is that the sole method of arriving at the truth in the long run is by the free competition of opinion in the open market. Another is that, since men will inevitably differ in their opinions, each man must be permitted to urge, freely and even strenuously, his own opinion, provided he accords to others the same right. And the final assumption is that from this mutual toleration and comparison of diverse opinions the one that seems the most rational will emerge and be generally accepted."[9]

Hardly anyone advocates completely untrammeled freedom of expression, although there are vast differences of opinion about the extent and nature of the permissible limitations. The Western point of view was perhaps best stated by Justice Oliver Wendell Holmes: "The question in every case is whether the words used are used in such circumstances and are of such a nature as to create a clear and present danger that they will bring about the substantive evils that Congress has a right to prevent. It is a question of proximity and degree."[10]

To the Communists, on the other hand, the ideal is that of a managed press taking a positive role in organizing the Communist state. Early in this century Lenin wrote: "A paper is not merely a collective propagandist and collective agitator, it is also a collective organizer."[11] Later Stalin declared: "The press is the prime instrument through which the Party speaks daily, hourly, with the working class in its own indispensible language. No other means such as this for weaving spiritual ties between Party and class, no other tool so flexible, is to be found in nature."[12]

At times, Communist statements seem to parallel those from the Western world; and because they use many of the same terms, one may conclude that there is agreement when really there is none at all. For example, Article 125 of the Constitution of the USSR states: "In conformity with the interests of the working people, and in order to strengthen the socialist system, the citizens of the USSR are guaranteed by law: (a) Freedom of speech; [and] (b) Freedom of the press. . . . These civil rights are ensured by placing at the disposal of the working people and their organizations printing presses, stocks of paper, public buildings, the streets, communications facilities and other material requisites for the exercise of these rights."[13] A careful rereading of the introductory phrase shows that there is freedom of speech only for those who will use it to support the established order and not for those who wish to question its basic principles. The mass media are not to present uncensored information from a wide range of sources; they are to play a positive role in developing the socialist system.

Additional perspective is provided by the press law of Yugoslavia, a country of Communist doctrine, even though it vigorously maintains its independence of the USSR. The Yugoslav Law on the Press and Other Media of Information, like the Soviet Constitution, guarantees freedom of expression but only to achieve certain objectives: "In order to ensure the democratic rights of citizens, to strengthen the role of public opinion in social life and to provide the fullest possible information . . . on events and developments in all domains of life in the country and abroad, the freedom of the press and other media of information is guaranteed."[14] It also pledges that there will be "no censorship of the press or other media of information, except in the case of war, or . . . danger of war," and promises that the exchange of information between Yugoslavia and other countries "can only be restricted . . . to protect the country's independence, security and free development, and to ensure the full respect of human rights and freedoms, of public law and order, and of international cooperation in the spirit of the United Nations Charter."

But the press law qualifies these rights by specifying that they "shall not be misused for the purpose of undermining the foundations of the socialist democratic government established by the Constitution, for the purpose of jeopardizing peace or the international cooperation and independence of the state, for the purpose of stirring national, racial or religious hatred or intolerance, or for the purpose of initiating criminal actions, nor shall they be misused to the detriment of public morals." It is further specified: "The publication of information which damages the honour, reputation or rights of citizens, or the interests of the social community, constitutes an abuse of freedom of information, and incurs responsibility as provided for by this Law. . . . The dissemination of information can be restricted only to prevent abuse of the freedom of information, and in cases specifically provided for by this Law."

In summary, then, the Western theory is that within practicable limits all points of view should be heard, under the assumption that the best ideas finally will prevail. Nevertheless, if the things said "are of such a nature as to create a clear and present danger," they may be censored. The totalitarian point of view, on the other hand, is that the press should be used, as the Soviet Constitution declares, "In conformity with the interests of the working people, and in order to strengthen the socialist system."

Each side claims to advocate freedom of speech, although as one Russian broadcaster remarked to me: "Freedom of speech is freedom to tell the truth." The Communists state that they jammed the Voice of America because its falsehoods might have caused unrest or even revolution. As mentioned before, this is the same argument advanced by the British for jamming Greek broadcasts to Cyprus in 1956. It also is the reason some American extremists want to limit the activities of certain groups, whose preachments, they feel, could overthrow the American government, or at least might undermine some cherished American institutions and beliefs.

Evidently, the Holmes dictum is accepted by both East and West as the basis for operations. To be sure there are important differences: The democratic countries believe that extensive discussion is inherently good, while the totalitarian countries limit debate and use the communications media to organize support for the government and its policies. Furthermore, the more secure Western democracies can allow much more questioning of basic concepts before approaching their danger points, whereas the younger and less well established totalitarian countries can afford public debates only about details within the system. But actual practice on both sides seems to be predicted on the "clear and present danger" theory.*

The systems of broadcasting which have grown up under these theories may be classified in several ways: some are monopolistic; others competitive; some are supported entirely by public funds; others depend wholly or partly on advertising revenue. But the most helpful classification from our point of view was provided by Albert Namurois,

* The applications of these theories to program planning are reviewed on pp. 119–123 below.

legal adviser to the Belgian broadcasting organization, who put the broadcasting systems of the world in four categories, ranging from complete state control at one extreme to private operation with very limited government involvement on the other.[15]

The first category is that in which the state itself runs the service, setting it up either as a government department or as a unit under direct control. Broadcasting in the Soviet Union and most other countries of Eastern Europe is of this type. In the second category the state creates a public corporation or authority, granting it considerable independence, though retaining final control. The best known examples are the BBC and ITA in the United Kingdom, although the systems in France, West Germany, and Belgium also belong here.

The third category Namurois describes as "partnerships in the public interest," in which a private corporation is set up, with the state either as the sole stockholder or as a partner along with private interests.[16] The government still retains final control, but legally the corporation is private rather than public. Italy, Sweden, and Switzerland belong here. Finally, there is private enterprise operation, with the state serving only as the licensing and regulating authority. Although the United States and Japan are the best known examples, on the European continent this is the pattern for the private commercial stations of Andorra, Luxembourg, Monaco, and the Saar.[17]

State-Operated Services

A state-operated broadcasting service is one in which radio and television are assigned to a government ministry, department, or completely nationalized administration. As a natural consequence of their basic broadcasting objectives, most Communist countries follow this procedure. Furthermore, countries which distrust private enterprise would almost certainly assign anything as important as broadcasting to a government-controlled agency.

The USSR and Other Communist Countries

In the Union of Soviet Socialist Republics responsibility for broadcasting rests with the State Committee for Radio and Television Broadcasting.[18] This is one of approximately twenty departments whose chairmen are listed in the masthead of the Soviet government and outranked only by the Council of Ministers and the heads of the various ministries. Broadcasting, therefore, is put at the same level of importance as aviation, foreign economic relations, labor and wages, defense technology, ship building, banking, cultural ties with foreign countries, atomic energy, and state planning.*

Although state control of broadcasting has never relaxed since the early days of the Soviet regime, procedures have varied. In 1924 there was a Joint-Stock Company for Radio Broadcasting owned by the trade unions and the educational authorities. In 1928 responsibility was assigned to the Ministry of Posts and Telegraphs, which was succeeded in 1933 by the All-Union Committee for Radio Broadcasting under the Council of People's Commissars. The present committee, the State Committee for Radio and Television, was established in 1957. This committee consists of seventeen members appointed by the Council of Ministers; it is based in Moscow and also serves as the committee for the Russian Soviet Federated Socialist Republic. Each of the fourteen other independent republics of the USSR has its own committee, in addition to which there are regional, district, and local committees. A considerable degree of autonomy is allowed these groups, as their members are quick to point out.

The state committee is responsible for all aspects of both domestic and foreign broadcasting except studio equipment, interconnecting lines, and transmitters which, as in many European countries, are administered by the Ministry of Postal Services and Communications. Under the committee's control, however, are extensive studio and office buildings in Moscow besides production, recording, and experimental facilities. A staff of 35,000 reports directly to this committee or the other committees mentioned above.

The chief officers of the state committee include the chairman and four deputy members who head the major departments of Soviet broadcasting: domestic radio; domestic television; broadcasts for reception abroad; and administrative, technical, and financial operations.† The preparation of programs for the five domestic radio networks is done by fourteen departments organized according to functions and geog-

* Michael T. Florinsky, ed., *Encyclopedia of Russia and the Soviet Union*, p. 207. There is, however, a Postal Services and Communications Ministry which provides all technical equipment, although it has no authority over broadcasting.

† Engineering facilities are described on pp. 26–27, 30–31, 38–39, 42, 45 above; program services on pp. 127–128, 131 below.

raphy. Principal divisions include information (including news programs); propaganda (news, talks, and lectures dealing with political, economic, industrial, agricultural, international, and scientific affairs); programs for children (all types of programs from entertainment to propaganda); programs for youth; literary programs; music (concerts and music education); broadcasts for the Moscow area; audience research (based principally—though not entirely—upon letter analysis); and radio and television exchanges with foreign countries (involving eighty-six countries throughout the world). Another major division deals with domestic television. There are fourteen subsections dealing with such program areas as information, politics, music, drama, and education; presentation aspects such as films, set design, and production; and programs for special age groups like children and youths.

Although international broadcasting is not a major consideration of this study, it should be mentioned that the international broadcasting services of the Soviet Union are the largest in the world, and the deputy in charge of them bears major responsibilities. Also important are the administrative, financial, and technical problems assigned to the fourth deputy. These include the department of personnel, concerned with selecting and training staff; engineering planning and operations; a research division, which among other things reports on the activities of both Soviet and foreign broadcasting organizations, and arranges conferences; publications, which puts out articles in fifty-three foreign languages every day; financial planning; labor and wages; and correspondence.

To supplement its national services the USSR also has decentralized regional and local broadcasting in sixty different languages as well as program distribution by wire. These are administered by fourteen committees in the various Soviet Socialist Republics and twenty in the autonomous republics, as well as by 112 regional (oblast) committees, seven autonomous regional (oblast district) committees, and 153 city committees. Although subordinate to the state committee to the same extent as are their local governments to the Moscow authorities, the local committees nevertheless have much freedom of action. Basically, though, they are organized according to the pattern described above for the state committee.

Despite the fact that broadcasting in the Soviet Union is the formal responsibility of the State Committee for Radio and Television, which reports to the Council of Ministers, the Communist party is a big factor too, as with all important functions in the Soviet Union. The Council of Ministers always is subject to the ultimate power of the top party organs. Furthermore, most if not all the members of the state committee as well as the key officials in the broadcasting organization belong to the party.

Party influence is exercised indirectly when its Central Committee publishes edicts criticizing the operations and output of Soviet broadcasting. That happened in 1960 and again in July 1962, when a detailed analysis of shortcomings was issued that could hardly have been overlooked by the state committee or its staff.[19] In April 1966 at its twenty-third Congress the party stated: "Fuller use must be made of the press, radio, television, and the cinema in order to mold a Marxist-Leninist outlook and promote the political and cultural development of all Soviet People."[20]

The other Eastern countries follow a basic pattern very similar to that of the Soviet Union. Most of them have a broadcasting committee or authority subject to the top organs of government and party, and many followed the same 1957 time schedule in arriving at their present structures. In Czechoslovakia broadcasting formerly was under the Ministry of Information, but in 1948 when the Communist party assumed control it became a national undertaking. Section 22 (2) of the Constitution of that year stipulated that "the right to provide a sound radio and television service is an exclusive prerogative of the government," while section 148 stated that "broadcasting and motion pictures are susceptible only of state ownership."[21] In 1957, Czechoslovak radio and television were moved from the Ministry of Culture and given independent status under a Committee for Radio and Television operating under the Council of Ministers with the director general responsible directly to it.*

Polskie Radio, created in 1945 as a state enterprise, after several transformations in 1960 became the National Radio and Television Committee, appointed by the Council of Ministers.[22] An Advisory Program Council, whose chairman is also the chairman of the National Radio and Television Committee, is appointed by the chairman of the Council of Ministers acting upon suggestions submitted by the chair-

* Czechoslovakia, Hungary, and the Netherlands are the only European countries where radio and television are entirely separated.

man of the committee. The program council includes representatives of the Council of Ministers, trade unions, workers in such fields as music, art, journalism, and the cinema, and some members from the broadcasting organizations themselves. The national committee is in charge of all aspects of broadcasting except the collection of fees, long lines, and transmitters which are the responsibility of the Ministry of Telecommunications.

The five sections of the Polish broadcasting organization, each headed by a vice president, are similar to those of the USSR: domestic radio, domestic television, broadcasting abroad, technical problems, and general administration. There also are several advisory bodies including program, scientific, and technical councils. Although the separate national units are firmly united at the top, they are allowed considerable operating independence and regional studios also enjoy much local autonomy.

Hungarian broadcasting became a state monopoly in 1925, the program service subsequently being assigned to a company known as the Hungarian Central Office of Information, with share capital divided among various political parties and trade unions.[23] This office also was responsible for telegraph service and advertising. In the early 1930's a new corporation with private shareholders was granted an exclusive franchise to engage in commercial broadcasting, subject, however, to regulation by the Ministry of Posts, Telegraph, and Telephone. This evolved into the Office of Hungarian Radio in 1950. Jurisdiction was transferred to the Government Information Office in 1952, and to a new Hungarian Radio and Television Service (Magyar Radio es Televizie) in 1958, within which radio and television are organized separately. This agency now is responsible for all broadcasting in Hungary although transmission facilities are controlled by the Ministry of Posts, Telegraph, and Telephone.

The fact that the new Hungarian, like the Czechoslovak, authority was set up the year following the reorganization of Soviet broadcasting may account for certain similarities in pattern. The top policy group is an advisory council of seven members, made up of the president of Hungarian broadcasting, his administrative assistant, the four vice presidents, and the secretary of the Hungarian Socialist Workers party. The president holds ministerial rank and participates in the government. The main department heads are appointed by the Council of Ministers: There are two vice presidents for radio and two for television. In both media the program activities have been divided into four areas: politics; music; literature and youth; and children's programs. Each of these has its own advisory committee. Asked to characterize the relationships between the broadcasting organization and the Communist party, an official of Hungarian broadcasting replied: "The closest and friendliest relations exist." Another spokesman stated that the president of the broadcasting board reported both to the Council of Ministers and to the party secretary.

Rumania has a broadcasting charter under a decree of 1949 which grants a broadcasting monopoly to a state enterprise directly controlled by the government.[24] Section 1 of this decree states that "the right to broadcast words or music, as also pictures by television with or without wires belongs to the State." Section 2 assigns this right to a Broadcasting Committee under the Council of Ministers of the Rumanian People's Republic which appoints the main officials. The system in Bulgaria does not differ fundamentally from that described above for the other Eastern countries.[25]

In broadcasting as in so many other respects, Yugoslavia departs from the pattern followed by the other Communist countries. Like West Germany and Switzerland, federated Yugoslavia has a considerable measure of decentralization which is evident in its broadcasting too. Each of the six Yugoslav republics as well as the two autonomous regions has its own broadcasting organization. Although independent they exchange radio programs and contribute to a common television service, achieving coordination through a voluntary national association.[26]

The legal basis for Yugoslav broadcasting is supplied by a law which became effective in 1965. There now are eight main broadcasting organizations plus forty-nine local stations, all of which enjoy a considerable measure of independence. Each is a collective headed by an advisory council elected by the employee members from their own ranks.[27] The stations are independent financially, even to the point of setting different license fees for their respective areas.

Membership in the nationwide organization, Jugoslovenska Radiotelevizija, is not obligatory, though all the individual stations belong. This association has a governing assembly composed of five representatives from each station; a managing board elected by the assembly from its own ranks; and a three-man board of supervisors also chosen by the assembly from its members, charged with "supervising the material and financial operations of the association."[28] There also are operational committees dealing with such subjects as spoken word and political broadcasts; cultural, artistic, and entertainment programs; foreign contacts; music; television; technical problems; personnel training; technical matters; and supplies and finance.

The Yugoslav national press law parallels portions of the Soviet Constitution, and procedures under it are not as free as in the democratic Western countries. Yet in structure and practice, Yugoslav broadcasting provides an ideological bridge between the typical Communist and democratic systems.

The Public Corporation

In some countries broadcasting is done by a public corporation chartered by the state. Such organizations normally are not subject to direct government supervision, although they receive policy guidance from a board of directors which often is appointed by the government. Liaison with the state usually is through the ministers of posts, telephone, and telegraph, or education and culture. Although there always are some programing requirements and prohibitions, when the system works well the responsible minister resists pressures to regulate program content. Once the government has laid down basic policies, it usually allows the broadcasting organization much initiative and freedom, including the right to expend funds within the broad limits imposed by charter and license. Yet such corporations always are subject to some supervision and final review, and in extreme situations the state has authority to suspend their operations.

The examples of public corporations treated here are those in France, West Germany, and Belgium. The unusual system of the Netherlands also is described in this category.

FRANCE

The creation of the Office de Radiodiffusion-Télévision Française (ORTF) in June 1964 was a consequence of widespread criticism of French broadcasting. Specific complaints about program service and inadequate personnel were accompanied by charges that French radio and television were dominated by the executive branch of the government. The main objective of the new organization, therefore, was to provide more autonomy for broadcasting. The ORTF, managing its own budget and running its own affairs, was to be governed in matters of broad policy by an administrative council with private as well as government members, and no longer was to be controlled by the minister of information, even though still to be under his tutelage.

The history of French broadcasting reveals that the role of the state has been dominant. A French law of 1923 gave the state a monopoly over radio and television.[29] Between 1923 and 1941, France was served by a combination of state stations operated by the Postal and Telegraph Authority and private commercial stations. Legislation enacted in 1944 following the liberation of France ended all private broadcasting, and Radiodiffusion et Télévision Française (RTF) came into being on March 23, 1945. A subsequent ordinance on February 4, 1959, provided the legal basis for French broadcasting until the recent act of 1964.

The act of 1964 was precipitated by strong criticisms of French broadcasting.[30] There were complaints that the RTF was controlled by the Ministry of Information; that it employed unnecessary and unqualified staff members because of pressure from members of Parliament; that some of the periodic strikes were really protests against government control of news programs; and that even simple projects required high-level—and thus delaying—financial approval. There were frequent changes of top management, coupled with widespread press criticism of state control. This had been bad enough when one party regularly succeeded another in power, but the long De Gaulle regime tipped the scales consistently in one direction. One critic asserted that between 1956 and 1959 French television did not devote a single program to the Algerian revolt, and it was generally agreed that during the 1962 campaign to amend the Constitution so as to strengthen the presidency, the Gaullist position was enormously favored by television.[31] Another famous incident occurred in February 1963 when the RTF canceled television interviews with Nikita Khrushchev and Marshall Rodion Y. Malinovsky.

During the parliamentary debates on the new legislation, the minister of information, Alain Peyrefitte, spoke very frankly about the problems the reorganization was intended to eliminate.[32] He cited two indications of inadequacy in the RTF: the loss of listeners and viewers to stations in adjacent countries and the frequent strikes of RTF staff. He then listed several basic defects in the present organization: unnecessarily stringent financial controls, particularly the requirement for financial approval before all major expenditures; bureaucratic weaknesses within the RTF; the development of small power cliques which interfered with efficient operation; and the susceptibility of the RTF to political pressure.

The solution to these problems, according to Mr. Peyrefitte, was to give the broadcasting organization greater autonomy. There apparently was permanent confusion about which decisions came from the RTF and which came from the government. An example was the Khrushchev-Malinovsky interview. This had been canceled, he said, because Mr. Khrushchev, invited to record an interview for February 7, 1963, commemorating the twentieth anniversary of the Battle of Stalingrad, used the occasion to violently attack the government of West Germany and Chancellor Adenauer. Had this been broadcast it might have been misunderstood in West Germany as an expression of official opinion at the very time the French government was working for rapprochement with Germany. The solution, therefore, was to make the broadcasting organization autonomous so that no one could regard it as an official mouthpiece.

Alain Peyrefitte concluded by outlining "the three attributes of autonomy" to be given the RTF. First was financial autonomy: Like other French public enterprises the new ORTF would be free to determine its budget, subject only to a posteriori review. Second would be the substitution of tutelage (*tutelle*) for government control (*autorité*.) Third would be the creation of an administrative council, with both government and private members, to determine basic policy, operations being left to the ORTF. In summary Mr. Peyrefitte declared: "We hope this will constitute a break with the past. The government-controlled RTF disappears, to be succeeded by an autonomous Office, free of government domination, administered by a Council which will guarantee its impartiality, under a distinguished president, and with a director general really responsible for the administration of the organization."[33]

During the three-day debate in Parliament the Gaullist majority showed some hesitation about surrendering state control of broadcasting because of the hostility of the press to De Gaulle. On the other hand the opposition alleged that, though this was a step in the right direction, the government would still have too much influence, in view of its power to appoint half the members of the administrative council, as well as to appoint and discharge the director general.[34] Nevertheless, the bill was passed by the National Assembly on May 28, 1964, by a vote of 276 to 181, and became law on June 27, 1964.[35]

The new statute describes the Office de Radiodiffusion-Télévision Française as a "public state establishment of industrial and commercial character," created to maintain a "national public service of radio and television" in order to "satisfy the public's need for information, culture, education, and entertainment."[36] Like other French state organs "of industrial and commercial character," the ORTF has an administrative council and is under the *supervision* rather than *control* of a minister. It is the minister of information who safeguards the ORTF's broadcasting monopoly; sees that its public service obligations are discharged; approves the budget jointly with the minister of finance and economic affairs; and checks the use made by the ORTF of its resources.[37]

A decree of July 22, 1964, set the administrative council at sixteen members, half representing the state, and the other half viewers and listeners, the press, the ORTF staff, and the public. All appointments are made by the government with private members chosen from lists drawn up by representative organizations. Council membership is for three years although the terms of office can be ended at any time at the mandate of the members representing the state.[38] This administrative council determines ORTF policy and budget. It also assures itself of the quality and morality of the programs; ensures the objectivity and accuracy of all information broadcast; and sees that the programs reflect the country's main trends of thought and opinion.* The director general and the two deputy directors are appointed by cabinet decree, rather than, as some members of Parliament had hoped, by the administrative council.[39]

ORTF financing is from license fees, and by implication—although the law does not say so—advertising is prohibited.† Financial supervi-

* *Statuts*, Art. 4. It was Parliament that requested the council be responsible for ensuring not only the quality but also the morality of programs.

† But there is periodic speculation on a possible change of policy on this point, partly because of the ORTF's regular deficits. (*New York Times*, November 9,

sion is assured by requiring the minister of information to discuss ORTF financial plans with parliamentary representatives at least once every three months.[40] Nevertheless, the new law provides much more financial independence than did the old one, since the ORTF now is subject only to those controls normally prescribed for a national public undertaking. Accordingly, there now is only a posteriori rather than a priori financial reviews as before. Parliament wanted to insert in the law a guarantee for a right of reply by persons considering themselves injured by materials broadcast. The government did not accept this proposal, but did instruct the director general to preserve recordings for examination by those who believed themselves wronged.

On July 22, 1964, the government published five decrees implementing the new legislation. One of them set up radio and television program committees, appointed by the minister of information. One-third of the members of each committee represent public services, and are chosen after consultation with certain designated ministers; one-third are persons particularly competent in family, social affairs, and news problems; and the remaining one-third come from the arts and entertainment fields. These committees advise the broadcasting authorities on program policies. The director general does not have to follow their advice; but if he ignores it, production of the broadcasts in question may be held up until he has reconsidered his original decision.[41]

Although the new law had the objective of releasing French broadcasting from government control, it still contains many provisions which the government could use to influence, if not control, the ORTF. Thus, the minister of information retains various supervisory prerogatives; the government appoints all the members of the administrative council, as well as the director general and the deputy directors; and Parliament maintains certain financial controls. There also is authority for the government to require the broadcasting of any statements or communications it considers essential, though these must be identified by source.*

The chances for government influence and control surely are less

1964, p. 10; *Variety,* November 17, 1965, p. 27; *Broadcasting,* February 1, 1965, p. 62.)
* *Statuts,* Art. 5. The last requirement was inserted to eliminate embarrassments like that caused by the cancellation of the Khrushchev interview since it distinguishes publicly between broadcasts made by the ORTF on its own authority and those made at government request.

under the new law than under the old one, but such possibilities still exist. For example, during a parliamentary debate which took place the year following the enactment of the new legislation, the minister of information, Alain Peyrefitte—the same man who had told the National Assembly that the purpose of the new law was to free the ORTF from government control—stated that, in view of the virtual monopoly of the printed press by De Gaulle critics, television might properly provide a counterbalance by favoring the General![42] Needless to say, the opposition parties did not accept this theory of the role of the ORTF. But during the presidential election of December 1965 the rival candidates were given air time as never before; and even though they still complained about their treatment, one foreign reporter wrote: "It is something quite new for French people to have five challengers for the presidency, during the lunch hour and at night, dominating the screen with an incessant attack on the regime."*

GERMAN FEDERAL REPUBLIC

The organization of West German broadcasting reflects that country's postwar status and problems. Because Germany was the major defeated power its rebirth was carefully supervised. The occupying victors, aware of its potential strength, organized West Germany as a federal republic divided into a number of separate states or Länder.

---

* London *Times,* December 2, 1965, p. 10; *Variety,* December 1, 1965, p. 23; *New York Times,* January 26, 1966, p. 5. The treatment of elections by the ORTF is discussed further on pp. 153–155.

Rather than draw hasty conclusions about the influence of government on broadcasting from a literal reading of legal documents, one must examine these situations in their national settings. Thus, the BBC and the ITA are two public corporations generally agreed to be quite free of government control. Yet the British government may appoint or dismiss the governors of the BBC at will; revoke its charter for "reasonable cause"; assign or withhold radio frequencies and television channels; determine the amount of money payable by the Treasury to the Corporation; nationalize the BBC in an emergency; or revoke its license for unsatisfactory performance. The postmaster general may, if he wishes, dismiss members of the Independent Television Authority and review the Authority's accounts. The Television Act of 1964 devotes several pages to program standards; furthermore, under the terms of the act, the government has laid down strict regulations for advertising. The British government has the authority to initiate or veto programs on both BBC and ITA. The BBC license states that the Corporation, "whenever so requested by any Department" of the government, is to broadcast "any announcement . . . which such Department may request." (*1962 Licence,* Sec. 15 (3).) There is a similar requirement in the Television Act of 1964 which established the ITA. (*Television Act 1964,* Sec. 18 (1–4).) See also Paulu, *British Broadcasting in Transition,* pp. 15–16 and 39–40.

Divisions of authority between the federal and local governments roughly approximated those in the United States and led to the same kinds of jurisdictional problems, one of the most interesting in regard to television. Broadcasting was organized on a state rather than federal basis because of the unfortunate use of centralized mass communications by the Nazi party.

In the early 1920's there were nine regional broadcasting companies in Germany.[43] These soon banded together as the Reichsrundfunk-gesellschaft (German Broadcasting Company), which continued in existence, though with some changes, until 1945. Following the war, first the transmitters of the occupying forces were developed, after which public broadcasting corporations were set up in the Western zone, beginning in 1948; the last of these was the Saarländischer Rund-funk, organized in 1959. What finally emerged was a system in which nine organizations assumed responsibility for all domestic programing in the eleven Länder. Federal responsibility is limited to assigning technical facilities and to developing such obviously national functions as broadcasts for listeners abroad. The entire system is financed through a combination of license fees and advertising, and the responsibilities for transmitting facilities are shared by the broadcasting organizations and the Post Office.

The nine separate and independent broadcasting corporations are as follows (in alphabetical order with the studio center location and area served by each): Bayerischer Rundfunk, Munich (Bavaria); Hessischer Rundfunk, Frankfurt am Main (Hesse); Norddeutscher Rundfunk, Hamburg (Lower Saxony, Schleswig-Holstein, and the free Hanseatic City and State of Hamburg); Radio Bremen (Bremen); Saarländischer Rundfunk, Saarbrücken (Saar); Sender Freies Berlin (West Berlin); Süddeutscher Rundfunk, Stuttgart (North Wurttemberg and North Baden-Wurttemberg); Südwestfunk, Baden-Baden (South Baden, South Wurttemberg part of Baden-Wurttemberg and Rhineland-Palatinate); and Westdeutscher Rundfunk, Cologne (North Rhine-Westphalia).

The broadcasting corporations are similarly organized although they are set up under the laws of the individual Länder and are quite independent of each other. Each corporation has the objectives of balancing the various social and political forces, and guaranteeing all important elements access to the airwaves, while assuring individual organizations a high degree of autonomy.[44] A broadcasting council, chosen to represent a wide range of constituent interest, is in charge of the corporation. Some members are elected by Land parliaments though most councils also have members appointed by local governments, churches, employers' and workers' groups, educational agencies, the press, and other organizations. Usually government representatives constitute only a minority of the membership.

These broadcasting councils are in effect boards of directors functioning on the policy level. One of their most important tasks is to appoint the administrative councils, which occupy the next level in the hierarchy. Although in certain Länder some administrative council members either are government appointed or hold office ex officio, the majority are chosen by the broadcasting councils. The administrative councils in turn usually appoint the intendants or directors general. Some Länder also have program advisory councils, elected by the broadcasting council and certain local governmental units. Though without authority to enforce their recommendations, these councils are expected to advise the intendants on program matters.

The intendant is responsible for administering the organization according to the general policy directives laid down by the various councils and committees, and he is subject to various legal stipulations that he serve the religious, educational, and cultural needs of the community. Thus, it normally is required that news be of general interest, independent, and objective and that programs not serve the prejudices of any one party, pressure group, philosophy, or creed. With such general requirements, the intendants and their staffs have a high degree of independence.

The individual corporations soon realized that in the absence of a coordinating agency they would have to provide their own national association.[45] Consequently, informal cooperation on such matters as program exchange, technical and legal problems, and long-range plans, led to the organization on June 9, 1950, of the Arbeitsgemeinschaft der öffentlich-rechtlichen Rundfunkanstalten der Bundesrepublik Deutschland (Consortium of Chartered Broadcasting Corporations of the Federal Republic of Germany). Its constitution declares it to be the purpose of the ARD "to further the common interests of the broadcasting organizations," and "to deal with common programme problems and common questions of a legal, technical, and operational nature." This has come to include relations with the federal government and international organizations; contracts with authors, publishers, and artists; the engaging of news facilities; and negotiations concerning technical, allocation, and transmitter problems.

To keep the organization as simple as possible no new administrative offices were set up and each member served in turn as official spokesman. However, as individuals in various regional organizations developed particular skills in dealing with continuing problems, they retained this responsibility. Annual general and committee meetings give direction to ARD activities.*

In the early 1950's ARD members joined forces to develop a short-wave program for listeners abroad as well as a propaganda service for other countries in Europe, with special attention to East Germany. Later, however, these activities were transferred to the federal government. In 1954 ARD began a television program exchange which grew into West Germany's first nationwide network, although individual members continue to do regional programs, and in 1963 the Länder set up another public corporation to operate a second national television network, Zweites Deutsches Fernsehen.

The constitution for the Federal Republic proclaimed "freedom of broadcasting" as a fundamental right but did not specify whether the federal or state governments should legislate in that field.[46] This led to a long and bitter dispute in which each claimed control of the second television network. The federal government insisted that broadcasting was included under "telecommunications," a subject reserved to it. The Länder, while willing to concede control of technical facilities, argued that program control should be exclusively theirs on the grounds that everything not expressly assigned to the federal government is allocated to the states. When finally resolved by a court decision in 1961, there was clarification, not only about the television network but also about the legal status of broadcasting in general.

Shortly after the founding of the Federal Republic in 1949, Bonn had begun to show an interest in broadcasting. A decade of negotiations between the federal government and the Länder culminated in the introduction of a Federal Broadcasting Bill into the Bundestag on Sep-

* At present the ARD also includes the Deutschlandfunk for programs to East Germany and Deutsche Welle which presents all other programs for foreign reception. RIAS participates as a guest. Zweites Deutsches Fernsehen emphasizes its separate identity by not belonging to ARD though it does associate and cooperate with ARD members.

tember 30, 1959. This proposed three federal broadcasting organizations, to be responsible respectively for overseas short-wave services, broadcasts to listeners in other parts of Europe, and a second television service, the latter to be financed primarily from advertising revenue. The three organizations were to be joined together in a public corporation called the Deutscher Rundfunkverband (German Broadcasting Association).

The federal government's plan to enter domestic broadcasting precipitated a violent controversy.[47] On the surface it appeared that the proposal would only establish a corporation like Britain's ITA, which then would contract with private companies for program production. But since the federal chancellor, Konrad Adenauer, in effect was to be sole shareholder there were fears of political control, particularly since the new network was to begin operations in 1961, shortly before the next general election. In addition, the fact of commercial support raised questions about program quality and advertiser control. Accordingly, there were vigorous objections from official Länder spokesmen, as well as from churches, trade unions, and many private citizens. Four Land governments—Hesse, Lower Saxony, Hamburg, and Bremen—brought suit, questioning the constitutionality of the plan.

The matter was finally resolved on February 28, 1961, when the Federal Constitutional Court at Karlsruhe ruled the proposal unconstitutional. The court held that the plan for a second television program violated the constitutional division of authority between the federal and Länder governments. Domestic broadcasting, said the court, is within the competence of the latter; and furthermore the proposal threatened freedom of the air, since the Constitution requires that broadcasting be surrendered neither to the state nor to any single social, political, or economic group. Although the assignment and operation of transmitting facilities is properly a federal activity the federal government should have no control over programs.

On the other hand, because the federal rather than the Land government is responsible for international relations, it could set up the Deutschlandfunk to broadcast to other countries in Europe, as well as the Deutsche Welle, which thereupon took over the short-wave service previously operated by the ARD. Accordingly, both organizations began operations July 1, 1962, with headquarters in Cologne. They are comparable to the Land domestic broadcasting corporations in organization and enjoy a high degree of autonomy. The central government does not directly supervise their programs. Their boards of directors include representatives of the federal government, Land governments, Parliament, the churches, and employers' and employees' organizations. Neither corporation produces anything except news and current affairs programs, however, the remainder being supplied by the Land organizations. Both Deutschlandfunk and Deutsche Welle belong to the ARD.

Left in sole control of domestic television, the Länder decided that competition would be better than monopoly and accordingly set up a new public corporation with offices in Mainz, which took over the second television network, Zweites Deutsches Fernsehen, on April 1, 1963. ZDF enjoys autonomous status and is not subject to direct government control. Its board of directors includes representatives from various governmental and public groups, as does each board of the nine ARD corporations. Cooperation between the first and second network organizations is required by law, so that viewers will be assured of balanced and contrasting programs.[48]

This review of the conflict between the federal and state governments over television does not exhaust the list of controversial problems facing German broadcasting. There also is a running battle between the broadcasters and the press about the propriety of a public corporation deriving income from advertising.[49] Some press spokesmen have argued that because public broadcasting agencies benefit from tax exemption they should not receive income from advertising. Furthermore, commercial broadcasting by a government corporation endangers the economic survival, and hence the independent operation of newspapers. With these arguments have come suggestions that one television network be operated by a group of newspaper publishers. The leader of this campaign is Alex Springer, Europe's largest publisher, who already commands a one-third share of the West German press circulation.

The German example supplements that of France in the public corporation operation of broadcasting. The difference between them is that the centralized French government made the nationwide ORTF a logical development, whereas the division of Germany into highly independent Länder resulted in the creation of nine separate broadcasting corporations to serve their respective areas. Any broadcasting system with state involvement faces the possibility of government influence, so that battles over the control of German broadcasting will never be finished. But decentralization makes it easier for the Germans than for the French to keep broadcasting free from domination by either the government or political groups, thus leaving the program staff independent to do its work. While the French for a time at least encountered a considerable amount of government interference, the Germans, partly because of their experiences with state control in the 1930's, and also because of their balance of parties, utilized both pressure and law to continue a system of independent and decentralized operation.

BELGIUM

Belgium has separate broadcasting corporations to serve the highly antagonistic Walloon and Flemish population groups. There are three public corporations, one each for French and Dutch programming, and the third is jointly administered by the other two to provide technical and administrative services for both.[50]

Broadcasting in Belgium developed in the early 1920's with programs in French and Dutch produced by two private companies and supported by advertising. Some private activity continued up to World War II, but since then the country has had neither private nor commercial broadcasting although periodically there are pressures on the government to reintroduce commercial broadcasting, a movement which may grow now that the Netherlands has introduced commercial television. In 1930, the Belgian Parliament set up a public corporation called the Institut National Belge de Radiodiffusion, which continued operations until the present Organic Act became effective in May 1960.

The new law created three broadcasting institutes. One is responsible for French-language programs (Radio-Télévision Belge—Emissions Française); a second is responsible for Dutch programs (Belgische Radio en Televisie—Nederlandse uitzendingen); the third is the Common Services Institute (Radio-Télévision Belge—Institut des Services Communs). As their names suggest, the first two are responsible for both radio and television broadcasting in the languages named. The third holds title to and administers the premises and technical equipment, and maintains certain administrative and financial activities common to both, including the symphony orchestra, the record and music libraries, and the central reference library. The Common Services Insti-

69

tute also is responsible for domestic broadcasts in German, as well as for all overseas broadcasting and relations with foreign broadcasting organizations.

The first two institutes have separate boards of management of ten members each, appointed by Parliament from panels submitted by various educational, artistic, and public service organizations. The Common Services Institute is governed by these two boards acting jointly as a single general council. The Belgian government, acting upon the advice of the two boards of management, appoints a director general and two program directors for each institute, as well as the two directors general—one for administrative and the other for technical operations—of the Common Services Institute.

An interesting feature of the 1960 Act is the authorization to assign the production of certain types of religious and educational programs to accredited associations in those fields. This has led to the presentation of religious programs under the auspices of Catholic, Protestant, Jewish, and other organizations; cultural and educational programs by religious and philosophical groups; and educational programs by educational institutions, trade unions, and other interested agencies.

In Belgium as in France, the basic broadcasting legislation clearly permits close government regulation. The Organic Act provides for government supervision of purchasing and budgeting; authorizes the minister of cultural affairs to participate in meetings of the board; specifies the appointment of top personnel by the crown; requires government approval of administrative rules and staff regulations; and authorizes government determination of salaries and pensions. There also is provision for the appointment of an advisory committee by the government and authorization for the state to request up to ten hours of broadcast time each month. The institutes are forbidden to schedule broadcasts contrary to law or public interest, harmful to public peace or morality, or likely to offend anyone's convictions or be offensive to a foreign state.

On the other hand, the law states that "news broadcasts shall be given in a spirit of strict objectivity and without any prior censorship," and it is Parliament rather than the executive branch which is concerned with appointments to the boards of management. The ten hours per month requirement is intended to apply only to emergency announcements or programs, and all such broadcasts must be preceded and followed by statements indicating that they are being presented at government request.

While this surely permits day-to-day supervision, the apparent purpose of the act was to provide equality of representation, both to cultural groups and political parties, under situations in which pressure groups would cancel each other out. The principal legal authority on Belgian broadcasting, while admitting that this is "a most complex piece of machinery, whose complications stem from the desire to incarnate the principle of cultural autonomy," nevertheless concludes "that the new charter for broadcasting gives the institutes of the RTB a definite measure of independence from the reins of Government."[51]

THE NETHERLANDS

Broadcasting in the Netherlands is unusual for its division of program responsibilities among several private independent broadcasting societies, all coordinated by a public foundation made up of government and private representatives.[52] Between 1920 and 1926, in recognition of the social potentialities of radio, certain religious and political groups set up their own broadcasting organizations. Each obtained a concession from the government, and after an initial conflict, air time was divided under a law of 1930, the four larger groups getting equal shares whereas the smaller groups received a total of seven hours per week.

Early in 1947 the five organizations then in existence joined to found the Nederlandsche Radio Unio (NRU), and agreed to administer jointly their buildings, studios, technical equipment, and music and record libraries. The NRU also controlled such combined units as orchestras, choirs, and a drama repertoire company; standardized the conditions of employment and social benefits for all personnel; and assumed responsibility for regional broadcasting at home and liaison with broadcasting organizations abroad. Each society, however, remained responsible for its own programs, although machinery was set up for coordinating their output.

Television experimentation began in the Netherlands as far back as the 1920's, some of it under the auspices of the world-famous Philips electronics firm in Eindhoven.[53] After World War II experiments were resumed privately, being taken over in 1951 by the Netherlands Television Foundation (NTS), established in that year by the five broadcasting societies to coordinate television as the NRU did radio.

Although commercial television has been earnestly discussed in a number of European countries, the Netherlands is the only place where it led to the resignation of the Cabinet.[54] In 1961 a bill was introduced into the Dutch Parliament providing for a second television network with commercial support, after the pattern of the British Independent Television Authority. Parliament did approve a second television network, but only on a noncommercial basis. On November 12, 1962, the government introduced another commercial television proposal, this time suggesting that one third of the second network's programs be provided by the already existing noncommercial NTS, with a commercial concessionaire responsible for the remaining two thirds. When a third network was eventually set up, it would be assigned entirely to the NTS, with the commercial contractor then taking over all of the second network. Anticipating objections, such safeguards as profit limitations and requirements for high-quality programing were provided. But this proposal too was rejected.

Debates over commercial television in the Netherlands raised the same issues as elsewhere. There was disagreement about whether the introduction of advertising would raise or lower program quality. A lobby, known as OTEM, made up of various banks, newspapers, and industrialists seeking a commercial television concession, was organized to support the proposal. However, except for the few newspapers with financial interests, the press opposed commercial television, anticipating a loss of revenue and fearing that some of the smaller newspapers, holding minority viewpoints, might thereby be eliminated. The four larger broadcasting societies opposed the proposal bitterly: they had entered radio forty years before in recognition of the social importance of broadcasting, and they did not want to lose or share control now. At the same time, other groups in the population objected to the current arrangements, feeling that they were inadequately represented in the programing. An important factor on the side of commercial television was the favorable audience reaction to TV Noordsee, the short-lived commercial station which was suppressed in 1964. (See p. 24.)

On February 27, 1965, the Netherlands government resigned after a week of crucial meetings could not produce agreement on radio and television policy, including the possibility of advertising.[55] At that point the Liberal party and some Protestant ministers were advocating a limited form of commercial television, whereas other clergymen, though willing to accept advertising, objected to having private contractors produce any programs. Fears that the existing broadcasting societies might be discriminated against were another factor in the fall of the Cabinet.

In June 1965, the new government issued a memorandum on broadcasting, which, after being debated in Parliament, led to the promulgation, effective December 1, 1965, of a transitional radio and television system, pending the passage of a definitive act.[56] It continued the division of major program responsibilities among the existing broadcasting societies, while opening the possibility of licensing new organizations. In April 1966, a draft bill was submitted to Parliament. This was passed in the Second Chamber on January 18, 1967, and in the First Chamber on February 28, 1967, and is expected to take effect not later than 1968.

The new law continues the country's traditional dependence on broadcasting societies as the main source of programs, while reorganizing the coordinating body and introducing advertising as a supplementary source of revenue.[57] General responsibility for broadcasting rests, as before, with the Minister of Social Welfare and Culture. Through a commissioner appointed by and responsible to him, he is in ultimate control of programing, though he has no right of prior censorship. In theory, this commissioner has extensive supervisory powers: He can attend the meetings of the Netherlands Broadcasting Foundation and its principal management (but not program) committees; he can inspect programs; and he has limited disciplinary authority over the people who present them. It is expected, however, that these powers will seldom be used.

The two previous radio and television organizations—the Netherlands Radio Union (NRU) and the Netherlands Television Foundation (NTS)—are merged into the Netherlands Broadcasting Foundation (Nederlandse Omroep Stichting, or NOS).[58] The president of the Foundation is appointed by the crown on the advice of the government, as are a quarter of the members of the general board. Another quarter are appointed by various cultural and social organizations after consultation with the Minister of Culture, and the remaining half are nominated by the broadcasting societies. A Board of Directors, consisting of the President and six members of the Council (three from the broadcasting societies, two from the cultural organizations, and one representing the crown members) is responsible for day-to-day decisions. They are assigned, respectively, to general affairs, technical affairs, financial affairs, personal affairs, regional broadcasting, radio programing, and television programing. There are separate program councils for radio and television, one third of the members of each being nominated by the broadcasting societies, one third by the cultural organizations, and one third by the government. The NOS coordinates over-all program output, is in charge of broadcasting properties, directs domestic regional broadcasting, and represents Dutch broadcasting in its relations abroad, including the exchange of programs with foreign countries.

The new act liberalizes the conditions under which new and minority groups receive air time. It categorizes broadcasting societies according to size (over 400,000, 250,000, and 100,000 members, respectively) and recognizes the claims of other interested groups, such as churches and political parties, for occasional broadcast periods. To be eligible, an applicant society must meet certain standards: its main purpose must be to do radio or television broadcasting; it must be prepared to present a complete and balanced schedule, covering all kinds of subjects; it must not be commercially oriented; and it must have at least 15,000 license holders as members or contributors. The NOS itself is directly responsible for at least 15 per cent of the radio and 25 per cent of the television time, though its maximum total is not to exceed 40 per cent. Most of the remaining time is assigned to the large broadcasting organizations in the ratio of 5:3:1, although there are guarantees of limited air time for some other groups.

Six such societies are now active: the Algemene Vereniging Radio Omroep (AVRO), of no definite leanings; the Katholieke Radio Omroep (KRO), Catholic; the Nederlandse Christelijke Radio Vereniging (NCRV), Protestant; the Omroepvereniging (VARA), Socialist; the Vrijzinnig Protestantse Radio Omroep (VPRO), liberal Protestant; and the newest society, the Televisie en Radio Omroep Stichting (TROS), which was admitted May 11, 1966, and started broadcasting October 1, 1966. These are very large organizations: their total membership of more than two million constitutes 20 per cent of the entire population of the country and more than 50 per cent of all Dutch families.*

* The *Manchester Guardian Weekly* characterized the five older societies as follows: "One staunchly Socialist, one properly Protestant, one militantly Catholic, one

The four main societies must devote some of their time to programs of general interest not limited to their specific points of view, including the news service and other general information programs. Time also is allotted to churches, which are authorized to transfer production responsibility to organizations appointed or created for that purpose. Some Protestant churches assign responsibility to the IKOR (the Radio and Television Commission of the Ecumenical Council of Churches), the CVK (Convention of other Protestant Churches), and the Humanist Confederation. The RKK (Roman Catholic Association) is responsible for Roman Catholic broadcasts. Broadcasting time also is allocated to the RVU (University of the Air), to the National Art Collections Foundation, and to the Foundation for the Promotion of Social and Cultural Aims via Television and Radio (SOCUTERA). Nine of the ten political parties represented in the Netherlands Chamber of Deputies are allowed to broadcast, including—since 1965—the small Communist party.

From 1924 to 1940, broadcasting was supported entirely by the broadcasting societies, which depended upon contributions from their members, but after World War II they began to share the receipts from receiver licenses with the Postal Administration. They also received some income from their program journals, all of which carry advertising. Under the new law, broadcasting budgets are submitted to the government through the responsible minister, and when approved, funds are allocated from the traditional sources listed above as well as from advertising.

The current Dutch system is too new to be judged. On paper, however, it has certain advantages over the previous arrangements. For one thing, it minimizes the role of the older broadcasting societies, making it possible for new groups, representing new interests and points of view, to become active. It simplifies coordination, by centralizing responsibility in a single organization. Finally, the additional income from advertising will provide more resources, particularly important as additional television program hours place even greater demands upon the producing organizations.*

implicitly Conservative, and one (the smallest and some say the brightest) liberally non conformist." (February 4, 1960, p. 5.)

* Since the possibility of commercial support for broadcasting was the key issue that brought down the Cabinet in 1965, the new arrangement deals at length with broadcast advertising (see below, p. 109).

Private Corporations

Namurois describes the broadcasting organizations of Italy, Sweden, and Switzerland as "partnerships of public authorities and private interests."[*] Legally, these are private corporations in which the government, sometimes together with private interests, holds stock while reserving certain ultimate control powers. Thus, the government may take a part of the capital for itself; it may insist that private stockholders be nationals of the country; it may retain more voting power than its stockholdings merit; and it may control a certain number of seats on the board of directors, often sufficient to ensure a majority. Some of these companies—that in Sweden, for example—actually have provided some profit returns for private stockholders. The broadcasting organizations of Italy, Sweden, and Switzerland are examples of private corporations over which ultimate control is exercised, in theory at least, by their respective governments.

ITALY

The Italian Postal and Telecommunications Code stipulates that broadcasting services belong to the state, which may operate them directly or delegate them by special agreement.[†] Accordingly, Italy's first broadcasting organization, Unione Radiofonica Italian, a limited company, was set up in 1924 for six years. This was succeeded in 1927 by Ente Italiano Audizioni Radiofoniche, with a twenty-five-year franchise, which changed its name to Radio Audizioni Italia (RAI) in 1944. In 1952 the charter was rewritten to include television and extended to 1972. In 1954, with the inauguration of a regular television service, the name of the company was changed to RAI-Radio-televisione Italiana.

---

[*] Such an organization, he says, is "a private corporate entity whose purposes are to serve the public interest, and which on that account enjoys the organic participation of the public authorities and is accordingly subject to regulations which depart somewhat from those of ordinary commercial or civil law." (Namurois, *The Organization of Broadcasting*, p. 78, hereafter cited as Namurois.) Terrou and Solal put Italian broadcasting in the category of "enterprises taking the form of commercial companies." (Terrou and Solal, *Legislation for Press, Film, and Radio*, p. 163, hereafter cited as Terrou and Solal.)

[†] The following reasons are given for the state broadcasting monopoly: It avoids the private monopoly which would result from the scarcity of wave lengths if broadcasting were done privately; it guarantees service to all parts of the country including lightly populated areas where private commercial broadcasting might not be economically feasible; and it provides better guarantees of impartial and objective programing than would private enterprise. (RAI, *This Is RAI*, pp. 1–2; Namurois, pp. 79–82; RAI, *RAI*.)

STRUCTURE AND ORGANIZATION

The present concession gives RAI a monopoly of all radio and television broadcasting in Italy as well as control of program distribution by wire.

Legally RAI is a private corporation whose relations with the Italian government are regulated by a contract. The majority of its shares belong to the Istituto per la Ricostruzione Industriale (Institute for Industrial Recovery, or IRI), the government agency administering most of the state's holdings in industrial, commercial, and banking concerns. The remaining shares are privately held.

RAI is constituted so that the government is assured of being able to control its policies and procedures. The majority of stock in the general meeting of shareholders must be held by the government agency, IRI, so that the government is certain of a majority of the votes. Thirteen of the twenty members of the board of managers are elected by that general meeting, and the other seven appointed by various government ministries. Although the board of managers may elect its own chairman and vice chairman (from its members), as well as the managing director and director general of the company, all these appointments must be approved by the minister of posts and telecommunications after consultation with the council of ministers. There also is a board of auditors presided over by an official of the state general accounting office. Furthermore, the constitution and rules of the company must be approved by the minister of posts and telecommunications, after consultation with the special parliamentary committee set up to supervise RAI.

In addition to these direct administrative controls, RAI is required to submit its program plans for quarterly approval by the Ministry of Posts and Telecommunications, which, however, is expected to be guided by a committee in determining cultural, artistic, and educational policies. The 1952 charter gives the government some controls over news programs, "which might prejudice international relations or the good name of the state, or general interest." There is a parliamentary committee of thirty members, representing both houses and all parties, whose function it is to ensure political independence and news objectivity. On the technical side, the Ministry of Posts and Telecommunications must approve in advance all major technical installations and alterations, as well as supervise their performance, although RAI operates its own transmitting facilities. Finally, financial, administrative, and accounting checks are provided by the Treasury, the Ministry of Posts and Telecommunications, and the state auditing office. (RAI revenues consist of the proceeds from license fees, as well as the receipts from radio and television advertising.)

Internally RAI is departmentalized for administration, radio programming, television programming, news, radio engineering, television engineering, and foreign relations. There also are service departments for personnel, building, research, and technical studies, as well as the Telescuola Center. The latter, incidentally, has been given a measure of independence from other program activities since its head reports to the director general, rather than to the director of television programming.

In 1956, a private company challenged the RAI monopoly by applying to the Ministry of Posts and Telecommunications for permission to develop a commercial television service.[59] In the ensuing case before the Constitutional Court in 1960, the company argued that because the Italian Constitution of 1947 guarantees all men freedom of expression through all media, as well as freedom for the arts, sciences, and private enterprise, the state cannot monopolize broadcasting. In opposition, however, RAI maintained that the Constitution also authorizes the operation by the state, "in the general interest," of certain activities involving "essential public utilities" or "monopoly situations" which are "preeminently a public service." In its decision the court ruled against the private company, reasoning that because of the limited number of channels, television is in the "monopoly situations" category; that it is "preeminently a public service"; and that reasons of "general interest" justify a state monopoly.*

The decision also pointed out, however, that the monopoly status of RAI carried with it an obligation to make air time available to all points of view. Article 2597 of the Civil Code, in fact, requires that anyone operating a statutory monopoly is legally obliged to give equal treatment to all.[60] The court even went so far as to state that the situation required additional legislation to that effect.

In view of the potential for government control built into the RAI legal structure, it is important that the government leave the organization freedom of operation, if that is its intention. Some critics, however,

---

* The decision applied to television broadcasting only, but it is likely the same reasoning would have been applied to radio if the RAI radio monopoly also had been questioned.

have claimed that the Italian government often has gone in the opposite direction. Using its authority to name the principal RAI officers, the Catholic-oriented Christian Democratic party, long dominant in Italian politics, usually assigns these positions to party members. It also has been claimed that, in the years since the decision, neither the government nor RAI has done what it could to bring more points of view to the air.* But a review of RAI operations leads to the conclusion that, on the whole, the system works well. The range of offerings is wide, and in addition to much fine educational and cultural material includes many political and controversial programs which the government would suppress if it wanted to. Perhaps the best comment was provided by the staff member who remarked that, while Italy's RAI may not be as free as Britain's BBC, in view of Italy's Fascist background, RAI is very free indeed, and is making steady progress in the right direction.

Four other corporations are directly associated with RAI. The first is ERI—Edizioni RAI-Radiotelevisione Italiana—RAI's own publishing company, which produces the weekly program guide, *Radio Corriere-TV*, and many program bulletins and brochures, in addition to small luxury editions of art books and similar publications. The second, SIPRA—Societa Italiana Pubblicita Radiofonica Anonima—of which ERI and RAI are the sole shareholders, handles all radio and television advertising. The third is SACIS—Società Per Azioni Commerciale Iniziative Spettacolo—the RAI agent for the rental and purchase of films for television; and it conducts all RAI negotiations with the commercial film industry, including the rental of feature films. The fourth, TELESPAZIO, created in October 1961, operates an experimental satellite receiving station and is responsible for the reception of signals for both telephone and television communications.

SWEDEN

Sveriges Radio is a limited-liability company with a monopoly of radio and television broadcasting in Sweden. Supplementing the Arti-

---

* One critic ended his analysis of RAI operations with this statement: "The conclusion to which an attentive observer is inevitably led on assiduous observation of the production of the Italian radio and television is then that a good technical and artistic level shadows but cannot hide the central problem of free expression, which remains unresolved. Only an independent Authority, directly responsible for its production and organizationally pluralistic can satisfy the requisites of objectivity and wealth of information, of cultural vitality and liberty, and of recreational shows

cles of Association which constitute the company is an agreement with the government about programing. Operation of the transmitters and connecting links, however, is a responsibility of the Telecommunications Administration. Sveriges Radio also is in charge of broadcasts for listeners abroad, as well as of the preparation of transcriptions for use in other countries.

Although broadcasting in Sweden grew out of the activities of various amateur radio clubs, it has been the monopoly of a single company since 1925.[61] Sveriges Radio, as it has been called since 1956, is a private corporation, in which, unlike the situation in Italy, the state has no stock. Ownership of shares must be one-fifth by the press; three-fifths by large national organizations and popular movements; and one-fifth by business and industrial interests. None of the shares are held by individuals. The board of governors consists of a chairman, ten other members, and ten alternates chosen to represent various cultural, social, administrative, economic, and technical interests. The government appoints the chairman and half the board members and alternates, the others being elected by the stockholders at the annual general meeting.

Conditions for broadcasting are governed by an agreement between Sveriges Radio and the government, which runs for five years and is automatically renewed in the absence of notice to the contrary. The government reserves the right to allocate license revenues through the Ministry of Communications, and to determine the number of broadcasting hours. Programs must inform, instruct, and entertain; be objective, impartial, and varied; and be presented with full regard for the potential of broadcasting in the cultural and social life of the nation. There is a government-appointed broadcasting council of twenty-four members which reports to the minister of communications once a year. It is to exercise retrospective surveillance over programs, and to make certain that Sveriges Radio lives up to the terms of the broadcasting agreement, but it has no powers of censorship, and it cannot give any kind of directives either to the director general or the board of governors. It also deals with complaints about the program service. Commercial broadcasting is prohibited, and, except for the right of certain state

of dignity and intelligence, which are the very foundations of a forward looking democratic society." (Cesare Mannucci, "Structure and Policy of the RAI-TV," *Gazette*, 11 (No. 1):67 (1965).)

authorities to make announcements of great importance to the public, the corporation acknowledges no outside claims on program time.

Although the board of governors is the final authority within Sveriges Radio, it is concerned with general policy rather than day-to-day problems, ultimate responsibility for the latter being vested in the director general, who is appointed by the board. Under him are separate radio and television organizations, each with its own program director, as well as heads for music, drama, overseas broadcasts, publications, talks, administration, and technical services. The central news room, which provides basic material for both radio and television, reports to the director general.

To make long-range plans a government commission was appointed in 1960 to study the growth and financing of radio, its assignment being extended in 1962 to include television.[62] On April 7, 1965, the commission published a 750-page report, which soon came to be regarded as the Swedish counterpart of the British *Pilkington Report*. The committee recommended that Sveriges Radio be transformed into a foundation, the nearest practical equivalent in Swedish law to the public corporation encountered in many countries; that the board of governors be reduced to half its present size; and that the organization be generally streamlined. However, Parliament rejected the first two proposals. Various suggestions were made for restructuring the program departments: One was the further development of regional broadcasting centers, and another a comprehensive plan for three day-long radio services. In addition, a second television network was proposed beginning in 1968, although this will not begin until 1970. Special attention was given to educational programs for both radio and television. Other proposals concerned financial matters and it was suggested that, although advertising was barred, radio licenses be abolished and total costs borne by an increased television license.

The committee recommended against advertising, but the subject of commercial broadcasting came up during public discussion of the committee's report, partly because of the development of pirate stations in the vicinity of Sweden. There are pressures for and against commercial television and it would not be surprising to find it emerging in Sweden as it has in other countries. If the pressures for it become strong, however, Sveriges Radio probably would react sympathetically, in order to put itself in a position of influence and control. All things considered,

Sweden seems an outstanding example of a country which allows its broadcasting services operational freedom, even though its laws contain the potential for government control.

SWITZERLAND

The broadcasting organization of Switzerland, as mentioned before, was designed with special consideration of that country's three major linguistic groups and the feelings of separate identity which characterize the individual cantons. The Swiss national broadcasting system is divided into three quite autonomous sections for day-to-day operations.*

The basic concept of decentralization within a single organization was established on October 14, 1922, by the first federal broadcasting law. This made broadcasting a state monopoly, with the responsibility for programs assigned to the Société Suisse de Radiodiffusion and for transmitters and transmission lines to the Ministry of Posts and Telegraphs. The SSR included several regional radio companies, each responsible for broadcasting in its area and subject to the basic broadcasting law and to coordination by the central organization.

The emergence of television in the early 1950's, however, brought special problems.[63] As the public began to demand a television service, and citizens on the borders began tuning in programs from adjacent countries, the federal government decided to create a constitutional basis for controlling television. Accordingly, in July 1953, the federal council proposed an article for the Constitution which read as follows: "Legislation on radio and television is a federal matter. The erection and operation of transmitting stations is the responsibility of the Confederation. The Confederation shall entrust the programme service to one or more public or private institutions. It shall see to it that the spiritual and cultural needs of the cantons, of the different parts of the country, of the various classes of the population, and of the various linguistic regions are fairly taken into consideration."[64]

Commenting on this draft the council declared: "Since radio and television are of a public nature and cater for the whole of the population,

* There are four official languages in Switzerland. French is used by 20 per cent of the inhabitants, who live mainly in the western portion of the country; Italian by 6 per cent living mostly south of the Alps; and German by the 73 per cent majority, in the northern and eastern areas. The fourth language, Romansch, is spoken by about 1 per cent of the population living in the Grisons in the eastern zone of the country.

constituting a community of feeling and intellect upon which they exercise an influence, it is necessary to introduce special rules regarding the legal status of these institutions. As the subject-matter of a public utility, the programmes must serve the interests of the country and of culture, as well as meet the wishes of subscribers and the authorities. Radio and television accordingly cease to be a private affair for those very reasons. . . . The close relationship between radio and television compels us to lay down their legal status in one and the same Article."

The new article, which would have granted the Swiss Confederation the right to legislate on matters pertaining to radio and television program services, was made the subject of a national referendum on March 3, 1957.* With 58 per cent of the eligible voters participating, the proposal was rejected by a margin of 427,859 (57.3 per cent) to 319,634 (42.7 per cent), with 11½ cantons in favor of it and 10½ against. The defeat of the proposal may best be explained by saying that its adversaries feared it would give the central government a free hand to use public funds to finance television.†

After several more years of discussion it was decided to reorganize Swiss broadcasting without special constitutional provisions in order to simplify its structure, lower its costs, and improve program services. Accordingly a new license was granted to the Société Suisse de Radiodiffusion et Télévision effective on November 1, 1964.[65] The SSR's nine member societies have been absorbed by three new regional organizations, each of which represents one of the three major language areas. The Swiss government appoints the chairman and seven members of the seventeen-member central committee, and also nominates a minority of the members of the three regional organizations. The governing body, the annual general assembly of 103 members, is made up of some delegates appointed by the three regional organizations mentioned above, along with representatives from the regional program committees, the national television committee, the short-wave program committee, and the central committee.

The new license granted to the SSR by the federal council gave the

* It should be noted that the referendum forms an important part of the Swiss Constitution, and that it is obligatory to submit all constitutional amendments passed by the Assembly to popular vote.

† Pigé, p. 93, wrote: "One should not infer from this decision a condemnation of television as such; it essentially was a matter of control by federal authority." See also *EBU Review*, 47B:25 (February 1958).

organization a monopoly in radio and television broadcasting.* The Ministry of Posts and Telegraphs was given control of transmitter and linking facilities, which are operated in accordance with whatever national obligations are assumed by the Swiss government. Acting under authority of the law, the federal council designated the Department of Transport, Communications, and Power (formerly the Post and Railway Department) to supervise the functions performed by both the SSR and the Ministry of Posts and Telegraphs.

The programs "must defend and develop the cultural values of the country and make a contribution to intellectual, moral, religious, civic, and artistic education."[66] They must supply objective information, as well as "meet the need for entertainment." Programs also "must serve the national interest, consolidate national unity and harmony, and contribute to international understanding." It is expressly forbidden to present "broadcasts likely to endanger the internal or external security of the confederation or the cantons, their constitutional order, or the relations of Switzerland with other countries." The government "reserves the right to name the sources from which news for broadcasting shall be drawn." Although the government may require official communiqués or urgent police messages to be broadcast, "It is forbidden to demand that specific works or ideas shall be broadcast. . . ."

The new license also guarantees proportionate representation in the SSR organization to the "four linguistic regions," and assures program service to the small minority using Romansch.[67] But at the same time that it promises regional autonomy, the license holds the SSR responsible for coordination and exchange among the regions. The central organization also is to arrange foreign short-wave broadcasts and program distribution by wire. New to Swiss broadcasting was a provision allowing commercial support of television—but not radio—broadcasting, subject to rules laid down by the government.[68]

The SSR license brings to Swiss broadcasting the same spirit of compromise that permeates the country's entire structure. The three language groups—each jealous of its individuality, though never hostile to

---

* Arts. 1–4. Though there is little likelihood that the federal council would break the monopoly on domestic broadcasting assigned the SSR, it is quite possible that a concession for international broadcasting may be granted in a few years to a Protestant organization, Emetteur Protestant International, which has applied for one. This would not replace the present government-operated international broadcasting service.

the point reached by the French and Flemish groups in Belgium—are guaranteed separate services, although as parts of a single organization. The legal structure of the SSR could be used for government domination: The federal council which grants the license also designates the supervising body (the federal Department of Transport, Communications, and Power); it appoints the president of the central committee; and it must approve the appointment of the director general. Broadcasts likely to endanger the security of the country are prohibited; and the government even has the right to name the sources from which news shall be drawn. Still, the committee members appointed by the federal council are numerically in the minority and in fact broadcasting proceeds on the same even keel as do most things in Switzerland, with little if any evidence of government interference with freedom of expression by individuals or groups.

Private Commercial Stations

Private commercial stations are the fourth category of broadcasting organizations. But the state must be somewhat involved even with them, not only in assigning technical facilities but also in chartering the broadcasting organizations, determining the nature of their financial support, and asserting certain minimum program requirements.

Europe's four private commercial stations are located in three small countries, Luxembourg, Monaco, and Andorra, and in the Saar, formerly attached to France and now a part of Germany. Except for Luxembourg, which has regular programs in other languages too, these stations broadcast mainly in French for French audiences. Of interest and importance is the fact that the stock of all of them is mainly French-owned, and that three—Radio Monte Carlo, Europe 1, and Radio des Vallées in Andorra—are controlled by the wholly French government-owned corporation, Sofirad (Société Financière de Radiodiffusion), even though they compete with the programs of the noncommercial ORTF.

The best known of these stations is Radio Luxembourg. The present corporation, following some early experiments and succeeding a previous company founded in 1929, was set up as the Compagnie Luxembourgeoise de Radiodiffusion (CLT) on May 31, 1931.[69] Operating first as a high-powered radio station and adding television in 1955, the CLT became an extremely profitable operation.[70] With long-wave, medium-wave, FM, and short-wave transmitters, and a power potential of up to a million watts, its radio programs in French, Dutch, German, and English are clearly designed for foreign listeners. Luxembourg television uses the 819-line system and is programed in French for viewers in France and Belgium.

Radio Luxembourg was founded under a law passed December 19, 1929, which conferred upon the Ministry of Posts, Telephone and Telegraph the right to license and supervise broadcasting stations. The law required that the majority of the administrative council and station staff be Luxembourg citizens; that equipment, so far as possible, be purchased within the Grand Duchy; and that a government commissioner, advised by technical and program committees appointed by the minister of posts, telephone and telegraph, may attend but not vote at meetings of the administrative council. The station is obliged to maintain "complete neutrality in political matters," in addition to which its programs must maintain an "elevated cultural level."

Approximately 58 per cent of the stock of the CLT is held by French interests and 37 per cent by Belgian. The Luxembourg government was somewhat concerned over a newspaper report in May 1965 that Sofirad was about to purchase some of the stock.[71] As the story put it: "In official circles, the participation of Sofirad could have but one objective: to facilitate the coordination of programs and advertising among the several stations located on the periphery of France." Sofirad already held 80 per cent of the stock of Radio Monte Carlo; 97 per cent of that of Radio des Vallées, Andorra; and 39 per cent of that of Europe 1. But as things turned out, Sofirad did not purchase any Radio Luxembourg stock.

The status of Europe 1, the commercial radio station in the Saar, was complicated by several changes in the Saar's international legal status. After World War II, this territory was under French administration until January 1948; it had semi-autonomy from then until June 1956; and thereafter was united politically with the Federal Republic of Germany in 1957 and economically in 1960.[72] In 1952 commercial radio and television stations were established in the Saar by the Société Saaroise de Télévision which belongs to the holding company Images et Son, controlled in turn by a group of which the largest stockholder is also the president of Radio Monte Carlo. When the Saar was united with West Germany in 1957, Federal Republic authorities took steps which, after extended litigation, led to the television station joining the Saarländischer Rundfunk. But Europe 1 was allowed to continue as a privately owned radio station, programed in French by direct line from Paris, even though its transmitter, with power up to a million watts on 182 kilocycles, is located in Germany. At present Sofirad holds around 39 per cent of the stock of Europe 1; however, since some of these shares have more than one vote on the board of directors, it in effect has a 43 per cent representation on the board. Incidentally, Europe 1 and Radio-Télévision Monte Carlo both have the same sales representative in Paris.

Broadcasting in Monaco assumes even stranger aspects. Radio Monte Carlo was begun during World War II by Joseph Goebbels in order to propagandize North Africa.[73] Now a private commercial corporation controlled by Sofirad, it presents commercial radio and television programs for a French audience over transmitters located on national military property across the Monte Carlo border inside France.* From time to time the ORTF has begun legal action against Radio Monte Carlo, and in 1959 it tried unsuccessfully to persuade the French Ministry of National Defense to revoke the authority it had given the station to locate its transmitters on French military property.

Early in 1965 Radio Monte Carlo, adding to its other high-powered transmitters, began to broadcast experimentally with 1,250,000 watts on 218 kilocycles, thus becoming the most powerful long-wave station in the world. In this way it hoped to cover much of southern France, although its use of such high power on a frequency assigned to Oslo, Norway, brought vigorous objections from the Norwegians.

In the summer of 1964, Sofirad purchased a controlling interest in Radio des Vallées in Andorra, of which it now owns 97 per cent of the stock, thus completing its ring of stations around France. It invested a million French francs in modernizing the station, which at certain hours relays Monte Carlo programs.†

There are a number of explanations about why the French government has purchased stock in these stations. One is that because many Frenchmen listen to them, the government wanted to be certain they

---

* Because of the low altitude of the Principality of Monaco, it was necessary to seek the 3,281-foot altitude of Mont Agel, seventeen miles away, in order to achieve wide coverage.

† Andorra has a second commercial station, Radio Andorra, which also uses high-powered transmitters to broadcast in French or Spanish, but which does not belong to the Sofirad group.

broadcast Gaullist points of view.[74] With the ORTF often regarded as a government mouthpiece, it was hoped that these stations, whose ownership was not widely known, would be very effective supporters of government policies. On the other hand, ORTF spokesmen point out that since these virtually are French stations anyway, so far as their audience is concerned (except for Radio Luxembourg), the government is justified in controlling them to the same degree it does those on its own soil. In the absence of extensive documentation the observer must choose his own explanation.*

All European systems are closer to their governments than are broadcasters in the United States, which is inevitable with government-chartered organizations. To an American this may seem to guarantee government involvement, but this is not always the case. The basic question is how does the system work, not how does it look on paper. Laws and regulations for broadcasting are meaningful only in their national settings. No country allows its broadcasting organization absolute freedom. At the very least the assignment of technical facilities is supplemented by some stipulations for program performance. All broadcasters are

*In this connection it should be noted that many French listeners depend on Europe 1 and Radio Luxembourg for news because they believe that the reports on these commercial stations are more dependable and objective than the broadcasts of the ORTF.

In both Portugal and Spain national and private systems operate side by side. The official Portuguese service, Emissora Nacional de Radiodifusão, is run as a public corporation by the state. (Mario Moreira da Silva, "The Legal Position of Broadcasting in Portugal," *EBU Review*, 82B:53–61 (November 1963); Pigé, pp. 83–84; Walter Emery, *Five European Broadcasting Systems*, pp. 39–51.) Its director general, as well as the directors of the technical and administrative services, are all appointed by the government. Financing is mainly from license fees. In addition there are two stations in Lisbon and Oporto run by a Catholic organization and a number of commercial stations operated by four licensees. International radio services are provided by the Emissora Nacional de Radiodifusão. Portuguese television is assigned to a private corporation in which the state has one-third of the capital and the private radio stations another third, with the rest offered to public subscription. The corporation is directed by an administrative council of three members, the president being named by the state.

The Spanish system also includes public and private services. ("Spain: Reorganization of the Department of Broadcasting and Television," *EBU Review*, 47B:24–25 (February 1958).) The government service, Radio Nacional De España, also is in charge of short-wave broadcasting. In addition, there are the Falange network owned by the National Delegation of Press and Radio and operated by the political party, an educational network with transmitters in sixty cities, and a good many private commercial stations, most affiliated with one of four networks. The government stations are supported by government subsidies plus some commercial revenue. The single government-owned television service, operated by the Ministry of Information and Tourism, derives its support from advertising.

charged with certain educational and public service functions and in addition, in the democratic countries, there normally is a requirement for fairness in the treatment of controversial and political material. Furthermore, broadcasting is not to jeopardize law and order, nor are there to be programs which might endanger the neutrality or international political status of the country concerned. Programs designed primarily for foreign audiences invariably are under government control.

This chapter has grouped broadcasting organizations into four categories: state-operated services, with the government itself in direct charge; public corporations, chartered by the state, but highly independent; private corporations with the state a stockholder, either alone or together with private interests; and private enterprise operation. In the Soviet Union and the other countries in the first category, broadcasting is an integral part of a carefully managed information and press policy. No pretense is made of allowing the broadcasting organization any considerable independence. At the other extreme, in category four, are the private enterprise operations in which government involvement in program policy is minimal. Most West European broadcasting organizations, however, fall into categories two and three, which are more difficult to generalize about.

The question of whether a given system is a public or a private corporation seems to make no difference at all: Judgments must be made on an individual basis. The British Broadcasting Corporation and the Independent Television Authority are public corporations enjoying a high degree of freedom; West Germany, Belgium, and the Netherlands likewise are very independent; and if France, even while making progress, has not yet achieved the same measure of freedom, this is due to the climate of French politics rather than to the phraseology of the law. Among the private corporations, Sweden is as free as any broadcasting system anywhere, and Switzerland about equally so; Italy, though not as independent of government as either of those, has made remarkable progress since World War II.

CHAPTER IV

The Finances of Continental Broadcasting

ᴎ THE main sources of support for continental broadcasting are license fees, advertising receipts, and direct government grants. Subsidies obviously are necessary in countries like Vatican City and the Soviet Union, which do not require licenses and have little or no advertising revenue. They also are essential when license receipts and commercial income are inadequate, as during the early stages of a broadcasting service. In other instances operational deficits are covered by subsidies, while in almost all countries television is supported initially by a combination of diversions from radio funds and direct government grants. But in the last analysis, license fees and advertising income are the principal sources of support for most continental systems.*

License Fees for Radio and Television Receivers

Half the countries of the world, containing half the world's population, require radio and television set users to purchase yearly licenses.[1] On the European continent only Andorra, Monaco, San Marino, Spain, the Soviet Union, and Vatican City do not require licenses. Except for San Marino, which depends entirely on Italy for programs, all these countries have broadcasting services.† On the other hand, Luxembourg requires licenses, but turns the entire proceeds into the state treasury, supporting its broadcasting entirely from advertising revenue. Countries with both radio and television usually offer a choice of one license for radio or a combination license for a dwelling unit with radio and

* Although excise and sales taxes often are levied on receivers, these usually are sources of revenue for general government needs rather than for broadcasting.

† In Andorra and Monaco, broadcasting is commercially supported; in the USSR and Vatican City it is paid for out of the national treasury; in Spain it derives support from state subsidies and advertising.

television. In addition there often is a special license for homes receiving radio programs by wire. Normally, a combination of the licenses costs less than the total for individual ones.

When broadcasting grew up in the early 1920's, yearly taxes on sets were among the first methods of financing introduced. What could be more logical than that the listeners, for whom the programs were presented, should support the service? Yet in several countries, including the United Kingdom and the United States, the first program services were supported by set manufacturers in order to stimulate receiver sales. This pattern was repeated recently when the National Broadcasting Company, a subsidiary of the Radio Corporation of America, invested millions of dollars in color television programs to create a demand for color sets—RCA was not only the major manufacturer but also the holder of patents used by other manufacturers. As was pointed out above, licenses are required in Luxembourg, where broadcasting is both private and commercial; but the introduction of a commercially supported system in the United Kingdom in 1954 did not lead to any reduction of license fees for those people who claimed that, because they viewed the ITA and not the BBC, they should contribute nothing to the BBC. It also should be observed that, in a number of cases, countries withhold portions of license fee income for other government expenses.*

In the early years, when hardly any home had more than one receiver, there was no problem about assessing license fees for dwelling units with more than one set, but the question arose as people began to acquire additional radios. In most countries now, one license covers all the radios in a dwelling unit although additional licenses usually are required for receivers in automobiles and boats, and for portable sets. Some countries with wired distribution systems cover them with off-the-air licenses, while others require special licenses. Once television advanced beyond the experimental stage licenses were introduced

* Services for listeners abroad usually are financed directly by the government rather than charged against license or commercial revenue. The broadcasting organizations in France and Italy advance the necessary funds and then are reimbursed by their governments, and the BBC receives an annual grant-in-aid from the treasury. But in Belgium, although there is a government subsidy, broadcasting abroad is charged against license fees; and in Switzerland, short-wave costs are withheld from license fee receipts. ("Financing of Shortwave Services," *EBU Review*, 68B:12 (July 1961).)

for it too, with higher fees reflecting greater costs. Because most dwelling units with television have one or more radio receivers television licenses usually cover radio as well. The combined fee is often three or four times more than for radio alone and it can be seven times as much.

But there are exceptions to these generalizations.[2] Sets used in public places—television particularly—are charged higher fees, ranging from two times as much in Greece to eight times in France. In addition the French levy a supplementary charge on the gross receipts of the premises.* Under other conditions fees are reduced. As late as 1963 in Norway radio listeners living in fringe reception areas paid lower fees. In many countries, old-age pensioners, the disabled, and the blind either pay reduced fees or are entirely exempt. Sets in schools and hospitals also get special rates. In some cases the number of free licenses is quite large. Thus in Denmark there are approximately 110,000 free radio licenses to 310,600 paid; in France, 680,000 to 7,713,000; and in West Germany, 472,000 to 5,041,000. Perhaps because it is regarded as a luxury, or because it is not considered necessary to provide free television to the blind, the percentage of free television licenses is much smaller.

Licensing services normally are administered by the postal authorities although in some places the broadcasting agency itself makes the collections. In Italy, for example, radio fees are collected by 830 branch offices of the Ministry of Finance, while television fees are collected by RAI itself working from a computer center in Turin. In France an electronic installation in Rennes is taking over by stages all record keeping in connection with broadcast license fee collections.

Basic charges for the private use of a radio vary from time to time so that any set of figures will be somewhat in error when published.[3] However, typical rates (with rounded-off dollar equivalents) include Austria, 98 schillings ($3.80); Belgium, 204 francs ($4.15); Czechoslovakia, 60 crowns ($3.70); France, 25 francs ($5.00); Luxembourg, 96 francs ($2.00); United Kingdom, £1 5s ($3.50); and West Germany,

---

* In Europe even more than in the United States, because of lower personal incomes, there is extensive viewing in public places like restaurants and bars; this was particularly true during the early years of the service. But in France, because of the high tax on public sets, few are installed. In general, throughout Europe, only the newest and most luxurious hotels have television receivers in guest rooms.

24 deutsche marks ($6.00).* For the same countries the television rates (which include radio in all cases except Austria and Czechoslovakia) are as follows: Austria, 600 schillings ($23.50); Belgium, 960 francs ($19.50); Czechoslovakia, 180 crowns ($11.00); France, 85 francs ($17.50); Luxembourg, 192 francs ($3.85); United Kingdom, £5 ($14.00); and West Germany, 84 deutsche marks ($21.00).†

Where licenses are required ways must be developed to secure compliance.[4] In many cases dealers must either provide all new sets with licenses for the first year or furnish lists of purchasers to the proper authorities. Usually there are penalties for failures to secure licenses and for false declarations. Examples include a fine up to a hundred times the amount evaded (Austria); a fine of five times the amount evaded for first offense and ten times for second offense (France); and a fine of £10 ($28) for the first and £50 ($140) for the second offense (United Kingdom). Violators in Greece, Luxembourg, and Norway may even be imprisoned. Some countries have mobile vans equipped with detectors capable of locating FM radio and television sets. It has been found that the mere appearance of such units often motivates people to purchase licenses, even though—unknown to the general public—it is almost impossible to pinpoint the location of sets in areas with many receivers.

In 1963, 32,000 undeclared radio and 5,000 undeclared television receivers were discovered in France, and in the area served by the Süddeutscher Rundfunk in West Germany, 14,000 unlicensed radio and 10,000 unlicensed television sets were located. One writer estimated that in all of West Germany, in addition to approximately 11,-000,000 registered television sets, there were between 1,000,000 and 2,000,000 unlicensed "black watchers" and "black listeners." In Britain it is believed that one household out of every eight is operating a set without a license, with a consequent yearly loss of over £10,000,000 ($28,000,000) in revenue to the BBC, equal to about one-sixth its total income.[5]

Administrative costs, ranging from as low as 3 per cent in Belgium and Sweden up to 20 per cent in West Germany and Austria, normally

---

* When an extra charge is made for wired receivers the rate usually is the same as for off-the-air receivers.

† It must be recognized that a given amount in dollars does not represent the same real costs in all countries, and that with the Eastern countries especially, where exchange rates are rigidly controlled, dollar equivalents may mean very little.

are deducted from gross license revenue.[6] But all the rest does not necessarily reach the broadcasting organizations since the state often levies a tax on this revenue—10 per cent in France, for example. For a long time the British treasury kept a large portion of the net revenue and the amount withheld between 1927 and 1955 ranged from nothing at all up to 52 per cent, with the proportion seldom dropping below 15 per cent.[7] After collection costs have been subtracted and any government levy withheld, the remainder either is given to the broadcasting organization or divided between it and the postal authorities in those cases where the latter provide transmitter and other technical services. This division of revenue is sometimes automatic; in other countries, as in the United Kingdom, an act of Parliament appropriates the sums previously agreed upon by the BBC and the government.[8]

Revenue from Advertising

There is advertising on all the broadcasting systems of Europe except in Albania, Belgium, Denmark, France, Norway, Sweden, and Vatican City.* North America and Europe, however, do not define commercial broadcasting in the same way. The Continent has commercial stations, such as those in Andorra, Luxembourg, Monaco, and the Saar, with both spot advertising and sponsored programs. But the usual European procedure is for the broadcasting organization to permit commercial announcements under strictly controlled conditions, excluding sponsors, who in return for purchasing time and perhaps providing program content may identify themselves with the entire production. The relationship between advertising and program material resembles that between the news and advertising columns of a newspaper, rather than that found in the typical American commercial station. This is the basic pattern followed in West Germany, Italy, Switzerland, the United Kingdom, and the Netherlands. There also is advertising in most of the Communist countries where news and announcements about state industries

* Although France carries some institutional commercials for such state-operated monopolies as Air France, the ORTF normally is classed with the noncommercial systems. All European broadcasting organizations, both commercial and noncommercial, are confronted with the attempts of advertisers to get free publicity by erecting signs in sports stadiums, particularly when continent-wide distribution on Eurovision is scheduled. For example, the Austrian Broadcasting Corporation discovered early in 1967 that the stadium in which some ice hockey games had been scheduled had rented more than sixty advertising spaces which were sure to be picked up by cameras following the play. (*Variety*, February 15, 1967, p. 27.)

are broadcast; but except for Yugoslavia, the emphasis is more on information for the audience than on increased sales for the product or income for the broadcasting organization.

Private commercial broadcasting grew up in Europe in the early 1920's along with the noncommercial systems (see pp. 259–260 below). The state systems as a whole looked down on the commercial stations partly because they were commercial and partly for their light program fare. They also objected to the ways in which some of them usurped frequencies and operated with such high power that they interfered with authorized stations.*

Private commercial broadcasting fell somewhat by the wayside during World War II but the development of television brought a new set of pressures for advertising. High costs led some broadcasting organizations to seek commercial support at the same time that advertisers and agencies became aware of the power of television as a sales medium. In some cases there were complaints from manufacturers that industries in neighboring countries could advertise on programs received on both sides of the border, while they could not use television to boost sales at home. Other supporters included dissatisfied groups and individuals who believed that new stations under different management and with increased finances might do better broadcasting. There also were private entrepreneurs seeking profits who wanted to establish and operate the stations themselves.

But the pressures were not all in favor of commercial television. The other information media, particularly newspapers and magazines, opposed it, anticipating a loss of advertising revenue. Churches, educators, and public-spirited citizens often objected, fearing that the introduction of advertising, particularly on private stations, would substitute market for public service values. Finally, the state broadcasting agencies, well entrenched and strongly backed by the national establishment, often fought the introduction of advertising especially if the creation of competitive broadcasting organizations also was involved.

On theoretical grounds the basic issue usually has been whether a commercially supported organization, particularly if privately owned,

---

* For details of the BBC's attempts in the 1930's to curtail the growth of Radio Normandie and Radio Luxembourg, see Briggs, *The Golden Age of Wireless*, pp. 360–369. Other commercial stations with English-language programs were Radio Toulouse, Radio Côte d'Azur, and Radio Ljubljana in Yugoslavia.

could consistently maintain high program standards. Related to this has been concern that the commercials themselves would be objectionable. The high cost of television advertising has raised the argument that since only the larger firms could afford it broadcast advertising would be a step toward monopoly control of industry. During the discussions there always has been frequent reference to the United States, it being argued on the one hand that American broadcasting contains many undesirable excesses directly related to its commercial nature, and on the other that America's combination of competition and extensive financial resources has led to more imaginative and varied programing. Because of these conflicts most of the larger European countries which have introduced broadcast advertising limit it to short announcements in programs controlled by the traditional broadcasting organizations, rather than creating new private stations or allowing program sponsorship. In Europe the American pattern is followed only on the Iberian peninsula and by some of the private stations in small countries.

PRIVATE COMMERCIAL STATIONS

The private commercial stations in Andorra, Luxembourg, Monaco, and the Saar are much like those in the Western Hemisphere. They accept both spot announcements and sponsored programs and have no special limitations on the things advertised, except that they do not carry political programs for reception abroad. Their radio commercials consist partly of copy read by announcers, plus recorded spoken and singing commercials. Television advertisements also follow American patterns although they tend to be more ingenious than their American counterparts.

For example, Europe 1, the private station in the Saar owned mainly by French stockholders and programmed in French by telephone line from studios in Paris, publishes a rate card ranging from 650 French francs ($130) for a thirty-second announcement broadcast between 11 P.M. and 1 A.M. to 3,500 French francs ($700) for one aired between 7 and 8:30 P.M.* For commercials of forty-five seconds duration the basic rate is increased by 20 per cent. Announcements placed immediately before, after, or during news broadcasts pay a 20 per cent premium. As

---

* These quotations were provided by the station. For information about the control of Europe 1 by the French government, see pp. 86–87 above.

in the United States, Europe 1 and the other private European stations offer discounts up to 15 per cent for quantity purchases.

Radio Luxembourg has separate rate cards for broadcasts in English to the United Kingdom, and in French, Dutch, German, and Luxembourgian for countries speaking those languages.* English-language programs may be recorded in Britain and the tapes mailed to Luxembourg for broadcast. Spot announcements from seven to sixty seconds in length are available. During the winter season, time costs for a sixty-second announcement in the British service range from £90 ($252) at 6:00 P.M. up to £193 ($540.40) between 9:00 and 10:30 P.M. A thirty-minute segment of air time costs from £50 ($140) to £115 ($322), in addition to which advertisers must meet all program costs. On programs for France the rates for a sixty-second announcement range from 1,150 to 1,190 French francs ($234 to $241). Thirty minutes of air time, with a maximum of two minutes of commercials, costs from 1,440 to 2,300 French francs ($293 to $465) plus program expenses.†

Télé-Luxembourg rates cover both spot announcements and sponsored periods. A sixty-second spot announcement costs from 1,150 to 1,900 French francs ($234 to $388), while a thirty-minute sponsored program with a maximum allowance of two minutes of commercial time, will range from 1,400 to 2,300 French francs ($284 to $465) plus program costs. All radio and Télé-Luxembourg quotations are subject to reductions for purchases in quantity.

Radio Luxembourg maintains agency representatives in Great Britain, Belgium, Germany, France, Luxembourg, the Netherlands, Switzerland, Italy, Spain, and the United States. Some American firms advertise on the station, and Radio Luxembourg broadcasts paid religious programs of American origin on both the standard and short-wave bands.[9] The articles advertised include petroleum products, wines and spirits, cosmetics, confections, food products, and beverages. The company's

---

* Rate information was provided by the station. For other references to Radio Luxembourg, see pp. 14–15 and 85–86 above.

† In view of Radio Luxembourg's very high power and limited commercial competition, it is almost impossible to make meaningful comparisons between its rates and those of American stations, but it might be noted in passing that Radio Luxembourg's charges for a sixty-second announcement are higher than those for any New York City radio station. (*Standard Rate and Data Service, Spot Radio Rates and Data*, October 1, 1966, pp. 559–569.)

business is large and lucrative: In 1964, the gross income from programs beamed to the United Kingdom alone reached £640,000 ($1,792,000).

The more usual pattern for commercial broadcasting in Western Europe is one in which the traditional broadcasting organization retains absolute control of programs while allowing a limited amount of advertising, usually concentrated in several short periods. West Germany, Italy, Switzerland, and the Netherlands are examples.

West Germany. Advertisements were first introduced to German radio on September 15, 1924, and were continued until January 1, 1936, when they were banned by the Nazi government. RIAS first reintroduced radio advertising on February 1, 1948, being followed by Radio Bremen on August 1, 1948, the Bayerischer Rundfunk on July 1, 1949, the Südwestfunk on August 1, 1949, and the Hessischer Rundfunk on January 4, 1954. Currently seven of the nine broadcasting companies have radio advertising, the two exceptions being the Norddeutscher Rundfunk and the Westdeutscher Rundfunk.

While details vary from one Land to another, radio commercials usually are limited to specified periods during which spot advertisements are presented on popular music programs as in the United States. The Hessischer Rundfunk, which may be taken as an example, accepts advertising for its first network on weekdays only between 8:15 and 9:00 A.M., 11:10 and 11:30 A.M., and 1:10 and 2:00 P.M., and for its second network weekdays from 10:10 to 10:30 A.M., and 2:10 to 3:00 P.M.[10]

On both radio and television time is sold only for commercial products thus ruling out advertising for individuals, groups, churches, political parties, or organizations attempting to promote ideas or points of view. However, there are no official restrictions on the types of goods, commodities, or products that may be sold, although the same general standards and requirements apply to the advertisements as to the accompanying program material. Rates range from DM 15 to DM 20 per second ($3.75 to $5.00), with discounts from 5 to 15 per cent for quantity purchases. There are no legal restrictions on the amount of advertising although in the interests of good programming it never exceeds 25 to 30 per cent of the total time allocated for commercial programs. In view of the limited periods available it is clear that schedules cannot be overburdened with commercial material.

Only with the advent of television did advertising become an important factor in German broadcasting. Before this there had been no great need for additional revenue in view of the generous license fee returns. But beginning in the 1950's, because of television's potential power, its need for additional revenue, and the temptation of profits for private entrepreneurs, television advertising became a national issue. Television advertising was begun in West Germany by the Bayerischer Rundfunk on November 3, 1956.[11] On January 2, 1958, the Südwestfunk, Sender Freies Berlin, and Hessischer Rundfunk began to participate in the advertising programs of the Bayerischer Rundfunk, being joined later by the Süddeutscher Rundfunk. The Norddeutscher Rundfunk and Westdeutscher Rundfunk began television advertising April 1, 1959, and the Saarländischer Rundfunk on November 9, 1959. On January 2, 1960, Sender Freies Berlin and the Hessischer Rundfunk dropped out of the Bayerischer Rundfunk network and began their own advertising programs, although the Südwestfunk and Süddeutscher Rundfunk still have a joint program. At present all commercials on the first German network are regional; those on the second network, Zweites Deutsches Fernsehen (ZDF), are produced at its headquarters in Mainz for nationwide distribution; while the new third stations have no commercials at all.

There are differences among the various regional corporations in advertising as in other respects, but the basic pattern, for them as well as for the nationwide ZDF, is illustrated by the Norddeutsches Werbefernsehen GmbH (North German Commercial Television, Ltd.) in Hamburg, which is responsible for the areas served by the Norddeutscher Rundfunk and Radio Bremen.[12] This corporation, founded in October 1958 and in operation on April 1, 1959, is entirely owned by NDR and Radio Bremen which remain legally responsible for both its advertisements and programs. Because income tax must be paid on all the profits from commercial operations, if advertising were conducted by the broadcasting company itself taxes might have to be paid on total income, including license revenue. Thus, the new company was created to handle all advertising so that taxes are levied only on commercial revenue.

The Norddeutsches Werbefernsehen GmbH assumes complete responsibility for all television broadcasts on NDR-Radio Bremen from 6:00 to 8:00 P.M. on the six weekdays when advertisements are broadcast. It sells the time—usually to advertising agencies—and administers the regulations, in addition to being responsible for all the informational and entertainment material presented during those two hours. Originally the company was responsible only for the period between 7:25 and 8:00 P.M., during which up to nine minutes of advertisements could be broadcast; but with the expansion of the total period to two hours the commercial allowance was extended to twenty minutes. All the Land governments now have officially decreed a maximum allowance of twenty minutes of commercials per day to be broadcast before 8:00 P.M., with no commercials on Sundays or holidays. The same regulations apply to the nationwide Zweites Deutsches Fernsehen.

Television advertising consists entirely of filmed spot announcements concentrated in four blocks of five minutes each, placed between—but never within—programs. Sponsorship is forbidden. Advertisements may deal only with commercial matters and may include tobacco products and alcohol. A point is made of separating advertising from program content, and advertisers are prohibited from doing anything to suggest or imply that they provide program material. The participation of well-known actors during commercial periods on the same evenings they appear in entertainment programs is discouraged. Advertisers may use newspapers to call attention to their television spots but may not mention the adjacent programs. Although West Germany's commercial companies are legally separate and distinct from each other they cooperate in various ways, such as acquiring the entertainment portions of the programs which they produce themselves or purchase from outside sources.

Rates vary from region to region depending upon audience size. For Sender Freies Berlin tariffs range from DM 650 ($162.50) for fifteen seconds up to DM 4,000 ($1,000) for sixty seconds.* In the NDR-Radio

---

* European rates are generally in line with those in the United States. But in order to make direct comparisons, one would have to match continental and American stations in population potential (easy), extent of set ownership in area served (possible), and amount of set use (difficult, in view of the differences in methods of audience measurement). Related to these factors would be audience size: The European situation normally is that of monopoly, the American of competition; furthermore, audience measurement data would seldom be directly comparable. Then one would have to compare the purchasing power of the two audiences (complicated), and compensate for the differing costs of broadcasting (very hard to do, in view of equipment, labor, copyright, and other variables).

Nevertheless, one might contrast the rates for Sender Freies Berlin television, serving an audience of about 2,175,000 in West Berlin, with the two highest priced

Bremen area, however, tariffs go from DM 950 ($423.50) for fifteen seconds up to DM 12,000 ($3,000) for sixty seconds. Advertisements broadcast between 6:00 and 6:54 P.M. pay a lower rate than do those aired between 6:54 and 8:00 P.M. There are discounts of from 5 to 10 per cent for quantity purchases.* Rates on the nationwide ZDF are somewhat higher since the audience is national rather than regional. ZDF's lowest quotation is DM 3,750 for fifteen seconds ($937.50) and its highest DM 24,000 for a minute ($6,000), again with reductions of from 5 to 10 per cent for quantity purchases. To these amounts must be added the costs of preparing and recording the spots. In West Germany, as in most other West European countries with television advertising, demands for time greatly exceed the supply; in fact, all commercial time is sold by September 1 of the previous year.

Although the profits from German television advertising are considerable, expenditures for it do not constitute any substantial portion of national advertising allotments, largely because the limitations on time severely limit the amount of advertising that may be scheduled.[13] In 1962, for example, DM 1,403.2 million were spent on newspaper advertising; DM 1,097.4 for advertising in periodicals; and DM 281.8 for television, which constituted only 5.3 per cent of the total. The major categories of goods advertised on television during 1964 included alcoholic drinks 7.80 per cent; nonalcoholic drinks 1.73 per cent; clothing 6.04 per cent; electrical household appliances 4.58 per cent; tobacco and tobacco products 6.80 per cent; candies 4.86 per cent; coffee, tea, and cocoa 5.72 per cent; cosmetics 5.69 per cent; mouthwashes and toothpaste 2.88 per cent; and washing supplies 7.49 per cent.

Nevertheless, in Germany as in other countries there have been strenuous objections by the press to broadcast advertising. An example is

stations in the four-station market in Minneapolis and St. Paul, Minnesota, whose potential audience is a little below that figure. SFB's charges for a single spot announcement range from $162.50 for fifteen seconds up to $1,000 for one minute. Rates for comparable announcements on one large Twin Cities station range from $34 to $1,000 (the former rate being for a low-audience hour when the Berlin station is never on the air), and on the other from $270 to $800. (American rates are taken from *Standard Rate and Data Service, Spot Television Rates and Data,* September 15, 1966, pp. 245–246.)

* The population covered by NDR and Radio Bremen television is about 11,-841,000, while that of greater New York City is some 16,000,000. The top rate for a single one-minute announcement on WCBS-TV in New York is $3,100; the highest charge for a twenty-second announcement is $2,900. (*Standard Rate and Data Service, Spot Television Rates and Data,* September 15, 1966, p. 246.)

provided by the law drafted by the German Newspaper Publishers Association in March 1965, which if enacted would have forbidden all radio and television advertising.[14] These objections have been supplemented by complaints that charges are unreasonably high in view of the size of the audience reached, a situation possible only because of the great demand for time and the limited amount available.*

Italy. Italian radio permits both spot announcements and a very limited form of direct sponsorship on both its first and second networks, as well as on some regional and local services.[15] But the third program, with sophisticated intellectual fare, excludes advertising lest it interfere with program enjoyment. Short messages are the only form of radio advertising permitted. At times radio broadcasts may be preceded or followed with an announcement to the effect that Company X "invites you to hear"—or "hopes you have enjoyed"—this program; but in all such cases the programs themselves are planned and presented by RAI and contain no other advertising message. Spot announcements often are interspersed in musical programs, or grouped around time announcements. Radio commercials are read by the announcer on duty which has led to complaints by some advertisers about the quality of delivery. The commercials may be presented at any time of day, however, rather than being limited to several short early evening periods as with television.

Italian television began on January 1, 1954. The government decided that RAI would accept advertising only when the number of receivers reached 100,000 (later raised to 150,000), so that television advertising would be justifiable for both the advertiser and RAI, providing a good service to the former and adequate income to the latter. In response to pressure from the press, the RAI Charter of January 26, 1952, decreed that advertisements could not normally exceed 5 per cent of total program time, although this could be raised to 8 per cent by the minister of posts and telecommunications if in his opinion circumstances justified it. Actually, however, this level has never been reached; in 1962 for example, only 2.6 per cent of all radio and 3.1 per cent of television time were taken up by advertisements.[16]

Its charter permits RAI to handle broadcast advertising either directly or through a separate corporation. Italy, like Germany, decided to follow

* *Variety*, February 9, 1966, p. 40. In reply, though, it could be observed that if the rates really were too high, the natural reaction would be a decrease in time purchases—but that is not the case.

the latter procedure and set up SIPRA (Società Italiana Pubblicità Radiofonica Anonima) which is now Italy's largest advertising agency. Seventy per cent of SIPRA's capital is owned by IRI (Istituto per la Riconstruzione Industriale), the same government agency which owns a majority of RAI shares, and 30 per cent by RAI itself, so that SIPRA is in effect a completely owned subsidiary. However, because broadcasting in Italy is not decentralized as in Germany, one company serves the entire country. Under SIPRA rules television advertising contracts must be for a series of advertisements rather than for single announcements. Accordingly, there are from six to ten contract periods per year. A system of rotation gives all advertisers equal exposure, since a given spot is used first in one transmission, second in another, and so on through the series. Once a contract is made, operational details are arranged by SACIS (Società Per Azioni Commerciale Iniziative Spettacolo), which must approve a detailed production plan including story, script, set design, music, cast, directors, and shooting specifications. Then the advertiser must record his program on film and deliver it to SACIS for presentation by RAI.

Italian television started commercials on February 3, 1957. Advertising is limited to twenty-eight spots a day, concentrated during six evening broadcast periods, and individual advertisements range in length from 10 to 40 seconds. There are five daily commercial periods on Network 1 and one on Network 2. First in point of time is "Girotondo," broadcast at 5:30 P.M., which consists of four announcements, none exceeding 20 seconds in length. The second, "Gong," broadcast at 7:15 P.M. following the day's first television news program, contains two announcements ranging in length from 30 to 40 seconds. "Tic-Tac," at 8:07 P.M. following the sports news, with a time signal between the third and fourth announcements, consists of six short commercials, each from 30 to 40 seconds long. Shortly afterwards around 8:30 comes "Arcobaleno," six short announcements of 35 seconds each, with a weather forecast between the third and fourth announcements.

The longest commercial period—and most popular—is "Carosello" which is broadcast at about 9:00 P.M., following the second news program and preceding the major evening broadcasts. This runs 12 minutes, consisting of five sections each lasting 2 minutes and 15 seconds, of which 35 seconds is advertising and the remaining 1 minute and 40 seconds entertainment material. "Carosello," almost a national institution, is very popular because of its ingenious short sketches presented by some of the country's outstanding entertainers. The only advertising on the second network is "Intermezzo," five short announcements each lasting from 30 to 40 seconds, broadcast at 9:10 P.M. following the news.

Rates range from 150,000 lire ($247.50) for 10 seconds on the late afternoon "Girotondo," when about a million viewers are available, to 3,600,000 lire ($5,940) for each of the 2-minute 15-second shorts broadcast on "Carosello" at 9:00 P.M., when the audience reaches 10,000,000. Since advertisers must cover their own production expenses the total cost for a single spot may range between 500,000 and 1,000,000 lire ($825 and $1,650), while an insert for "Carosello" may run between 1,000,000 and 1,500,000 lire ($2,475). Time buyers work through their own agents or buy directly from SIPRA. All television advertising is national since Italy does not yet have local television services, but radio commercials can be purchased either on a national or local basis.

There are strict rules. Advertisements, which—in the words of a RAI official—must be "honest, true, loyal, clear and complete," may deal only with commercial goods, with no references to politics, religion, or controversial issues. Certain commodities, such as tobacco, some medicines, or articles of personal apparel like brassières, may not be advertised. Advertisers are permitted to refer to their broadcasts in the press and in the case of "Carosello" may mention the entertainment portions as well. Broadcast advertising is prohibited on certain holidays, such as Easter Sunday, and also following the death of a well-known political or religious leader when the ban is effective for several days. There is a limitation on the repetition of old commercial spots although advertisers may reuse them in cinemas.

Commercial television has had no marked effect on the Italian press because of its limited amount. Only about 30 per cent of the funds for Italian broadcasting come from advertising and the rest from license fees. RAI, in fact, intentionally allows only enough advertising to support its activities adequately without seriously affecting press income. Consequently, only about 10 per cent of the country's gross advertising outlay goes to broadcast advertising. All the television advertising periods are sold out during the winter, when there is a backlog of orders, although there is free time in the summer. From the standpoint of advertisers, however, the limitation on broadcast time is not entirely desirable since it deprives them of the greater use of two effective media and makes it impossible to build advertising campaigns mainly around broadcasting.

Switzerland. Switzerland provides an excellent case study of the introduction of television advertising into a country which previously had only a noncommercial system. When financial needs led Swiss broadcasters to seek additional revenue from advertising, the country's publishers, fearing a loss of income, offered to subsidize television in return for a guarantee of its remaining noncommercial. But this arrangement also proved insufficient so a compromise was worked out through which television accepted a limited amount of advertising.

Experimental telecasts began in Zurich, Switzerland, in July 1953, although regular service was not initiated until 1958. Between 1951 and 1953, some 900,000 francs ($211,500) of radio funds were diverted to the experimental television service and after 1955 radio's contribution totaled some 5,000,000 francs ($1,175,000). In December 1957 the Swiss Parliament voted a loan to television of 8.4 million francs ($1,974,000) to be paid back in ten years at 3 per cent interest.[17] Anticipating a need for even more money, a group of Swiss advertisers offered in May 1957 to provide from 2 to 3 million francs ($470,000 to $705,000) per year in return for the right to present a half hour of commercials each day.[18] This led to a counter proposal from the newspaper publishers to subsidize Swiss television to the extent of 2,000,000 francs ($470,000) per year for ten years.

After extensive discussions involving the publishers, the broadcasters, and the government an agreement was signed March 14, 1958, under which the publishers set up the Association for the Development of Television, which committed itself to subsidize the SSR provided it carried no advertising. During 1958, therefore, the television budget received 2,500,000 francs from license fees, 2,500,000 from the state loan, and 2,000,000 from the publishers for a total budget of 7,000,000 francs. The association was to be released from its commitment when the number of sets reached 180,000, at which point it was expected license fee receipts would balance the television budget. This point was predicted for 1967 but was reached in 1961; the publishers discontinued their subsidy the following year.

Under the agreement, the Association for the Development of Television could have prevented Swiss television from carrying any advertising until 1968; but it did not do so because rising costs confronted

Swiss television with a disastrous financial situation. Broadcasting in Switzerland is expensive for several reasons. The country is small, with fewer than 6,000,000 inhabitants. As previously mentioned, it must maintain three separate broadcasting services (for each of its major language groups, in addition to some broadcasts in Romansch, the fourth official language). The better supported French, German, and Italian systems inevitably subject the Swiss output to difficult comparisons, so that the Swiss have viewed a great deal of foreign television, although since financial reorganization and the consequent improvement of programs, this has decreased.

The publishers agreed to commercial television partly in recognition of the national need and partly to put themselves in a position to limit the amount of commercial time. Accordingly, they and the SSR drew up an agreement, officially approved by the Federal Council, which established the Society for Swiss Television Advertising, effective July 3, 1964 in Berne, with a share capital of 500,000 francs, divided as follows: 40 per cent to the Association for the Development of Television (the publishers group which previously had provided the 2,000,000 franc annual subsidy); 40 per cent to the SSR itself; 8 per cent to the Committee of the Swiss Association of Commerce and Industry; and 4 per cent each to the journalists (Swiss Press Association), the Swiss Farmers Association, and the Swiss Trademens' Union.[19] A board of management of twelve members was set up representing the major stockholders. This corporation is in charge of all television advertising. It accepts or refuses orders for time; allocates the periods available; enforces the advertising rules; collects the fees; and passes on the net proceeds to Swiss television.

The Federal Council laid down the rules as follows:[20] (1) Only commercial advertising is authorized. A broadcast is deemed an advertisement when its transmission benefits, in the first instance, those who wanted or requested it. (2) No advertising is allowed on Sundays or official holidays. (3) Religious and political propaganda are prohibited. (4) Advertising must not offend against morality. (5) False or misleading advertising, and advertising constituting unfair competition, are prohibited. (6) Prices may not be compared, or reference made to charge accounts or installment buying. (7) Advertisements for alcoholic beverages, tobacco, or medicine are prohibited. (8) Only national advertising is allowed, local commercials being excluded. (9) Every effort must be made to prevent television advertising from injuring the Swiss press or the national economy.

Commercial broadcasts began February 1, 1965. Advertising is limited to twelve minutes a day and is presented in three blocks between 7:00 and 8:30 P.M., the duration of individual advertisements being either 20, 30, 40, or 60 seconds. (If financially necessary, upon request of the SSR advertising time could be extended to fifteen minutes a day by the Federal Department of Transport, Communication and Power, the government ministry with ultimate control over broadcasting.) The three blocks of four minutes each are broadcast at 7:30, 7:55, and 8:15 P.M. in the French and German regions, and a little later in the Italian-speaking area. Advertising, of course, is completely separated from program material, there being only spot announcements and no sponsors.

The basic rate is 6,000 francs ($1,410) per minute for the entire national network; 4,800 francs ($1,128) for German-speaking Switzerland only; and 2,000 francs ($470) for either the French- or Italian-speaking sections. Advertisers must meet all production costs, and once it is approved deliver their material on film to the Society for Swiss Television Advertising ready for broadcast. Initial applications were accepted beginning August 1, 1964, and in six weeks all the time available in 1965 had been sold—orders equaled 130 per cent of the supply. Orders for 1966 totaled 155 per cent of the available time.

Gross income from advertising during the eleven months of commercial broadcasting in 1965 exceeded 25,500,000 Swiss francs (about $5,900,000), and income for all of 1966 was expected to total 28,000,000 Swiss francs ($6,460,000).[21] In 1965, 427 advertisers bought time in the following product groups, arranged in declining order: soap; food; hot drinks; textiles; beverages; cleaners; automobiles; chocolates; cosmetics; dairy products; hairdressing products; publications; household products; dental products and mouthwashes; oils and fats; and cameras and optical equipment. The net increased television income (18,000,000 francs or $4,230,000 in 1966) made possible various improvements in program service. Effective in February 1965, evening broadcasts began at 7:00 rather than 8:00 P.M.; Tuesday broadcasts were added (previously Swiss television had been off the air on that day for reasons of economy); Sunday programs extended; and news services augmented and improved.

Considerable ingenuity and taste are shown in the preparation of the commercials. Each unit is introduced and concluded by several cartoon characters, a cliff-hanging episode at the beginning not being resolved until the end. Picture material is well produced, and sound, often with music, effectively done. For the most part the same visual material is used for all three parts of the country, language being changed as required.

Most advertisers were pleased with their first year on Swiss television, viewers at least were not particularly displeased, and the effect on the press was slight. Some advertisers complained about the shortage of time, but this, of course, was planned for the protection of press advertising revenue. Total expenditures on television advertising for 1965, including the costs of production, came to 35,000,000 Swiss francs ($8,100,000), or only 4 per cent of the national expenditure on advertising.

Television advertising represented no problem for the national newspapers, though it did affect specialized periodicals and weeklies. In many cases the advertising volume of the latter dropped from 15 to 20 per cent. In 1965 the leading newspapers (defined as those covering an entire linguistic area), lost 2 per cent of their advertising orders from the manufacturers of some brand-name products. The illustrated newspapers lost some black and white but no color advertising.* Because local advertising is prohibited, local newspapers did not suffer at all. However, there was a reduction in income from advertising films shown in cinemas, a type of advertising much more important in Europe than in the United States.

The man who represented the publishers in the negotiations leading to the arrangements for television advertising summarized the first year's experiences by saying that "constructive cooperation between television and the press, such as would maintain the independent newspapers and defend the freedom of the press, seems possible to us on the following conditions: (a) that the quota system be applied to the total volume of television advertising broadcasts; (b) that the maximum time of each spot be limited so as to satisfy the greatest possible number of advertisers; [and] (c) that the sponsor system—a serious affliction of American television—be banned, because . . . it helps to foster dan-

---

* Swiss television will not add color until at least 1968.

gerous and regrettable confusion in the minds of the public between television programmes and television advertising."[22]

The Netherlands. Since it was the issue of commercial radio and television that brought down the Dutch Cabinet on February 27, 1965, notice should be taken of the new arrangements for broadcast advertising which became effective January 2, 1967.[23] Ultimate control rests with the Minister of Social Welfare and Culture, the same minister responsible for the program aspects of broadcasting. A royal decree of November 11, 1965, provided for the appointment by the Minister of a sixteen-member advertising council to represent various organizations, including the broadcasting societies, the press, advertisers, advertising agencies, and some cultural and social groups. This council has such policy responsibilities as making regulations and setting rates. The actual management of broadcast advertising is assigned to an independent foundation—Stichting Ether Reclame (STER)—managed by a board of six members appointed by the Minister to represent the various interested media. The foundation, however, does not produce the advertisements itself, but rather arranges for the broadcasting of material provided by others. Should there be any differences of opinion between the foundation and the advertising council, the Minister has authority to resolve them.

Following the practice observed in West Germany, Switzerland, Italy, and some other European countries, there is strict separation of advertising and program material. Advertising is not to exceed fifteen minutes a day on either of the two television networks and twenty-four minutes a day for each of the three radio networks. Tobacco advertisements are excluded, and there is no advertising on Sundays or holidays. During the first experimental year it was decreed that television advertising would consist of three three-minute periods daily on the first network, and two three-minute periods on the second, with total advertising not to exceed ninety-five minutes a week.[24] Net advertising proceeds are devoted to financing programs, although during the first three years 40 per cent of the revenue is being held in reserve to assist the press in the event advertising losses owing to radio and television place it in financial jeopardy.*

* As in some other countries, the Dutch press had claimed that it alone should be charged with arrangements for broadcast advertising. This position was rejected, although there was much sympathy for it in Parliament. ("The Press and Radio-TV

BROADCAST ADVERTISING IN COMMUNIST COUNTRIES

Countries in which the state owns the principal means of production and distribution, and in which it directly operates radio and television as well as all advertising, clearly do not have the same approach to broadcast advertising as do those with competitive private enterprise. When there is radio and television advertising in Communist Europe it is presented more for public information than to increase sales—except in Yugoslavia. In any case, the costs are low. When one state industry charges another one for services, there is no national advantage in setting high rates. It also should be noted that news broadcasts in these countries devote much time to such things as the opening of new stores and impressive industrial achievements, all of which constitute a type of institutional advertising.

All East European radio and television organizations except those in Albania carry some advertising, which is limited mainly to various state products and industries. In the USSR, for example, broadcasting stations allocate short periods of time, once or twice a day, to new products and items in generous supply, or to such public events as plays, concerts, and movies.* At the most 2 or 3 per cent of the total air time is devoted to advertisements, from which an insignificant amount of revenue is derived. Czechoslovak television carries short filmed advertisements about travel and the output of various nationalized industries. After noting that their charges were negligible, one broadcasting official went on to say: "But it all comes from and goes to the state anyway." The total income thus received in Czechoslovakia covers only about 1 per cent of all television expenses.

Advertising was eliminated from Hungarian radio by the Communist regime in 1949 but was restored in 1958. Commercials are restricted to socialized products and services and are run off in a block lasting fifteen to twenty minutes two or three mornings each week.[25] Hungarian television carries advertisements for ten minutes on Sunday afternoons only. These advertisements are filmed by the state advertising agency

Advertising in the Netherlands." Fédération Internationale des Editeurs de Journaux et Publications, *Bulletin d'Informations,* October 1965, pp. 26–27.)

* "How to Advertise to the Russians," London *Times,* February 7, 1967, p. 15. In September 1966 during an interview with Soviet broadcasters, I asked if, after the pending air exchange agreement between Aeroflot and Pan American Airways was signed, they would allow Pan American to advertise on Soviet radio and television. It will be interesting to see if their "yes" answer is borne out by experience.

and deal with such items as clothing, insurance, and airlines; and a spokesman has declared they would be willing to advertise other airlines than their own. Again, income is not a major factor, the main purpose being to help various cooperatives sell their products. Rumania advertises concerts and plays along with products like wine, cosmetics, and confections. When asked if time would be provided to other than Rumanian nationalized industries, a representative said they would be willing to carry advertisements for Air France, one of the airlines serving Rumania, but never have done so.

It is not surprising that Yugoslavia, with a favorable attitude toward competitive industry, broadcasts far more commercials than the other Communist countries.[26] Each of its eight decentralized radio services has from one to four periods of commercial announcements per day. In Belgrade, for example, in 1965, 6.14 per cent of radio program time was given to commercial material; the national average was 5.56 per cent. Yugoslav television devotes about 3.5 per cent of its national time to advertisements in addition to local advertising periods. Yugoslavia even has sponsored broadcasts in which "advertising is introduced in a discreet and unobtrusive way, recommending or calling attention to the sponsor's product." The main product groups advertised, in descending order, are foodstuffs, textiles, chemicals, electrical appliances, and personal care items. Advertisers and sponsors represent the national chemical, food, textile, electrical, tobacco, chocolate and candy, timber, and metal industries as well as a general category described as "institutions, business associations, and fairs." Yugoslav radio and television also carry advertisements for foreign products like Swiss watches and services such as Air France and Pan American Airways, all of which are available in Yugoslavia, as well as advertisements for cigarettes and liquor. The broadcasting organization provides all the editorial content for sponsored programs and produces the advertisements itself.

The financial importance of advertising is revealed by the balance sheet for Belgrade radio and television for the year ending December 31, 1963.[27] Total receipts for both radio and television from all sources were 5,279,519,000 dinars. Of this, 2,305,620,000 or 43.6 per cent came from radio licenses; 891,979,000 or 16.3 per cent from television licenses; and only 232,835,000 or 4.4 per cent from advertising. Some of the other Yugoslav broadcasting organizations, however, realized a greater percentage of income from advertisements. Zagreb radio and television, for example, had total receipts of 3,177,003,000 dinars, of which 2,521,974,-000 or 79 per cent came from radio and television licenses, and 278,-643,000 or 8.7 per cent from commercials.[28] For Ljubljana the total income was 2,159,724,000 dinars, of which license fees accounted for 1,558,185,000 or 72 per cent, and commercial revenue 202,627,000 dinars or 9.4 per cent. Obviously, in Yugoslavia commercial revenue plays a much greater role than in the other Communist countries, which is consistent with its greater emphasis on decentralized controls and competitive enterprise.

Operating Expenses

It is difficult to deal meaningfully with the operating budgets of foreign broadcasting organizations. A very large budget for a small country may be a small budget for a large one, and differences in the cost of living complicate attempts to make comparisons. Even if figures were available for the Communist countries it would be almost impossible to translate their costs into Western currency equivalents. Furthermore, no two countries use the same accounting system. For these and other reasons the figures cited below must be used with great care. Nevertheless, in order to give some idea of the finances of European broadcasting, a few data are quoted; these come partly from published accounts and partly from information received from broadcasting authorities in the countries concerned.[29] However, these figures are incomplete because of their several sources and no information is available about the means of meeting deficits or disposing of surpluses, if any.

Sweden is a country of 449,000 square kilometers (173,314 square miles) with a population of 7,775,000. In 1965 it had approximately 3,000,000 radio licenses, each of which cost 35 kronor ($6.79), and a little over 2,000,000 television licenses which cost 100 kronor ($20.37) each. The full-time radio program staff included 541 employees and the television staff 1,070, in addition to 869 employees shared by the two media. Tables 1 and 2 give statistics for the income and expenditures of the Swedish broadcasting services.

The area in northern Germany served by the Norddeutscher Rundfunk has a population of 11,000,000 and a territory of 63,797 square kilometers (24,625 square miles). In the middle of 1966 it had 3,480,761 radio licenses each costing DM 24 per year ($6), and 2,472,858 television

THE FINANCES OF CONTINENTAL BROADCASTING

Table 1. Swedish Broadcasting Income

Source of Income	Amount of Income	
	Kronor	Dollars
Radio		
License fees	67,300,000 kr.	$13,056,200.00
Publications (both radio and television)..	336,566	65,294.00
Subsidies and grants	247,773	48,068.00
Other	272,442	52,854.00
Total radio income	68,156,781	13,222,416.00
Television		
License fees	112,490,000 kr.	21,373,100.00
Subsidies and grants	270,000	51,300.00
Other	793,013	150,673.00
Total television income	113,553,013	21,575,073.00
Total income	181,709,794	34,797,489.00

Table 2. Swedish Broadcasting Expenditures

Type of Expenditure	Amount of Expenditure	
	Kronor	Dollars
Radio programs and administration	62,190,034 kr.	$11,816,106.00
In-school and overseas broadcasts	9,259,879	1,758,377.00
Television programs and administration	89,852,238	16,071,925.00
Transmitting facilities		
Radio	24,831,000	4,717,890.00
Television	23,401,000	4,446,190.00
Total	209,534,151	38,810,488.00

licenses which sold for DM 60 ($15) if purchased with a radio license or DM 84 ($21) without one. The radio and television staff included 2,879 full-time and 12,000 free-lance and occasional employees. Tables 3 and 4 give figures for the income and expenditures of the Norddeutscher Rundfunk, one of the two West German broadcasting organizations without radio advertising.

Italy had a population in 1965 of almost 53,000,000 with a territory of 301,224 square kilometers (116,272 square miles). There were 4,664,-433 radio licenses at 3,400 lire ($5.60) each, and 6,059,384 television licenses at 12,000 lire ($19.80). At the beginning of 1965 RAI had 1,478 radio program and 1,487 television program employees, plus 2,888 engineering employees. In addition there were 1,955 administrative staff and 15,000 free-lance and occasional staff members. Table 5 gives statistics for Italian broadcasting income and expenditures.

113

Table 3. Norddeutscher Rundfunk Income

Source of Income	Amount of Income	
	Deutsche Marks	Dollars
Radio		
License fees	DM 65,000,000	$16,250,000.00
Other	478,000	119,500.00
Total radio income	65,478,000	16,369,500.00
Television		
License fees	75,000,000	18,750,000.00
Advertising	18,000,000	4,500,000.00
Other	12,982,000	3,245,500.00
Total television income	105,982,000	26,495,500.00
Miscellaneous	3,600,000	9,000,000.00
Total income	175,060,000	43,765,000.00

Table 4. Norddeutscher Rundfunk Expenditures

Type of Expenditure	Amount of Expenditure	
	Deutsche Marks	Dollars
Program		
Radio	DM 31,925,000	$ 7,981,250.00
Television	50,265,000	12,566,250.00
Miscellaneous	16,530,000	4,132,500.00
Total program expenditure	98,720,000	24,680,000.00
Engineering	25,435,000	6,358,750.00
Administration	5,510,000	1,377,500.00
General services	11,455,000	2,863,750.00
Board	335,000	83,750.00
Management	1,715,000	428,750.00
Depreciation	15,000,000	3,750,000.00
Miscellaneous	12,830,000	3,207,500.00
At disposal of board and management	8,000,000	2,000,000.00
Total	179,000,000	44,750,000.00

Yugoslavia, the only Communist country for which figures are readily available, had a population of 19,622,000 at the end of 1965, and occupied 255,804 square kilometers (98,740 square miles) of territory. In that year it reported 2,782,889 radio licenses at 72 dinars ($5.76) each and 577,227 television licenses at 240 dinars ($19.20). Yugoslav broadcasting had 5,829 radio and 1,215 television employees, including both programming and engineering personnel.

The total national radio and television income was 262,626,430.00 dinars, ($21,010,114.40) of which 85 per cent came from license fees, 6 per cent from broadcast advertising, and 9 per cent from other sources.

THE FINANCES OF CONTINENTAL BROADCASTING

Table 5. Italian Broadcasting Income and Expenditures

Type of Income and Expenditure	Amount of Income and Expenditure	
	Italian Lire	Dollars
Radio and television income		
License fees	L61,582,228,015	$101,610,676.00
Radio advertising	10,191,762,790	16,816,409.00
Television advertising	13,248,880,825	21,860,653.00
Other	1,106,735,828	1,826,114.00
Total income	86,129,607,458	142,113,852.00
Major expenditures		
Programs	28,618,799,136	47,221,019.00
Engineering	22,191,752,299	36,616,391.00
Other	36,948,635,756	60,965,249.00
Total expenditure	87,759,187,191	144,802,659.00

In the Belgrade region, which may be taken as typical, the proportionate expenditure for radio and television in 1965 was as follows: programs, 36.9 per cent; engineering, 20.7 per cent; license collecting, 8.0 per cent; administration, 11.4 per cent; and investments, 23.0 per cent.

In the examples given above the proceeds from license fees and advertising are the principal sources of support for broadcasting, and this is generally the case throughout Europe. In all the state systems license fees are far more important than advertising despite the great amount of discussion that usually has preceded the introduction of commercial broadcasting. If it ever happens that the time available for advertising is substantially increased this situation may change. Countries such as the USSR, of course, without license fees and with negligible advertising income, necessarily must support broadcasting by government subsidies. Other possible sources of income are the excise taxes sometimes imposed on radio and television sets in Italy or the purchase taxes levied on receivers in other countries. But income received in this way usually goes directly to the national treasury rather than being allocated to broadcasting. In most countries programs designed for reception abroad are supported by special grants rather than by license fees or commercial receipts. This follows from the assumption that while it is proper for the users of a service to pay for it, it is unfair that people with broadcast receivers be required to support an international propaganda service designed to benefit all citizens equally.

CHAPTER V

Programs: Information

ꟷＵLTIMATELY, we must judge broadcasting systems on the basis of their programs, since they are the final product. Facilities, organization, and finance all exist to serve that objective. An examination of programs, therefore, is necessarily the heart of any study like this one. But before such an analysis can be made, we must realize that radio and television programs do not develop spontaneously in a vacuum; they are the result of environment. Certain conditions, favoring one or another program policy, are basic to decisions about broadcasting. These factors will be considered as various types of programs are described below, but it might be helpful to review them briefly at the outset.

One important—and obvious—consideration is the extent and nature of government involvement in broadcasting. The basic attitudes of a country toward the mass media, expressed in law and applied in practice, inevitably affect program output. Countries with close government supervision will not have the same types of programs as will those with free systems.

Another factor is the presence of powerful neighbors whom it may be judicious not to disturb by severe treatment on the domestic airwaves. Even the American Communications Act of 1934 gives the President authority to "suspend or amend" the rules and regulations applicable to broadcasting stations "in order to preserve the neutrality of the United States."* If American law admits this possibility, how

* Sec. 606 (c). "Upon proclamation by the President that there exists war or a threat of war, or a state of public peril or disaster or other national emergency, or in order to preserve the neutrality of the United States, the President, if he deems it necessary in the interest of national security, or defense, may suspend or amend, for such time as he may see fit, the rules and regulations applicable to any or all stations or devices capable of emitting electromagnetic radiations within the jurisdiction of the United States. . . ."

can broadcasters in little Finland be unaware of their powerful Soviet neighbor? Can Austria forget that its neighbors include several Communist countries which at times during the last twenty years have been under close Soviet control? Can Yugoslav broadcasters overlook the fact that in the summer of 1965 their famous writer, Mihajlo Mihajlov, received a suspended sentence for an article allegedly insulting the Soviet Union, and that in 1967 he was sentenced to four-and-a-half years in prison for propaganda against the state?

Also important is the type of financial support, which often is related to the issue of competition versus monopoly. A competitive commercial system usually places high values on programs with large audiences; a noncompetitive monopoly, even if partially dependent on advertising revenue, is less concerned about audience size as an end in itself. Examples might include the different program policies of the BBC and ITA in the United Kingdom; the commercially competitive program services of Portugal and Spain; West Germany's monopoly with limited advertising; and Luxembourg's highly competitive commercial company.

But there are other ramifications of competition besides commercialism. The commercial stations in Luxembourg, the Saar, Monaco, and Andorra compete with domestic broadcasters for audiences in France, the Low Countries, Germany, and the United Kingdom. The pirate stations on the high seas have been discussed in the British House of Commons, have caused certain changes in Britain's home radio pattern, and brought Melody Radio to Sweden. The domestic broadcasting organizations of the two Germanys are well aware of listeners and viewers on the other side of the boundary. Many residents of Belgium, the Netherlands, Switzerland, Austria, Czechoslovakia, Poland, Hungary, and Yugoslavia understand the languages of their neighbors, and have good reception of domestic programs from abroad. The nine broadcasting organizations of West Germany serve not only people in their own areas, but also many in adjacent Länder. So, competition—with or without advertising—must be regarded as an important factor in European radio and television.

There also are internal language and cultural problems which have been mentioned before. (Belgium and Czechoslovakia must broadcast in two main languages, and Switzerland and Yugoslavia in three.) Countries often feel obliged to provide programs for residents speaking minority languages: Norway does some broadcasting in Swedish, Danish, French, and German; Sweden and Norway cooperate in broadcasting to the Lapps in their own language, while Sweden also presents programs in Finnish; the Finns operate one radio network using Finnish and Swedish; Italy broadcasts in Slovene, Czech, and German; Czechoslovakia serves minority groups in Hungarian, Polish, Ukrainian, and German; while Yugoslavia, besides broadcasting in its three main languages, uses a number of minority tongues. Again, the prime example, of course, is the USSR. In addition to program complications resulting from eleven time zones, it presents domestic programs in sixty different languages and uses fifty-four languages for international broadcasting. More than 120 different languages and dialects are spoken in the USSR but Russian is the official tongue. Since the presence of multiple languages usually indicates contrasting and often competitive groups these countries must develop programs with reference to the cultural, religious, and attitudinal—as well as linguistic—differences of their populations.

But while these differences create problems they also offer opportunities for international cooperation. Thus, French-speaking France, Belgium, Luxembourg, and west Switzerland as well as far-off French Canada regularly exchange programs, and join forces for occasional elaborate joint productions. A similar relationship has grown up among West Germany, German-speaking Switzerland, and Austria. The Scandinavian countries, with similar though not identical languages, have developed exchanges too (such as Nordvision).

In some situations the availability of technical facilities influences program trends. During the early stages of television most countries continue certain types of radio programs better suited to television until wide television coverage is achieved. Although all of France and much of the Soviet Union are within range of their respective first television networks, the coverage by subsequent services has been much less complete. Therefore, programs intended for the entire country must be assigned to the network most generally received, second and third networks being reserved for supplementary offerings.

Finally there are problems of money and talent. The larger and economically more advanced countries normally have advantages in equipment, talent, and funds. Countries with several main language groups may have to maintain two or more separate services at disproportionately high cost. The fact that the best known entertainers are apt to be nationals or residents of the larger countries raises problems for the smaller countries with those languages. An example is the influence of the major French- and German-speaking countries over broadcasting in some of their neighbors. Minority language groups in the Soviet Union raise a problem too, but the total resources of the country are enormous, and Russian is a widely understood language.

In this study programs are divided into two general groups. After a consideration of various factors basic to all types of programs, this chapter deals with those that are mainly informational in nature: news and public affairs, politics and controversy, religion, education, agriculture, and international broadcasting. Chapter VI will take up programs with an emphasis on entertainment: music, drama and documentary, light entertainment, and sports. Chapter VI also reviews certain data about the audiences for continental broadcasting.

Program Objectives

The two basic information theories already have been reviewed.* The Western concept "is that from . . . mutual toleration and comparison of diverse opinions the one that seems the most rational will emerge and be generally accepted."[1] The totalitarian approach is that the press must be "a collective propagandist and collective agitator," as well as "a collective organizer."[2] An important footnote was added to this by a distinguished Russian jurist: "In our state, naturally, there is and can be no place for freedom of speech, press, and so on for the foes of socialism. Every sort of attempt on their part to utilize to the detriment of the state—that is to say, to the detriment of all the toilers—these freedoms granted to the toilers must be classified as a counter-revolutionary crime. . . ."[3] Yet, as was observed earlier, countries everywhere, whatever their theoretical positions, tend to decide indi-

---

* See pp. 48–51 above. For generalizations about the influence of geography, history, culture, etc., on broadcasting, see pp. 5–7 above. For an interesting appraisal of press freedom, in which countries are rated on a scale of 1 (high) to 9 (low), see Raymond B. Nixon, "Freedom in the World's Press: A Fresh Appraisal with New Data," *Journalism Quarterly*, 42 (No. 1): 3–14, 118–119. In the European area, Professor Nixon gives "1" ratings to Belgium, Denmark, the Netherlands, Norway, Sweden, Switzerland, and the United Kingdom. Ranked "2" are Austria, Finland, France, the Federal Republic of Germany, Ireland, and Italy. Ratings of "7" are assigned to Hungary, Poland, Portugal, and Spain, and "8" is given to Bulgaria, Czechoslovakia, the German Democratic Republic, and the Soviet Union.

vidual cases according to Justice Holmes' famous dictum: If a given publication or broadcast is considered a "clear and present danger" to state or society, it is apt to be suppressed, although countries differ widely in determining the danger point.

No broadcasting system anywhere has finer objectives than the BBC, though its charter and license make very few references to programs.* The charter states only that the BBC is "To provide . . . broadcasting services . . . for general reception," because of "the great value of such services as means of disseminating information, education and entertainment." Its license requires it to "send efficiently programmes . . . from such stations as . . . the Postmaster General may . . . prescribe," and also to "broadcast an impartial account day by day . . . of the proceedings in both Houses of the United Kingdom Parliament." This is the extent of the program requirements specifically imposed on the domestic services of the corporation by either charter or license.[4] When the creation of the commercially supported Independent Television Authority in 1954 caused the BBC to re-examine its program policies, the director general stated that it was the duty of the BBC "to provide a balanced and comprehensive output in our sound and television services, ranging from one end of the scale to the other and covering all types of material that can be conveyed by broadcasting."[5] The Television Act of 1964, largely reiterating the original act of 1954, states: "It shall be the duty of the [Independent Television] Authority—(a) to provide the television broadcasting services as a public service for disseminating information, education, and entertainment; (b) to ensure that the programmes broadcast by the Authority in each area maintain a high general standard in all respects, and in particular in respect of their content and quality, and a proper balance and wide range in their subject-matter . . . and (c) to secure a wide showing for programmes of merit."[6]

For the most part statements of program objectives in Western countries are very brief. Programs in Denmark are to be "versatile, cultural, and educational."[7] Broadcasting in France is "to satisfy the need for information, culture, education, and entertainment for the public."[8] In

* As stated before, the United Kingdom is outside the scope of this study and reference is only made periodically to the BBC and the ITA, in view of the very considerable influence that British—and especially BBC—practice has had on the various continental services.

general the broadcasting laws in Western Germany say that "in addition to the dissemination of news . . . radio must provide presentations of an instructive, educational, and entertaining character. One cannot fail to perceive the very clear hint that an appropriate cultural standard must be maintained."[9] Specifically, the law for Hesse states: "It is the task of the Hessischer Rundfunk to broadcast news and productions of educational, instructive and entertaining character. For this purpose, it will procure and operate broadcasting stations."[10] Recent legislation in Turkey contains the requirement that programs be "prepared having regard to the basic ideas and principles underlying the Constitution and to the aims of the Atatürk revolutions as well as to the new ideas and way of life which they introduced into the country." Furthermore, these programs are to be "satisfactory from the standpoint of culture, education, and social development."[11]

In Switzerland, programs "must defend and develop the cultural values of the country and make a contribution to intellectual, moral, religious, civic, and artistic education." They also must supply "objective" information, "meet the need for entertainment . . . serve the national interest, consolidate national unity and harmony, and contribute to international understanding."[12] It is expressly forbidden to present programs "likely to endanger . . . the relations of Switzerland with other countries." One other example, in keeping with the general trend, is Luxembourg, whose broadcasts are required to maintain "complete neutrality in political matters," in addition to which programs must maintain an "elevated cultural level."[13] Many countries forbid their broadcasting organizations to present programs which might jeopardize international relations. Belgium and Italy are examples (see above pp. 70 and 77).

The Eastern countries give firmer assignments to their broadcasters. The Deputy Chairman of the East German Radio Committee declared: "There is no doubt that at present radio is one of the most important mass media of propaganda, since it can at any time and in any place address itself to the population of any region. In addition, socialist radio aims not only at providing various strata of listeners with entertainment, information and education, but also at attracting and mobilizing them to take an active part in the socialist transformation."[14] The chairman of the committee wrote in a similar vein: "By means of ideological and educational broadcasts from the main centres of the Republic, radio and television [must] aid the building-up and victory of socialism. The ideological struggle against the opinions disseminated by numerous transmitters hostile to our country plays an important role in our broadcasts."[15] Sofia spoke likewise: "Bulgarian Radio is continuously fighting to realize the policy of the Bulgarian Communist Party and the People's Government to build-up socialism and communism in our country. In its broadcasts it explains their measures, it mobilizes the working people to fulfil the set tasks and it carries our socialist truth to the remotest corners of the country. . . ."[16]

The basic objective of Czech broadcasting is to "promote the policy of the Communist party of Czechoslovakia with all the means available."[17] This also is the main purpose of broadcasting in Hungary; furthermore, as previously mentioned, the Hungarians, like the rest, can discuss the differences within the system, but cannot oppose its basic ideologies. One purpose of Polish radio is to raise the culture of society to a higher level. An official of Rumanian Radio concerned with children's programs, perhaps with an eye toward the Soviet Union, stated that it is important to inform children of the trials of their ancestors so they will understand the importance of fighting for their independence. "The basic task of television in Yugoslavia is to contribute, by its programmes and specific ways of expression, to the country's socialist development, and thus to the creation of better living conditions for all the working people."[18]

Spokesmen for the Soviet Union speak firmly and frankly about the role of broadcasting. The director of political programs for television wrote: "Our chief task is to ensure that TV programmes contribute to the successful realization of the Party programme: the creation of the material-technical basis of communism, the formation of communist social relations, education of the people of the communist society."[19]

On a lofty note one Ukrainian broadcasting executive wrote that "Soviet Radio aims to spread the truth and promote friendship among the nations as a firm foundation for peace and progress."[20] The president of the Radio and Television Committee of the Byelorussian Soviet Socialist Republic, writing under the title "The Way to Human Hearts," stated in 1961: "We consider it our sacred duty to help the State and Party in educating new, politically broad-minded people with communist traits and widely developed aesthetic tastes. This noble aim is pursued by each of our programmes—no matter whether it be a classical music concert, a theatrical play, a commentary, or an 'on-the-spot report.' "[21]

After several weeks of discussion with Soviet broadcasters in the fall of 1958, I attempted to summarize their opinions as follows: "Support of the basic ideologies of Communism, of the Communist Party, and of current government policies and practices, is the principal, underlying and continuing objective of all Soviet broadcasting." Several key broadcasting executives in Moscow, Leningrad, Tbilisi, and Kiev endorsed this without hesitation. One of my four American traveling companions, noting that all programs had a propaganda objective, remarked that Soviet broadcasting might be considered a commercial for the state 50 per cent of the time. Our hosts reacted vigorously: If you want to put it that way, they said, better count it as 100 per cent!

At first it might appear that the totalitarian and democratic points of view are diametrically opposed because totalitarian broadcasting almost always reflects current government opinion whereas democratic broadcasting may not. Superficially this is true: Totalitarian broadcasting is under strict censorship and must support the government, while democratic broadcasting, with relatively few controls, makes a great point of its freedom to agree or disagree with prevailing official opinion. But the real truth is more fundamental.

Broadcasting always implements national policies on information media. The programs are different not because some reflect government policy while others do not but because the underlying concepts are different. Totalitarian countries everywhere, believing it best that the media support official policies, give the government control, and then use the media only to advance those policies. The democracies, on the other hand, believing that society is best served if all points of view are reported and discussed, allow and encourage the airing of all shades of opinion. The starting point in both cases is the underlying concept. These fundamental ideologies determine what is done; it is not that one system reflects national information policy whereas the other does not.

Europe's Stations and Networks

To the extent permitted by their national economies, all European countries have established, or are attempting to establish, multiple radio and television services. Typically these stations and networks are supplementary and contrasting rather than duplicating and competitive. Most European countries have three radio networks, one or two of which offer regional or local services during certain periods each day. Customarily the first and second programs are broadcast simultaneously on AM and FM while the third is on FM only. Procedures vary from country to country but several may be chosen to illustrate the general pattern.*

The British Broadcasting Corporation, whose basic policies were established before the commercially supported and competitive Independent Television Authority went on the air in 1955, is a good one to start with, since it has been taken as a model by a number of continental countries. The BBC operates three nationwide radio networks, all available on both AM and FM, and was scheduled to add a fourth popular music network in 1967.[22] The Home Service is a middle-of-the-road program with both serious and light material. At certain periods of the day some of its transmitters carry regional programs. The Light Programme is a light entertainment and popular music network which also offers brief news summaries, light drama, musical comedy, and various types of public service information. The Third Network carries four types of programs: The Music Programme from early morning until late afternoon broadcasts music ranging from jazz to symphony; the Sports Service presents continuous sports commentaries on Saturday afternoons; the Study Session brings an hour of serious instructional materials early each evening; and the Third Programme—the world-famous highbrow service—serves sophisticated audiences weekday evenings from 7:30 until midnight and during longer periods on Sundays.†

French radio changes more frequently than does British but nevertheless follows the same basic pattern.[23] France has four nationwide networks; two are combined during certain hours of the day. Among them they offer choices similar to those of the BBC, with the added feature that France-Musique broadcasts almost nothing but serious mu-

---

* In Europe the term "program" often is applied to a network as well as to an individual broadcast. When used at all, the word "station" usually means an individual transmitter, not a studio-transmitter combination as in the United States. Seldom is a single transmitter programed independently; normally at least two or three are joined together to provide maximum coverage of a metropolitan area or region.

† Reference also should be made to the pirate stations broadcasting to Britain, described above on pp. 21–25. Although these do provide programs for British listeners they are in no sense an official part of the United Kingdom's radio service.

sic. Some of these networks become regional services during certain periods each day. Three of the four are on both AM and FM, although the all-music network is on FM only. There also are AM and FM stations in Paris which carry educational broadcasts from the Sorbonne. Like Britain, France has service from stations outside its borders: Luxembourg, Europe 1 (in the Saar), Monaco, and Andorra (see pp. 85–88 above).

In West Germany, as already has been pointed out, domestic broadcasting is conducted by nine independent and separate corporations organized under the laws of the individual Länder.* Most Länder operate three radio services of contrasting and supplementary nature, the first broadcast on AM and FM and the others on FM only.[24] In some cases there are short-wave relays too. Almost anywhere in Germany it is possible to tune in at least two FM services, and half the population can receive four or more programs on that band. Although there are some exchanges among the various Länder basic program planning is regionalized because these are not true nationwide networks, although each organization in turn provides an all-night music program carried by all of them.†

Normally the first and second networks are general services while the third network's programs are specialized, being somewhat influenced by the Third Programme of the BBC. As the director of the Norddeutscher Rundfunk Third Programme in Hamburg put it: "This Third Programme is neither a university of the air nor a radio adult education course, nor for that matter a playground for intellectual snobs; it is a reflection of the intellectual, artistic and political trends which are part of the particular decade of the century in which we live, and which the Third Programme has set itself the task of observing, reporting and describing."‡ However, the third programs also are

* See pp. 63–69 above, for a description of the basic legal structure of broadcasting in Western Germany.

† For example, the Süddeutscher Rundfunk in 1963 obtained only 11.4 per cent of its first and 7.8 per cent of its second network's program from outside sources. (*Internationales Handbuch 1965/66*, pp. C124–125.)

‡ "Significance and Aims of *Norddeutscher Rundfunk's* Third Programme," *EBU Review*, 72B:30 (March 1962). During the winter of 1964–65, the Third Programme of the Norddeutscher Rundfunk and Sender Freies Berlin combined to develop a pattern in which Sunday evenings were devoted to theatrical and dramatic presentations, Monday to jazz and other music, Wednesday to an opera, and Thursday to a major concert. In many cases the programs for an entire week were built around a

used for other kinds of minority services, including programs in Turkish, Greek, Italian, French, and Spanish for foreign workers.

The Italian programs are also patterned after those in the United Kingdom. Since 1951 the RAI has operated three nationwide networks, now on both AM and FM. The National Program is a "middle" program, somewhat like the BBC Home Service; the Second Program is essentially an entertainment service; while the Third Program—of "cultural character," to quote RAI—shares time with the Third Network, a serious music service.[25] These are supplemented by the five channels of the excellent wired radio service, Filodiffusione, run by RAI, which began in 1958 in four major cities and now is available in a dozen metropolitan centers. Three channels carry the broadcast services, the other two being devoted to serious and light music, including some stereophonic transmissions. There also are local broadcasts in approximately twenty cities; services in some areas in German, Slovene, and other minority languages; and an all-night music program.

Sveriges Radio maintains three domestic radio services. Program 1, on the air from 6:00 A.M. to 11:00 P.M., stresses material of general appeal, mostly spoken word programs such as news, talks, and discussions, along with dramatic, religious, and children's programs. Program 2 presents school broadcasts from 9:00 A.M. to 2:00 P.M. and serious music from 7:30 P.M. to midnight; thus during those hours it is Sweden's "good music" network. Program 3 is a light music service on the air twenty-four hours a day. Various combinations of AM, FM, and short-wave stations carry these programs, with most complete coverage by FM transmitters which bring the three services to all parts of the country. Yugoslavian broadcasting is decentralized, there being eight broadcasting organizations. Belgrade transmits three radio programs and the other centers from one to three each, all on both AM and FM. In addition there are forty-nine local stations in various cities.[26]

Fundamental procedures are the same in Eastern Europe. Czechoslovakia, for example, maintains two national networks on AM and FM, though this comes down to one for the Slovak population in the east and another for Czech-speaking citizens in the west.[27] In addition there is regional broadcasting from various centers which also make contributions to the national networks, along with some local program-

single theme. (Norddeutscher Rundfunk, Sender Freies Berlin, *Das Dritte Programm Frühjahr 1965.*)

ming in Russian, Spanish, Bulgarian, Polish, German, and Hungarian. Future plans are for three networks offering the familiar light, standard, and highbrow choices, with the latter on FM only. Rumania has two programs for the entire country on long- and medium-wave; an emerging third FM-only service which is entirely music; and some regional broadcasting including programs in German and Hungarian.

In Poland, Program 1, on the air from 5:00 A.M. to midnight, is broadcast to the entire country by a high-powered long-wave station and some reinforcing FM stations.[28] Program 2, on the air during the same hours, is distributed nationally by a combination of medium-wave and FM stations. Program 3, on FM only, which began October 1, 1966, is broadcast from 6:00 to 12:00 P.M. Starting in January 1968 this will be extended to eight hours and in 1969 to ten hours a day. The third program at present covers 64 per cent of the population, and is expected to be available to the entire population by 1970. There also is some local broadcasting. Poland favors the block programming concept, devoting extended periods on successive evenings to such areas as programs for young people, science, literature, and music.

The Soviet Union operates five radio networks from its Moscow headquarters.* The first and most basic, intended for the entire USSR, is on short-wave, relayed by local medium-wave transmitters throughout the country, and offered by all of the wired distribution centers.† This is a general service with information, literary and dramatic material, plus programs for young people. The second program, Majak (the word in Russian means "beacon" or "lighthouse"), also is distributed nationwide and is on the air twenty-four hours a day. It consists mostly of light music with news and information on the hour and half-hour. Majak is the equivalent of an American news and music station, and foreign correspondents and missions in the USSR frequently monitor it around the clock to be informed of the latest Soviet developments. The third program, on the air from 5:00 A.M. to 11:00 P.M., is broadcast only in European Russia. It is essentially a literary and musical program with an educational emphasis and includes a daily children's hour. The fourth, on the air twenty hours a day, subdivided into sec-

* Information about Soviet broadcasting was supplied by the International Relations Department of the USSR State Committee for Broadcasting and Television. Data on technical facilities were given above on pp. 26–27.

† The Soviet Union has as many wired as off-the-air receivers: about 40,000,000 of each (see above, pp. 30–31).

127

tions "A" and "B," is intended for residents in Siberia. The fifth service is for Soviet citizens abroad, such as seamen, as well as for foreigners who understand Russian.

All these programs are carried by combinations of long-, medium-, and short-wave transmitters, with some—though not much—FM duplication. To supplement originations in Moscow there are centers in seventeen regions, most of whose boundaries approximate those of the fifteen Soviet republics, which in addition to broadcasting the national programs from Moscow offer one or more services of their own, often in several languages. For example, Radio Alma-Ata in the Kazakh Soviet Socialist Republic originates programs in Russian, German, and Kazakh and has a special service for farmers. Radio Leningrad, besides taking programs from Moscow, has two services of its own at certain periods of the day and originates special programs for seamen in the Baltic Sea and the North Atlantic.

Most European radio services are on the air from about 5:00 or 6:00 A.M. to midnight. A few still sign off during certain daytime hours, but that is becoming more and more unusual. Twenty-four-hour programming is rare, although France, Italy, Germany, Sweden, and the Soviet Union are among those broadcasting all-night musical programs. Czechoslovakia starts some services at 3:30 A.M. to accommodate shift workers, and reference already has been made to the extensive schedules of the Soviet Union.* Strict adherence to schedules is not so much the rule in Europe as in the United States, partly because time is seldom sold, and also because local stations are not always cutting in and out of networks as in North America. Consequently overrunning is frequent. But as networking becomes more widespread there is increasingly greater emphasis on close timing and most European broadcasting executives urge this on their staffs anyway.

Television is an extension of the radio pattern. There are from one to three television services in the major countries on both the VHF and UHF bands, and a number of countries are approaching almost complete coverage with at least their first service.† Since most European

* These time limitations do not apply to the international services broadcast by most European countries on a round-the-clock basis; their hours depend upon convenient reception times in the target countries.

† In 1967 the following European countries had three television services: United Kingdom (two BBC, one ITA); USSR (the third channel in Leningrad and Moscow only); and West Germany (the third on forty-one transmitters serving five or six

television services are noncompetitive, being operated by national monopolies except in Britain, they are planned to supplement and contrast rather than compete with each other. Again, the United Kingdom is a good starting point, since it was the first European country to offer regular television programs.

The BBC's first television service (which, as mentioned before, went on the air November 2, 1936, using a 405-line system, and was resumed following World War II on June 7, 1945), provides a complete range of programs from education to comedy and from public events to sports.[29] BBC 2 was inaugurated on April 20, 1964. Still not nationwide in coverage and not available to all United Kingdom sets because it uses a 625-line system in the UHF band, BBC 2 is being developed as a supplementary service. Britain also has the competitive programs of the commercially supported ITA, which like BBC 1 broadcasts in the VHF band using the 405-line system.

France maintains two television networks. The first, operating in the VHF band using the 819-line system, covers the entire country with thirty-five key transmitters supplemented by over three hundred low-powered relay stations. Most of the daytime periods are devoted to programs for schools, there are a few general interest programs including news at noon, and a general service for adults is scheduled from late afternoon to late evening. Certain transmitters on this service carry regional programs in addition to relaying Paris productions. The second program made its official debut April 18, 1964, and now is carried by 30 transmitters using the West European 625-line system on the UHF band.[30] With coverage only of larger cities, and with broadcast periods on most days limited to several mid-evening hours, it provides a supplementary rather than a basic service. But the second channel is not specialized as are the third radio and television services in West Germany and the Soviet Union. Like the first program it broadcasts entertainment, variety, drama, and news.

In most of West Germany viewers have a choice of two regional programs on VHF and UHF, and in some Länder also a third on UHF only. In addition the nine regional broadcasting corporations combine

Länder.) There were two services in Austria, Belgium, Finland, France, Italy, the Netherlands, and Spain. All the remaining countries had one network only. (Although Switzerland provides separate German-, French-, and Italian-language programs for its three major linguistic areas, these in effect are three sections of one network rather than three separate services.) (*EBU Review*, 102A:86 (April 1967).)

forces to present a common national program under the name of Deutsches Fernsehen on some of the same transmitters, with contributions proportionate to their basic program resources.* Programs for the second national all-UHF network, Zweites Deutsches Fernsehen, are originated primarily at the national headquarters in Mainz. The third television programs on UHF in some states† are the television equivalent of the third programs on radio, although they are more didactic, with formal lessons on such varied subjects as languages, arithmetic, motor repairs, and skiing as well as general cultural material. The aim of the service in Hesse, for example, is "to place television at the service of education for the people; in particular, to provide programmes for qualified minorities and courses for adults."[31]

Italy began its National Program in 1954 and the addition of another network in 1961 made it the second European country to offer an alternate television service.[32] The National Program on VHF has nationwide coverage and the Second Program on UHF reaches three-fourths of the population. Sicily and Sardinia receive programs by direct microwave connection. The National Program devotes its daytime periods to educational programs for schools (Telescuola) and broadcasts a general adult service from late afternoon to almost midnight. The Second Program, normally on the air for a little over two hours in mid-evening, is a supplement to the first. Each day of the week it features a different type of program; Sunday is set aside for variety, Monday for drama, Wednesday for cinema films, and Thursday and Friday for specials and documentaries.

Television is less advanced in the Eastern countries. East Germany, Czechoslovakia, Rumania, Hungary, and Yugoslavia have only one television service each; Bulgaria is just beginning; and Albanian television is still in the experimental stage. All these countries are planning to introduce second networks but will complete nationwide coverage with their first services before introducing second ones.

* The Westdeutscher Rundfunk contributes 25 per cent of the total; Norddeutscher Rundfunk 20 per cent; Bayerischer Rundfunk 17 per cent; Hessischer Rundfunk, Sender Freies Berlin, Süddeutscher Rundfunk, and Südwestfunk 8 per cent each; and Radio Bremen and Saarländischer Rundfunk 3 per cent each. (*Internationales Handbuch 1965/66*, p. C24.)

† As of 1966, they were presented by the Hessischer Rundfunk (Frankfurt); Bayerischer Rundfunk (Munich); Norddeutscher Rundfunk (Hamburg); Radio Bremen; and Sender Freies Berlin.

Moscow began regular transmissions from a single station on December 31, 1939. After an interruption due to the war, programming was resumed on December 15, 1945.[33] Moscow and Leningrad have three channels each, and much of the USSR west of the Urals can receive two services; but in the eastern part there is only one service if any at all. One hundred and twenty cities in various parts of the USSR can originate programs. In the eastern portion of the Soviet Union, where few if any stations are linked for live simultaneous broadcasting, programs are exchanged by recording. Educational channels have recently opened in Moscow and Leningrad. Depending upon the number of channels available, Soviet television is national, regional, or local in nature. Moscow, for example, originates one service for all of European Russia and another for the Moscow region, and also has an educational channel which concentrates on instructional and cultural materials for local use.

No European country has a round-the-clock television schedule such as one finds in many large American cities. Economic limitation is the principal reason for this but there also is the conviction, shared by many observers of the American scene as well, that there is not enough good program material to fill television screens from early morning to late night. Usually there is little if any broadcasting before the latter part of the afternoon, except for in-school and other educational programs, which occupy a good many hours in France, West Germany, and Italy. General programming normally begins in the late afternoon or early evening and runs until 11:00 P.M. or midnight. The British postmaster general limits the basic program hours for BBC 1 and ITV to 50 hours a week, plus time for certain religious, school, and educational broadcasts which bring the total for each to about 70 hours. BBC 2 is limited to 30 hours per week. The USSR does not depart significantly from the West European standard. In Moscow in 1966, for example, the three stations together were on the air an average of 16.4 hours per day, the first for 9.3 hours, the second for 4.5 hours, and the third for 2.6 hours. *

Europe's lovely woman television announcers—*speakerines* in French-

* At the end of 1966 program hours per week for first, second, and (when operated) third networks included Austria 47 and 14; Belgium 38 and 42; Denmark 30; Finland 47 and 23; France 67 and 26; West Germany 62, 47.5, and 20; Italy 84.5 and 25; Luxembourg 34; Monaco 30; Netherlands 37 and 21; Norway 29; Portugal 56.3; Spain 64 and 23; Sweden 42.2; Switzerland 50, 50, and 44; United Kingdom 72 (BBC 1), 33 (BBC 2), and 67.4 (ITA). (*EBU Review*, 102A:86 (April 1967).) In 1965 East German television was averaging 70 hours a week.

language countries and *Ansagerinnen* in German ones—deserve a paragraph to themselves. On almost all stations, both East and West, several carefully coiffured and neatly dressed young women, chosen for appearance, poise, voice quality, and diction, appear on screens at the beginning and ends of transmissions and between program features to make announcements, and, what is more important, to serve as hostesses and provide continuity for the program schedule. Some of these ladies have excellent linguistic accomplishments, and I have seen international broadcasts in which a young woman provided introductions in three or four languages with great ease and skill. After some months' viewing of European television I can only regret that the pressure for time to sell more twenty-second spot announcements rules out speakerines for American television!

There are no comparable percentages for different types of programs broadcast by various countries. In many instances such data are not available at all; and when they are, categories vary so widely that direct comparisons are impossible.* However, some figures are available, and from them a few generalizations may be made. Again the British Broadcasting Corporation is a good starting point. There are differences among the three radio services, since they are intended to contrast with and supplement each other.[34] If we average the entire output, however, during the fifty-three weeks ending April 1, 1966, 31 per cent of the time consisted of entertainment music and 25 per cent of serious music, while news ran 9 per cent and talks 10 per cent. General light entertainment constituted only 3 per cent of the radio output but it must be remembered that in Europe as in the United States light comedy and variety have been shifted to television and replaced on radio by music and talk.

The Bayerischer Rundfunk may be taken as an example for West Germany. On the two radio services broadcasting between April 1, 1962, and March 31, 1963, 58.17 per cent of all programs were musical: 24.85 per cent was dance and light music; 15.20 per cent middle range music; 15.30 per cent serious music; and 2.82 per cent folk music.[35] Of the remaining 41.83 per cent devoted to the spoken word, the larger categories included news for 3.72 per cent and in-school programs for 4.55 per cent of the time. The first network had relatively more political and economic

---

* A UNESCO publication has set out some "Suggestions for an International Classification of Radio Broadcasting Programs." (UNESCO, *Statistics on Radio and TV 1950–1960*, pp. 32–35.)

material while the second had more music and particularly serious music.

In 1965 Italy's three radio networks devoted 78.3 per cent of their national output to recreational and cultural programs and 17 per cent to information programs, the remaining 4.7 per cent being miscellaneous.[36] The largest single category was light music for 24.6 per cent of the time. Symphonic music took up 14.5 per cent, news 8.6 per cent, and entertainment and variety 7.5 per cent of the program time. Yugoslavia is another country which provides detailed statistics. Its main radio stations in 1965 devoted 29.90 per cent of their time to popular music, 20.78 per cent to classical music, and 12.50 per cent to folk music. Other major categories included news, 2.82 per cent; foreign affairs, 2.42 per cent; home affairs, 2.10 per cent; culture and the arts, 3.67 per cent; physical culture, 3.56 per cent; and sports and chess, 2.64 per cent.[37]

As to television, the BBC devoted 14.7 per cent of its national service during the fifty-three weeks ending April 1, 1966, to outside broadcasts (programs originating outside the studios, including mainly sports and entertainment, plus some public events); 12.8 per cent to "talks, documentaries and other information programmes"; 14.2 per cent to feature films and serials; 11.5 per cent to drama; 7.5 per cent to children's programs; 6.9 per cent to light entertainment; and 6.6 per cent to school broadcasts.[38] The largest individual classification for Italian television was 22.0 per cent for in-school programs, because of the extended daytime periods devoted to Telescuola. Following in order were news 10.9 per cent; films and telefilms 9.0 per cent; programs for children 7.5 per cent; cultural programs 6.4 per cent; and light entertainment 5.8 per cent.[39] The Yugoslav schedule for 1964 likewise shows an emphasis on the serious side. Informative programs took 29.3 per cent of the time; and "popular and humorous programmes" only 9.0 per cent. However, all types of films taken together occupied 11.7 per cent, these being mostly entertainment, while sports broadcasting took 10.1 per cent.[40]

Twenty per cent of Czechoslovak television is for children and youth; 11.5 per cent is news; 11 per cent is features; and 10 per cent each is education, sports, literary programs, light entertainment (except films), and film. Soviet authorities report that 42.6 per cent of Moscow-originated transmissions are of social and economic nature, 39.3 per cent artistic, and 10.6 per cent children's programs. One official stated that from 25 to 30 per cent of their television time was devoted to information, culture, and science; 30 to 35 per cent to fiction, art, spectacles, entertainment, concerts, operas, ballets, and drama; 15 to 20 per cent to youth and children's programs; 20 per cent to films; and 10 per cent to educational and miscellaneous.

It is clear that throughout Europe, except for the commercial stations in the small countries, there is more serious and less entertainment material than on any American network, even though light entertainment, light music, and sports together usually constitute over half the adult schedule. One gets this impression from hearing and viewing European broadcasts as well as from studying statistical tables. Supplementing these data is the additional fact that a much greater proportion of serious material is scheduled during mid-evening hours in Europe than in the United States.

Finally, something should be said about the relation between radio and television in Europe. The coming of television affected radio there just as it did in the United States. Initially, there was viewing in public places until people developed the interest and acquired the funds with which to purchase their own receivers. Then, as television viewing became more widespread, radio listening dropped, especially during evening hours.

But there are several basic differences between the American and European situations. For one thing, European radio and television services usually are operated by the same organizations, so that they are noncompetitive, supplementary services. Furthermore, since European television stations seldom broadcast during the daytime except to present limited-interest programs for in-school use, radio still has the field largely to itself until late afternoon. It also is important to note that in Europe the decline of listening has not lowered radio income, which is based largely on license fee receipts. In fact, the steady increase in the number of television sets has raised rather than lowered radio income since almost all countries require the purchasers of television licenses to buy radio licenses too. Europe's radio broadcasters, therefore, have not suffered from diminishing financial resources as have those in the United States.

However, once it is on the scene anywhere, television has certain predictable effects on the use of radio. People listen to the radio less as they view television more and radio listening becomes a background to other activities. Small transistor sets now are widely available in Europe, and one finds them on the streets, on the beach, and in restaurants. Dining in a Moscow hotel restaurant on the day of an important soccer match in the summer of 1965, for example, I noticed people at adjacent tables listening to the game on transistor radios.

The officials in charge of radio programming are well aware of these trends, and react to them as do their American counterparts.[41] In Western Europe schedules have taken somewhat the same trend toward music and news as in the United States; yet there still is much serious drama on European radio. The pirate stations in the northern countries also have been a factor in hastening the emergence of music and news formats. The Eastern countries likewise recognize the effects of television. A Czech spokesman told me that when television is available in the evening, radio must take second place, but pointed out that they meet this challenge partly by shifting some evening programs to late afternoon periods before television goes on the air, as well as by signing on at 3:30 A.M. to serve shift workers. A Hungarian radio executive noted, as have many people in Europe and America, that the intelligentsia prefer radio to television because "it provides greater appeal to the imagination." A Soviet spokesman emphasized that the USSR does not consider radio and television as rival media: Run by the same organization, both are operated for the good of all rather than for the enrichment of station operators—as, he declared, is the case in capitalistic countries. But radio programing has been changed everywhere: Most countries have more music and news than before; Sweden has Melody Radio; the USSR introduced "Mayda" with music, news, and information.

Program Exchanges

Broadcasting organizations turn to program exchange in order to maximize their resources. They hope, by sharing and exchanging programs and by some cooperative production, to extend the range of their offerings at the same time that they improve quality and reduce costs. It is for this reason that networks and other types of exchanges have developed in all countries. In Europe there first were informal bilateral exchanges; then organized exchanges among political, geographical, and linguistic neighbors; and finally such elaborate projects as West Europe's Eurovision and East Europe's Intervision.

One interesting project was set up in 1955 by France and the French-speaking portions of Switzerland, Belgium, and Canada.[42] During its first ten years this group exchanged some 10,000 items, in addition to providing programs for new countries in Asia and Africa in which French was the official or a supplementary language. A program bulletin issued in 1964 listed one thousand available programs. In May and June 1964 hookups twice a day expedited the exchange of 420 news items. This group also exchanges radio and television school programs.

The German-language services also have exchanges. In 1961, Bavaria, Austria, and German-speaking Switzerland, dividing costs on a 6-3-1 basis, cooperated on a series of television films, each ninety minutes long, which dealt in documentary fashion with such varied subjects as bird life, railways, games, and social institutions.[43] These services also exchange school features.

After several decades of team work in radio, the Scandinavian countries inaugurated the regular television exchanges of Nordvision on October 1, 1959.[44] This well-structured organization provides a constant flow of administrative, program, engineering, and legal information among its members although language problems are more difficult with Nordvision than with the French or German groups. Norwegian, Swedish, and Danish are somewhat similar but Finnish, related to Estonian, Hungarian, and Lapp rather than to any of the Scandinavian languages, is incomprehensible to Scandinavians without special language training.*

There is far more *ad hoc* program exchange and cooperative program development than even most Europeans realize. To cite several examples at random: In January 1964 West Germany's Hessischer Rundfunk organized a Hungarian Week on Frankfurt Radio, presenting forty-four broadcasts dealing with or prepared in Hungary.[45] Early in 1967, a Hessian television team flew to Moscow to make a color television documentary, "Medicine in the Soviet Union." In 1955 East German radio had contacts with sixteen foreign broadcasting organizations and by the end of 1960 was exchanging programs with sixty-two groups. By 1965 it was supplying musical programs of all types to the broadcasting systems of sixty-nine countries, including fifty non-Communist organizations in such places as Belgium, the United Kingdom, the Scandinavian coun-

* Although strictly speaking "Scandinavia" includes only Norway, Sweden, Denmark, and sometimes Iceland, the term "Scandinavian" as used by Nordvision includes Finland as well.

tries, a number of new African countries, Australia, and various Latin American countries.[46]

In 1963 Rumania sent 800 reports on various aspects of Rumanian life along with 166 hours of music to other Eastern countries, receiving in return 850 reports and 161 hours of music.[47] In addition it sent radio and television recordings of music by contemporary Rumanian composers to most of the West European countries as well as to various stations in the United States. In 1963 camera teams from Belgium, Czechoslovakia, Japan, and West Germany came to Rumania to make films and more recently Rumania drew up a television film exchange agreement with the United Kingdom. Normally the costs for these exchanges are borne by the host country which also provides technical equipment. By 1964 Rumania was exchanging broadcasts with sixty-five countries in all parts of the world, and on July 4, 1965, Rumanian television, under the terms of an agreement with the United States, broadcast a film about the music camp at Interlaken, Michigan, which was supplied by the United States government.

Czechoslovakia is very active and in 1963 provided material for 3,322 newscasts to Eastern and 519 to Western countries, as well as distributing 513 television films.[48] In 1964 Czech television cooperated with forty-three foreign teams including ten from West Germany, three from Austria, four from Japan, and others from the United Kingdom, the Netherlands, Sweden, Mexico, and Guatemala. These teams came to Czechoslovakia to do film reports on subjects such as the national health service, the care of mothers and children, universities, theaters, and Czech history.

In August 1964, Vienna and Prague produced live radio quiz programs which even ventured into topics like cultural relations across the Iron Curtain. Czech and Austrian artists appeared on a joint entertainment telecast from a Czechoslovak castle.[49] There also have been quiz exchanges between Vienna and Budapest. During the same year Czech Radio carried a live relay of Wagner's *Ring des Nibelungen* from the famous opera house in Bayreuth, Bavaria, and later broadcast Bayreuth recordings of *Tannhäuser* and *Tristan und Isolde*.

The radio and television program exchanges of the European Broadcasting Union and the International Radio and Television Organization will be mentioned frequently in this and the following chapter, as different types of programs are described in turn. The EBU was founded in Torquay, in the United Kingdom, on February 12, 1950, as the Western successor to the International Broadcasting Union, established in 1925, which divided into Eastern and Western organizations as a result of the international political strains that developed following World War II. The objectives of the EBU, as stated in its statutes, cover almost all aspects of broadcasting: "(a) to support in every domain the interests of broadcasting organizations which have accepted these Statutes and to establish relations with other broadcasting organizations; (b) to promote and coordinate the study of all questions relating to broadcasting, and to ensure the exchange of information on all matters of general interest to broadcasting services; (c) to promote all measures designed to assist the development of broadcasting in all its forms; (d) to seek the solution, by means of international cooperation, of any differences that may arise; (e) to use its best endeavors to ensure that all its members respect the provisions of international agreements relating to all aspects of broadcasting."[50]

The European Broadcasting Union is nongovernmental in contrast to the International Telecommunication Union, which has international legal status as an agency of the United Nations. Membership "is restricted to broadcasting organisations from a country that is a member or associate member of the International Telecommunication Union." Organizations from countries in the European area are admitted only as active members. In 1965 there were twenty-eight active members from twenty-five countries. Organizations from other parts of the world may become associate members. In 1965 there were forty associate members from twenty-nine countries, all except one from outside the European area. Eight commercial and educational broadcasting organizations from the United States belong to the EBU.*

The EBU's councils and committees deal with almost every conceivable aspect of broadcasting. In addition to programming problems in general, there also is consideration of special areas such as agriculture, programs for young people, light entertainment, music, news, drama, education, and sports as well as radio and television production.

* *Statutes of the European Broadcasting Union*, Art. 3. As of January 1, 1965, the broadcasting organizations of the following countries were active members: Austria, Belgium, Denmark, Finland, France, Federal Republic of Germany (2), Greece, Iceland, Ireland, Israel, Italy, Lebanon, Luxembourg, Monaco, the Netherlands, Norway, Portugal (2), Spain, Sweden, Switzerland, Tunisia, Turkey, the United Kingdom (2), Vatican City, and Yugoslavia. (*This Is the EBU*, pp. 5–8.)

The many-faceted legal problems that confront broadcasters everywhere are reviewed by committees of experts from member countries. The EBU also is concerned with engineering including basic research, standardization, and equipment design and operation. Staff training is another major concern and seminars are organized and brochures printed for this purpose.

The EBU works with many other groups. In addition to participating in internationally oriented projects organized by its members, such as the world conferences on educational broadcasting held in Rome in 1961, Tokyo in 1964, and Paris in 1967, its committees are involved in a wide range of radio and television competitions, ranging from popular music (Eurovision Song Contest), to the annual festivals held at Cannes, Montreux, Monte Carlo, Salzburg, Munich, and Berlin. It organizes training projects for Africa and Asia. Finally, the EBU supplements its own radio and television program exchange activities by cooperating with the corresponding Eastern organization, the International Radio and Television Organization, in many projects.

The EBU administrative office, at 1, rue de Varembé, in Geneva, houses the administrative, legal, and program departments. The technical center, at 32, Avenue Albert Lancaster, in Brussels, is supplemented by a receiving and measuring station in the same city. EBU publications include a *Review*, with alternate issues devoted to administrative programing and technical subjects, and occasional special brochures on matters of interest to its members. Administrative and program exchange costs are divided among active members in proportion to their resources, which are determined by criteria such as the number of receivers in each country; associate members pay annual contributions, also computed on the basis of total resources.

There was a long history of radio cooperation in Europe preceding World War II. An example of an exchange project developed by the EBU was the annual International Radio Week, which, though now discontinued, in 1965 presented *Tristan und Isolde* from Germany, *Boris Godunov* from Austria, and *Don Carlos* from Italy, as well as concerts by native composers from Denmark, Finland, and France and music from the time of Dante contributed by Italy.[51] Besides this there was a "Jazz Around the World" project organized by West Germany and "an experimental meeting between jazz and folk music" from Sweden. Over twenty-five copies of these programs were dispatched to

EBU members and associate members all over the world. There also were a series of carillon recordings coordinated by the Netherlands, broadcasts in translation of T. S. Eliot's *Murder in the Cathedral,* and some news exchange projects. To this France added an "International Forum" in which listeners from thirteen countries posed questions of substance to such celebrities as Jean Rostand, Julian Huxley, Frederico Fellini, and Ilya Ehrenburg. Some thirty-five EBU members were involved with International Radio Week in 1965. Currently all EBU radio exchanges are offered to OIRT stations automatically.

As early as 1948 it was suggested that the International Broadcasting Union set up a clearinghouse to expedite the exchange of television programs.[52] Accordingly, when the EBU was created in 1950 its legal, technical, and program committees began to study this possibility. After many meetings and much discussion Eurovision finally came into being on June 6, 1954. By the end of 1966, all the non-Communist countries of Europe except Greece and Turkey had connections permitting live program exchange, as did Yugoslavia. In addition Eurovision had a daily exchange of news items.

During the decade from December 1954 through December 1963 Eurovision's main product was sports broadcasts: The percentage of sports programs never dropped below 45 per cent and sometimes reached 70 per cent.[53] Few news items were transmitted before December 1960, but in 1963 and 1964 there were more news than sports items; in fact, during those two years news and actuality programs made up nearly 60 per cent of all Eurovision material.[54] Events like the common market negotiations; President Kennedy's trip to Europe and later his assassination; the death of Pope John XXIII; the trip of Pope Paul to the Holy Land; the visit of Nikita Khrushchev to Scandinavia; the death of Jawaharlal Nehru; the Congo crisis; and the United States presidential election were naturals for international exchange. As a consequence of the Early Bird satellite in 1965, the day-long transmission of live television across the Atlantic became technically possible at the very time there was increasing demand for news exchanges.*

* In 1964, twenty-eight Eurovision members originated 664 hours of programs. The principal contributors were Austria (131 hours—mainly winter sports); France (65 hours); BBC (62 hours); Italy (58 hours); and Japan (56½ hours—mainly Olympics coverage). The total was 1,134 separate news items originated. (J. Treeby Dickinson, "Eurovision in 1965," *WRTH 1966,* pp. 30–32, 48; "Eurovision

There should be at least passing reference to the legal problems of international exchange, which involve matters of copyright, mechanical rights (recordings, films, and tapes), performance rights, rights for sporting events, and union rights.[55] In 1954, three performers' federations attempted to boycott all international television relays until agreements were worked out to their satisfaction. Before Eurovision and Intervision could be developed on a large scale, therefore, these and many other barriers had to be surmounted through agreements involving the Council of Europe, UNESCO, the individual broadcasting organizations, the copyright owners, the manufacturers of films and records, all types of impressarios and promoters, and performers' unions. Little do Europe's viewers realize the legal groundwork which had to be laid before they could regularly view programs from abroad!

In 1960 East Europe developed Intervision under the aegis of the International Radio and Television Organization, which is set up in much the same way as the European Broadcasting Union. In 1966 there were twenty-four OIRT members of whom thirteen belonged to Intervision.[*] Between January 1960 and January 1965, more than 3,700 programs were transmitted by the Intervision network. A Russian television executive classified the programs as follows: sports, 43.5 per cent; topical, 30.5 per cent; cultural, 9.8 per cent; children's, 9.4 per cent; and

Programme Statistics: 1st January 1964–31st December 1964," *EBU Review*, 91B: 51–53 (May 1965).) This was still further increased in 1965, when the number of transmissions reached 1,551, and the total duration 969 hours, which indicated increases of 20 and 8 per cent respectively over the previous year. (J. Treeby Dickinson, "Eurovision in 1966," *WRTH 1967*, pp. 22, 26.)

[*] The International Radio and Television Organization is usually referred to by the initials of its French name, the Organization Internationale de Radio et Télévision. Founded in 1946, its members in 1966 included Albania, Bulgaria, China, Cuba, Czechoslovakia, Finland, German Democratic Republic, Hungary, Iraq, Mali, Mongolia, North Korea, North Viet Nam, Poland, Rumania, the United Arab Republic, and the USSR—including the Byelorussian SSR, Estonian SSR, Latvian SSR, Lithuanian SSR, Moldavian SSR, and Ukrainian SSR. (*WRTH 1967*, p. 16; *OIRT*, No. 6:3–8 (1966).) The address of the OIRT is 15, U Mrazovky, Prague 5, Czechoslovakia.

The thirteen Intervision members in 1966 were Bulgaria, Czechoslovakia, Finland, German Democratic Republic, Hungary, Poland, Rumania, and the USSR—including the Byelorussian SSR, the Latvian SSR, the Estonian SSR, the Ukrainian SSR, and the Lithuanian SSR. Albania, with only experimental television, was not a member. Finland, the only country belonging to both EBU and OIRT, received programs from both Eurovision and Intervision. Yugoslavia, which belonged to the EBU but not the OIRT, received Eurovision programs as an EBU member, and some Intervision programs as well. (Ales Suchy, "Intervision in 1965," *WRTH 1966*, pp. 38–39.)

entertainment, 6.7 per cent.[56] Between April 1 and June 30, 1965, Intervision offered its members thirty-six Eurovision programs, and reported that in return various Eurovision members received from two to twenty-five Intervision broadcasts, including three each taken by NBC and CBS, and seven by ABC. In 1965, a total of 1,700 programs were broadcast by Intervision including 100 programs contributed by Eurovision.[57] Of the Intervision broadcasts in 1965, topical and political programs represented 36.4 per cent of the total, just a few points below 39.3 per cent for sports; cultural programs, 10.7 per cent; entertainment, 7.8 per cent; and children's programs, 5.8 per cent. Although the percentage for sports programs still slightly exceeded that for topical and political programs, the ratio had changed since the previous tabulation, indicating that Intervision as well as Eurovision is shifting from sports programs to news and actualities.

News and Public Events Programs

News and public events programs are important because they are one of the best indications of a country's attitude toward broadcasting. If any programs are to be controlled, news broadcasts will be the first. The basic differences between countries with a free press and those with a controlled press have already been discussed. Among the former, freedom in news reporting is a matter of pride for all concerned, while among the latter there is complete frankness in stating that news broadcasts have a propaganda objective. "TV news is part of the political broadcasts of the propaganda department," stated a member of the Hungarian broadcasting staff writing on "TV News in the Framework of Television Political Programmes."[58] The same is true of news commentaries, which in Poland, for example, are "to explain the line of the Party and the Government." Not only government views must be reported, but also certain "individual opinions and judgments provided, of course, they are not harmful."[59]

Most European governments retain at least some potential for program control, whether or not they use it, and this raises certain problems not encountered in the United States. If the government has the power to regulate broadcasting there is always the possibility that a certain program may represent official opinion. For this reason the broadcasting organization usually has the right to indicate which announcements or programs are presented at government request. For example, the BBC's license states that whenever it is required to broadcast any kind of material, "the Corporation . . . may at its discretion announce or refrain from announcing that it is sent at the request of a named Minister." A similar provision governs relationships between the government and the ITA.[60]

The new French broadcasting law of 1964 not only permits but requires the ORTF to identify any such material as "coming from the Government."[61] This provision was introduced to eliminate misunderstandings such as resulted from the cancellation of the Khrushchev-Malinovsky interview in 1963 (see above, pp. 59–60). In Belgium also, whenever announcements are broadcast at the request of the government, they must be so identified.[62] The Swiss broadcasting corporation is not to present "broadcasts likely to endanger the internal or external security . . . or the relations of Switzerland with other countries." The government may require urgent police messages to be broadcast, but may not "demand that specific works or ideas shall be broadcast."[63] The law in Hesse authorizes the government "to use the broadcasting system to make known laws, ordinances, and other important information."[64] However, on the subject of news it also says: "Reporting must be true and objective. News and commentaries thereon shall be clearly separated from one another. Doubts to correctness must be expressed. Commentaries on the news must be designated as such, naming the responsible author."

All European broadcasting organizations present many news programs. In 1953 UNESCO reported that from 5 to 10 per cent of most radio air time in Western Europe was devoted to news.[65] A later UNESCO study found the percentages for radio to be in the same range, while news took from 10 to 25 per cent of television time.[66] More recent—and more exact—are figures from West Germany for news time which for radio ranged from 2.22 to 9.91 per cent, most services devoting around 6 or 7 per cent of their time to news. Bavarian television assigned 14.5 per cent of its time to news, while the Zweites Deutsches Fernsehen figure was 12.8 per cent.[67] In 1965, Italy assigned 8.6 per cent of radio time and 10.9 per cent of television time to news broadcasts.[68]

Many radio services present news on the hour or half-hour from

morning until night, besides longer roundups several times a day.*
RAI, in addition to national, regional, and local radio news (the latter
including some programs in German, Slovene, and French), offers an
almost continuous news service by telephone, revised several times
each day, which can be dialed in twenty cities. Switzerland, too, besides frequent radio newscasts has a day-long telephone news service
available nationally. In addition to frequent news on other services, the
Soviet Union on its second network, Majak, offers news and information every half-hour twenty-four hours a day. Almost all of these programs include not only the reading of bulletins by studio announcers,
but also some domestic and foreign actuality recordings.

There are fewer television newscasts, partly because the television
schedules themselves are shorter, and partly because television news-
casting has not yet fully developed in all parts of Europe. Where there
are noon services for the general public as in France, these often include news; but the major television newscasts, usually lasting from
fifteen to thirty minutes, are broadcast during the early and late evening hours, say at 6:00, 7:00, or 8:00 P.M., and again at 10:00 or 10:30
P.M.

News agency reports are the basic source for radio and television
news. All countries of any size have one or more agencies of their own,
usually private in the West and government monopolies in the East.†
Broadcasting organizations in most of the Western and some of the
Eastern countries also make wide use of such international organizations as the Associated Press, United Press International, and Reuters.
Hungary and Czechoslovakia, for example, receive service from UPI
and Visnews. Government controlled or not, there is wide exchange
among all these agencies. One example is the Soviet Union's Tass,
which supplements its own worldwide network of correspondents by
exchanges with some thirty foreign agencies. Tass, incidentally, sells its
services abroad in Russian, English, French, German, and Spanish versions.[69]

In earlier years some countries required that news bulletins be based

---

* For example, Czechoslovakia has twenty-three radio newscasts each day, plus a
daily 7:00 P.M. "World Tonight" roundup. (Alois Srubar, "The Czechoslovak Radio
Newsreel," *OIRT*, No. 5:197–200 (1960).)

† The latter are found in Albania, Bulgaria, Czechoslovakia, East Germany, Hungary, Poland, Rumania, Turkey, Yugoslavia, and the USSR. (UNESCO, *World
Communications: Press, Radio, Television, Film*, in articles on these countries.)

only upon certain designated sources. This was partly the result of the strong influence of the press, which wished to prevent the broadcasters from developing their own news-gathering organizations, and partly the consequence of fear that the broadcasting organizations might become too independent. Thus for a time in Sweden all news bulletins had to be edited by and broadcast directly from the office of Radiotjanst, the official state news agency, which is owned by the Swedish press. But since 1956 news programs also have been originated by Sveriges Radio, which now has complete access to AP and UPI service, and also has its own correspondents both in Sweden and abroad.[70] In its agreement with the broadcasting organization the Swiss government "reserves the right to name the sources from which news broadcasts shall be drawn."[71]

With the coming of television the need for news film was met partly by older agencies like UP, which set up United Press International News Film (known as UPITN after 1967, following a merger with Britain's Independent Television news), as well as by such new ones as Visnews, which grew out of the combined activities of the BBC, the Australian Broadcasting Commission, the Canadian Broadcasting Corporation, the Rank organization, and Reuters.[72] Visnews now has subscribers in more than sixty countries all over the world, including most of Europe as well as NBC in the United States. To supplement these agencies all the major European broadcasting organizations have set up their own extensive news-gathering facilities. The BBC, for example, after a modest beginning in 1938, operates what has become a twenty-four-hour, worldwide radio monitoring service and maintains seventeen full-time staff correspondents abroad, besides about fifty "stringers" who occasionally provide it with news.* France, Italy, Germany, the Soviet Union, and most other continental countries also have news representatives abroad. Consequently it is routine for Europeans to hear and see direct reports from "our correspondent" in, for example, New York, Moscow, London, or Cairo.[73]

An important television news source is the EBU exchange coordinated by the Eurovision office in Geneva. Advance information is dis-

---

* Michael Peacock, "News in Television," *EBU Review*, 77B:6–9 (January 1963); John Crawley, "At the Centre of the Network," *EBU Review*, 91B:21–23 (May 1965). See also John Campbell, *Listening to the World*. The purchase of these monitoring reports by news agencies explains why so much news from East Europe and China bears a London dateline.

tributed about scheduled events of international interest. Telephone conferences twice a day then confirm plans for transmitting news pictures over international video networks so that a video tape may be made of the picture material for delayed use on the local station. Each country later inserts commentary in its own language based upon information received during the telephone conferences. Intervision has a similar project, although less highly developed, and there is an increasing amount of exchange between the two groups.

News stories from overseas as well as special events frequently are transmitted by satellite, but this is not always practical because of the time differences between Europe and the United States (see above, pp. 43–45). For example, because of the six-hour difference between Chicago and Paris, an event available for satellite transmission at 6:00 P.M. Chicago time could not be received and processed for broadcast before 12:30 A.M. Central European time. But there are few television news programs in Europe before early evening, so it is just as satisfactory and much cheaper to record the material and ship it by air. There are no facilities to exchange programs among Western European countries by satellite, though there are reception facilities in the United Kingdom, France, and Italy. The USSR, however, has its own Molnya satellites to transmit programs within the Soviet Union, which also have been used to exchange black-and-white and color programs with France.

The basic procedures for producing news programs are the same everywhere. A good example is the newsroom in Hamburg, West Germany, which originates all national news for the first German network. There also is a newsroom for the second network, Zweites Deutsches Fernsehen, in Wiesbaden, in addition to local facilities for each of the nine regional broadcasting organizations. The head of the Hamburg news center, responsible to the directors general of the nine ARD companies, has a staff of fifty.[74] Sources for news and film include the West German news agencies, ARD foreign and domestic correspondents, Agence France Press, Associated Press, UPI, Visnews, EBU exchanges, and monitoring reports on other broadcasting organizations including East Germany.*

* There are facilities in Hamburg to record East German telecasts off-the-air. At times these are used on West German programs, though with the source identi-

The "Tagesschau" was begun at the end of December 1952 with three broadcasts a week, although there have been daily programs since October 1, 1956. Weekdays there is a summary of the previous day's news from 10:00 to 10:20 A.M., plus two five-minute afternoon newscasts, in addition to the main program from 8:00 to 8:15 P.M., and a late edition at 10:30 P.M. For all this the ARD has provided in Hamburg a special news studio with three remote control cameras operated from a well-equipped control room, together with all the paraphernalia necessary for rear screen projection, slides, still pictures, film, and special effects. The broadcasts maintain high professional standards and use one announcer who reads news on screen and another who does commentary for silent film and video tape. These daily programs are supplemented by occasional specials such as the comprehensive six-hour coverage—complete with computer predictions—of the German general election on September 19, 1965.*

Programs vary widely from country to country, depending upon the national approach to news policy as well as upon equipment, staff, and skill. Radio newscasts all over Europe combine straight news reading with recorded on-the-spot coverage and short interviews. Weather forecasts are an established feature of European broadcasting. Radio news programs usually include weather information, while on both East and West television, announcers or skilled meteorologists report weather trends, often with considerable skill, using ingenious maps and other appropriate devices. In response to public demand the Swiss supplement weather forecasts with reports on skiing and mountain driving, in addition to a telephone service for information on weather, skiing, and roads.

As has been observed, West Germany is among the leaders in television. The principal news programs on French television also are well done despite criticism of government control of content. Though not so

fied. The East Germans record Western programs off-the-air for incorporation into their news and commentary programs.

  * "Television Coverage of the Parliamentary Election in the Federal Republic, September 1965," *EBU Review*, 96A:71–72 (April 1966). The traditions of news handling in Western Europe sometimes rise to plague people who would like to forget the past. German radio news was censored even during the Weimar Republic, and, of course, was completely controlled by the Nazis. Recently it has been suggested that broadcasting be separated into journalistic and cultural divisions, with the former to become the responsibility of the federal government. Fortunately, though, this has not been done. (Thomas Petry, "West German TV—The Way Ahead," *Television Quarterly*, II (No. 3):61 (Summer 1963).)

polished as West Germany's networks, the ORTF also utilizes several announcers who alternate in reading copy, motion and still pictures being introduced as required. Since television news in Switzerland must be broadcast in three languages, pictorial material with "international sound" is transmitted from the Zurich headquarters to the German-, French-, and Italian-language regional centers where commentary is added.* Swiss television uses no announcers in vision and printed titles are given in all three languages. In November 1964, the Netherlands inaugurated a weekly one-hour television newsreel for the deaf, claimed to be a European first, in which narration is supplemented by subtitles although the original sound track is broadcast for viewers with normal or only slightly impaired hearing.[75]

The question of how well European broadcasters report the news must be answered in terms of their national information policies. Where freedom is allowed news services usually acquit themselves well; if control is the rule it will apply equally to all media. Few if any extensive studies of news broadcasting content have been made, although the viewing of many telecasts indicates that in the West news coverage is reasonably complete; and reports from critical residents usually support the conclusion that broadcasts are honest and objective in the central European countries. Complaints about slanted newscasts in France have lessened since the new broadcasting law took effect in 1964, and it is agreed that most Western countries have moved steadily toward freedom in news reporting since World War II.[76]

The Eastern countries proceed somewhat differently. Political objectives account for the great amount of time devoted to such items as national production or harvest norms, the completion of new buildings, and the opening of new factories. Not only does such news take a large share of program time but also frequently it provides the lead stories. An announcer may spend several minutes reading lists of production figures, and political commentaries without accompanying visual material often are included while human interest items are minimized. The conspicuous exception is East Germany. Forced to compete for audiences with Western services, the German Democratic Republic has developed a first-class news broadcasting organization which must appear to minimize propaganda if it is to hold its public. I had an opportunity

* "International sound" includes crowd noises and sound effects not dependent on language for meaning.

148

in September 1966 to compare West and East Berlin television news-casts on the day Chancellor Ludwig Erhard of West Germany was visiting in Washington and Walter Ulbricht, chairman of the State Council of East Germany, was in Belgrade. As would be expected, each service led with film reports about its own chief executive but both included some material about the travels of the other. The subject matter on the remaining portions of the two programs was largely duplicative.

While not accorded the luxury of questioning basic beliefs, Eastern broadcasters may criticize shortcomings within their systems. On a Moscow television news program during the summer of 1965, for example, I saw an exposé of the shortcomings of some public bathing beaches. Interviews with bathers emphasized such deficiencies as slow public transportation, inadequate snack counters, and poor dressing rooms. On a Belgrade program I saw a documentary treatment of the inadequacy of motel construction and operation, an important subject because of Yugoslavia's efforts to attract foreign tourists.

In program production the Eastern countries lag behind although when they have had time to construct better facilities and train more personnel, there is no reason why they should not be just as good as anyone else. But at present their news presentations often are stiff and stilted, with ineffective lighting, poor visuals, and slow camera work. Again, East Germany is the exception and has first-class production fully on a par with that in the West. As an added feature, East German television offers a young lady news reader who would do well in any country's beauty contest.

The shift of emphasis from radio to television news has gone less far in Europe than in the United States. There are proportionately fewer television sets in Europe and the schedules are shorter. Since the same organizations run both radio and television there is less incentive to regard them as competitive. Some European broadcasting executives even say that if people want more news, they always can listen to the radio. For these reasons the European public as a whole, in comparison with the American public, depends more on radio than on television as a basic news source.*

* In Sweden, radio and television news, though under the same ultimate control, were decentralized to dispel fears that the broadcasting monopoly would lead to identical news services on both media. (Olof Rydbeck, "Coordinating the Two Services," *EBU Review*, 91B:40–42 (May 1965).)

News from and about the United States figures prominently. All the major broadcasting organizations have one or more American correspondents to supplement news agency reports, and television organizations have access to extensive picture material about the United States. Most important American developments are reported, although European like American news editors sometimes feature what is interesting and sensational rather than important or—in the case of television—stories for which pictorial material is available. Furthermore, in all countries West and East, prejudices about the United States are apt to be documented and American foibles played for laughs, although this could be said about any country's coverage of foreign news.* However, major American events are reported and one regularly hears the voices and names and sees the faces of America's leaders on European programs. In the Eastern countries there is a much greater tendency to select news about the United States for its editorial effect. In the course of one thirty-minute evening television program in Moscow, for example, I saw only two items dealing with the United States: One showed colored people chaining themselves to the door of a Chicago courthouse, and the other showed Negroes being dragged unceremoniously from demonstrations in a southern state. The same pictures undoubtedly were used by many American television stations that same day but with balancing material.

European broadcasters make a great deal of state occasions and other public events. The Coronation of Queen Elizabeth II in 1953, which helped lay the foundations for Eurovision, is one of the best examples of how a country offered practically the entire world relays of one of its major state ceremonies.[77] Other events with extended radio and television coverage have included the Soviet Union's May Day parades and October Revolution anniversaries; the state visit of Elizabeth II to Germany in 1965; American presidential activities, ranging from inauguration to the assassination and funeral of the late President Kennedy; and the exploits of both American and Soviet astronauts. However, the Soviet Union has never covered the exploits of its astronauts in live broadcasts for either domestic or international audiences, as has

* The United States was so displeased with the "anti-American tone" of French radio and television coverage of the American role in Viet Nam that Ambassador Charles E. Bohlen called on the French minister of state to protest the ORTF's presentation. (*New York Times,* August 10, 1966, p. 9C; August 11, 1966, p. 2.)

the United States. Royal weddings, such as that of Holland's Crown Princess Beatrix to West Germany's Prince Claus von Amsberg in 1966, are natural material, as are parliamentary openings, major international conclaves, and sporting events.[78] When not of sufficient interest to justify extensive live coverage, film or video tape recordings are distributed.

When the country in which an event takes place cannot offer adequate origination facilities, one or more interested countries may dispatch a team to cover it, subsequently supplying programs to all of Europe and the world. Thus RAI reported the trip of the Pope to the Holy Land in 1964 with 200 staff members who used 27 vehicles in Jordan and 14 in Israel. This project provided ten hours of television and over thirteen hours of radio programs. RAI also covered the trips of the Pope to Bombay and the United Nations in New York.[79]

Cooperation between broadcasting organizations in Britain, Italy, and Switzerland made possible elaborate coverage of the successful climb of the Swiss Matterhorn on July 14, 1965, to commemorate the centenary of the first successful ascent of that famous peak.[80] More than ten tons of equipment were hauled by train to an Alpine meadow at an altitude of 7,000 feet; cameras and other facilities were taken by helicopter to posts at 9,300 and 12,009 feet; and the climbing teams were equipped with radio transmitters and accompanied by cameramen climbers. Commentary in three languages accompanied the pictures which were fed for live or recorded use in most of Western Europe, East Germany, Yugoslavia, and the United States.

Politics and Controversy

With political and controversial programs as with news, there is a difference between the democratic and totalitarian countries. Most of the former make time available to all major parties as well as for discussions of controversial issues, whereas the latter use the broadcast media to organize support for the single party allowed on the ballot, and for discussions confined to procedural variations within officially defined ideological limits.

The United Kingdom is again a good starting point because of the influence it exerts by its example.[81] Before each general election the BBC and ITA meet with representatives of the three major parties—

Labour, Conservative, and Liberal—to assign radio and television periods to each, the amount of time being proportionate to their strength in the House of Commons, usually about a 5-5-3 ratio. Minority parties, including the Communist, are allowed some time on the air provided they enter at least fifty candidates throughout the country. The programs are produced by the BBC and the commercial television companies may relay all—or at their choice none—of the television presentations. The BBC alone carries the radio programs.

There usually is also extensive news coverage of political campaigns, although this was not always the case, in addition to which both BBC and ITA arrange other programs pertaining to the election. During campaigns both broadcasting organizations in Britain, as well as many on the Continent, curtail entertainment, dramatic, discussion, and documentary programs with possible political implications in order to maintain strict impartiality. During periods apart from general elections other types of political broadcasts are scheduled, the assignment of time again reflecting party strength in the House of Commons. In addition to these formal broadcasts, both BBC and ITA frequently invite members of Parliament and other political figures to take part in discussions of political and controversial matters, and to make brief statements for news broadcasts.

The democratic countries proceed in a similar manner. The nine broadcasting organizations in the Federal Republic of Germany are required by law to make broadcast time available for all parties meeting the requirements to file for Parliament on nomination day.[82] The Hessischer Rundfunk specifically must provide equal broadcast time to all parties with candidates in all districts.[83] Hesse has had political broadcasting since 1948, with candidates and their spokesmen participating, although in effect the law excludes extreme left and right wing groups. Besides broadcasts at election times, which are developed jointly with the parties, Hesse provides time to party spokesmen at other periods.

Belgium follows somewhat the same procedure, though its history of political broadcasting dates back to 1930.[84] Both candidates and spokesmen may broadcast and exact hours are determined before each election. The three traditional parties (Social Christian party, party for Liberty and Progress, and the Belgian Socialist party) have equal time, the Communist party somewhat less. At other times each of these three is given an eight-minute period a week and the Communist party an eight-minute period every three months. During campaigns no other programs are curtailed or changed.

Current procedures for political broadcasting in Switzerland took effect in 1959.[85] As a rule, election broadcasts do not follow the customary format of periods assigned to parties or candidates, but rather are debates and discussions in which several parties participate. Air time is given to all parties in the national legislature, plans being worked out jointly by them and the broadcasters, but since the system is still experimental, new ground rules are drawn up for each election. To supplement these election programs, throughout the year politicians from all parties take part in regular discussions of both domestic and international issues.

As might be expected Sweden has one of the most advanced systems. Arrangements for political broadcasting grew out of negotiations between Sveriges Radio and the party leaders, since neither the law nor the accompanying contract between the state and the broadcasting organization refers to the subject at all.[86] Final responsibility rests with Sveriges Radio though it works cooperatively with the parties. Political broadcasting began in the late 1920's and has increased in amount ever since. Election programs start about four weeks before polling day. Only those parties in Parliament—the Social Democrats, Liberals, Conservatives, Agrarians, and Communists—may participate, although all five get equal time, and news programs cover the activities of parties not in Parliament. Apart from election periods, there is at least one broadcast series each year on which party spokesmen appear, and at any time, when party leaders make news, they may be interviewed for news programs.

The new French broadcasting law, which took effect in June 1964, had as one of its main objectives the equal radio and television treatment of all political parties (see above, pp. 58–63). Although things have improved, the government still is reluctant to relinquish its advantages. Thus, in response to opposition charges that President De Gaulle and his ministers monopolized radio and television, Minister of Information Alain Peyrefitte declared in 1965: "In ordinary times, it is not reasonable that the Opposition express itself as often as the Government. The Government has something to say, since it manages the nation's affairs. The Opposition can only criticize." Nevertheless, the minister announced that preceding the presidential election scheduled for December 5, 1965, the anti-De Gaulle candidates would divide a total of twenty hours of broadcasting time, while the Gaullist candidate —not yet known at the time the announcement was made on October 20, 1965—would have only four hours.[87]

As election time approached, some opposition candidates complained of censorship. They reported that they were forced to be personally present for all programs on which they appeared, often under very inconvenient circumstances; that there were limitations on who could speak on their behalf; and that they were denied the right to use certain films in expounding their positions. The failure of President De Gaulle to make full use of his allotted time was widely cited as one reason he failed to win a majority.[88] Public interest in the election was indicated by an increase in newspaper circulation and in the rental in Paris of even more television sets than during the recent Olympic games. Before the run-off election on December 19, 1965, a special control commission was set up to supervise the use of broadcasting by the two candidates, President Charles de Gaulle and François Mitterand. This time, though, both used all their allotments.[89] Following the election, perhaps in response to criticisms that the government was still dominating coverage of public issues, the French television network began a series of forty-five-minute interviews on which prominent political and public figures were questioned by panels of political writers.[90]

In November 1966 the Cabinet announced that preceding the elections to the National Assembly to be held in March 1967, time would be divided equally between the Gaullist majority and the opposition, with ninety minutes for each on radio and television.[91] But this obviously favored De Gaulle supporters, since the two Gaullist parties would share equally with the four principal and several smaller opposition parties. The Paris newspaper Le Monde considered this "obviously unacceptable" for a country with several opposition parties. Although candidates in French legislative elections are local and not national, broadcasting time was assigned on a national network basis only, thus denying broadcast exposure to all except the few candidates chosen as national spokesmen. The final blow, however, came on election eve, March 4, 1967, when General De Gaulle went on the air with a dramatic appeal for the election of his supporters to the National Assembly. On the pretext that he was not a candidate, De Gaulle took advantage of his

status as President to appear at a time so late as to preclude any broadcast replies. There were vigorous complaints from several of his political opponents and this broadcast may have been the factor that won
a narrow electoral margin for his faction. The problems of political
broadcasting in France are only partially solved.

In totalitarian countries radio and television are used to encourage
the public to vote rather than to expound different points of view. The
procedure in Czechoslovakia during the election for the National Assembly, and some other offices, on June 14, 1964, was typical.[92] Before
the election Czech television presented information about the lives and
records of the candidates: "The TV agitation centre was also in operation, fulfilling explanatory and propagandistic tasks during the preparation of the elections"; and there were reports on developments in various cities since the last elections. Election day coverage began at 9:00
A.M., and in the course of the day some older voters recalled election procedures between the two world wars. That evening Czech television
broadcast Smetana's famous opera, *The Bartered Bride*. In Spain, too,
broadcasting is used to organize support for an officially favored position, rather than to discuss the pros and cons of proposals, as for example with the national referendum on the new constitution held on December 14, 1966.[93]

Without exception European countries with commercial broadcasting
do not permit the sale of time for politics or propaganda. This includes
not only such national systems as Austria, Italy, Spain, Switzerland, and
West Germany but also the United Kingdom's ITA. The commercial
stations in Andorra, Luxembourg, Monaco, and the Saar do not sell time
either to their own politicians or to those of other countries who might
want to address their countrymen from abroad.

Discussions and debates appear on all broadcasting schedules. Most
democratic countries schedule at least a few programs—and some a
great many—on which basic beliefs may be questioned. In the totalitarian spheres, on the other hand, discussion is limited to procedural
matters within the limits of accepted and defined orthodoxy, though
this does not preclude searching analyses and debates within limits.
The basic techniques used are much like those found in the United
States: face-to-face confrontations of people with different points of
view; "Meet-the-Press" programs in which distinguished guests are
questioned by representatives of the information media; and programs

in which experts in a field answer questions from a studio or broadcast audience.

Austria has discussions of international and domestic affairs by journalists as well as "Meet-the-Press" programs. Beginning in 1964 it even developed some programs with three of its Eastern neighbors, including Vienna-Prague "Stadtgespraeche" ("City Talks"); a radio quiz exchange between certain smaller cities in Austria and Hungary; and a television discussion involving members of the philosophy departments of the universities of Cracow and Vienna.[94]

The broadcasting law of Hesse states that whenever spokesmen for political parties, or for religious, ideological, labor, or employers' groups, "are granted the opportunity of discussion, the possibility of expression of views in speech and reply shall be given them under equal conditions in each case."[95] The law limits this right of participation to parties with candidates in all election districts, to "those labor and employers' organizations as extend over the whole Land," and to statewide religious and ideological communities. But there is at least one limit to the range of topics; as a spokesman for the Hessischer Rundfunk put it: "according to our Land-Law the democratic character of the regime cannot be put in question."

Belgium is prepared to schedule discussions on such topics as An Analysis of Social Insurance; The Origins of the Government Crisis; The Origins and Political Repercussions of the Strikes in the Limburg Coal Mines; and Is There a Crisis in the Belgian Political System?[96] Some programs consist of answers by political leaders to telephoned questions from the audience. The organization of controversial programs in the Netherlands is complicated by the fact that the six broadcasting societies are free to broadcast their own opinions.[97] But most of them schedule programs presenting other points of view as well, and the coordinating NOS guarantees air time to minority groups. (See pp. 74–75.)

Sweden's democratic status is evidenced by its willingness to broadcast discussions of almost any subject within reason. As a spokesman indicated, "Even subjects of a so-called delicate nature, as homosexuality, can be freely discussed by scientists and/or laymen."[98] Although it might be difficult to find "one responsible person who would express the opinion that the whole parliamentary system ought to be changed . . . if we could find him, we would certainly arrange a debate between him and others." But "opinions contrary to the Western conception of democracy should not be allowed to stand un-answered." Still, Communists and people of neo-Nazi points of view are among those who may broadcast. Sweden also is prepared to schedule documentaries on social problems in which local authorities or private interests are attacked, though in that case the latter may appear to defend themselves on the same or on follow-up programs. Faced with the recurring problem of all broadcasters, whether a program must be balanced within itself or may be countered by another one, the Swedes believe that the "obligation to be impartial and objective refers to the total program output and that therefore a controversial opinion must not necessarily be followed in the same program by a contradictory view. Thus such 'answers' could appear in another program some other time."

An interesting discussion project is RAI's "Tribuna Politica" ("Political Platform"), scheduled during periods of normal political activity, which becomes "Tribuna Electorale" ("Electoral Platform") in election years.[99] Dates and rules are determined annually by the Parliamentary Committee for the Supervision of Broadcasting, made up of deputies and senators constituting a cross section of the national Parliament. During its first year in 1960, the project included ten press conferences and nine talks, the former averaging thirty and the latter ten minutes in length. By 1966 this had grown to a total of twenty-nine broadcasts, all except three on both radio and television.

The "Voice of the Parties" consisted of six broadcasts on which all the parliamentary parties participated, air time for each varying from eight to sixteen minutes, with total majority time totaling forty-six and opposition time fifty-four minutes. Nine broadcast periods were devoted to "Party Secretaries' Press Conference," during which journalists of widely varying backgrounds questioned the secretaries of the parliamentary parties in American "Meet-the-Press" fashion. The three hour-long television programs in the "Topical News" series were filmed comments by parliamentary party spokesmen on issues of current interest. During the eight "Debates," each forty-five minutes long, representatives of the national parties confronted each other, with two to four parties appearing on each program. Finally there were the three "Trade Union Debates" in which spokesmen for the larger trade unions and employers' associations took part. The elaborate rules laid down for these programs ensured fairness and equality of opportunity for all the interests and points of view represented.

Communist countries also schedule various types of discussion programs. Although most of the Eastern countries do not confront government officials with journalists, Yugoslavia, for example, might have a program on currency devaluation; but the government having decided to revalue the dinar, the discussion would deal with details of application rather than with the basic issue of devaluation.* In 1964 the Department of Contemporary Events of East German radio had a Tuesday evening series entitled "Journalists Put Questions." Ministers, scientists, and even party leaders were interviewed. "They answer outstanding and often burning topical questions and express their opinions to the wide audience of radio listeners."[100] Also in East Germany a radio series called "Frankly" was begun in 1964 to discuss "frankly and directly with our listeners all questions occupying their attention and concerning mainly political and economic life." Listeners in various regional studios outside Berlin telephone questions to a team of three well-known experts and a moderator in Berlin. Each half-hour program in the series deals on the average with from eight to ten questions. These range from "the relation of the German Democratic Republic toward West Germany and the friendship pact between the German Democratic Republic and the Soviet Union to the problems of reform in industrial prices, the technical revolution, distribution and trade." A point is made of transmitting the programs live to maintain higher listener interest.†

Religion

There are two important aspects to religious broadcasting: under what conditions are religious programs permitted? and what is the nature of the programs?

As to the first point, with religious as with political programs, the basic determinant is national policy. There are few religious programs in the Communist countries: Those which do tolerate religion take the position that even though permitted, religion is not to be encouraged,

---

* In 1965 16.65 per cent of all Yugoslav radio programs, including 47.75 per cent of all speech programs, were classified as "informative and political," while in 1964 and 1965 29.3 per cent of all television programs were in the "informative" category. (*Yugoslav Yearbook 1965*, pp. 70, 148.)

† Manfred Klein, "The Broadcast Called 'Frankly,'" *OIRT*, No. 1:8–9 (1965). The author referred to the case when a Dresden listener complained of red tape in the local travel agency. A member of Parliament who was on the panel promised to look into the matter, and on the following program explained when and how the problem would be solved.

and hence not much—if any—air time should be allotted. In those countries where only one church is active, broadcasts may be limited to it. Elsewhere, though religious freedom is practiced in theory, one church may be so dominant that there is little need or audience for broadcasts by others. Yet in some countries there is real religious freedom, whether or not there is a state church, with all—or almost all—denominations given air time.

Only the Roman Catholic Church may broadcast in Portugal and Spain.[101] Since 1957 Spain even has had a nationwide radio network Cadena de Ondas Populares Española (Network of Spanish Popular Stations), operated by the Episcopal Commission for Cinema, Radio, and Television of the Catholic Church.[102] In addition to one government and several commercial radio networks, there also is a government television network. On all stations, however, religious programs are accepted only from the Catholic Church. The operation of its own radio service is one of the prerogatives of politically independent Vatican City.[103] Studios are located within the walls of the Vatican, and transmitters—AM, FM, and short-wave—are at Santa Maria di Galeria in nearby Italian territory. Vatican Radio's sixteen hours of daily programing are in thirty languages, and, of course, are all Catholic in orientation. Along with the BBC, Voice of America, Radio Liberation, and Radio Free Europe it was among the stations which formerly were regularly jammed in Eastern Europe.

Although Turkey is predominantly a Moslem country it is committed by its Constitution to freedom of worship.[104] Yet "the primary concern is first to direct religious broadcasting from a single centre, in order to further the establishment of a secular social system, and, second, to broadcast programmes of an instructive and educative character in order to inculcate the idea of secularism itself." To keep broadcasting from being used by religious authorities as "the mere tool of religious interests," and because "The country's cultural development has not yet reached the point where religious fanaticism no longer constitutes a threat to society," the government keeps a firm hand on religious programing in order "to educate the nation in the principles of secularism and keep it on the alert against the threat of reaction."

According to the 1961 census approximately 7,500,000 Greeks belong to the Greek Orthodox Church, the Moslem faith ranking a poor second with only 112,665 adherents.[105] The Greek Constitution, therefore, refers

159

to the Greek Orthodox religion as "the predominant religion in Greece." Other religions are allowed freedom of worship, but their activities clearly are circumscribed by the constitutional requirement that "Proselytism or any other intervention against the predominant religion is forbidden." In view of this, the Hellenic National Broadcasting Institute permits only broadcasts by the Greek Orthodox Church.

Although France is predominantly Roman Catholic its approach to religious broadcasting differs from the examples cited above.[106] The majority of its religious programs on radio are Catholic, but there also is a Protestant service every Sunday plus special features during Lent and Christmas, and a Jewish broadcast every Friday along with special programs for the Jewish Orthodox minority. Television presents a Catholic mass lasting ninety minutes and a Protestant service for half an hour each Sunday, a Jewish service every fortnight, and occasional presentations for the Eastern Orthodox Church.

The Hessischer Rundfunk in West Germany is required by law to present religious services which shall not "offend moral and religious feeling," at the same time that it is forbidden to present programs "containing any prejudice or discrimination on account of nationality, race, color, religious, or ideological faith of an individual or a group."[107] Consequently the Hessischer Rundfunk presents occasional religious services from churches, synagogues, and cathedrals representing the major church groups. Belgium, over 93 per cent Catholic, broadcasts religious services only from Roman Catholic churches, but does have Jewish and Protestant as well as Catholic studio broadcasts.

Of the six associations in the Netherlands responsible for broadcasting, three have religious orientations: KRO (Catholic), NCRV (Protestant), and VPRO (Liberal-Protestant).[108] On their own programs these groups may express their respective viewpoints. But in addition, a Royal Decree of December 1955 declared that the minister of education, arts, and sciences is to "allocate television transmitting time to those church denominations that should apply to the Minister for same," although the time thus assigned is not to exceed 5 per cent of the total amount available. Following this requirement various other churches, including the Netherlands Reformed Church, Baptist, Evangelical Lutheran, Calvinist Churches, Salvation Army, and some others are assigned broadcasting time, and several production organizations set up to assist them. (See above, p. 75.)

Although Sweden has a state church, the Established Church of Sweden (Lutheran), to which 99 per cent of the population belongs, Sveriges Radio provides time to other denominations too, including Baptist, Methodist, and Roman Catholic, as well as the Salvation Army.[109] About half the time for religious broadcasts is given to the state church and the other Christian churches receive most of the remainder. In addition there are some nondenominational programs with religious orientation.

In almost all countries the heart of religious broadcasting is the presentation of actual services from cathedrals, churches, synagogues, and other places of worship. There are also studio broadcasts, talks, discussions of religious subjects, and short devotional periods and prayers. For the most part, however, religious programs on the Continent do not exploit the potentials of radio or television to the extent found in the United Kingdom or the United States, where great imagination has been exhibited in developing programs to attract the nonchurchgoing public.

But there are some interesting exceptions. In the Netherlands, the organization which provides liaison between Protestant churches has developed question-and-answer and current events broadcasts emphasizing religious information.[110] Other Dutch programs review religious publications, while KRO, the Catholic broadcasting association, broadcasts a monthly half-hour religious documentary. Religious broadcasts in Spain include cultural and recreational programs.[111] A series entitled "The Family from Within" presents family problems in dramatized format, followed by discussions of such issues as the unfaithful husband, jealousy, and even mothers-in-law!

In religious broadcasting the BBC and ITA use avant-garde techniques seldom found on the Continent.[112] In fulfilling their basic policy of serving all major faiths, they make a real effort to interest nonchurchgoers through hymn singing, discussions, dramatizations, and the insertion of short religious features in other types of programs. Even light entertainment techniques have been used in Britain to attract this audience.

Finally, something should be said about music and religion.[113] Inevitably, much religious music is broadcast by all countries especially during the major religious festivals. Eurovision too is involved: One of its first programs was a Whitsuntide ceremony from Rome in 1954; and the

Easter and Christmas periods always include programs from the Holy Land, midnight mass from famous cathedrals, and carols from England. Sound on all of these programs is excellent, and camera work often superb.

Educational and Children's Broadcasts

Europe does a great deal of excellent educational broadcasting: there are programs for in-school use; out-of-school programs for children and youth; and educational and cultural programs for adults.

Except for the commercial stations in Luxembourg, the Saar, Monaco, and Andorra, there is much more serious programming on European radio and television than in the United States. Any evening of listening or viewing will turn up far more significant drama, concert music, discussions, and documentary material than would a comparable period on American commercial stations. This is the principal reason Europe has so few educational stations. There are special services such as the German and Italian third programs for radio; good music networks like France Musique; and the emerging third television channels of West Germany and the Soviet Union. But most of these are not educational in a didactic sense, being rather of general cultural nature.

There are several important differences between the educational and cultural programs of Europe and those of the United States. Although the total funds available to them are limited by American standards, European broadcasters devote a larger proportion of their resources to serious programing. American commercial stations and networks, with potentially greater resources for serious programs, do not often use them that way except for sporadic educational and cultural spectaculars. At the same time, although America's educational stations have the will to produce such programs, they seldom can finance them adequately. There also is a difference in perspective. Most educational and cultural programs in Europe are developed by national organizations with national viewpoints, whereas in the United States they are produced by local stations with less comprehensive approaches. All things considered, therefore, Europe has better serious programs than does the United States. However, one must except the irregular but often superb productions of America's networks, as well as some of the output of National Educational Television, the educational television service supported by the Ford Foundation.

IN-SCHOOL PROGRAMS

Broadcasts for use in classrooms—in-school or school programs—
have long been a feature of the European scene. There was school
broadcasting in Germany in 1923, in the United Kingdom and Denmark in 1924, and in a number of other continental countries by 1930.
Following World War II the in-school radio services were resumed,
after which in-school television developed. Although experiments began
early in the 1950's, by 1959 only three countries—the United Kingdom,
France, and Italy—had regular in-school services. But European television generally was slow to develop, and educators there as elsewhere
had to be convinced of the value of the new medium. In any case, by
1970 virtually all European countries will have at least some television
programs for schools. Strangely enough, although the Soviet Union has
many out-of-school programs for children as well as instructional broadcasts for adults, it does very little in-school broadcasting through either
medium.[114]

Inevitably, in-school services develop along lines dictated by educational needs and practices. Thus, countries with centralized educational
systems like France, Italy, and Sweden have national in-school services;
decentralized West Germany and Yugoslavia organize their school programs regionally; multilingual countries like Belgium, Czechoslovakia,
and Switzerland broadcast programs in several languages.* It should
be noted that in the United States, too, decentralized education has led
to regional and local in-school broadcasting. The national schools-of-
the-air conducted years ago by NBC and CBS fell by the wayside, and
the six-state Midwest Program on Airborne Television Instruction cen-
tered in Indiana has encountered difficulties partly because of its attempts to cover divergent school systems; but local in-school services
have continued to thrive.

There is surprising agreement on the purposes of in-school radio and
television. The chairman of the School Broadcasting Commission of
Portugal spoke for all when he outlined the following general objectives
in 1962: "(a) development in the child of the realisation that he belongs
to a wider social environment than that which lies within the bounds

---

* To further complicate things, Switzerland is divided into twenty-five cantons
and half cantons, each with its own educational authorities. (René Dovaz, "The
Difficulties of Introducing Sound Broadcasting to Schools," *EBU Review*, 70B:40–
42 (November 1961).)

of his school; (b) widening of the pupil's cultural and affective horizons; (c) stimulation of his powers of initiative and of his desire for cultural development; (d) valorisation of teaching by the introduction of new and different elements into normal teaching practice; [and] (e) improvement of the technical and educational conditions in which teachers perform their task."[115]

Another point on which there originally was agreement was stated by a Belgian Commission in 1931: ". . . school broadcasts can never take the place of the teacher . . . the importance of broadcasting lies in its capacity to supplement and complement teaching; and . . . the guiding principle should be: do what the teacher cannot do and never what he can do better himself in school."[116] This was echoed by the head of school broadcasting in Denmark in 1961:[117] "Educational broadcasting *must not, cannot,* and *is not* intended to replace the teacher. . . . On the other hand the cooperation of the teacher is indispensable, and often a 'school radio lesson' must be reckoned to take up more of the teacher's time than a 'normal lesson' and on the whole to make heavier demands on him. . . . A broadcast is to constitute only a supplement to daily teaching. . . ."

Although most Western educators would disagree with the school broadcasting official in Poland who said that it was the function of "television . . . to aid the development of the scientific, materialist world outlook," many would agree with her that "it is not our task to replace the teacher but to develop his ideas and demonstrate what he himself cannot demonstrate in the course of his lessons. We do not want to teach, but to illustrate, to show how the objects and phenomena mentioned in textbooks look in reality."[118]

More recently, however, in Europe as in the United States, there has been a trend toward direct teaching because of the shortage of qualified teachers to deal with ever more complex subjects.[119] Beginning in the 1940's Sweden met the lack of English teachers through radio lessons; more recently France has developed science and language broadcasts especially for secondary schools with inadequate teachers; Yugoslavia has begun television programs in fields where there is a shortage of teachers; and Italy's Telescuola is basically a combination of direct teaching and correspondence study resulting from a severe shortage of both schools and teachers.[120] Back in 1947, Hungary had special broadcasts for children whose schools were closed because of inadequate heating, and in the same year Norway developed broadcast correspondence courses for children living a long way from schools.[121]

Changes in curricula and methods after World War II also affected school broadcasting. The point was well stated by the director of in-school broadcasting for Radio Zagreb in Yugoslavia: "The fundamental changes that have taken place in the country have profoundly altered the structure of the population and the standard of education, calling for a higher and higher level of general culture and technical knowledge. . . . School broadcasts in sound were brought in during the school reform period and developed their activity at a time when new curricula and working methods were being introduced into the schools, when free activity was beginning to take an important part in the educational programme. The spirit of our new schools has created conditions for the modernisation of teaching of which broadcasting is a part."[122] France, Italy, West Germany, Sweden, and Poland are five other countries whose postwar in-school broadcasting has been related to educational changes. Along with this have come special broadcasts for teachers in Denmark, Finland, France, Italy, Poland, and Sweden, among others, to improve their use of radio and television or to instruct them about new subject matter and teaching methods. Other countries have issued special brochures for this purpose.

Another universal problem is liaison between broadcasters and education authorities. Since advice from teachers is desirable if not indispensable, it is agreed that there should be regular contacts with an official agency like the ministry of education or with advisory teachers' committees, although in most countries the broadcasting organization rather than the education authorities is ultimately responsible for financing, administering, and producing in-school services.[123] In any case, decisions about using programs always are made by classroom teachers.

Supplementary materials to accompany broadcasts are the general rule. There are teachers' handbooks and wall posters with information about topics and schedules, along with brochures for pupils. On the whole these materials are well written and attractively printed. The Dutch claim that in September 1950 they were the first to introduce film strips to accompany radio broadcasts.[124] Slides and film strips now are available in Czechoslovakia, Finland, France, the Netherlands, Norway, and Sweden, to name just a few countries. Czechoslovakia, Norway, Sweden, France, and West Germany are among those making wide use of tape recordings to supplement radio broadcasts: in some cases the broadcasting organization itself circulates the recordings, while in others the schools themselves do taping off-the-air.

In-school programs cover almost every subject in the curriculum.* They range from 15 to 30 minutes in length, 15 to 20 minutes being the average, and frequently are repeated for the convenience of classes meeting at different hours. The total amount of time devoted to such programs is considerable. For example, Polish radio assigns 16½ hours a week to in-school programs; France, 15 hours a week to in-school television alone; while Italy with 6 hours a day devotes most of its daytime television schedule to such material.†

Some of Europe's best planning and production are lavished on these programs. Radio presentations are effective combinations of talks, dramatizations, and on-the-spot actualities, while television runs the gamut of production possibilities. For example, special camera crews frequently do location filming in such varied places as mountaintops, coal mines, tropical jungles, and European factories while studio presentations are carefully designed for maximum pedagogical effect. In Italy a special building was constructed to house the studios and administrative offices for Telescuola.

Though on the whole European broadcasters have been slow to develop audience research for their general program services, they have done well in studying in-school audiences. For one thing, these audiences are easily surveyed; for another, if there is to be continued cooperation from teachers and education authorities, there must be evidence of results. Therefore, questionnaires are circulated widely among teachers and school administrators, and meetings arranged with teachers, while in West Germany and Poland visiting teachers talk to teachers and students and observe programs in use.

France is a prime example of a country with a highly centralized educational system whose curricula are planned and administered on a national basis. Consequently most in-school programs come from Paris,

---

* The following subjects are typical: art, biology, chemistry, civics, current events, drama, drawing, economics, ethics, geography, geology, gymnastics, history, humanities, industry and industrial techniques, languages, literature, mathematics, medicine, music, news and news analysis, physics, religion, safety, science, social studies, sociology, travel, vocabulary building, vocational guidance, and zoology.

† One should note that since most continental countries have few daytime television programs for adults, they have plenty of time for in-school broadcasts.

although there has been some decentralization in recent years.[125] Programs are planned and organized by personnel from various state schools assigned for that purpose to the National Pedagogical Institute in Paris, although production is by the ORTF staff.

After World War II the French were faced with severe educational problems which they attempted to solve in part through television. At the same time that the country had a growing school population, it had to decrease the number of school dropouts; yet traditional French schools were never designed for large student populations. School television also was expected to bring rural elementary schools out of their isolation. For the most part the French believe radio and television should supplement rather than replace the teacher. Yet they have recognized the need for special instruction in such fields as languages, mathematics, and science where there is an inadequate supply of qualified teachers. The French also have given much thought to the problem of achieving the best results: students should be prepared before programs go on the air; there should be optimum reception conditions; and there should be carefully planned follow-up discussions. To improve utilization the ORTF presents study courses and special broadcasts for teachers, including refresher courses. In 1966 six thirty-minute evening television programs for teachers were presented each week, dealing with modern mathematics, the new physics, biology, and applied linguistics.

French school radio programs began in 1951, and offer all age groups a very wide range of subjects. Although most broadcasts are distributed nationally there have been experiments with local and regional programs too. School television programs, started in 1951, are broadcast during several morning and afternoon hours each school day, again largely to a national audience. Variations on standard patterns are provided by the broadcasts of the National Center for Teaching by Correspondence, some of which are designed for bedridden or isolated children, for adults wishing to complete interrupted studies, and for the children of families living on river barges. Instruction is basically by correspondence with broadcasts supplementing printed materials. An incidental feature of both radio and television has been the exchange of recorded programs with other French-speaking countries, including Belgium, Switzerland, Canada, and some French-speaking African countries. The ORTF also has prepared French-language lessons for broadcast in Denmark, Norway, Sweden, and Yugoslavia.

There is constant appraisal of these broadcasts. Over 10,000 questionnaires are filled out by teachers every year, the results being reported back through a bimonthly review (*Bulletin de la Radio Télévision Scolaire*). With its two supplements, the *Bulletin* reached a fortnightly circulation of 39,200 copies in 1966. Another measure of response is the distribution figures for the elaborate printed materials which accompany the broadcasts. In 1961–62, 12,000 booklets were distributed for a series on atomic physics; 16,940 for a series on English; 2,120 for some broadcasts on geography; 600 for programs about techniques of atomic science; and 4,360 texts for dramatic programs. During 1965–66, 455,000 booklets for radio language programs were distributed to secondary schools, and 1,900,000 booklets for singing programs to primary schools. The same year a survey of state schools equipped with receivers showed that 60 per cent of such schools were regularly using radio and nearly 20 per cent television programs.

French in-school radio and television are excellent. Programs are carefully planned and worked out; are accompanied by well-prepared and attractively printed handbooks for both teachers and students; and are well produced. An enormous amount of time and money has been put into these broadcasts, with splendid results.

In contrast to France is decentralized West Germany. Each of the nine Länder has its own schools and its own broadcasting; in fact, the German constitution specifies that education must be a state rather than a federal function. In-school radio broadcasting began in 1923, and developed extensively under the Weimar Republic. During the Nazi era it was terminated by Hitler himself, when the Hitler Youth and the Nazi Teachers' Organization were unable to agree on which should be responsible for school broadcasting. It later was resumed following World War II.[126] School television was begun in several Länder in 1961 and now is emerging in most of the others too. West Germany regards in-school programs as supplementary to the work of teachers, although responsibility rests with the broadcasting corporations rather than with the education authorities. German observers recognize drawbacks in the decentralized approach but point out the advantage of letting each section of the country develop those programs most suitable to its needs and problems. Noteworthy features of the German system include after-school preview broadcasts, so that teachers can decide whether or not and how best to use the programs, and schools are encouraged to tape both radio and television programs for delayed use. At least two German broadcasting organizations have visiting teachers to provide liaison between broadcasters and schools. There is an exchange of programs among the German services of Austria, Germany, and Switzerland.

Yugoslavia is another decentralized country and its education and broadcasting are decentralized too.[127] The first school radio programs in Yugoslavia were presented by Radio Ljubljana in 1945 and most other areas have had them since 1953; school television first appeared in 1960. Programs vary in length from ten to fifteen minutes, exact broadcast times depending upon local conditions. All told six federal units present six different sets of school programs in either the Serbo-Croatian or Slovene language, while three others broadcast in Albanian, Hungarian, and Macedonian. In some places these programs are the primary responsibility of the broadcasters and in others of educational councils. The wide range of subjects includes Russian, French lessons from Paris, and English lessons from London. Some broadcasts are repeated after school hours for other listeners. In the fall of 1956 Yugoslavia initiated an hour a day of in-school television, partly supplementary to the school curriculum, but including some direct teaching of subjects for which there was a shortage of qualified instructors. Despite Yugoslavia's 20 per cent illiteracy rate, however, it was decided not to use television to teach reading in the belief that the audience reached would be too small to justify the cost and effort involved. In order to evaluate the programs, there are periodic visits to schools by representatives of the broadcasting services; discussions with teachers and students; and questionnaire studies of results (some schools get television sets in return for reporting on the programs they use). Several schools have been set up as experimental centers, and there are regular meetings between educational advisory committees and school personnel.

Although some East European broadcasting objectives differ from those of the West, the operational approach to school programming is much the same everywhere. Polish radio presents some thirty in-school programs a week for use in 20,000 schools, and in 1961 Polish television broadcast thirty-six experimental half-hour in-school programs.[128] Rumania has no in-school broadcasting at all, though some of their many children's programs are used in classrooms. One reason is that much of the country is not electrified and hence has few receivers, in addition to which the two-shift system found in many schools would complicate reception schedules; but Yugoslavia, too, has many communities with two-shift schools, and yet does have in-school broadcasting. The Czechs, after some years of school radio, began school television in 1960 and by 1961 were devoting much air time to such programs.[129] Regular television programs for nursery schools were begun in 1958–59 and plans laid for daily in-school broadcasts by 1965. One interesting variation on the customary pattern is the presentation of some programs at 3:00 P.M., about the time schools are dismissed, so there can be collective viewing without interfering with regular class periods.

Radio programs for Italian schools began in March 1934, and after a wartime interruption were resumed in November 1945.[130] These cover all grades from primary through high school, and like most school program services are designed to supplement existing school activities. Subjects range from a news bulletin for very young listeners to stories, dramas, musical programs, and foreign languages for older children.

But Italy's real claim to fame is its Telescuola.[131] RAI launched its first experimental school television programs in 1954, intending to follow the radio pattern of supplying supplementary and enrichment materials. But a 1953 survey indicated that Italy had more than 700,000 unemployed young people between the ages of fourteen and twenty-one with an almost complete lack of professional qualifications. Out of every hundred students who entered primary school, only 25 per cent reached secondary school, 5 per cent finished secondary school, and 2 per cent went on to complete university training. Even as recently as 1962–63, nearly 3,700 communities out of a total of 8,000 had no secondary schools at all, while the shortage of adequate educational facilities in southern Italy was particularly marked.

Telescuola, therefore, grew up because there was a great need, a centralized school system that facilitated the nationwide project, and an available television network. Telescuola's aim was to enable children living in areas without secondary schools to attend school until age fourteen as required by law. The idea came from RAI, which at first had difficulty selling it to educators, but eventually Telescuola was worked out cooperatively with the Ministry of Education. The head of Telescuola reports directly to the director general of RAI, rather than to a television program executive, which emphasizes the importance of the project.

Telescuola began in 1958–59 with two half-hour lessons a day corresponding to the first year of the industrial-vocational syllabus.* By 1963–64 Telescuola was offering a three-year course that paralleled the combined secondary-vocational curriculum in effect after 1961. This requires some six hours of television time six days a week between 8:30 A.M. and 2:30 P.M., from October through June. Subjects now include art, civics, domestic economy, drawing, English, French, geography, gymnastics, history, Italian, Latin, music, mathematics, physical education, religion, science, and writing. There are frequent repeats, and the schedule is planned so that pupils in any class have intervals of twenty or twenty-five minutes between lessons during which to review the material just seen.

The twenty-two Telescuola teachers are carefully chosen from the more than 2,000 experienced teachers who apply each year from all parts of Italy. Two hundred are selected by a committee from the Ministry of Education and RAI to make test recordings, and then fifty are brought to Rome for the final eliminations. Those chosen are well paid and usually stay with Telescuola for three years or more. Six average pupils appear as a permanent panel on camera with each teacher, to give the impression of a classroom to student viewers, and to provide an immediate feedback. The programs are very well produced and care is taken to maintain the atmosphere of a teacher in a class rather than of a television show.

When Telescuola began in 1958, appeals were made to all parts of the country to provide television viewing rooms. At present, in addition to space in schools and public buildings, viewing centers have been set up in charitable institutions, reformatories, hospitals, and nursing homes. Viewing groups are organized as detached sections of the nearest regular state school, under the ultimate control of local authorities. Supervision is provided by paid coordinators who check attendance, keep order, administer examinations, and submit reports to the headquarters in Rome. Although originally most homework was corrected in Rome because of a shortage of qualified local volunteers this now usually is done by local coordinators, and only a few examples—chosen

*Strictly speaking the term Telescuola or Television School is applied not only to RAI's in-school series for children, but also to the literacy series "Non è mai troppo tardi" ("It's Never Too Late") for adults, but here the term is applied only to the in-school programs.

to illustrate the best and the poorest—are forwarded to Rome. Special textbooks, well organized and attractive, are printed for these programs and are free for pupils unable to pay for them.

The statistics for Telescuola are impressive. Each year 1,100 hours of lessons are viewed by 60,000 students—20,000 for each of the three years of the course—in over 2,000 centers.* But much remains to be done since there are over 200,000 children in need of this schooling. Unfortunately, it sometimes is difficult to persuade parents to send their children to Telescuola since not all of them understand the importance of schooling. Nevertheless, during the first three years 100,000 to 145,000 textbooks were distributed for six courses alone. At the end of each school year students may go to a state school to take supervised examinations. In 1961–62, over 11,000 students took these tests and 85 per cent of them passed. The best students are rewarded by money prizes and trips to Rome.

To supplement Telescuola, RAI began in June 1962 to broadcast during evening hours a pre-university science series to prepare high school pupils for university mathematics, physics, and chemistry. Since 1963 there have been after-school refresher courses for teachers on the program "The New Secondary School," necessitated by the periodic reforms of the school curriculum. Another series, "Looking Ahead," helps young people select occupations.

OUT-OF-SCHOOL BROADCASTS FOR CHILDREN

Any survey of out-of-school broadcasts for children and young people reveals certain interesting similarities and differences in objectives between some of the Western and Eastern countries. The chairman of the European Broadcasting Union's Study Group for Children's and Young People's Programmes referred to the exchange of such programs as "a powerful means whereby friendship and understanding between peoples can be furthered; and the seed of this friendly understanding cannot be sown too early in the hearts of the young." Commenting on German children viewing a program from Amsterdam, he said: "We saw the pretty, happy [Dutch] children laughing and waving on the screen as if they were beckoning to us . . . and the German children

---

* The regular state schools seldom use Telescuola, although there are enrichment radio programs for them. There is no Telescuola for primary schools since there are adequate schools for children of that age.

watching laughed back, with shining eyes. . . . Someone remarked quietly: These children could never shoot at one another. . . ."[132]

Statements from Eastern Europe often stress the solidarity of the Communist countries. A Russian writer was pleased to report that through "school clubs of international friendship children organize correspondence with their contemporaries of many countries, [and] exchange souvenirs and songs. . . . The program exchange among radio organizations—OIRT members—helps us considerably in the preparation of broadcasts with themes of international education."[133]

Under the title "Socialistic Programmes for Children on German DDR Television," an East German wrote that one of the themes of children's television plays was the "history of the German and international children's movement, working youth and workers, the struggle of the working people in Europe against fascism, [and] the struggle of progressive elements in Federal Germany against the seeds of German fascism and militarism."[134] An article on Rumanian radio programs for children and youth reported: "Materials describing the life and activity of pioneers in friendly countries, and those reflecting the hard life of the children of working people in capitalist countries and colonies are included to [in] this programme, too."[135]

On the other hand, many generalizations by Eastern writers could be accepted by broadcasters everywhere. Thus, a Soviet children's program executive wrote: "In radio broadcasts for school children we talk about people marked by high moral standards whose love for their homeland, discipline, audacity and faithfulness to friendship and many other noble traits represent an example to be followed by young people."[136] Reflecting a universal observation of parents, he continued: "In this age of the speedy physical and intellectual development between childhood and adolescence it is very important not to lose influence over the young people and to find a way to their minds and hearts. It is well-known that adolescents are often skeptical to [of] the opinions of adults, have their own ideas of life, the surrounding world, and painfully receive every discrepancy between the words and deeds of adults." A Rumanian wrote that "the aim of broadcasts for school children is not to replace the educational influence of the family and school, being rather to assist those directly concerned with the education of children."[137]

A Czech writer expressed concerns shared by commentators on children's programs in many countries.[138] "Articles by physicians, psychologists and pedagogues appearing in Western magazines often point out the ill effects of television on the development of children." Unfortunately, "by sitting in front of a TV set the child learns only to accept passively a ready-made programme which captures all its senses, causing it to discard books and more complicated toys without interest. . . ." To avoid this, the writer went on, Czechoslovak television encourages children to engage in activities. Small children are asked to draw pictures or find mistakes in pictures shown on the program. Older children can reply to questions put to them. At all times children should be led from the "active viewing of programmes to creative work of their own after the program is finished." The author suggested that parents limit the amount of television viewing and select only those programs suitable for children. Finally, he said, young children should go to bed at eight o'clock, right after the television news.

East German television urges children to work puzzles, do manual work and drawing, conduct chemical experiments, and take part in cultural, technical, and group activities.[139] One way to do this is to have child artists, poets, and writers take part in programs. Belgian television also tries to have children sing, draw, dance, play music, and engage in handicrafts.[140] A writer from Finland stated: "Among the most important aims is the activating of the children both as listeners and as performers in the programmes."[141] In fact, children in many countries take part in radio and television programs as announcers, actors, singers, and performers.[142]

All countries devote much late afternoon and early evening time to programs for children. Outstanding is a program exchange project, the International Children's Magazine, developed in 1955 by the European Broadcasting Union's Study Group for Children's and Young People's Programs. Austria, Belgium, Denmark, France, Italy, the Netherlands, Norway, Sweden, Switzerland, West Germany, and Yugoslavia are the European countries which devote from fifteen to sixty minutes a month to this project, program contributions being made by twenty countries, four of them—the United States, Canada, Australia, and Japan—outside of Europe.[143]

Soviet radio devotes a total of seven hours a day on its various networks to children's programs.[144] These attempt to help the parents of very young children acquaint them with the surrounding world. Other programs include early morning newscasts; English, French, German, and Russian lessons; fairy tales; book talks; and musical programs, with some distinguished artists taking part. The Soviets are among those countries utilizing the technique of simulated journeys to introduce travel information.

Rumanian radio offers twenty-four hours a week of broadcasts for children and young people ranging in age from five to twenty.[145] There are news bulletins; concerts with a chorus of 180 children (their *Radio Times* sometimes prints the music and texts for these programs); and an imaginary rocket ship which can travel anywhere, backwards or forwards, in time or space, in order to present a wide range of facts and ideas. Programs for older children include discussions and entertainment.

European broadcasts for children are of every imaginable type from direct instruction to pure entertainment. Every kind of music is played from folk songs to symphony, from musical comedy to the latest popular hits. Instruction ranges from science to literature and from simple health hints to philosophy and politics. There are single as well as serial broadcasts. Varied and ingenious techniques are used to make these programs attractive. Europe still has its equivalents of the uncles, aunts, grandfathers, and other personalities who introduced children's programs in the United States in the early days of radio. Films include some imported from North America as well as many made in Europe. Puppets and marionettes are popular, especially in countries like Portugal, Czechoslovakia, and the USSR which have cultural traditions in those media. Clubs and societies are another device to involve the young audience. Some countries have repertory companies of actors and singers as well as children's orchestras and bands. Distinguished adult educators, actors, musicians, and entertainers also take part.

One does not have to agree with all of the basic concepts underlying these programs to recognize that by and large they are very well done. Many hours of air time are devoted to them and they receive some fine writing and production. Staffs usually consist of dedicated and skillful people.* Despite differences in objectives between East and West the

* The East Germans have required authors, editors, producers, and artists on children's television programs to live and work four weeks each year in the country, small towns, and factories so that "A fresh wind will blow in our studios and many new, hitherto unknown faces will appear in the children's broadcasts on our tele-

best programs from many countries, if language barriers could be surmounted, would meet with approval by children and parents everywhere. The finest work of all is on programs of pure fantasy and entertainment without propaganda objectives. In Europe there is very little of the intense excitement, violence, and shoddiness which so often mars children's programs on American commercial radio and television. Europe's broadcasts for children are not always as exciting as those in the United States, but on the whole they deserve a higher rating.

INSTRUCTIONAL PROGRAMS FOR ADULTS

Instructional programs for adults have been a feature of European broadcasting for many years. In addition to the cultural, documentary, and informational broadcasts which form such a large part of European radio and television, there are many formally organized instructional programs, although very little has been done with courses for credit.

Denmark started adult education radio broadcasts before World War II and extended them during the German occupation.[146] Although at one time there were 900 study groups all over the country, these died out after the war and most listening now is done individually, though with study guides. Over fifty such brochures have been published and one of them achieved a sale of 80,000 copies. In 1958 Denmark began a "Sunday University" which offered Sunday morning lectures on subjects ranging from Martin Luther to the Danish farmer, and from the insect world to the principles of Marx and Lenin.

In the spring of 1964 the Television Academy Foundation of the Netherlands (TELEAC) was set up to provide direct teaching for adult viewers during early and late evening hours. Some vocational education courses were offered for young people in industry, while other more general courses were broadcast for the general public. TELEAC has its own board of management with an advisory council representing various educational and public groups. Courses cover such subjects as first aid, pedagogy for elementary and secondary school teachers, Greek Tragedy, on-the-road automobile repairs, and modern logic. Initial responses were excellent and audience reaction was very encouraging, as indicated by the sale of brochures and general audience surveys.

vision screens. . . ." (S. Böhme, "Socialistic Programmes for Children on German GDR Television," *OIRT*, No. 2:51 (1960).)

The term "university" crops up all over, though hardly ever with reference to courses for credit. In 1959 Poland introduced a "Radio University" of which the chief aim was "Development of the listener's capacity of independent thinking and critical assessment of observations."[147] This noncredit project offers programs on three levels of difficulty. There also is a Polish "Television University" which deals with art, history, mathematics, and some other subjects.

But the most ambitious Polish experiment began in the fall of 1966.[148] After a successful pilot project earlier the same year, this new enterprise, developed jointly by the Polish educational authorities and the UNESCO Department of Mass Communication, was set up on a six-year basis, with UNESCO providing funds for additional television equipment and Poland conducting research. The original announcement in January 1966 brought 58,000 requests for study guides, although the long-term project was not expected to accommodate more than 12,000 students. During the first year there were five half-hour programs a week, chosen from courses in the first year of a four-year college curriculum. In subsequent years there were to be ten broadcasts each week from the first and second years of study. Programs were scheduled at four o'clock in the afternoon—the Polish factory day normally ends at two or three—and there also were evening repeats. Students were to get time off from work to study and attend meetings, going every six weeks to study centers for personal conferences, discussion, and laboratory work.

In January 1963 Rumanian radio and television started a "Technical University" consisting of lectures on metallurgy, chemistry, engineering, and industrial electronics.[149] In the same year Belgium's "Popular University" offered sequential programs on astronomy, painting, and law.[150] Czechoslovakia's "Radio University," with about 600 registrations per quarter, offers no credit but does give certificates to listeners. Sometimes as many as 1,000 free scripts are distributed during a quarter, while from 20,000 to 200,000 printed script collections have been sold at nominal prices.[151] Bulgarian radio has its "Pupil's University," through which lessons are given by "outstanding scientists-popularizers," who also answer questions mailed in by listeners.[152]

The USSR has a "Radio University of Literature and Art," though this is "only a symbolic title, since it does not in the least offer a 'University' education." However, the programs do attempt to "incite listeners' interest in books, theatre, music, and fine arts."[153] The "Radio Cultural University" of the Ukraine, begun on September 1, 1960, deals with Soviet and world literature, music, and art.[154]

One of the most ambitious projects is in East Germany, which has applied the term "Television Academy" to its adult education since February 1961.[155] Though holding that "all broadcasts must serve educational purposes," "educational broadcasts" are defined as those "whose prime objective is education, i.e., the systematic transmission of knowledge and data." Such programs constitute from 4 to 5 per cent of the seventy-hour weekly television output of the German Democratic Republic. Series have included one on mathematics comprising ninety-five weekly broadcasts of forty-five minutes each, fifty-five broadcasts on chemistry, and forty-five on physics. Other programs have been on the Russian language, natural science, the technology of production, agricultural technology, and livestock breeding. Since November 1964 the Television Academy has been expanded to include some programs for high school children.

Although these courses are not for credit, students watching them and reading the accompanying materials may take examinations at evening schools and receive certificates. Viewer response is very impressive: The ninety-five broadcasts on mathematics brought in 200,000 letters; those on chemistry and physics about 100,000 each; while the eighteen Russian lessons had over 500,000 responses. Forty thousand viewers who satisfied all the necessary requirements have been awarded "diplomas of honour of the Television Academy." Thirty-five per cent of the viewers are teachers and students, and 30 per cent industrial and agricultural workers. The largest age group (35 per cent) was between 25 and 30 years of age and the next largest (30 per cent) 11 to 16 years old.

An ambitious current project in West Germany is the Bavarian Television College which began January 2, 1967. This is being developed cooperatively by the government and the broadcasters, with the state education officers organizing the instruction, correcting the homework, conducting regular discussion groups, and giving certificates, while the broadcasting organization produces the programs. There is direct teaching, with accompanying materials, of German, English, history, mathematics, physics, chemistry, biology, geography, technical drawing, commercial arithmetic, industrial management, and nutrition.

Viewers successfully completing the courses and passing the examinations are eligible to receive a certificate normally available only after regular attendance at a vocational secondary school.

Initially some 15,000 students were enrolled. Broadcasts are presented every evening on the first and third Bavarian television channels. It is expected that the complete cycle of television college studies, to include about thirteen subjects, will run approximately two-and-a-half years. New beginner's courses will begin every year so that after three years three levels of courses will be on the air. Tuition is only nominal, and most of the accompanying materials are available free-of-charge. The broadcasting organization, however, is investing 10,000,-000 DM (approximately $2,500,000) in the project and the state 5,-000,000 DM ($1,250,000).

France has neither radio nor television networks exclusively for education though it does have France Musique plus an experimental educational radio station. But the total amount of time it devotes to educational broadcasts is very large. The French tele-clubs were an interesting pioneering television adult education experiment.[156] In the early 1950's a number of small retarded rural communities within reach of Paris television formed viewers' cooperatives to purchase large-screen receivers, which usually were placed in school buildings for in-school use in the daytime and adult viewing at night. By 1954 there were approximately 180 clubs which met regularly to view all types of programs. In 1952 French television authorities, recognizing this potential, began to organize programs especially for these groups. A series of thirteen telecasts, "Etat d'Urgence" ("State of Emergency"), was organized to deal with such typical rural problems as control of forest lands, drainage, water and plumbing, local family life, mechanization of agriculture, country women, and rural youth. These were broadcast on thirteen evenings from January through March 1954, and the accompanying research indicated favorable acceptance by the intended viewers.

Since 1952 France has had language and general cultural broadcasts for pupils in technical colleges, as well as a "College of the Air" for out-of-school listening. In February 1962 an experimental series over an FM transmitter in the northeastern part of the country included adult courses in mathematics, French, physics, chemistry, bookkeeping, and English as well as some specialized college-level courses on science, law, and medicine.[157] More recently, the ORTF and the National Pedagogical Institute have cooperated to produce programs dealing with written and oral communication, nuclear physics, and modern European history on Saturday afternoons and Sunday mornings, and plans for 1967 included programs on mathematics, reading, and economics.[158] In Paris, Radio Sorbonne carries thirty-eight hours a week of lecture courses from the University of Paris on subjects ranging from the classical languages to science.

Since 1949 France has served as the center for an ambitious International University of the Air. Begun as a radio exchange project, it now embraces television as well.[159] At present forty nations, including both East and West European countries, contribute to these programs. Scripts written by experts are translated and read in the languages of the countries broadcasting them. Recordings and video tapes also have been exchanged. Between 1961 and 1963, sixty-nine different subjects were treated on International University of the Air broadcasts, including twenty-nine series on science, six on music, twenty-three on history, and eleven on legal and sociological subjects. These broadcasts, however, are not for credit, the term "university" again being used only in a general sense.

Language lessons are among the most widespread types of adult education programs, being broadcast by almost every country in Europe.[160] English, French, and German are among the most popular languages but the complete list includes all the major European languages plus Esperanto. Radio and television lessons in French and English have been prepared by the ORTF and BBC respectively for use in a number of countries. Particularly ingenious are the BBC's "English by Radio" and "English by Television." In 1966, 260 stations in 90 countries were broadcasting "English by Radio" while the television series, first available in January 1963, was being used by 42 countries, including most of Western Europe, Hungary, Poland, and Yugoslavia. These now are available in bilingual form in which commentary in the language of the country is interspersed with dramatic bits in English involving two attractive young Britishers, Walter and Connie. The dramatic parts appear as well in the all-English versions. In Europe alone over 300,000 copies of the accompanying booklets have been sold and in Germany it even became a national best seller. The programs are designed not only to teach English but also to expound British viewpoints. I saw one program in Warsaw in which the English language interludes dealt with a court trial for a minor traffic offense. The script managed to demonstrate the fairness of British justice, which Polish viewers might well have noted gives more rights to the accused than does their own legal system.

One of the most dramatic uses of television for organized instruction is RAI's "Non è mai troppo tardi," a literacy series for adults.[161] As with Telescuola, it was a tremendous challenge that gave rise to a major project. In 1951, 11.5 per cent of Italy's 41,500,000 inhabitants were illiterate, the rate in certain areas being as high as 27 per cent. Although this had decreased to 4 per cent by 1960 there still was a great educational need, and so in October of that year "Never Too Late" was inaugurated.

The first year's courses taught adult illiterates reading, writing, and arithmetic. The success of the initial venture led to a second series in November 1961 which introduced the writing of simple compositions, and in the summer of 1962 to a third project for all adults of limited education, planned especially for people using the reading centers established by the Central Service for Adult Education of the Ministry of Education. For "Non è mai troppo tardi" students, RAI provides a textbook, an exercise book, a ruler, and a pencil.

Instructors are chosen from qualified primary teachers in Rome and great care is taken to select people attractive to adult illiterates; yet the broadcasts definitely are lessons rather than shows. Most viewing is done under school conditions in groups of twenty-five, since the majority of the intended audience cannot afford individual receivers, although there also is much viewing in homes. With each group is a teacher who spends two hours with his students per evening: half an hour for preparation; half an hour watching the program; and one hour for follow-up exercises. The thirty-minute programs are broadcast six nights a week during early evening periods.

For the first six months of broadcasts between November 1960 and April 1961, 3,305 viewing groups were organized all over Italy, though predominantly in the south where the need was greatest, and some 20,000 free textbooks were distributed to over 48,000 viewers, of whom 34,000 or about 80 per cent passed the examinations. During the first four years the average percentage of passes ranged from 70 to 77 per cent, 36 per cent being by students under twenty years of age. In 1961,

41 per cent of these were women, and in 1964 47 per cent. Although the project was originally designed for adults many young people and even some primary grade children view the courses with profit. The average audience for "Never Too Late," including both those in viewing centers and at home, is about 1,500,000.

Europe's broadcasters must be praised for their adult education programs. In addition to general cultural offerings, serious music, and fine drama, both radio and television present a very wide range of instructional materials during prime evening hours. Whenever there are two or more radio and television services in a country, the second and third invariably are programed to contrast rather than compete with the first service, a policy that facilitates the scheduling of significant materials at convenient hours. On the whole, however, adult education materials are not as skillfully produced as are in-school broadcasts. Many radio and television lectures are uninspired, often being little more than the reading of erudite essays. East European presentations sometimes are so heavily loaded with propaganda as to alienate their audiences. Nevertheless, the balance sheet is in favor of the Continent's broadcasters. For providing so many excellent serious programs for the adult audience they deserve higher ratings than do most American stations or networks.

The majority of the programs described above are broadcast by regular rather than specialized educational stations. America's educational stations, licensed mainly to colleges, universities, public school systems, or noncommercial corporations created for that purpose, grew up because economic pressures made it impossible for commercial stations to provide adequate educational services. But in Europe the national networks, even though sometimes partially dependent on commercial support, have many daytime periods available for school broadcasting and make it a point to do some general educational and cultural programing during peak evening hours.

Britain's famous Third Programme for radio, which provided the pattern for various continental services, was the first European network to be devoted primarily to cultural and serious material. But it was not regarded initially as "educational" by the BBC, although the transmitters carrying the Third Programme now broadcast a sixty-minute "Study Session" during early evening hours. The third radio services in West Germany and Italy, and such good music networks as France

Musique, put the emphasis not on direct teaching but on general cultural programs.

The new third television services in West Germany and the Soviet Union, however, are devoted more to instructional materials.[162] Experimental third television channels began to go on the air in Germany in 1964. In 1965 19 per cent of the Bavarian television budget was assigned to its third channel, despite an expected audience of less than 10 per cent of the viewers, while the first channel, a general service program, received only 29.1 per cent of the total funds.[163] Typically the German third services broadcast from 7:00 to 10:00 P.M. with organized courses and lectures on languages, science, technology, politics, drama, literature, and music along with information about such practical subjects as motor repairs and skiing. It is expected that eventually these stations will be linked as a network with programs originated in turn by the several Länder.

The third television stations which went on the air in Moscow and Leningrad in 1964 are definitely instructional. They began with language broadcasts and branched out into forty-five minute lectures on subjects like mathematics, mechanics, physics, and chemistry for groups in polytechnic colleges as well as for home audiences. Viewing groups are expected to have follow-up discussions and home viewers may call in questions by telephone. There are plans for third television programs in other large Soviet cities too but there is no immediate intention of linking them as a network.

Although Europe has had in-school radio and television programs for over forty years, there is hardly any use of such programs in colleges and universities, nor are there many closed-circuit television installations on the Continent, despite their rapid development in the United States. Closed-circuit television was first used in medical teaching in the Netherlands, Paris, London, Geneva, Rome, Turin, and Naples. It also was used in West Germany for magnification in chemistry and physics classes, in a polytechnic institute in Zurich, and experimentally for science teaching in Belgium. In the spring of 1964 there was a small experimental installation at the Bonn Educational Academy in West Germany for training primary teachers.*

* *Television and Adult Education*, July 1964, p. 33. Although beyond the scope of this study, reference should be made to some experiments in the United Kingdom. Beginning in the fall of 1965, the direct teaching of mathematics and French by

There was a more extensive experiment at Sèvres, France, in 1958–59, when one studio and three receiving rooms were used to test a projected series of programs; to train secondary school teachers; as a production laboratory; and for psychological and pedagogical research.[164] Since then eight French secondary schools have been equipped with closed-circuit television and video tape recording facilities, and have exchanged tapes of their own productions. In September 1966 a new experimental secondary education complex, based on team teaching, closed-circuit television, and learning laboratories, was opened at Marly-le-Roi near Paris. On the whole, however, Europe lags far behind America in developing the educational uses of closed-circuit television. Although European like American institutions of higher learning are under great pressures to expand, the situation is nowhere near as dramatic as in the United States, except perhaps at the University of Paris which has over 90,000 students. In any case, European educators are even more conservative than their American colleagues in adopting new media.

Agricultural Programs

With agriculture such an important part of the economy, and with so many people engaged in activities related to it, programs for and about farming appear on all broadcasting schedules. Normally these are some combination of news, weather, and related information presented during early morning hours (usually an hour later in the winter), plus longer informational and instructional programs at noon or in the early evening. Farm broadcasters everywhere are agreed that their programs should be as interesting as possible to urban dwellers as well as to farmers and residents of small villages. In East Europe, where the rural population is larger, there are many programs designed particularly for villagers.

Reference already has been made to the tele-clubs of rural France, for which one of the most highly praised early educational television programs was devised (see p. 179 above). In addition to them,

closed-circuit television was made available to 215 Glasgow schools. Initial results were so encouraging that plans are under way to extend its use in the Glasgow area and to initiate similar projects elsewhere. Plans also are in the talking stage for linking a number of universities for exchanges of instruction, as well as for a university of the air on broadcast television. (London *Times*, September 5, 1966, p. 16, and October 11, 1966, p. 19.)

French television has had other types of agricultural programs since 1957. In the words of their director: "For most town dwellers in France the farmer is a rather rough individual, living in a mean squalid farm and using completely outdated working methods." One of the purposes of these programs, therefore, is to show that farmers are progressing and to report innovations in agriculture.[165]

The farm editor of Sveriges Radio reports that even though 50 per cent of the population in the countryside moved into cities during the last decade, there is growing antagonism between city and rural dwellers. One of broadcasting's functions, therefore, is to bring these two groups together. In Sweden, incidentally, agriculture is defined to include forestry.[166] Danish television builds some of its programs around a real "TV Farm" close to Copenhagen, selected partly because the housewife from eastern and husband from western Denmark have different dialects. Their farm is the setting for a series of programs dealing with agricultural problems.[167]

One of Eurovision's first projects was an International Agricultural Newsreel. Most members make six or more contributions per year, preference being given to subjects of instructive and informative nature such as new developments in agriculture or methods of work. An attempt is made to select items which, even though produced with the farming public in mind, are of general interest.[168]

Agricultural broadcasters in Communist countries write in much the same vein as do their democratic colleagues, although they are more conscious of "agricultural propaganda." Thus the main task for rural broadcasts in Bulgaria is "set up by the Communist Party of Bulgaria and the needs of socialist building-up regarding agriculture in Bulgaria."[169] One of the main objectives in Hungary is to explain and popularize the party's agrarian policy; in fact, 70 per cent of the broadcasts for rural listeners have this purpose.[170] In Poland one of the most important tasks is the "building-up of socialism."[171] In 1960, the Soviet Union broadcasts to agricultural workers to persuade them to introduce progressive methods and to fulfill the Seven-Year Plan.[172]

But this emphasis on propaganda does not mean that there are no agricultural experts in Eastern broadcasting, nor does it indicate any lack of initiative in developing effective methods of presentation. Rumania, for example, had a radio quiz for agricultural workers, the questions being "closely associated with the progressive practice of socialist cooperative agricultural units in our country."[173] The main subjects for the competition together with reading lists were distributed to contestants thirty to forty-five days beforehand. Public interest was shown by the fact that audiences with as many as 3,500 people attended the broadcasts. East German radio devotes four hours a week to agricultural programs for which it has a staff of twenty-eight.[174] Polish radio devotes six hours a week to agricultural broadcasts from Warsaw, in addition to which programs are originated by regional stations. The Warsaw staff alone has fourteen members including two agricultural engineers, one forestry economist, and two agricultural economists.[175]

International Broadcasting

Although this study deals primarily with domestic broadcasting, notice should be taken of the international services maintained by almost all countries. Some of these programs are intended for nationals abroad or at sea, though most are propaganda for noncitizens.* The total amount of international broadcasting is very considerable.[176] In March 1966 the USSR led the world with 1,381 program hours per week, while all the other European Communist countries combined (Albania, Bulgaria, Czechoslovakia, the German Democratic Republic, Hungary, Poland, and Rumania) broadcast 1,211 hours. Other countries with large outputs included China, 1,105 hours; the United States, 909 hours; the German Federal Republic, 689 hours; and the United Kingdom, 663 hours.[177] The Soviet Union broadcasts in 54 languages, and its schedule includes 5 hours a day for North America. The USSR also presents some television programs in Finnish for viewers in Finland.[178]

There also are the broadcasting services developed in Central Europe by the victorious allies of World War II to propagandize each other.[179] The United States sponsors RIAS in Berlin (Rundfunk im Amerikanischen Sektor Berlins), mainly for East Germans; Radio Free Europe in Munich (some transmitters in Germany, most in Portugal), for Communist East Europe except the Soviet Union; Radio Liberty in Munich (transmitters in Germany, Spain, and Taiwan), for an audi-

---

* As pointed out previously, the word "propaganda" does not necessarily have bad connotations. It is defined by Funk and Wagnalls' *New Standard Dictionary* as "any institution or systematic scheme for propagating a doctrine or system." Webster's *Third New International Dictionary* defines it as "a group or movement organized for spreading a particular doctrine or system of principles."

ence in the USSR; as well as some Voice of America relay stations in West Germany, Greece, and the United Kingdom. Berlin also is the outlet for an organization called "Broadcasts of the Soviet Committee for Cultural Relations with Fellow Countrymen in the German Democratic Republic."

Somewhat related to these are the services maintained by the occupying powers for their own troops, since many of their programs are heard by Europeans, particularly the younger generation who tune in for the latest in popular music and foreign language practice. These include the American Forces Network, the British Forces Broadcasting Service, Radio Canadian Army Europe, Radio Forces Françaises de Berlin, and Radio Volga.

There are some interesting aspects to the broadcasting competition between East and West Germany. Each has a radio and television propaganda organization in addition to many domestic programs planned with the other Germany in mind.[180] In border areas some programs from the previous evening are repeated the next morning for viewers across the boundary. Each country video-tapes programs from the other off-the-air which might be useful for reference or rebroadcast to either audience. Program planners, East and West, are quite aware of cross tuning. An East German television executive told me in August of 1965 that all their broadcasts are planned with the assumption that the German public hears and views both sides, so that the two must compete for audience and build up their reputations for accuracy.

Western radio and television programs designed for the domestic audience are received in East Germany, Czechoslovakia, and Hungary.[181] At times attempts are made to discourage this, even to the point of dismantling television aerials pointed across the border, but this campaign currently is in abeyance. Along with this electronic communication war, however, is a limited amount of cooperation in program exchange. Thus a West German television team was authorized to make a documentary film on East Berlin and some other East German cities. West German newspapers and virtually all West German radio and television program magazines carry East German television schedules, though this is not reciprocated. The British Broadcasting Corporation even was able to arrange a publicity display at the International Trade Fair at Brno, Czechoslovakia, in September 1965.[182]

Reference already has been made to the radio and television exchanges arranged by the EBU and the OIRT (see above, pp. 135–142).

As noted earlier, during the last several years there has been very little jamming by East European countries although some RIAS transmissions are jammed in East Germany. The cessation of jamming probably resulted from a combination of factors. The countries feel more secure internally, and hence can tolerate some dissenting points of view. With better domestic programs they can compete for audiences with foreign services. There also is the fact that, in spite of the great difficulty and expense of comprehensive jamming, it is virtually impossible to blanket out all foreign signals completely. But the jamming transmitters are still there, and surely will be used again if the international situation becomes sufficiently tense.

CHAPTER VI

Programs: Entertainment

ᐃALTHOUGH European broadcasters take justifiable pride in the prestige programs described above, over half their schedules consist of materials with entertainment potential. It is to these that the average man tunes most frequently. This chapter deals with music and drama, which can be either culture or entertainment, and with light entertainment and sports, which are first in program preference everywhere.

Music

Europe has long and enviable musical traditions. While the average European probably does not achieve the level of appreciation for serious music accorded him by most Americans, a high value certainly is placed on music by the people who directly and indirectly determine broadcasting policy. Furthermore, the monopoly structure and the lack of sponsors in continental broadcasting are conducive to such programs. Therefore it should come as no surprise to find that European radio and television make a great deal of their musical programs.*

While America still debates whether or not to support the arts with public funds, this has been an accepted procedure in Europe for many years.[1] There is a precedent for using some of the money collected for broadcasting to subsidize the composition and performance of fine music: Even private commercial stations like those in Luxembourg and Monaco, despite a great emphasis on disc jockeys and popular music, invest much more in live concert music than do America's stations and networks.

Over half of Europe's radio time is devoted to music, along with a good share of its television time. Of Norddeutscher Rundfunk's three

---

* This section deals principally with serious music. Light music is discussed under "Light Entertainment" below, pp. 207–211.

services in 1963, the first devoted approximately 33.9 per cent of its schedule to light music, 10.2 per cent to serious music, and 9.6 per cent to musical entertainment. For the second service the figures were 16 per cent for light music, 19.3 per cent for serious music, and 18.2 per cent for musical entertainment. The more sophisticated third program devoted only 8.1 per cent to light music, and 11.8 per cent to musical entertainment, but 32.5 per cent to serious music.[2] Of Süddeutscher Rundfunk's first program in 1963, 55.5 per cent was music; of this amount, light music was 37.6 per cent, symphony and opera 8 per cent, chamber music 4.9 per cent, folk music 3.2 per cent, and church and choral music 1.8 per cent.[3] The second program was 56.1 per cent music, including light music for 31.2 per cent of the time, symphony and opera 13.6 per cent, chamber music 8.5 per cent, folk music 1.4 per cent, and church and choral music 1.4 per cent of the time. There is less music on television, but nevertheless the second German network, Zweites Deutsches Fernsehen, devoted about 7 per cent of its schedule in 1964 to the combined category of "Theatre and Music."[4]

Musical programs illustrate very well how European networks are planned to be complementary rather than competitive. In 1965 RAI devoted 14.5 per cent of its radio time to symphonic music, the percentages for its four networks ranging from 0.7 to 45.1 per cent. The chamber music total was 11.3 per cent, with individual networks varying from 1.1 to 33.3 per cent. Opera, often regarded as the Italian "national sport," received 6.69 per cent of all radio time: While one network devoted 3.0 per cent of its time to opera, another assigned 12.0 per cent. But in Italy as elsewhere light music was the largest category, the average being 24.6 per cent, with the highbrow network carrying none at all and the light program 46.4 per cent.[5] The two television networks combined devoted 1.1 per cent of their time to symphonic and chamber music and 1.2 per cent to opera and ballet. Light and entertainment music took 7.7 per cent of the total time, 20.1 per cent on one network and only 4.4 per cent on the other one.[6]

Yugoslavia illustrates even more strikingly how programing may vary from one network to another. In 1965 the country's fifteen domestic radio broadcasting units devoted from 57.94 to 83.98 per cent of their time to music, the average being 63.20 per cent. Percentages for serious music ranged from 10.80 to 79.86 per cent, with these extremes represented by two of the three stations in Zagreb. The national average for serious music was 20.78 per cent, for popular music 29.90 per cent, and for folk music 12.50 per cent. In 1964 and 1965, 3.3 per cent of all television time was devoted to opera, ballet, and serious music.[7]

The East European countries emphasize music to the same extent, though fewer statistics are available about their radio music output. The Soviet Union, on its five nationwide networks and many local services, puts out 67½ hours of music every day, ranging from concerts and music appreciation lectures to light and dance music.[8] About 60 per cent of all programs are music, 70 per cent of this consisting of light music. Twenty-two per cent of Rumania's musical programs are serious, 34 per cent light and jazz, 15 per cent folk music, and 11 per cent opera and operetta. Figures for the other Eastern countries are similar.

Music is broadcast by all European stations although there is an increasing tendency to set up all-music radio services emphasizing either serious or light music.* Thus France Musique, RAI's Network Three, and the Third Radio Program in Hungary consist almost entirely of serious music. All television services devote a fair amount of time to symphonic music, opera, and ballet. When there are two services one may telecast opera, concert music, or ballet against lighter material on the other network. As third services emerge most of their music either is serious or is music education material. Light music too gets its due: There is music for every taste including standard popular music, operetta, serious jazz, and current fads like rock and roll and pop music. Broadcasters both East and West are concerned with raising the standards of light music programing.[9] There also are the wired sound services, as in Switzerland and Italy, which provide music of all sorts.

To fill the hours with music, and to present occasional public concerts, most continental broadcasting organizations maintain large permanent staffs of musicians, and also frequently draw upon other organizations and soloists. French radio established a full-time symphony orchestra in January 1934.[10] The Norddeutscher Rundfunk maintains a symphony orchestra of 109 musicians; two other concert orchestras, one of 71 and

* Most European radio organizations play short musical themes during station breaks to identify themselves. These are compositions by native composers, national folk songs, or themes composed especially for the purpose. Identifying themes—though not necessarily the same ones—also are used on many short-wave services, and the European Broadcasting Union has themes to introduce its radio and television exchanges. The radio section of any edition of the *World Radio TV Handbook* lists many of these.

the other of 59 players; dance and light music orchestras of 40, 34, and 27 members respectively; a tango orchestra of 27; a big band of 17; and a combo of 9.[11] The Süddeutscher Rundfunk has a 96-piece symphony orchestra in addition to other orchestral groups consisting of 46, 37, and 16 musicians respectively. The Südwestfunk has a concert orchestra of 94, and other groups of 45, 20, and 17 members. RIAS, though not strictly a German organization, maintains a symphony orchestra of 120, a youth orchestra of 76, a choir of 40, and a dance orchestra of 34.[12] For its music RAI supports 100-piece symphony orchestras in Rome, Turin, and Milan besides a chamber orchestra of 44 members in Naples. Choral ensembles of 50 to 70 members are attached to each of these.[13]

The State Broadcasting Committee of the Soviet Union has the Bolshoi Symphony Orchestra which also plays for the Bolshoi Opera and Ballet; the Opera Symphony Orchestra; the Theatrical Orchestra; the Orchestra of Native Instruments; the Bolshoi Choir; the Choir of all Union Radio; the Choir of Russian Songs; vocal soloists; and groups of instrumental soloists and accompanists. These groups contribute to both radio and television and also present concerts in Moscow and other cities. In East Berlin the radio symphony orchestra of 112 is supplemented by a 17-piece dance orchestra, a 66-voice choir, and various other musical groups while in Leipzig there is a symphony orchestra of 105, a concert orchestra of 57, a light orchestra of 30, a wind group of 31, a dance band of 17, and a 60-voice choir.[14] Hungary, in addition to a 70-member music department, maintains a symphony orchestra of 96 and a chorus of 65, along with a dance band, two small dance groups, a children's chorus, and a gypsy orchestra.

It should be noted that these extensive musical establishments are not limited to the larger countries. There is an excellent 90-piece symphony orchestra in Belgium; several symphonic broadcasting groups in the Netherlands; and symphonic and light music orchestras in Denmark and Sweden. Clearly, continental broadcasting does not lack for live music, one respect in which it is far ahead of the United States, where the limited amount of live serious music is hardly ever presented by groups maintained by the broadcasting organizations themselves.

Extensive use also is made of other organizations. Most broadcasting headquarters are located in capital cities which have fine symphony orchestras and opera companies. In addition to its radio symphony orchestra, West Berlin has the Berlin Philharmonic and an opera company, while East Berlin can supplement the DDR Symphony Orchestra with its own symphonic and operatic groups. Budapest has three full-sized symphonic organizations in addition to a fine broadcasting orchestra; Prague supplements two radio orchestras and the State Film Company Orchestra with a chamber group and two other symphony orchestras. The many summer festivals are another resource. To name only a few, Germany has them at Bayreuth and Munich and there are others in Copenhagen, Monaco, Prague, and Salzburg. These are broadcast nationally, fed live to radio and television services in all of Europe, and tape recorded for distribution abroad.[15]

Supplementing live music, and indeed providing the heart for music schedules, are extensive libraries of recordings. Most major broadcasting units have enormous disc and tape collections from all over the world, in addition to many recordings of their own broadcasts, some of great historical value. By 1963, for example, RAI had a 2,000-title catalogue of stereophonic recordings of serious music. In 1965 Yugoslavia's eight radio stations reported having 73,395 records and 149,538 tapes.[16] In the Netherlands a whole new building to house music and recordings recently came into use.[17] The collection at present includes 150,000 scores, over 150,000 78-rpm records, 50,000 long-playing records, and 60,000 45-rpm records. There are 70,000 records made by the broadcasting organization itself, 4,000 sound effects records, and over 80,000 audio tape recordings. The building also contains thirteen listening cubicles where producers may monitor records and tapes. An interesting production note is the fact that some European organizations —including most of those in West Germany as well as in Hungary— broadcast few if any discs. If they are unable to buy tape recordings initially, they copy everything onto tape, believing this ensures higher quality at the same time that it eliminates deterioration due to record wear.

Copyright laws in Europe give record manufacturers the right to collect royalties for broadcasts of recordings, something not covered by American legislation. This adds a big item to program costs, and sometimes leads to prolonged disputes such as that which kept most records off West German stations for six months in 1966.[18] In response to a request to increase their annual performance fees ten times over the $625,000 already being paid, the stations virtually stopped using recorded music. Broadcasting was resumed January 1, 1967, under an agreement for annual payments of $1,350,000 for thirty-five hours a week of recorded music, rates in subsequent years to depend upon increases in the number of receiver licenses.

The objectives for music broadcasts in Western Europe, when stated at all, follow the familiar line that they provide enjoyment and inspiration, and contribute to the better life.[19] In contrast to this was the statement of a Soviet writer: "The most important task of the [television] musical department is to propagate, by means of music, those contemporary ideas which dominate the Soviet people and which determine the basis of our life. These are the ideas of struggle for constructing a Communist Society, the struggle for peace and friendship between peoples; the ideas of Soviet patriotism and the spiritual development of the Soviet People."[20]

The chief editor of the Department of Musical Broadcasts of Soviet Central Television remarked that it was difficult to devise programs of popular music "because we must protect our youth against evil influences, banality, decadent moods, naturalism, vulgarity, and erotic lyrism."[21] Dance telecasts, he said, must avoid "exaggerated twisting of the hips, an unnatural stance with the legs astride, and . . . erotic movements," and he quoted with approval—this was 1964—a statement by Nikita Khrushchev: "We are for melodious music which moves human souls . . . music without melody cannot arouse anything but irritation." He also condemned the banality of popular song texts, a subject of frequent complaint in all parts of the world: "Composers and poets writing songs full of the spirit of decadency, inconsolable languor, endless repetition of the theme of unrequited love, and cheap lyrism have been sharply criticized."

Whatever may be the proper objectives for music broadcasts, with much time available, splendid performers, and extensive libraries of recorded music, the musical repertoire of Europe's broadcasting organizations is extensive enough to satisfy almost any taste. It ranges from esoteric chamber works to serious jazz, from folk music to opera, and from standard light works to symphonic music of every type. Most major live programs originate in studios or concert halls with audiences present, though in some cases broadcasting groups give public concerts which are not broadcast. A few examples will illustrate the wide range of repertoire.

In 1965 Italian radio broadcast 3,484 concerts, of which 1,106 were symphonic music, 933 chamber music, 892 opera, and 553 miscellaneous. These included performances from festivals in Austria, Czechoslovakia, Finland, Greece, Hungary, Rumania, South Africa, the Soviet Union, Switzerland, the United Kingdom, the United States of America, the Vatican, and West Germany. In addition, there were over 564 concerts of folk music ranging from Italian folk songs to compositions for carillon.[22] The Italian television output also was impressive, including 96 instrumental concerts, 39 operas, and 15 ballets.[23]

Small countries too do some very imaginative work. Belgian radio sponsored an impressive series of modern music concerts in the fall of 1964 in which soloists and conductors, both Belgian and foreign, participated, and the radio symphony orchestra played unfamiliar works by such established composers as Claude Debussy and Arnold Schoenberg, plus avant-garde works including electronic music by Karlheinz Stockhausen.[24]

New idioms include both jazz and electronic music. Western Germany, for example, produced "Jazz Around the World," while Czech radio makes a great deal of the various International Jazz Festivals held in Prague.[25] A number of countries are working on electronic music. The world's first demonstration of electronic music, claimed two Soviet writers, was given in Moscow in 1921.[26] Up to the time of their article in 1963, fourteen types of electromusical instruments had been used in the Soviet Union as solo instruments and to provide background music for plays. After noting the existence of electronic studios in Cologne, Milan, New York, Paris, Tokyo, and elsewhere, the authors emphasized the seriousness of the Soviet experiments by reporting that it had taken three months to prepare one five-minute composition. Italy began experiments in 1956 and Poland in 1957.[27] In 1964 and 1965 Sveriges Radio assigned funds for the construction of a special studio for experimentation with electronic music. An Italian legal expert in "Notes on the Subject of Electronic Music" remarked that "delicate problems" were raised by such music, and concluded that Italian copyright law probably covers it, although "it might be difficult to establish a case of plagiarism of an electronic work owing to the absence of any reliable written record of the work itself."[28]

All the European television organizations work with ballet. Belgium commemorated ten years of television ballet with a handsome 80-page brochure reviewing a repertoire which ranged from *Airs et Danses Anciens* with music from the sixteenth and seventeenth centuries, to *Zone Interdite* with music by Kresimir Sipush.[29] In July 1965, I attended the première of a new choreography of Stravinsky's *Rite of Spring* in the Bolshoi Theater in Moscow, and observed television cameras recording the performance which I saw on Russian television several evenings later.[30]

One of the most important activities of European broadcasters is the encouragement of new music. Many offer prizes and commissions for original works, and almost all broadcast a great deal of new music by both native and foreign composers. In fact, continental radio and television now are among the world's foremost patrons of contemporary composers, and also commission some ballets. This work goes forward all over Europe despite the low ratings it receives since audiences everywhere prefer familiar to new and modern music.

Of all program types music lends itself most readily to international exchange, since there is no language problem at all with instrumental works and no serious one for vocal compositions.* In the light music project of Nord-Ring Tour, organized by the North Sea countries, each participant contributes one outstanding variety artist to a touring group which goes from country to country giving concerts broadcast by all the members. The first time around in 1964, performances were given in Antwerp, Hanover, Hilversum, London, Oslo, and Stockholm, with Britain's BBC as executive producer and Belgium as tour manager. The Music Committee of the European Broadcasting Union has developed projects to commission original compositions; auditioned recordings of new works in order to bring the best of them to the attention of major performers; arranged a jointly produced Christmas carol program; organized a series on "Old Organs of Europe"; did a similar project with European carillons; organized performances by children of songs written for them; and developed a historical series about barrel organs.

* Although not discussed here, European broadcasters encounter copyright and union problems which on the whole are even more difficult than those faced in the United States. Musicians' unions are as strong in Europe as elsewhere, even though American companies often find it advantageous to record abroad, and the amount of negotiation necessary to arrange elaborate international exchanges is tremendous. Copyright is another problem that is greatly complicated by international exchanges. Each issue of the *EBU Review* contains a section on legal problems, and some *OIRT Reviews* also contain such articles.

I heard a radio competition of new compositions for brass band relayed from Belgium, and later saw a superb telecast of the annual New Year's Day concert by the Vienna Philharmonic Orchestra, in which a delightful combination of ballet and other visual accompaniments was added to the traditional Strauss concert in such a way as to make it an excellent television program without detracting from the enjoyment of those who saw it in the hall or heard it on radio. I saw a performance in Moscow relayed from Italy's LaScala Opera during which Russian explanations were presented between the acts. More and more of Eurovision's music is being transmitted by Intervision and vice versa, although Intervision—like East European countries generally—emphasizes folk music more than does the Western group.[31]

Normally concerts and music appreciation lectures are kept apart, although continental broadcasters make a good deal of music education, not only through their wide range of repertoire, but also in the presentation of accompanying materials.[32] Consequently France Musique introduces many recordings with descriptive notes, and some lectures on the International University of the Air heard over France-Culture deal with musical topics. In addition, one might hear in Switzerland an ingenious presentation of recordings by the late Wilhelm Furtwaengler; in Rumania, both radio and television broadcasts about—and by—their famous composer-pianist-violinist-conductor Georges Enesco; in Czechoslovakia, programs designed to popularize chamber music, which there, as elsewhere, usually has few followers; and in East Germany, elaborately organized music education programs for both in-school audiences and adults.

Most continental broadcasting organizations have one or more large studios designed especially for concerts: There are good examples in Brussels, Bucharest, Copenhagen, Frankfurt, Geneva, Hamburg, Luxembourg, Naples, Paris, and Stockholm. These usually have seating for audiences, and the newer studios are equipped for television too. Most new European concert halls are planned for broadcasting. Although the famous Bolshoi Theater in Moscow, completed in 1824, must assign television cameras to boxes at the side or back of the auditorium, the new Palace of Congresses within the Kremlin walls, completed in 1961, has permanent camera positions. In any case, microphones, cameras, control rooms, and the rest are fundamentally the same wherever encountered, as are the techniques and methods of reproducing sound and transmitting pictures.

Most radio broadcasts of music are competently done. The performances usually are by experienced professionals, and the producers have mastered the basics of sound reproduction. The world audience for recordings has contributed to standardization at a high level of perfection, since Europe's principal broadcasting orchestras and opera companies make recordings sold everywhere. Thus producers in every country may study the world output without the problems of translation faced by workers in language programs.

Greater variations of skill are manifested in the telecasting of music, even though Western and Eastern producers say about the same things. For example, the head of music production for BBC television pointed out that "music is the main concern, and any visual image which detracts from the viewer's concentration on the music is in error." He went on to say that camera treatment "cannot be merely improvised, with the cameras ranging more or less at random over the orchestra: the camera director must know the score almost as thoroughly as the conductor, and must so plan and arrange his shots that every one is meaningful and helps to bring out the musical thought. The temptation to offer pictures, however effective, without adequate musical motivation must be ruthlessly resisted. It is generally best to begin a performance with an establishing shot of the whole orchestra: thereafter shots will be dictated by the course the music takes."[33]

A Moscow producer voiced agreement. A general view of the orchestra, he wrote, "can interest for a moment only and then we would like to observe the action of the conductor and that group of instruments, which at the given moment hold the main musical theme. . . . The best way is when the mounting of pictures coincides precisely with the movements of the conductor's baton and switches over to this or that group of the instruments at the moment before they start performing. Such a presentation of the orchestra requires a perfect knowledge of the score according to which the pictures are then made. . . . It is extremely important that the main producer of the telecast be a musician who knows the score, the beginning and end of a musical thought, and the character of the transition of one piece to another."*

* "Music on Television," OIRT, No. 1:1–6 (1960). After producing some telecasts by the Minneapolis Symphony Orchestra in Minneapolis in 1953, I wrote in much

But in music as in other fields, television production still is more advanced in the West than the East, however similar their theories may be. Consequently one sees little televised music in the West that is not well done, and much that is superb, while in the East the average production level is low. Here, as in other areas, however, more and better equipment and greater experience will close the gap.

Concern with mechanics, however, should not draw attention away from the fine work of European broadcasting organizations in advancing the cause of music. Freed from the economic pressures of American-type commercial broadcasting, it is possible for them to commission new works and regularly present new compositions of all types; broadcast the great works of the standard repertoire; exercise leadership in developing musical taste; and contribute in important ways to the creation and performance of music in their respective countries. Work in music represents one of the finest—if not the very finest—contribution of Europe's broadcasters to life and culture on the Continent.

Dramatic and Documentary Programs

Any American surveying European broadcast drama immediately will notice two things: The growth of television has not materially reduced the quality or quantity of dramatic programs on radio; and the widespread popularity of light entertainment has not eliminated serious drama from television.

The continuance of radio drama may be due partly to the lower value placed on audience ratings: European broadcasting organizations receive much or all of their income from license fees, and radio's share has not been reduced by the increased popularity of television. In most cases people must secure a radio license if they want a television license so that any reduction in the use of radio does not lower its income. Another reason is the emphasis given to education and culture: because good radio drama has artistic merit it is continued. Finally, since there are proportionately fewer television receivers in Eu-

the same vein: "Throughout this series the musical content of the selections being telecast, rather than the pictorial possibilities of the instruments playing, determined the production techniques used. Television served musical objectives, and technique never became an end in itself. Thus, there were no harp-violin supers or other pretty or trick shots without musical justifications." (Paulu, "Televising the Minneapolis Symphony Orchestra," *Quarterly of Film, Radio, and Television*, VIII (No. 2):160.)

rope than in the United States, radio still is the dominant medium in some areas; so it is necessary to continue radio drama if many people are to have broadcast drama at all.

Any large continental broadcasting organization could provide examples of the continued vigor of radio drama. For example, the main Yugoslav stations broadcast 452 radio plays in 1963 and 526 in 1964.[34] This two-year period included 90 premières of radio originals by foreign authors, and 103 of adapted works by foreign authors. There also were 105 original Yugoslav radio dramas plus 47 premières of adapted ones. Included were Dylan Thomas' *Under Milk Wood* as well as Richard Hughes' *Danger,* the world's first original radio play.[35] The repertoire also contained adaptations of works by Shaw, Shakespeare, Giraudoux, Hemingway, and Schnitzler. The *Yugoslav Yearbook* stated with pride that radio plays by Yugoslav writers were becoming "an integral part of foreign broadcasting stations' programmes": Czech and Polish radio in 1964 organized festivals of Yugoslav radio drama, while North German radio had a "Week of Yugoslav Radio Drama."

Italian radio also has maintained a high level of dramatic output. In 1965 RAI devoted 2.9 per cent of its air time to 451 radio plays, of which 208 were adaptations of stage plays, 84 radio originals, and 147 adaptations of other literary works, and 12 were classified simply as "varied."[36] Adapted stage works were divided about equally between those by Italians and those by foreigners, though in both cases the authors included literary figures like Luigi Pirandello, Jean Anouilh, Georg Büchner, Miguel de Cervantes, John Dryden, Hugo von Hofmannsthal, Eugene Ionesco, Alexandre Dumas, William Shakespeare, August Strindberg, Harold Pinter, Wolfgang Goethe, Alfred de Musset, William Inge, and Molière. There were adaptations of novels by Jack London, Edgar Allan Poe, Thornton Wilder, Oliver Goldsmith, Mark Twain, William Thackeray, Herman Melville, and Bertolt Brecht. The "varied" category in 1964 included a series of twelve programs to commemorate the 400th anniversary of Shakespeare's birth.

Swedish radio also has done imaginative work with drama. Sophisticated repertoire is drawn from the entire world of literature, and sometimes is presented in the original language. At the same time a real attempt is made to involve native authors, and many new Swedish radio plays are broadcast, along with standard works and serializations of novels. To avoid the concentration of dramatic experience in a few large metropolitan centers, provincial theaters are given broadcast opportunities too. For some series there are listeners' handbooks as well as oral introductions during the broadcasts. Examples of accompanying handbooks chosen at random include an abridged Swedish translation of Goethe's *Faust*, a 158-page brochure dealing with the plays of Eugene O'Neill, and a 248-page commentary with English-language texts for six Shakespearean plays. Each play in the Shakespearean series was the subject of three or four broadcasts, the first two or three consisting of short excerpts and explanations, the last a sequence of scenes tied together by narration.

West German radio also regards drama seriously.[37] Approximately 200 radio dramas have been published in Germany since 1927, some in editions as large as 100,000; and of these 160 appeared after 1945. European radio drama, writes one observer, "has acquired literary status. [It is] . . . an art form whose literary station is taken seriously throughout Europe."[38] The various German broadcasting organizations publish attractive brochures listing authors, titles, broadcast times, and other information about the plays presented.

East Germany too places a high premium on radio plays.[39] The deputy chief dramaturgist of German Democratic Radio referred to radio drama before the Nazis as "the first golden age of the radio play." Only "modest" results were achieved following 1933, however, when some "fascist bards" tried to put the radio play to the service of the "blood and soil myth." In the 1950's original radio plays were still "on the decline," but since then a new generation of experienced radio playwrights has emerged. Accordingly, he noted with pride, "the radio play in the German Democratic Republic has attained a reputation in the last few years and in spite of many people pointing to the spectacular development of television, it has strengthened its position."

Both theater and television have on occasion adapted radio plays, and in 1964 East German television transmitted seven such plays. The author complained that with the exception of Bertolt Brecht's *The Trial of Lucullus*, "only a single radio play from the German Democratic Republic has been presented by a West German station." Since the station he cited—Beromünster Radio—is Swiss rather than West German, he in effect said that no West German station had ever broadcast radio plays by East German authors. However, he was pleased to note an exchange of plays among stations in Prague, Bratislava, Budapest, Warsaw, Ljubljana, and Zagreb. In 1964 an OIRT radio drama festival, which in the German Democratic Republic was combined with the "Third Week of the International Radio Play," included material from Czechoslovakia, Hungary, Poland, Yugoslavia, France, Great Britain, Sweden, Switzerland, and Japan.[40]

In 1958 Hungarian radio presented 158 major literary works in a series entitled "The Theatre at the Microphone," of which 42 were relays from theaters, the remainder being studio presentations.[41] These 158 presentations exceeded the total number of performances given by all the theaters in Budapest the previous year. The practice of relaying programs from theaters has been much more popular in Europe than in the United States. The BBC did so until rather recently, while the Eastern countries continue this on both radio and television. The explanation probably is that less sophisticated audiences like to be "in" the theater, and are willing to overlook certain technical limitations in order to have this experience. A Hungarian writer observed in 1960: "A listener living far from a communal centre and with no possibilities to go to the theatre, is taken there via the radio. He hears not only a play, but an opera or a concert and thanks to the broadcast, the theatre can influence him."

Five years later another Hungarian producer reported on the success of serial radio plays.[42] The author mentioned the many years of BBC success with "Mrs. Dale's Diary" and "The Archers," the nearest British equivalents of America's soap opera serials, and compared them to the Polish "Matysiak Family" series broadcast since 1957. The British series, she said, counseled surrender: "That is life. Not only you, but also other people have it hard and one must put up with it." On the other hand, the Polish series aims "to educate a feeling of responsibility and social consciousness in people. . . . [It] also attempts to contribute to the formation of social opinion by showing conflicts and contradictions between the private and social, stimulating listeners to improve and change the present state of affairs." Speaking almost like the representative of an American network, the author also said: "The number of individual instalments is not determined in advance. They are written week by week. The 'families' live as long as they interest the public." But this family seems assured of a long lease on life. On January 17, 1966, the twenty-first anniversary of the liberation of Warsaw, the Polish Radio and Television Committee opened to old-age pensioners the doors of the Matysiak House, constructed with public contributions invited by the broadcast series.

A number of European broadcasting organizations—particularly Eastern ones—also have regular novel and poetry readings. Poland, for example, did so before World War II and resumed them in 1947.[43] Averaging from twenty to thirty minutes in length, and usually on the air twice a week, these range from simple narrations to broadcasts with backgrounds of sound and music. Czechoslovakia devotes thirty minutes a day to novel readings; Hungary has a twenty-minute program three times a week on which actors read from five to six complete novels a year; Rumania, in addition to programs about new books, has readings, often by the authors themselves. Bulgaria, supplementing readings by native and foreign authors, has a series, "Fifteen Minutes of Poetry," with definite political overtones: "At the time of the excited discussion of UNO on the question of abolition of colonialism the wrathful protest of African poets against imperialist oppression could be heard over our radio, while at the time of the threats of American imperialism to the Cuban people poetry of heroic Cuba was broadcast."[44] There also is "Our Sonorous Language," with "recordings of talks by popular narrators, [and] recordings of talks by people from various parts of the country and various strata of the population, in correct and incorrect dialects, etc."

Most European broadcasting organizations do good work in radio drama. They select excellent repertoire, both native and foreign, and make sincere attempts to encourage creative writing. Production has been standardized at a high level and acting is well done either by broadcast repertory companies or free-lance performers. To judge the fine points, of course, would require knowledge of Europe's many languages; but the production is good.*

---

* European writers on radio drama come to many of the same conclusions about its opportunities and problems, as well as about the roles of sound, music, and special effects, as do their American counterparts. Representative articles from Eastern Europe include Khristo Kovachev, "Sound in Radio Plays," *OIRT*, No. 4: 10–11 (1961); Miloslav Jares, "Music in Literary and Dramatic Broadcasts," *OIRT*, No. 4:3–6 (1962); Ivan Teren, "Radio Play—the Art of Our Century," *OIRT*, No. 5:23–28 (1962). Mr. Teren devotes an extensive footnote (p. 23) to the Hughes play broadcast by the BBC on January 15, 1924, mentioned above on p. 200. Although both Western and Eastern Europe make a great deal of broadcast drama, the Eastern *OIRT Review* has many more articles about it than has the Western *EBU Review*, except for the several *EBU Review* issues devoted to television design.

Television drama also is impressive for high quality of repertoire and performance. In Europe serious drama has not been replaced by the telefilms and light entertainment that have driven most significant dramatic programs off American television. This may be explained by some of the same reasons given above for the continuance of radio drama. Program quality rather than audience rating is the dominant value. Continental countries with two or more television services deliberately plan contrasting schedules, rather than letting their several networks compete for the maximum audience with the same types of programs. It therefore is normal to schedule major dramatic programs for relatively small audiences on one network while another is serving larger numbers of viewers with entertainment, sport, or other contrasting materials. In any case, the amount of time devoted to drama is extensive: broadcast periods of ninety minutes or longer permit the presentation of significant plays with few cuts. Despite a renewed interest in significant drama which began to emerge in 1966 and 1967, America's television networks still are a long way behind European standards.

Monday is drama night on the second Italian network, in addition to which there are other dramatic programs on both networks.[45] In 1965 RAI television devoted 5.6 per cent of its time to 195 dramatic programs, including eighty-two adaptations of stage plays, thirty-three scripts written for television, seventy-three adaptations of other literary works, and seven miscellaneous presentations. Most of the television originals and about half the adaptations were by Italian authors. Foreign names included Truman Capote, Anton Chekov, Noël Coward, T. S. Eliot, Graham Greene, James Joyce, Ferenc Molnár, J. B. Priestley, Terrence Rattigan, and Leo Tolstoi.

Both Germanys pay much attention to television drama. Each of the two national networks in West Germany averages two dramas a week, from one to two hours often being assigned to a play, with repertoire ranging from the classics to avant-garde originals. By way of promotion some of the broadcasting corporations prepare attractive illustrated brochures listing titles, casts, and dates and times of performances.[46] It is interesting to note that both West and East Germany make a good deal of plays by Bertolt Brecht despite the fact that in his later years he lived and worked in East Berlin.

The German Democratic Republic frankly emphasizes the ideological potentials of broadcast drama.[47] Television plays are "a weapon of propaganda." In the early days of television a drama department was set up to produce "humanistic and socialist works of world literature" so as to lead viewers "towards becoming an 'educated nation.'" However, a play "wins real success [only] if it is based on a clear political conception."

Since three plays are broadcast each week, a hundred new ones are needed every year.[48] Between 1952 and 1964 East German television produced 780 television plays in addition to 117 television dramas and art films, of which many were recorded for foreign distribution. To promote their use East German television has issued an illustrated catalogue of 191 pages, with text in German, French, and English. The programs range from a few serials with episodes thirty to sixty minutes long, to full-scale productions running from an hour and a half to two hours or more. Some obviously have propaganda messages, but others are straight entertainment. Both photographs and descriptions suggest that sex is so much a factor that many of them could not be aired in the United States. This emphasis may be an outgrowth of the competition between East and West Germany for audiences on both sides of the border, or it may merely be the television equivalent of theaters whose marquee advertisements are more flamboyant than the films running inside.

Poland has its "Television Theatre," with repertoire ranging from the Greek Aeschylus to the Polish Zeromski, a series to which it devotes from sixty to one hundred minutes per program.[49] Rumania thus far has emphasized adaptations more than originals.[50] Yugoslavia, with about 4.5 per cent of its schedule devoted to plays, has increased presentations by native authors to the point where half its television drama is by Yugoslavs.[51]

An interesting international project is Eurovision's "Largest Theatre in the World," for which the European Broadcasting Union commissions original scripts by well-known playwrights of international renown.[52] Its purpose is to stimulate both new and higher standards of work in television writing and production. Plays have included originals for television, serializations of great literature, serious productions, and comedies. There are no restrictions on the writing except that programs are to run from sixty to ninety minutes, must have international appeal, and must not offend the moral, political, or religious feelings of any substantial part of its audience. So far as possible, an attempt is made for all participating services in Europe and elsewhere to televise the plays on the same day. Once a script has been written, each country does its own translation and production. Examples have included Terrence Rattigan's *Heart to Heart,* broadcast in December 1962, and Diege Fabbri's *One Among You,* in December 1965.

Standards of television drama vary widely, far more than with radio. The major presentations of many Western countries—France, West Germany, Italy, and some of the smaller ones too—are very well done in settings, lighting, acting, and production.[53] East Germany likewise does some superb work. But in the other Eastern countries, which frequently have had very limited experience, halting production reflects the embryonic stage of their dramatic work. One even encounters programs televised from stages set up in studios, complete with curtain and proscenium arch, on which all camera work is from the vantage point of the audience. All this, of course, is the result of inadequate studios, limited equipment, and inexperience. In due time any country with good theater will develop equivalent skill with television drama.

Both radio and television have fine documentary programs. The BBC's early example was influential, since for years British "Feature Programmes" and their television successors provided models for the Continent; in fact, the BBC still provides such programs for its colleagues. In 1960 the European Broadcasting Union sponsored a cooperative film series, "Town Building and Town Planning." In addition to an introductory program on "The Modern City," subjects included "Rotterdam—Reconstructed Port"; "Copenhagen—Design for Living"; "London—the Fight Against Size"; "Philadelphia, an Old City Strikes Back" (done by the United States Information Agency); "Chandigarh—One Man's Dream," a program showing what can be achieved with a completely planned city; and "Venice and Bruges—Great Cities of the Past."

Belgium, France, Hungary, the Netherlands, and the United Kingdom are examples of countries which recently treated World Wars I and II in television documentaries. The BBC provided a history of the 1914–18 war with sound tracks in several languages which was widely shown on the Continent. East Germany had a comprehensive series, "The German Destiny: History and Stories of Twelve Decades," which dealt with the period from 1848 to the present in fifteen forty-five-minute programs. "The scientific conception of the series was drawn up by historians of the Marxist-Leninist Institute on the basis of the proposal of the 'History of the German Workers' Movement.' . . ."[54]

Although a small country with limited resources, the Netherlands has produced many documentaries on an impressive range of subjects. Examples include the disastrous hurricane and high tide of 1953; a five-installment study of Japanese-Nepal-Pakistan relations; a series on Dutch settlers in Israel; the hundredth anniversary of the abolition of slavery in the Dutch colonies; the new highway between Scandinavia and West Europe; the problem of the unwed mother; the story of 40,000 Austrian children sent to the Netherlands after World Wars I and II; the fiftieth anniversary of the Royal Netherlands Air Force; the unfaithful husband; "Erasmus and His Times," developed jointly with the Flemish service of Belgian television; the problem of home construction; "The Fortress City of Maastricht"; the hundredth anniversary of the First Socialist International; life aboard a Dutch inland waterway motor vessel; "Unfinished Coverage of Spain in Europe," so named because four members of the production team were arrested by the Spanish Secret Police and some of their film confiscated; "The Occupation," a twenty-one installment series on the Netherlands in World War II; a program based on film from Nazi archives and on recordings of East German television about former Nazis holding high office in the West German government; two programs about the effects of the Wall Street crash of 1929 on political and social developments in the Netherlands; American business in Europe, with special reference to how some Dutch industries may be merely a front for American interests; and a ninety-minute production commemorating the twenty-fifth anniversary of the invasion of the Soviet Union by Germany on June 22, 1941, based upon filming done in the Soviet Union by a Dutch camera team during a three-month journey, as well as on documentary materials from the Moscow State Film archives used for the first time on television.[55]

It is clear that the range of subjects treated in European broadcast documentaries is tremendous. Although some of these programs are superficial, many are first rate. Seldom are there the resources to mount elaborate documentary extravaganzas such as one occasionally finds in the United States; but Europe's best are honest, sincere, and well produced—and there are many of them.

Light Entertainment

In Europe as elsewhere light entertainment takes up a large part of radio and television time, reflecting universal interest in such programs.

Yet the Europeans seldom write about these programs. This may be because government-chartered monopoly broadcasting tends to emphasize education, culture, and public service rather than entertainment. But in any case, there are many such productions, and they are very popular with their audiences.

To take a few statistics at random, in 1962–63 Bavarian radio devoted over half its time to music, and half of that to dance and light music. The figures for North German Radio are approximately the same.[56] In the entire Federal Republic of Germany approximately 33 per cent of all television time was used for plays, films, and entertainment.[57] In 1965 Italian radio assigned 24.6 per cent of its schedule to light music and 7.5 per cent to comedy and variety. In the same year RAI television devoted 9 per cent of its time—the largest single adult category—to films and telefilms, 5.8 per cent to variety and musical comedy and 1.9 per cent to light music.[58] But exact comparisons are impossible since not all countries publish such figures and those that do define program types differently.

European radio always has broadcast much light music, and the amount has increased since television eliminated some radio light entertainment and drama. Its importance is indicated by the appointment of light music committees for EBU and OIRT. This music is both live and recorded: All major European broadcasting organizations have large numbers of staff musicians, and engage many more on a free-lance basis. Radio Luxembourg, Europe 1, Radio Monte Carlo, and the various floating pirate stations in the North Sea follow the American pattern of "personality" disc jockeys to introduce the "top 40" with much banter about music and artists. But the national networks also broadcast a great deal of popular music; in fact, most countries have one service devoted entirely to it. For example, the USSR has Mayda or Light House; Sweden has Melody Radio. The announcers on the national services are not so blatantly "folksy" as those on the commercial stations, but nevertheless cultivate a friendly and informal manner.

Light music on European radio and television runs the gamut from current jazz through standard popular music and operettas to folk music. A good deal of it comes from the United States. Younger generations in Central Europe have listened for years to the American Forces Network and the Voice of America; furthermore, films and recordings have helped develop international styles in popular music along with world audiences for certain orchestras and vocalists. Tastes in popular music are much the same everywhere although each country has some music peculiarly its own, plus a few native stars not known elsewhere. Generally speaking, although clothing fashions move from Europe to America, tastes in popular music travel in the other direction. The most conspicuous lag is in East Europe. My own sampling has convinced me that much popular music there approximates that prevailing in West Europe and the United States twenty years ago, although there is an avant-garde group which keeps abreast with the latest in Paris, London, and New York. In East Europe one also hears much native folk music.

Fads in popular music change rapidly, so that a current example may not be valid a year later. But to illustrate a point, reference can be made to the British Beatles. Eastern as well as Western Europe is quite aware of them, their manner of composition and performance, and their hair and dress styles. One American reporter wrote from Berlin that the question of accepting the Beatles (along with a native "anarchistic individualist" poet-singer named Wolf Biermann) constituted a "cultural dispute" which was "creating the greatest internal turmoil in East Germany since the Berlin wall was erected."[59] The story quoted a Communist official as saying that the Beatles would be accepted "because they are more like folk singers," but the Rolling Stones would be ruled out as "too animalistic." However, such entertainers have followings on both sides of the Iron Curtain. While the state-controlled systems can exclude their music from the air, some of it is broadcast nevertheless, partly in response to popular demand, and partly because listeners thus have less incentive to tune in foreign stations.

Eurovision provides much light entertainment through both the creation and the exchange of programs. An example is the annual Eurovision song contest, begun in 1956, the first program to be produced jointly by Eurovision members. Its purpose is to stimulate the composition and performance of popular songs.[60] Eighteen countries entered the tenth competition held March 20, 1965, when the program originated in the RAI production center in Naples. An elaborate arrangement permitted jury members from all the participating countries to vote, except on performances by their own entries. The winner that year was a young lady from Luxembourg.

Although this project has slight artistic merit, it attracts so much attention that the 1965 presentation, in addition to Eurovision distribution, was carried by Intervision to Eastern Europe where it was seen in Czechoslovakia, East Germany, Poland, Hungary, Rumania, and the Soviet Union and also was broadcast by most European radio stations. The total estimated television audience was over 150,000,000. All concerned must have judged the venture successful, since the following year's contest, held in Luxembourg March 5, 1966, was carried by the eighteen countries taking part plus Czechoslovakia, East Germany, Hungary, Morocco, Poland, Rumania, and the Soviet Union. This time Austria was the winner.

In Europe as in America the development of variety and light entertainment programs for television has been accompanied by a cutback of such programs on radio. Europe, of course, still has radio variety shows, although neither radio nor television ever developed anything on the order of America's soap opera serials. Most light entertainment formats, however, are basically similar to those in the United States, although the transition from other media to television is less complete. But with Ed Sullivan presenting vaudeville acts to large American audiences week after week, one cannot complain if many European television programs are organized the same way.

Stars of stage and screen are presented regularly, either in solo programs or with other entertainers. A common setting is a simulated cabaret or night club, with the viewers invited to "join" the audience. One example is the USSR's "Blue Fire," broadcast Saturday evenings.* There are two or more masters of ceremony and almost all the guests do entertainment turns. Holland and Hungary also utilize cabaret and night club settings. Circus acts, which have held up better in popularity than in the United States, also appear frequently on television. Europe seldom has a long series of programs built around a single star who sings, dances, or engages in comedy skits with other members of the cast. But once a decision has been made to schedule any kind of variety program, it may receive lavish production, with elaborate sets, ingenious lighting, and many special effects.†

* Vladimir Merkulov, "Blue Fire," *OIRT*, No. 5:6–7 (1963). "Obviously the custom of visiting friends exists in every country. We say in this case to go to the fire and as the TV screen is considered to be blue we have painted our invitations with this colour too."

† I recall a French program in which some popular stars appeared to sing while riding horses and engaging in other strenuous outdoor activities, a procedure which obviously required pre-recording of the sound with subsequent miming of the vocalization.

Even though Holland is a small country it produces some interesting programs.[61] There is "Look at Rigk," built around a cabaret personality. A program with a run of forty broadcasts, "Top or Flop," similar to the BBC's "Jukebox Jury," featured a jury which rated popular recordings. One program presented a man playing an organ accompanied by changing light patterns. Holland also has puppet shows; its own version of "Candid Camera"; a jazz pianist serving as hostess in a night club; a program in which older artists interview younger ones; and—like many European systems—ballroom dancing demonstrations. In addition to exchanges with Sweden, Denmark, Norway, Finland, and Belgium, Dutch television presented Sammy Davis, Jr., in a program developed cooperatively with the Belgian and French services; a two-hour version of the London Theatre workshop project *Oh What a Lovely War*; a Barbra Streisand program from CBS; and the Sophia Loren tour of Rome from ABC. A special which received an international award was a program in which a man, a young female singer, and a chimpanzee performed on a set in a circus ring surrounded by water. The theme of the program was Robinson Crusoe on an uninhabited Pacific island.

Language is a constant problem in terms of both production and cost, since the combination of different languages and small countries makes it difficult to spread the costs of expensive programs over sufficient numbers of viewers. There are frequent exchanges of stars among the French-speaking services of France, Belgium, and western Switzerland; between Holland and Dutch-speaking Belgium; and among the German-speaking populations of Germany, Austria, and northern Switzerland. But nowhere in Western Europe is there the single-language audience for entertainment one finds in the United States. Nor are there sufficiently large audiences anywhere for second runs of programs in French, German, or Italian, such as the United States has in English-speaking Canada and England. This limitation, of course, does not apply equally to musical programs, since lyrics in a foreign language are not the barrier to enjoyment represented by foreign-language comedy routines, which often are not translatable.

Quiz and give-away programs are very popular. In its heyday Italy's "Double or Quit," with a top prize of $10,000, created almost as much furor as did the "$64,000 Question" in America.[62] A visitor to Italy in 1957 reported that toward 9:00 P.M., when "Double or Quit" was scheduled, the streets in Milan were half deserted, while in the cafés not a chair with a view of the television screen was unoccupied.[63] In another successful Italian series, "Il Musichiere," contestants were given large prizes for identifying popular tunes. Audience interest was further heightened by the appearance of such guest stars as Jayne Mansfield and Gary Cooper.[64] Swiss television has a sort of "Information Please" in which several experts answer questions about their respective fields, and West Germany formerly had a radio lottery which gave large sums of money to charity.[65] A Polish radio series, "Guess, Guesser," with questions about contemporary Poland, was repeated from recordings on Bulgarian, Czech, East German, and Hungarian radio.[66]

Europe has done much more than America with political satire. The BBC's "That Was the Week That Was," in addition to inducing a short run by a similar program on America's NBC, served as the prototype for "That's How It Happens to Be" on Netherlands television. Despite strong parliamentary reactions to several episodes the Dutch series was continued.[67] Even some East European countries have broadcast political satire, though they cannot do as much as West Germany, for example, which makes a good many such programs.

Widely discussed was the Norddeutscher Rundfunk series "Panorama," which provided a forum for social and political issues. Although it has been severely criticized from time to time by the government, the Catholic Church, the press, and various special interest groups, the program survived.[68] Another series, "Report," produced by the Süddeutscher Rundfunk and the Bayerischer Rundfunk for the first television network, went so far during a critique of automobile price increases as to represent Chancellor Ludwig Erhard as a traffic policeman who allowed Volkswagen prices to drive ahead without interruption.[69]

Reports indicate that the German government has at times brought pressure against the electronic as well as the printed media for being too outspoken. But nevertheless, programs such as "Panorama," "Report," and "Hello Neighbor," which satirize political, economic, and social issues much more than does American broadcasting, do continue. If American networks were that frank, they too would be subject to at least some pressures to curtail their freedom of expression.[70]

A large percentage of European television time is devoted to films, including telefilms made for television and some produced originally for theater showings. In 1965 RAI broadcast 303 films, including 165 telefilms, 26 cartoons, and 112 cinema films.[71] Telefilms, mainly but not exclusively from the United States, carried names and titles like Fred Astaire, "Bonanza," Dick Powell, Desilu, Alfred Hitchcock, "Dodge City," and "Perry Mason" while the cartoons came almost exclusively from such American sources as Screen Gems, Associated Artists, and Walt Disney. In 1964 cinema films featured directors and actors of the caliber of Ingrid Bergman, Spencer Tracy, Sergei Eisenstein, and John Huston. Some were arranged in sequence to illustrate themes: "Great Interpreters of the Cinema"; "The Cinema and Resistance in Europe"; "Masters of the Cinema"; and "Gangster Films."[72]

Like most broadcasting organizations in countries dependent upon foreign sources of supply, RAI was asked why it used so many American programs.[73] In reply it explained that between 1963 and 1966 it used 348 feature films of which 13.5 per cent were made in Italy. But Italian films were both less accessible and more expensive, and few telefilms were made in Italy except those which RAI itself produced. Actually RAI used a larger percentage of Italian films than did the cinema houses: Only 25 per cent of all films shown in Italian cinemas after 1936 were of Italian origin, whereas since the start of television in 1954 RAI averaged 31 per cent Italian to 69 per cent foreign offerings.

The Russians too use a great deal of film material. According to one report films make up from 30 to 40 per cent of all Moscow television.[74] Another Russian source says that in 1964 the programs of Central Television in Moscow were 16 per cent movie films and 12 per cent television films. In 1962, for example, the USSR produced twenty-five television films on such subjects as the Cuban novel, Mozart and Salieri, and *The Taming of the Shrew*. In 1963 Soviet films received prizes at the International Television Film Festivals at Monte Carlo and Cannes. Because of the growth of amateur film making, USSR television in recent years has shown 142 films produced by amateurs. Cinema film showings include Russian films from all periods, often grouped into such cycles as "Classical Russian and Soviet Film Dramaturgy," and "Films of Past Years." There is a weekly three-hour program which includes a portrait of a well-known producer and the showing of one of his best productions.

When Europe schedules foreign films, it often has a language problem. In the larger countries dialogue usually is rerecorded in translation, and with such skill that there is a surprising amount of lip synchronization, even though the dramatic effect is often lessened. It is thus possible to hear British and American actors speaking fluent French, Spanish, German, Italian, or Rumanian as the case may be; and the impact of American cowboys speaking Hungarian is devastating to one accustomed to the original.* Sometimes, as occasionally in Poland, there is simultaneous translation by a single voice. In certain Scandinavian countries and the Netherlands, where foreign languages are widely spoken, films often are broadcast in English, German, or other languages without subtitles.

Cinema owners everywhere complain about the effects of film broadcasts on theater attendance. They also point out that they are at a disadvantage because it is impossible to enforce on television audiences the age limitations that often are applied in theaters.† Also opposed to imported films are local entertainers, musicians, and film producers as well as those national treasuries concerned about foreign exchange.‡

All this has led to various limitations on the telecasting of films. Eastern Europe, where there is government control of both films and broadcasting, is less strict than are West Europe and the United States, where these two groups are highly competitive. For a time Hungary and the Soviet Union imposed no delay at all between the release of films to cinemas and their use on television, but Hungary now requires a six months' waiting period, while the USSR requires six months' delay with fiction films although none for documentaries. In any case, Soviet television need only meet the costs of the film print, there being no royalty payments.

The main source of television films is the United States, where film exports totaled $76,000,000 in 1965 and were expected to reach $80,000,000

* One reason given for the great popularity of Westerns in Europe is that Europeans learn cowboy and Western tunes from the American Forces Network and the Voice of America, although the popularity of such programs in all parts of the world must depend in the last analysis upon their satisfying basic entertainment needs. Germany has some eighty Western clubs from which a thousand members gather once a year for a three-day Indian Council at which they wear Western and Indian clothes, dance square dances, play lacrosse, and elect chieftains for the coming year. (London *Times,* June 9, 1966, p. 11.)

† In Switzerland, for example, very few films can be seen by young people under eighteen even if accompanied by their parents, although many of the films thus proscribed seem to an American to be quite harmless.

‡ For these reasons the amount of foreign material on British television, both ITA and BBC, is held to about 15 per cent by informal agreement, although attempts to write such limitations into the law setting up the ITA in 1954 were defeated. (Paulu, *British Broadcasting,* p. 53; Paulu, *British Broadcasting in Transition,* pp. 41–42; *House of Commons Debates,* 528:621, 639–640 (May 27, 1954).) The *Television Act 1964,* Sec. 3 (1, c) says only "that proper proportions" of the programs must be "of British origin and of British performance."

in 1966.[75] The biggest markets in 1966 were Canada ($20,000,000), Australia ($16,000,000), Japan ($12,000,000), Latin America ($11,000,000), and the United Kingdom ($7,000,000) with all of Western Europe buying only $7,500,000 worth of telefilms. Prices charged depend upon what the market will bear. Canada, the United Kingdom, and West Germany are at the top with an average of $3,000 for a thirty-minute program, and $5,000 to $6,000 for an hour's program. All of America's major networks and film producers have European offices to sell their products, as well as to represent them in securing European talent and programs for use at home. In 1964 CBS, operating in 170 countries, was the world's largest exporter of television films, with NBC selling programs to 300 markets in eighty countries.

Those well-known American names and titles which appear regularly on foreign screens include Perry Como, "Peyton Place," "Daniel Boone," "Beverly Hillbillies," Jackie Gleason, "Gunsmoke," Ed Sullivan, Gary Moore, "Candid Camera," "The Virginian," Milton Berle, "Stage 67," "The Man from UNCLE," "Bonanza," "I Love Lucy," "Gomer Pyle," "Perry Mason," "Lassie," "Flicka," "Rin Tin Tin," and "The Untouchables." Overseas program sales are apt to be of those shows currently on American networks, although this trend has been discouraged by the frequency with which highly touted programs have been canceled after short runs because of low domestic ratings.

The truly international aspects of the business are illustrated by the fact that "Bonanza" has been sold in sixty-three markets where it was viewed by over 350,000,000 people. "Perry Mason" has been seen in fifty-eight countries, having been dubbed into German, Spanish, Japanese, Portuguese, French, Italian, Arabic, Korean, and Thai, and broadcast with subtitles in Dutch, Flemish, Danish, Swedish, Norwegian, Greek, Finnish, Malay, Polish, and Chinese.[76] The Soviet Union and Bulgaria do not take any American telefilms, although the other Eastern countries do. From Poland the USIA reported: "A Radio and TV Magazine carried resumes of six of the 'most interesting film serials appearing on Polish TV.' All of them were American productions, but the magazine omitted that fact."[77]

Other major telefilm sources are Canada, which sells both its English- and French-language product in Europe, and the United Kingdom, where the private program contractors and the BBC compete for foreign markets.[78] Television films also are made by the various continental broadcasting organizations, including France, West Germany, and Italy. Some are exchanged via Eurovision and others are sold.

It is more difficult for European broadcasting organizations to sell telefilms to each other than for the United States to sell to any of them. The United States can undersell them, since it can recover basic costs from broadcasts at home, something much harder to do in smaller countries. While the American thirty-minute program may not permit as much character development as do Europe's longer segments—RAI, for example, did *Les Misérables* in ten episodes totaling eleven hours and twenty minutes running time—such programs are easier to fit into schedules. Finally, many more countries can broadcast English-language programs without translation than can use German-, Italian-, or French-language films. France can sell to Belgium, Canada, Switzerland, and parts of Africa; and Italy to Switzerland and perhaps New York City; but the United States has most of Canada, Australia, and the United Kingdom, plus many other countries for which English is a second if not the native language. Since it may cost twice as much to dub new dialogue as to buy the film itself, the economics are all in favor of the American product.

The great preponderance of American films leads inevitably to questions about the cultural consequences of foreign programs. What is the result of concentrating so much American material in peak viewing hours?* Do American programs really contradict European values? Are they influential enough to justify concern? An intensive study of the facts and philosophies involved would be necessary to provide the answers. But nevertheless, some foreign television organizations are concerned about showing American films, at the same time that many Americans fear that money, rather than cultural values, international understanding, or the American image abroad, determine policy in international telefilm sales.†

---

* On one occasion Swedish television approved for broadcast only seven or eight out of a series of thirty-nine American Western programs. (Kenneth Adam, "Aspects of European Television," *Listener*, August 18, 1960, p. 257.)

† In a study of *The Impact of American Commercial Television in Western Europe*, the United States Information Agency reported that the European viewing public voted two to one that American telefilms left good rather than bad impressions, although the sample polled was exceedingly small. But a United States Information Agency foreign service officer involved with television program exchange,

PROGRAMS: ENTERTAINMENT

Sports

Anyone who believes that European broadcasting, because it is free from the economic pressures of American commercial broadcasting, consistently gives the public what it "ought to have" rather than "what it wants," should note that sports and light entertainment constitute two of its major program categories. This follows naturally from the fact that Europeans like everyone else want to be entertained, and that sports, along with comedy, light drama, and popular music, are universally enjoyed.*

If there is any important difference between public reactions to spectator sports in Europe and in the United States it might be that the Europeans are even more enthusiastic than the Americans. The sports themselves are often different, and some may appear amusing to Americans simply because they are unfamiliar. Universally popular are automobile and motorcycle racing, boxing, equestrian contests, sailing, soccer, tennis, and track and field events. Of intense local interest and importance are bullfighting in Portugal, Spain, and southern France; bicycle racing in Belgium, France, Italy, Czechoslovakia, and Poland; dog racing and cricket in the United Kingdom; and skiing in mountain areas in every country.

One evidence of the status of competitive sports is the number and size of the large stadiums in most of the principal cities. Berlin, Bucharest, Hamburg, Leningrad, Moscow, Paris, and Rome are among the places with stadiums seating 100,000 people or more. Anyone who has attended a major event in Europe, and felt the intense enthusiasm and partisanship of the crowd, knows that American baseball, basketball, and football are not the only contests in which there is great public interest.

while asserting that our record in exporting television films "is better than most critics of U.S. television are willing to concede," nevertheless concluded that we should be "represented on overseas television by something more than the standard formula of cowboy serials, detective films, pratfall comedies, and an occasional news documentary. An overseas viewer would be hard put to believe, from what he sees on his screen, that contemporary America is a leader in the lively arts such as drama, architecture, painting, and sculpture, or to understand the workings of our economic system or our current struggle to build a truly democratic multi-racial society. These subjects are seldom raised in the bland products that make up most of the U.S. television export package." (Wilson P. Dizard, *Television: A World View*, pp. 284–285.)

* For references above to various aspects of sports broadcasting, see pp. 43, 45, 140, 142.

217

Television devotes more time to sports than does radio.* For example, in Switzerland in 1964, an average of about 3.5 per cent of all radio time was given to sports, while the German- and French-language television networks devoted 19.3 per cent of their time to sports, and the Italian network 25.7 per cent.[79] During the same year in Italy an average of 2 per cent of all radio time was spent on sports: The first and second (more popular) services devoted respectively 3.2 and 2.4 per cent, while the third program had no sports at all. Eleven and eight-tenths per cent of all television time was spent on sports, one network assigning 11.1 and the other 14.0 per cent.[80]

The absolute numbers are even more impressive.[81] Italian radio had 6,085 sports programs, of which 5,599 were news programs and 486 actuality broadcasts of automobile racing, bicycling, boxing, soccer, tennis, and the Winter Olympics in Innsbruck. Television offered fewer but longer programs. There were 1,074 all told, including 687 news programs and 334 actualities covering almost the complete range of sports; auto racing, bicycling (with extensive coverage of a bicycle race around Italy), boxing, hockey, motorcycle racing, relays from Innsbruck, soccer, tennis, thirty relays from the Olympic Games in Tokyo—and one baseball game! Figures from Germany will complete the picture. In 1965, five of the West German radio services devoted between 1.01 and 3.77 per cent of their time to sports; the second German television network allocated 18.8 per cent; while East German television assigned 13.4 per cent one year and 15.4 per cent the next.[82]

A spokesman for Czechoslovak television provided an interesting rationale for sports broadcasting.[83] Sports broadcasts, he wrote, were so popular with viewers that they were the most popular single type of program, occupying almost one-fifth of all television time. Play-by-play accounts should do three things: they should inform; they should propagate and instruct; and they should entertain. The first function needed no explanation. As to the second, "every relay should be a mass instruction for thousands of sportsmen." Figure skating and handball were two sports whose current popularity he ascribed to television coverage. "It is also our wish that all our relays be not only a school of the rules of the

---

* A UNESCO study published in 1963 reported that in five European countries the percentage of sports programs on television ranged from three to five times what it was on radio. (UNESCO, *Statistics on Radio and Television 1950–1960*, p. 35.)

game concerned, but also of fair play and correct conduct on the field and beyond the barriers. We wish to contribute considerably to the moral education of sportsmen." In regard to item three, television wishes to entertain its viewers and "to provide them with thrilling and good entertainment after which they can return refreshed to their own work."

Engineering and production staffs take great pains in sports coverage. Between June 25 and July 16, 1961, to cover the Tour de France, the immensely popular bicycle race, a combination of live and recorded transmissions was used. There were radio flashes every hour plus special television reports. Radio coverage required three technical vehicles, one motorcycle, and one airplane; television used one stationary vehicle, one remote pickup unit, one motorcycle, one helicopter which followed the main body of cyclists, and a technical team of eighty persons.[84]

In 1964 in East Germany, for coverage of "the largest amateur cycling race in the world, the Peace Race," a relay van with reporters from East Germany, Poland, and Czechoslovakia transmitted reports to an airplane which, by a complicated series of relays, fed them to the East German, Polish, and Czechoslovak radio networks.[85] The head of the East German television sports department, who supplemented experience in co-production with Polish and Czech television by viewing broadcasts from Austria, England, France, Italy, Sweden, Switzerland, the United States, and West Germany, reported that it was not unusual to use a dozen cameras to cover certain competitive sports.[86] For the world motorcycling championship at Sachsenring, DDR television used 11 cameras to cover 80 per cent of the track and in 1962 broadcast a description of the Baltic Sea Regatta from a tugboat three miles off shore. A description of the seventy kilometers of a bicycle race was broadcast from a helicopter flying above the track, and there were twenty-second film portraits of all the racers ready to insert into the programs to supplement the live reportage.

Another example of the trouble and expense incurred in order to carry a major athletic event was the elaborate hookup devised so that Eurovision could take a soccer match between Portuguese and Dutch teams on May 8, 1963.[87] The game was in Lisbon but at that time the Portuguese network was not connected to that of any other country. It was necessary, therefore, to improvise a relay over some 230 miles of mountainous territory between Lisbon and Guadalcanal, Spain, the nearest terminus of the Eurovision network. This was done in less than a week by the Portuguese and Spanish authorities, with assistance from the Dutch who chartered an airplane to fly in six engineers and nearly three tons of equipment. Consequently it was possible not only to bring the game from Portugal to the Netherlands but also to arrange the first direct Eurovision transmission from Portugal.

The most elaborate setup of all, however, was that developed jointly by the EBU and the Japanese NHK for covering the 1964 Olympics in Tokyo.[88] The seven-story building assigned as headquarters contained almost everything required from restaurants to sixty radio studios. Two thousand NHK staff members were available, and for its various services the European Broadcasting Union had 650 microphones, 600 amplifiers, 500 audio tape recorders, 1,000 telephonic stations, eighty-five television cameras, forty-six video tape recorders, twenty mobile television trucks, twenty film cameras, and a helicopter, plus some other equipment.

For the radio transmissions to Europe there were cable connections from Tokyo to London via California and New York, and then to the Continent. At first television programs were video tape recorded in Tokyo and flown by jet plane to Hamburg for network distribution. This later was speeded up through Syncom 3 relay from Japan to California; microwave transmission from Los Angeles to Montreal for tape recording; and then a jet plane flight to Hamburg. Plans are being laid for even more elaborate coverage in color of the Mexico City Olympics in 1968, with Intervision participating and sharing costs.

In all these capitalist countries the sports promoters must be reckoned with. The most important contests are arranged by individuals or syndicates for financial gain, and promoters naturally are unwilling to lose revenue because of broadcasting. Some events, therefore, are blacked out entirely or delayed for twenty-four hours; others aired only when the broadcasting organizations guarantee to make up any losses in estimated attendance; and in almost all cases, broadcast rights are sold for considerable sums. Since many events are distributed by closed-circuit television for viewing in theaters to which admission is charged, there sometimes is hard competitive bidding between the closed-circuit television and broadcasting groups.*

* At a meeting of West European television program directors in Berlin in 1965, I made a plea for the educational uses of closed-circuit television. Their unenthusiastic response was explained to me later as the result of their associating closed-circuit television not with education, but with competition for telecasting sports

Sports programs are among the staples for international exchange, since the most exciting contests usually are between teams from different countries. Consequently in radio and television there are bilateral as well as multi-national play-by-play transmissions. The first extensive interconnections of European television stations involved sports programs. In Eastern Europe, early in 1956, several stations in East Germany and Czechoslovakia broadcast Olympic hockey matches relayed by Eurovision from Italy.[89] Subsequent relays linking Czechoslovakia and East Germany led to Intervision in 1960. During its first year, 269 of Intervision's 572 program hours were sports, and during 1961 the figure was 189 out of 454 hours. Between January 1960 and January 1965, of the more than 3,700 programs transmitted by Intervision, 43.5 per cent were sports broadcasts, with the second largest category, Topical Programs, making up only 30.5 per cent of the programs. But during 1965 with 1,700 relays, news and political programs forged ahead to 36.4 per cent while sports dropped to 39.3 per cent.[90]

Sports relays in Eastern Europe have included the world ice hockey championships in Switzerland; the 1961 Peace Cycle Race between Warsaw, Berlin, and Prague; the world motorcycle championship at Sachsenring; the world cycling championship in Switzerland; the world rowing contest in Prague; the European boxing championship in Belgrade; and periodic relays of football games. There was a USSR-USA athletic contest in Moscow which was broadcast live for viewers all over Europe and recorded for delayed use in America. Intervision also broadcast film recordings of the winter Olympic Games in Squaw Valley, California, and more recently carried relays from the 1964 winter Olympics in Innsbruck and summer Olympic Games in Tokyo.

The same situation exists in Western Europe. During the first eight years of Eurovision, sports constituted the major type of transmission. Thus in 1956, after two years, 70 per cent of all programs were sports. Subsequently, however, the proportion decreased, so that by December 1964 only 40 per cent of Eurovision programs were sports, the major category then being news.[91] It should be noted, however, that during 1963 and 1964 there were especially compelling developments, including the Kennedy assassination and funeral, the trip of Pope Paul to

events. More recently, however, the use of closed-circuit television in teaching on the Continent has grown.

the Holy Land, and the United States presidential election, so this higher rating for news may be only temporary.

For producers the international coverage of sports events is very complicated. It is not so hard for radio: Each country has its own announcers, and if there are enough circuits, play-by-play reports are brought directly to the home audience. But television is more difficult, not because of pictures but because of sound. There usually are enough cameras to provide good coverage and the pictures are fed to all countries along with "international sound"—crowd noises and other nonlanguage backgrounds which can be used anywhere. But there must be an individual circuit for each announcer. This is the reason news pictures of international television pickups often show a long line of announcers in isolated booths. In some cases countries with a common language share announcers, although European like American networks often want to build their own sports personalities, so this solution is seldom followed except when the game is so distant that circuits are limited or very expensive. At times only pictures and international sound are sent out, with local announcers describing the action "off the tube" in their own studios. In either case, there is much use of superimpositions giving the countries, names, and performance records of the contestants, along with time and speed indicators at the edge of the screen to assist viewers in following the action.

Essentially sport broadcasts are of two types: news reports, consisting of scores and general information; and play-by-play descriptions. Sport news usually is either incorporated into other newscasts or scheduled adjacent to them. Play-by-play reports are much the same everywhere. One gets the same impression of excitement from the voices of announcers describing bicycle races in France or ice hockey games in West Germany as from football announcers in America. Television coverage is basically similar in all countries: Cameras follow the center of interest, cutting back and forth or zooming as required. In Europe as in the United States, television with its pictures requires less commentary than does radio.

For the most part European broadcasters do well with sports. Widespread interest forces the broadcasting organizations to employ experts as producers and commentators: A Spanish bullfighting *aficionado,* a French cycle enthusiast, a German boxing fan, and a Swiss skier are just as merciless in judging inept camera work or faulty descriptions as are American fans in condemning poor coverage of the World Series.

On the whole, though, European coverage is more relaxed. I have seen broadcasts of skiing and equestrian contests which lasted two or three times as long as they would in the United States. Where an American station would record an event in order to broadcast its high points, picking up live only the moments of greatest interest, a European network might cover the whole performance from start to finish. But this slower pacing is typical of other programs too, and may merely reflect national differences in taste and temperament. It also may be a result of the greater amount of time on European stations, as well as of the absence of competition. But if Network 1 transmits ski jumping *in extenso,* while Network 2 is presenting a symphony concert or serious drama, why should anyone complain?

The Audience for Continental Broadcasting

Broadcasting always is accompanied by some research, even though it may be very elementary. At the least broadcasters want to know who listened or watched and what they thought of the programs. Research begins when a broadcaster discusses a program with one or more members of his audience. This leads to mail analysis, and later to much more sophisticated studies in which scientific methods are used to gather and interpret information from a carefully selected audience sample.

The nature and extent of research are closely related to the motivations behind it. Because the funds initially available for broadcasting in most European countries were largely dependent upon license fees, the first data published often pertained to the number and distribution of licenses. Thereafter, curiosity about the audience, reinforced by the conviction that knowledge of the public is necessary if programing is to accomplish its objectives, led to more thorough studies.

The growth of commercial broadcasting has been a major stimulus because of the effect of audience size on income. This is one reason America leads the world in broadcast research. It also explains why research in the United Kingdom expanded so much following the introduction of commercial television in 1954. Another factor is the development of mass communications research in general, dealing with press and cinema as well as broadcasting. Also important are university activities, which at once have contributed to and been stimulated by the research of the broadcasting organizations.

An example of a steadily emerging point of view was the Dutch decision in September 1964 "to institute a continuous inquiry into the listening and viewing habits" of the public in recognition of "a growing need of systematic insight into audience structure and the reactions of listeners and viewers to the various programme items."[92] Because press reports and unsolicited communications from listeners and viewers could "never be representative of the whole," the Netherlands henceforth would set up panels and circulate questionnaires. The work was to be done by the Institute for Applied Market Research in Hilversum under the direction of a committee representing the country's five broadcasting associations, the Netherlands Radio Union, and the Netherlands Television Foundation. At the same time, a quarterly was established to publish mass communications studies.

The Bureau of Studies of Radio-Télévision Belge conducts a "permanent inquiry into programs," from which have come more than fifty reports on the size, nature, and habits of Belgian audiences. These are supplemented by a quarterly founded in 1963 which, in addition to providing information for staff members, also aims to contribute to an awareness of the RTB in the professional and university worlds. The opening issue observed that while literature on radio and television was abundant in the United States, Germany, Italy, and Japan, the French language had a paucity of such material. In addition to articles on the theory and practice of broadcasting, this publication provides abstracts of articles and books, together with research reports from many countries including the United States.[93]

Italy's RAI has a Department of Service and Studies whose output includes descriptions of broadcasting in other countries, reports in depth on various aspects of Italian broadcasting, and a well-edited and detailed yearbook. The considerable amount of audience research in Germany reflects the general interest of German scholars in psychological and statistical studies. In addition to publications by broadcasting organizations, there is the Hans Bredow Institute for Radio and Television at the University of Hamburg, which supplements its very useful *Internationales Handbuch für Rundfunk und Fernsehen* with a variety of reports by individual staff members.

After only four or five years of broadcast research, Yugoslavia devoted eighteen pages of its 290-page yearbook in 1965 to a summary of findings, which it said were "becoming more and more indispensable in the work of broadcasting stations." This was the third year in which Yugoslavia published a yearbook in English.*

Although East Germany is a latecomer it plans to use the most modern devices in its research. As one of its radio staff members wrote: "The contents, forms and methods of radio work change together with the changes in society. Radio research work must serve as . . . guide in this field. . . . If this is not the case, radio lags behind the requirements of Society."[94] Continuing developments dating from 1963, the Council of Ministers of the German Democratic Republic resolved in April 1965 "to build an information and documentation system in the field of social sciences," making the greatest possible use of electronic equipment, even though it might not be available until 1967.

The Poles believe that public opinion research in Communist countries must differ from that in capitalist countries, because "the formation of a new, socialist community," rather than profits, is the basic motivation.[95] When Polish broadcasting set up its own research center in 1958, it limited itself initially to analyzing the 100,000 letters received each year, but it now has some fifty workers and more than 1,800 volunteers in all parts of the country who interview selected cross sections of the population. To provide perspective for its findings this center also studies such related topics as the use of leisure time and the living patterns of different social groups. The Center for the Study of Public Opinion is another Polish organization that does research on the mass media as well as on major social, political, cultural, and economic problems.

The Czechoslovaks believe that "If television is to fulfill its cultural-political mission it is necessary to learn some facts about the viewers, their approach and reactions to programmes."[96] The Czechoslovak Study Department, organized in 1946 though not active until several years later, cooperates with the Institute of Psychology at Charles University in Prague in making many types of listening and viewing studies involving carefully chosen samples. Like Belgium, Czechoslovak broad-

---

* *Yugoslav Yearbook 1965*, pp. 7, 196–214. Yugoslavia probably is the only country publishing an entire yearbook in a foreign language, although Italy, the Netherlands, and East and West Germany are among those countries providing various descriptive materials in foreign languages.

casting publishes a journal which digests articles from foreign periodicals and reports research findings.

Although these countries are not the only ones engaged in broadcast research, their activities are typical. All countries, in fact, do some research, and by now most have advanced considerably beyond the stage of analyzing letters. Surprisingly, the USSR limits its audience research largely to the work of the Department of Letters of Central Radio which receives, analyzes, and answers some of the 500,000 letters received each year from the domestic audience.

Various European journals deal with broadcasting. The *Review* of the European Broadcasting Union published in Geneva, and the *Review* and *Information Bulletin* of the International Radio and Television Organization in Prague, contain some articles on research along with much statistical and factual data. There also are the quarterly review, *The Training of Journalists,* published by the International Center for Higher Education in Journalism at the University of Strasbourg, and the *News Bulletin* of the International Federation of Editors and Publishers (*Bulletin d'Informations,* Fédération Internationale des Editeurs de Journaux et Publications) in Paris.

Supplementary studies have been made by various propaganda organizations. The United States Information Agency publishes regular reports on reactions to the Voice of America as well as to RIAS. Surveys are conducted by Radio Free Europe (which broadcasts to the satellite countries) and Radio Liberty (whose target is the Soviet Union). The BBC also does extensive research on the audiences for its various overseas services.

Taken together these sources provide a good deal of information about European audiences. It is not as complete or systematic as that available in either the United Kingdom or the United States; many of the findings of the broadcasting organizations are not published; much of what has been published is meaningful only to people in the country concerned; and no comprehensive attempts have been made to summarize or correlate the results.[97] Nevertheless, there is more information available than most people—surely most Americans—realize, and some of this has been drawn upon for the paragraphs which follow, although in order to have comparable data from a number of countries, special questionnaires were sent to some continental broadcasting organizations.

As mentioned before, most of the Continent can receive one or more radio and television signals, and the more populous countries are covered by several radio services, plus at least one television network. The extent of receiver distribution varies widely, depending upon national economic levels, and with television on such factors as the length of time service has been available. The European Broadcasting Union publishes annual reports on the number of receiver licenses in most European countries. Table 6 shows that at the end of 1966, the widest radio

Table 6. Number of Radio Licenses and Radio Licenses
per Hundred Inhabitants, by Country

Country	Number of Radio Licenses	Radio Licenses per Hundred Inhabitants
Sweden	2,948,203	37.88
Luxembourg	125,997	37.81
Finland	1,594,147	34.21
Germany (East)	5,811,731	34.03
Denmark	1,560,975	32.74
France	15,861,411	31.91
Belgium	3,047,476	30.47
Germany (West)	18,232,133	30.39
United Kingdom	16,432,184	30.19
Austria	2,167,753	29.88
Norway	1,110,346	29.48
Switzerland	1,684,867	28.65
Czechoslovakia	3,828,957	26.78
Bulgaria	2,144,082	25.88
Netherlands	3,135,190	25.02
Hungary	2,497,000	24.56
Italy	11,162,904	21.09
Ireland	550,309	19.10
Spain	6,010,000	18.78
Poland	5,592,751	17.59
Yugoslavia	3,003,321	15.09
Portugal	1,235,484	14.34
Greece	893,078	10.51
Turkey	2,636,685	8.40

distribution was in Sweden, which had 37.88 licenses per hundred inhabitants. Luxembourg was second with 37.81. The northern countries were in the lead; Portugal, Greece, and Turkey at the bottom; and the Communist countries in the lower half, except East Germany which was fourth from the top.*

* Based on "Radio and Television Licence Statistics, 1966," *EBU Review*, 102B: 36 (March 1967). Although more recent figures are available from some countries, reference here is to EBU data only, in order to have comparable information for all

Most European countries do not report the percentage of homes which have receivers. Some that do supplied the following data: Belgium 97 per cent; Switzerland 97 per cent; Sweden 94 per cent; United Kingdom 93.25 per cent; West Germany 93.08 per cent; Italy 74.75 per cent; Yugoslavia 60 per cent.[98] (In the continental United States, 98 per cent of all homes have radios (*Broadcasting Yearbook Issue 1967*, p. 18).)

Television set ownership was much below the radio level, as would be expected, although the rate of increase once service is available is often astonishing. Table 7 shows that again Sweden was ahead with 27.75 licenses per hundred inhabitants, and Britain was a close second with 25.57. Those countries with very few receivers usually are of lower economic status, or have relatively new television services, two factors which tend to be related. Countries providing data as to the percentage of homes with television receivers include: United Kingdom 78.20 per cent; Sweden 77.70 per cent; West Germany 62.51 per cent; Belgium 50 per cent; Italy 43 per cent; Switzerland 40 per cent; East Germany 51 per cent; and Yugoslavia 17 per cent.*

Information about the social composition of the receiver-owning public is very incomplete. In Italy in December 1961, when 64 per cent of all families had radios, 79 per cent of families in towns with a population of over 100,000 had receivers, while only 55 per cent of families in towns with less than 5,000 inhabitants had them.[99] The reasons for not having radios included the lack of an electricity supply, no interest in radio, and financial inability.

In the Netherlands in the autumn of 1962, when 1,234,000 television receivers were owned in the population of around twelve million, there was a close relationship between set ownership and socioeconomic sta-

countries. Licenses for both off-the-air and wired receivers are included. (For a discussion of wired receivers, see pp. 29–31 above.) All these figures are for licenses and not receivers, except for Spain where licenses are not required. Since most countries require only one license per household, the number of radio receivers is greater than the number of licenses. Furthermore, there are some unlicensed sets in all countries—estimates often running as high as 10 per cent (see above, p. 93). Some data on receivers in the Soviet Union are given on p. 31 above. Very few statistics are published as to radio-equipped automobiles, although it appears that their number is quite small. Italy, however, reported that in 1954, 2.67 per cent of all automobiles had radios, the number increasing steadily until by 1965 11.90 per cent were radio equipped. (*Annuario RAI 1966*, p. 366.)

* In the continental United States, 94 per cent of all homes have one or more television receivers. (*Broadcasting Yearbook Issue 1967*, p. 18.)

Table 7. Number of TV Licenses and TV Licenses per
Hundred Inhabitants, by Country

Country	Number of TV Licenses	TV Licenses per Hundred Inhabitants
Sweden	2,160,435	27.75
United Kingdom	13,919,191	25.57
Denmark	1,140,371	23.92
Germany (West)	12,719,599	21.20
Germany (East)	3,559,240	20.84
Netherlands	2,369,997	18.91
Finland	822,691	17.65
Czechoslovakia	2,375,318	16.61
Belgium	1,659,955	16.60
Norway	573,757	15.23
France	7,471,192	15.03
Italy	6,874,543	12.99
Switzerland	754,161	12.83
Austria	834,999	11.51
Ireland	320,061	11.11
Luxembourg	36,297	10.89
Hungary	1,000,000	9.84
Poland	2,540,064	7.99
Spain	2,325,000	7.26
Yugoslavia	777,299	3.91
Bulgaria	287,880	3.47
Portugal	210,913	2.45

tus, since higher income was found to be a stimulus for the purchase of television receivers.[100] On the other hand, people with elementary school educations were more apt to own sets than those of higher educational achievement. An interesting relationship was found between set ownership and church attendance: 56 per cent of the receivers were owned by people who did not belong to any church; regular churchgoers constituted only 41 per cent of the owners; and irregular churchgoers 53 per cent. The ownership rate was lower in rural and higher in built-up areas, although reception was about uniform everywhere.

There are relatively few data concerning set use. Those countries which have provided figures about daily listening in radio homes include the following: Belgium, 1 to 1½ hours in the summertime, approximately 2 hours in the winter; West Germany, from 1½ to 2 hours; and Yugoslavia, 3 hours. In West Germany television sets are turned on an average of 2½ hours a day; while Yugoslavia reports 4 hours of daily use. Adults with access to television view an average of 2 hours a day in Belgium, 2 hours in Yugoslavia, 2 hours and 10 minutes in the Netherlands, and from 2 to 3 hours in Czechoslovakia. In the Netherlands, 70 per cent of set owners watch television each evening, although those on the upper socioeconomic levels do less viewing.[101] In Czechoslovakia it was reported in 1961 that 65 per cent of sets were used daily.[102] Few European stations broadcast all day long, and most daytime programing is for schools. Therefore, these figures cover mainly evening viewing.*

Reports on audience tastes in Europe will not surprise readers familiar with data from anywhere else: The whole world prefers entertainment to education and escape from reality to serious thought. There is a close correlation between the amount of broadcast time given to different types of programs and their acceptance by the audience, since in all countries there is much pressure on the broadcasting authorities to provide programs of high interest. Consequently, schedules throughout Europe always give a great deal of time to light music, entertainment, and sports, the extensive coverage of international soccer matches and the Olympic Games being dramatic examples of the latter (see above, p. 220).

In Czechoslovakia I was told that light music is preferred along with plays, sports, and entertainment. In Hungary, the audience likes quizzes, light entertainment, and drama, with high interest in news and news commentaries, but shows a lack of enthusiasm for agricultural and industrial production data. In the USSR, preferences are for sports, news in general, and especially news about the achievements of Soviet astronauts. The Spanish public likes football, bullfighting, and American telefilms.

In view of the widespread belief that most Italians like opera, it is interesting to examine some data from RAI about the musical tastes of the Italian radio public. In April 1962, asked to indicate interest in different types of music on a scale of 100, respondents placed popular songs at the top with 73, followed by light orchestral music 54, operetta 47, opera 42, jazz 25, symphony 21, and chamber music 14.[103] Young people preferred light music while older listeners were more apt to favor opera, although age differences were slight in regard to symphonic and chamber music. When the public was divided into four levels of educational

* In the United States the average television viewer watches television about 3 hours a day, and in addition listens to the radio about 2½ hours—most television viewing occurring in the evening and radio listening in the daytime. The television set in an average home is turned on about 6½ hours each day. (*Broadcasting Yearbook Issue 1967*, p. 20.)

achievement, the results were what would be expected: Those with elementary education preferred popular music and university groups liked symphonic and chamber music. But although respondents with less education disliked jazz, opera, symphony, and chamber music, the differences among other educational categories over jazz and opera were not pronounced.

Italian television viewers in April 1964 gave films a top 77 rating, after which came news with 74 and telefilms with a 68, followed closely by several other types of entertainment programs.[104] The rating for sports was a surprisingly low 43. Opera ranked below sports with 33 and symphonic music at the bottom with 18. The middle educational category showed the greatest interest in sports, with the top group next and the elementary group—surprisingly—below it. The most pronounced educational differences were with symphonic music where there was a steady progression from 13 for the lowest category up to 35 for the university group.

Figures from the Netherlands based upon actual viewing surveys produced results similar to the interest indications reported from Italy. During all of 1965, the largest audience—94 per cent of all sets—was for an entertainment program, "Toon Hermans' One-Man Show." The Eurovision Song Festival and a Dutch-Spanish soccer match tied for second with 89, while third place with a rating of 88 was shared by "Holiday on Ice" and the "Netherlands Song Festival."[105] Most of the other very popular programs were entertainment too although occasionally there were high ratings for news broadcasts. One edition of "That's How It Happens to Be" received a rating of 77. Occasionally an American telefilm made the Netherlands top ten, as did the "Beverly Hillbillies" and "Bonanza" in 1965; but for the most part, although American telefilms and other entertainment programs frequently attract large audiences in Europe, the top ratings almost always go to national productions.

In Belgium, results from questionnaires about preferences were very similar to reports of actual viewing. In both cases, feature films, entertainment, comedy, and telefilms ranked at the top and jazz at the very bottom, with serious music and opera somewhere between. Programs of information and news also were in the middle range.[106]

A number of European countries have developed networks for people of sophisticated and specialized tastes following the pattern of the BBC's Third Programme introduced in 1946. The consistently small audiences for these services support the data given above in showing a lack of wide interest in broadcasts of serious material. The French-speaking service in Belgium began its third program in 1961.[107] On the average only 1 or 2 per cent of all listening is to this program. The median age for listeners is 38, only 2 per cent being under 18. Professional groups provide most of the audience; laborers and workers hardly any of it. The data RAI collected about its third program in 1957 are very similar.[108] Only 1 per cent of the public listened "daily or almost daily" to the service. Regular listeners came from the upper educational and professional classes although the very top level listened a bit less than did the second one.

The influence of television upon audiences for the older media of radio, cinema, and theater follows the same pattern reported earlier in the United States and Britain. One of the first effects of television is to reduce radio listening during those hours when television is on the air. An Italian survey made in March 1963 showed that the highest level of radio listening was at 1:00 P.M. when over nine million people were tuned in. The evening radio peak of less than six million came at approximately 8:00 P.M., at which hour television was attracting thirteen million viewers.[109] At 8:00 P.M., 34 per cent of the adults with radio but without television were listening to the radio. Only 5 per cent of people with television were listening to radio, although 21 per cent were watching television. By 9:00 P.M., 23 per cent of the radio-only adults were listening compared to only 1 per cent of those with television, whereas 65 per cent of the television group were then watching television.

Similar results were reported from a Belgian study the following year.[110] During one week in February 1964 approximately 40 per cent of the non-television public listened to the radio at 1:00 P.M., while less than 30 per cent of the television public did. At 7:30 P.M., over 45 per cent of non-television adults were listening to the radio, compared to less than 5 per cent of the television public. The radio-only public maintained a 30 per cent or better listening level from 7:00 to 10:00 P.M. and the television public's listening declined steadily from 5 per cent at 7:00 to the vanishing point at 10:00 P.M.

A Belgian inquiry made in 1953 found that as television ownership grew, participation in other activities declined, although television was not necessarily the cause of all the changes.[111] Between 1958 and 1963, the population of the country grew only slightly but the number of television sets increased from 223,168 to 1,200,000, the number of persons per set declining from 40.6 to 7.7. Between 1953 and 1962, while total expenditures on leisure-time activities went down by a third, expenditures on television grew from .52 to 8.99 per cent of the national leisure-time budget. Cinema attendance dropped consistently from 1946 through 1961, the number of admissions declining from about 100 million in 1958 to 65 million in 1962. A comparative table of cinema attendance in Belgium, France, Italy, West Germany, the Netherlands, the United Kingdom, and the United States showed a striking decrease in all cases, but most of all in the United Kingdom and the United States, which had had television for the longest time. But ownership of television did not lead to a decrease in the purchase of newspapers though it may have led to their being read less carefully. Data on the effects of television on attendance at sports events were incomplete, but the evidence available to the Belgians led sports promoters to conclude that television had reduced their audiences.

A Hungarian broadcast monitored in 1964 reported that only a quarter of those people who had gone to the cinema one or more times a week continued to do so after buying television sets, and that over two-thirds of those who had attended the theater frequently reduced attendance after acquiring television.[112] Also reported were sharp drops in radio listening and attendance at variety shows and sports events. On the other hand, after getting their sets, nearly three times as many people watched films and ten or fifteen times as many viewed plays on television as had previously attended cinemas and theaters.

In June of 1965 it was reported from Poland that coincident with a 6 per cent increase in the number of television license holders during the first half of the year came a reduction in cinema and theater audiences, along with a drop-off in radio listening.[113] In Warsaw, for example, there was 5.2 per cent less attendance at theaters and concerts than during the comparable period the preceding year, and a 13.3 per cent drop in cinema-going. A report from Yugoslavia indicated that on Saturday evenings, because of the number of live entertainment programs on television, attendance at coffee houses, restaurants, theaters, and cinemas has been reduced by 50 per cent, and that radio listening falls off considerably after 7:30 P.M.

From all this several conclusions can be drawn even though both the range and extent of European data are limited. Program preferences in radio and television are basically the same the world over. Many Americans believe that public taste in Europe is more sophisticated than in the United States, but the data do not support that thesis: in fact, the same types of programs are liked and disliked everywhere.[114] By and large, the same things are happening on the European continent that occurred previously in Britain and the United States, where the television cycle began earlier. The status of radio both declines and changes as a consequence of television. Theater and cinema-going and reading are affected too, although television's relationship to the latter is neither so direct nor clear. Television has affected all the other mass media although it should neither be credited nor blamed for all the changes that have taken place.

CHAPTER VII

Conclusions and Comments

A CHANGE of scene provides new ideas and experiences and an opportunity to appraise one's normal environment with the greater understanding that grows out of a different perspective. Four-and-a-half years of residence in various European countries have led me to certain conclusions about the theory and practice of broadcasting both there and in the United States. In the process I have become aware of the extensive misinformation underlying the opinions and conclusions of most Americans about foreign broadcasting. I also have learned to appreciate how much broadcasters everywhere can benefit from regular exchanges of information, and particularly how certain attitudes and points of view, taken for granted in European broadcasting but unfortunately largely absent in the United States, might better become a part of the American heritage.

It is fundamental that radio and television be regarded as integral parts of the countries they serve, since they cannot be understood without reference to their historical, political, economic, social, religious, educational, and cultural settings. Unfortunately, much that is said about broadcasting overlooks its dependence on environment. People often mistakenly appraise foreign broadcasting as though it were taking place in their own country. A similar error is that another system is often explained by reference to factors impressing the observer because they differ—or seem to differ—from what he is used to at home. An example is the American fondness for characterizing European broadcasting as monopolistic (which it is); noncommercial (which it is not, for the most part); and subject to strict government control (which is only partly true). To the extent that these generalizations are correct, they are important; but they by no means explain all the distinctive aspects of European broadcasting. Furthermore, the broadcasting systems in different

235

European countries vary among themselves just as much as the countries do.

Americans, who like to think that no country could possibly approach the technical achievements of their own, fail to appreciate the quantity and quality of radio and television facilities in Europe. In fact, they are almost shocked when they first realize the amount and excellence of much European equipment; the size and elaborateness of many European radio and television buildings; and the extent of the remote pickup arrangements used for major public ceremonies and sporting events. While American radio is being cut back, there are new studio centers in many European cities—for example, Stockholm's Radio House and the superb Maison de Radio in Paris—that are lavish by any standards. Then there are the vast installations of the USSR. Although Soviet studios and equipment often appear drab to West Europeans and Americans, the extent of facilities in this huge country cannot fail to impress even a casual observer.

Nationwide FM has recently come to the United States. Thus, it is important to notice the extent of its growth on the Continent where it is emerging as the dominant sound broadcasting medium. Also noteworthy is the dissemination of programs by wire. In Italy a five-channel system serves subscribers in a number of larger cities; Switzerland's nationwide six-channel system distributes programs both from home and abroad; while in the USSR approximately half the radio receivers are fed by wire.

Although these developments are good, the lack of standardization in television surely is lamentable. It was bad enough to have four incompatible black-and-white systems—in the United Kingdom, France, Western and Eastern Europe—but much worse to permit two color systems. Yet Europe now is committed to one color standard for France and the Communist countries and another for everyone else. Even though conversion techniques will make possible the exchange of programs among countries, and dual-circuit sets will enable people living in border areas to receive programs on two standards, the absence of agreement will introduce confusion, lower technical performance, and increase costs. Europe's problem, of course, is basically political rather than technical: The engineers could easily have resolved their differences but national pride and ambition made agreement impossible. In this respect North America has the advantage of a single 525-line system, even though some observers believe that a higher definition should have been adopted.

Any consideration of broadcasting's legal structure must begin by classifying countries as democratic or totalitarian. Traditionally, the democratic ideal encourages a wide exchange of information so that the public may be informed in order to judge. Yet, as Justice Holmes wrote, freedom of expression may be limited if "The words used are used in such circumstances and are of such a nature as to create a clear and present danger." The totalitarian countries believe in a managed press taking a positive role in organizing the state, although they usually insist on their belief in freedom of expression. But the USSR constitution guarantees freedom of speech only "In conformity with the interests of the working people, and in order to strengthen the socialist system." Furthermore, the Soviets insist that freedom of speech is freedom only to tell the truth.

Yet, on the operational level, in deciding whether or not to censor a given statement, both sides proceed in much the same way: They accept the Holmes dictum and allow freedom of speech only up to the point where it poses a "clear and present danger." Most democratic countries are strong enough to permit a wide diversity of opinion, whereas the totalitarian regimes, usually younger and less secure, feel that the danger point is reached much sooner, and hence limit most debates to details rather than permitting public discussion of fundamental concepts.

But whatever the basic theories may be, in both democratic and totalitarian countries there always is more regulation of the electronic than of the printed media. This follows initially from the obvious need to assign frequencies and channels. But in addition broadcasting has a great potential for being beneficial or harmful. It can influence public opinion; it has spread confusion and induced riots; it can be received in the home without previewing; its domestic output often can be heard abroad. For these or other reasons, most enabling legislation requires broadcasters to provide information, education, and culture as well as entertainment. Furthermore, in countries without free discussion the system is operated to exclude unwanted opinions, while in countries with freedom of expression the law assures equal expression for all points of view.

The extent to which European broadcasters are free from government control is greatly underestimated in the United States. In those countries which do not permit freedom of information the output is carefully regulated, of course; but in Western countries with a high degree of press freedom, such as Switzerland, the Scandinavian countries, and West Germany, the broadcasters definitely are free from government interference.

There probably is no important difference anywhere between the freedom to broadcast and the freedom to print (with the possible exception of France), even though most European broadcasting organizations are state-chartered, whereas the Western press is not. But in this connection it should be noted that critics of American broadcasting often claim that its program policies are strongly influenced by the economic importance of advertising in the system, if not directly dictated by the advertisers themselves. However this may be, one must judge a broadcasting system only on the basis of how it actually functions. The point is not how it appears on paper, or how it would work in another country, but how it performs in its own environment.

In most of Europe broadcasting is regarded as a public service, whereas in the United States the broadcasters refer to themselves—and usually act—as an industry. The fact that in most European countries broadcasting developed originally as a government-sponsored noncommercial monopoly is undoubtedly the basic reason for this emphasis on service, just as American broadcasting was molded by its competitive and commercial nature.

Except for Portugal, Spain, and the United Kingdom, European broadcasting is noncompetitive within countries although the commercial stations on the periphery of France compete with the ORTF, and the radio pirates with the BBC. There is the competition of international broadcasting but domestic monopoly is the rule and competition the exception.*

Monopoly has both its good and bad aspects. It is conducive to balanced and supplementary rather than competitive programing. Network one can play symphonic music while network two is attracting the majority audience with a sports broadcast. On the other hand, it may explain a lack of initiative in devising new program services. Without the

---

* Throughout this chapter generalizations made about European broadcasting pertain to the major national systems and not to the private commercial stations in Luxembourg, Monaco, Andorra, and the Saar, or to the radio pirate stations, unless so stated.

spur of competition, policies may develop without reference to the interests, needs, and limitations of the audience. In the United States, on the other hand, there usually is too much concern with the audience: ratings and profits become the main consideration. In Europe monopoly appears to have had more good than bad results, although there is a constant need to guard against the complacency that may follow from a lack of competition.

European broadcasting is depending more and more on advertising for support. In fact, the only countries in Western Europe without some type of commercial broadcasting are France, Belgium, Norway, Denmark, Sweden, and Vatican City; practically all the Communist countries have some advertising; and it is quite possible that before the decade is out there will be commercial broadcasting in France, Belgium, and Sweden too.

The introduction of advertising has been preceded by much debate, with the United States cited to illustrate all points of view. One basic issue is whether commercially-supported systems can maintain high program standards. The high costs of television, particularly when second networks are planned, have led some broadcasting organizations to seek advertising, while others have opposed advertising lest it lead to the deterioration of programs. Advertisers advocate broadcast advertising, regarding it as an effective means to increase sales. On the other hand, the printed press usually opposes commercial broadcasting fearing a loss of revenue, or else wants to do the broadcasting itself in order to reap the profits. For the most part, disinterested public leaders, educators, and guardians of the established way of life have objected to advertising believing that it would lower program quality or lead to influence or control by advertisers.

As a consequence of all this, advertising has been introduced under conditions designed to avoid its possible disadvantages and excesses. Program control has been left to the traditional broadcasting organizations, and advertisements, limited to short announcements, are, on television, concentrated in a few early evening periods. The commercials themselves are carefully controlled—some countries exclude tobacco advertising, for example—and are scheduled between rather than within programs. Sponsorship has been eliminated; that is, advertisers may neither provide nor associate themselves with program material. The relationship of advertising to programs, therefore, is similar to that between the news and advertising columns of a newspaper.* To alleviate fears that commercial broadcasting might seriously injure the press, the amount and nature of advertising often have been limited, and in the Netherlands provision was made for a share of the proceeds to be assigned to the press should that prove financially necessary.

Europe has found a way to introduce broadcast advertising without affecting program balance or quality that deserves careful consideration in the United States. The fact that the major European systems are national monopolies whereas our stations are privately owned and competitive would make entirely unrealistic any attempt to completely adopt the European pattern. But the principle of separating responsibility for advertisements and programs, and of rigorously controlling both the amount and nature of advertisements, is attractive, and deserves thorough and sympathetic consideration.†

Despite fewer stations than the United States, European broadcasting achieves wide diversity in its programs. To the extent permitted by their economies all countries maintain multiple radio and television services. But since all networks and stations usually are controlled by a single organization, balanced and supplementary rather than competitive programing is the objective. Consequently, European audiences often have more real choices than do those in many American cities. One reason for this is that radio has not been reduced by television competition to the music and news format so dominant in the United States. Europeans visiting here often complain that although we have many stations the basic choices are limited and certain types of programs are not available at all during much of the day.

Although European radio services extend from early morning to mid-

* This is not the pattern, however, for Europe's private commercial stations, which are in the American style. The United Kingdom's ITA permits commercials at "natural breaks," but excludes them entirely from certain types of programs, including news.

† In this connection it should be noted that the Commission on Freedom of the Press offered as one of its conclusions in 1947: "We recommend that the radio networks, radio stations, the National Association of Broadcasters, and the organizations of writers, directors, and commentators, jointly or severally, establish the practice of separation of advertising from programs (this not to prevent the selling and programming of unrelated advertising announcements preceding or following programs). If the industry or its agencies fail to assume this responsibility within a reasonable time, we recommend that the F.C.C. set up this separation as a regulation or standard of performance to be considered in the license or relicense of stations." (Llewelyn White, *The American Radio*, pp. viii–ix.)

night or later, there is only a limited amount of daytime television, and most of that is for use in schools. The basic reason is economic, although many Europeans stress the virtual impossibility of obtaining worthwhile programs at any price to fill an eighteen- or twenty-four hour television day. Were it not for the financial advantages of long schedules, American stations might agree with this judgment, as do many of their critical viewers.

Compared to the United States, the over-all European emphasis is on serious rather than light programs, although much popular music and entertainment are broadcast. But one should not equate European networks with American educational stations: The European services have much greater resources and offer a full range of programs from light entertainment and sports to news, serious drama, and all types of music.

On the whole, program quality is high. Great emphasis is placed on news. All countries have extensive facilities for gathering and disseminating news, supplemented by international exchanges. This is one of the most exciting aspects of Western Europe's Eurovision, which, among other things, arranges for daily exchanges of television news via special microwave connections. Eastern Europe's Intervision now is beginning to participate too. American as well as European news is covered, and the balance and freedom of reporting are in keeping with the respective national information policies.

Political broadcasting is arranged in an interesting way. Observant Europeans have remarked that Section 315 of the American Communications Act of 1934, which requires stations to treat all candidates alike, has the effect of dividing time on the basis of party treasuries. Although this rule was temporarily suspended for the Kennedy-Nixon debates by an amendment which relieved stations of the obligation to give equal time to minority candidates, it remains the basic policy. European practice, on the other hand, is to divide time in proportion to party strength in the national legislatures, the main parties sharing about equally, with minority and splinter groups getting a few broadcasts each. Periods for political or controversial material are never sold in those countries with commercial broadcasting, and the total amount of time assigned is much less than in the United States, so the airwaves are not surfeited with politics in the weeks before elections.

The European record with educational and children's programs is superb. Most daytime hours on television and many on radio are devoted to programs for use in schools, in addition to which many educational, cultural, and documentary features are broadcast almost every evening at peak hours. While the very finest American public service programs often are superior to Europe's best, the Europeans lead when all the programs are considered.

America has developed educational stations to compensate for the shortcomings of its commercial broadcasters. Unfortunately, these educational stations seldom are adequately supported, for which reason their work usually is much below the serious output of Europe's national broadcasting organizations. Recently there has been a commendable surge of interest in these stations: The satellite proposal of the Ford Foundation, the searching probe of the Carnegie Commission, and the several proposals for federal support have illustrated recognition of the inadequate programing of commercial stations, and of the insufficient resources of their educational supplements. Europe, too, has some specialized services. But their development has not reduced the number of serious programs presented by the full-range networks, so that the casual tuner in Europe—who, like his American cousin is not usually seeking third or quality programs—is more apt to encounter a serious program than is an American dial-hopper sampling American commercial stations.

The Europeans do less well with light entertainment. Their resources are not always adequate to command the best stars, and even though their variety production sometimes is very elaborate, it frequently is ineffective. This is one reason a fair amount of continental television consists of American and British telefilms, usually with dialogue rerecorded in the local language, thereby raising some difficult policy problems. In addition to the financial and union aspects, there is much discussion of the cultural and educational effects of entertainment from abroad, so that almost all European broadcasters are under pressure to curtail if not eliminate such programs. Yet, because they are relatively inexpensive and are very popular, a fair number are scheduled by most countries, including those in the Communist bloc, except for the Soviet Union.

There also is the question of how much good or harm the extensive use of these films does the United States. The United States Information Agency has sponsored public opinion polls which support the conclusion that while the results are mainly good there still are some bad effects.[1] My own observation has been that however the average European viewer may react, professional groups tend to take a dim view of this American material, even though it contains some excellent, along with many trivial, programs. For us the problem is whether a country dedicated to freedom of information can prohibit or limit the exportation of what it views at home on the ground that its use abroad might be harmful to the national image. Probably not, except by persuasion. One practical recourse, however, is to encourage, through both private and government channels, the greater use abroad of other kinds of programs.

In sports Europe does very well. As a consequence of intense public interest, especially in international competitions, radio and television devote many hours to all major and minor sports. Until recently, when overtaken by news and public events, sports was the largest category for Eurovision and Intervision exchanges. Despite the periodic ups and downs of the cold war, East and West share planning and costs for the technical installations—often ingenious, elaborate, and expensive—necessary to cover these events.

The record with dramatic and musical programs is truly brilliant. Radio and television drama repertoires are amazing, and casts often include the finest actors available. Europe's broadcasting organizations are major sources of subsidy for all sorts of music. Most employ large permanent groups of performers, from jazz to symphony, and engage others as required. The live repertoire is magnificent, in addition to which enormous disc and tape collections provide many hours of material.

Inevitably one must compare the program services of the democratic and totalitarian countries. The fact that most of the latter are less fortunate economically necessarily limits the extent of their technical installations and curtails their program output. Surely they feel less impelled to respond to audience interests, even though well aware of audience needs as officially defined. There of course are basic differences of opinion about the proper role of the mass media. The democracies have more freedom and less guidance; the totalitarian states exploit the propaganda possibilities of all sorts of programs, from news to entertainment. While these conflicting concepts underlie some important variations in policy, program differences are not explainable solely on the grounds of ideology. Despite the strong propaganda motive permeating much of the totalitarian output, musical programs are affected very little; dramatic programs only partly; and most aspects of educational and cultural offerings to a limited—even though important—degree.

On the whole, though, much more imagination and skill are manifested in program planning and production in the democratic countries, the result both of superior financial resources and greater creative freedom. However, the musical and dramatic output of the Communist countries often is impressive. In television production there is no question at all about Western leadership, although East Germany's record is impressive. Perhaps its need to compete for audiences with West Germany is the main explanation.

Although conflicts persist between East and West, there are many exciting projects for program exchange. Neighboring countries with the same or similar languages have shared radio and television programs for many years. More recently the European Broadcasting Union's Eurovision and the International Radio and Television Organization's Intervision have encouraged the exchange of programs among their own members, and now there is exchange between the two groups as well. Program committees in each stimulate this activity, which includes everything from sports and entertainment to special events.

Here is a major project in international cooperation: EBU and OIRT members develop working relationships with each other at the same time they exchange programs which may in themselves advance international understanding. Even more important than the general educational objectives of such exchanges is their role in introducing new information and ideas into the Communist world. In view of television's great impact, surely these Eurovision-Intervision projects must open a new window on the West for Eastern viewers, at the same time that they provide additional information about the Communist countries to Western Europe and the rest of the world.

Although there has been a limited amount of audience research in continental countries, the results thus far show no basically important differences between Europe and the United States, and it is reasonable to assume that additional studies will contain no surprises for those who know the American record. Economic limitations seem to be the only barrier to nearly universal receiver ownership. The public's acceptance of television is just as enthusiastic as in the United States and the United Kingdom, both of which began the television cycle earlier. Television is having the same effect on the other media too, with decreased audiences for radio, theater, cinema, and sports. Program tastes are about the same everywhere, and with the same gradations for different social, economic, and educational levels. One point should be emphasized, however: while both Europeans and Americans prefer light entertainment and sports to more serious fare, and although American telefilms command good audiences in those countries using them, the very largest audiences almost always are for programs of local origin.

In the last analysis, judgment of a broadcasting system must be in terms of its objectives. Broadcasting is universally recognized as a medium of communication with consequent social obligations of a high order. Almost all the legislation recognizes this. The charter of the BBC —like the laws of many continental countries—refers to "the great value of . . . [broadcasting] services as means of disseminating information, culture, education, and entertainment." The American Communications Act of 1934 states that the FCC is to license broadcasting stations only after determining that "public interest, convenience, and necessity will be served." Stating the assignment in his context was the Soviet spokesman who wrote that the broadcaster's main task was to "contribute to the successful realization of the Party programme."

No broadcasting system, European or American, completely achieves its objectives. The best any can do is to maximize its strengths in an attempt to meet its challenges and solve its problems. Yet, on the whole, European broadcasting organizations perform very well. Most of the democratic countries have succeeded in maintaining freedom despite close government association. The totalitarian countries, on the other hand, measure their success in terms of how well they advance national and party objectives under close government supervision. But whatever their objectives, all concerned take a commendably serious view of their obligations toward society.

Europe can look to American broadcasting for enthusiasm and drive as well as for production ingenuity. But the United States can acquire from Europe the concepts that broadcasting is a public service rather than an industry, and that program policies should be determined by social values rather than investment returns.

APPENDIX

World Television Systems

The following tables provide information about the television broadcasting standards used in the principal countries of the world. The twelve major systems (designated by letters) are listed not only by the number of lines—the usual manner of identification—but also with reference to six of the other variables which distinguish them. The countries using each system are listed with information about channel limits. The tables have been adapted from the *World Radio TV Handbook 1967*, p. 243.

Appendix Table 1. The Twelve Major Television Systems*

System	Number of Lines	Channel Width Mc	Vision Band-width Mc	Vision/ Sound Separation Mc	Vestigial Side-band Mc	Vision Modu-lation	Sound Modu-lation
A	405	5	3	−3.5	0.75	Pos.	AM
B	625	7	5	+5.5	0.75	Neg.	FM
C	625	7	5	+5.5	0.75	Pos.	AM
D	625	8	6	+6.5	0.75	Neg.	FM
E	819	14	10	±11.5	2	Pos.	AM
F	819	7	5	+5.5	0.75	Pos.	AM
G	625	8	5	+5.5	0.75	Neg.	FM
H	625	8	5	+5.5	1.25	Neg.	FM
I	625	8	5.5	+6	1.25	Neg.	FM
K	625	8	6	+6.5	0.75	Neg.	FM
L	625	8	6	+6.5	1.25	Pos.	AM
M	525	6	4.2	+4.5	0.75	Neg.	FM

SOURCE: CCIR Report No. 308, 10th Plenary Assembly, Geneva, 1964.

* For all systems the field repetition frequency is 50 per second except for the 525-line system, used principally in North America and Japan, for which it is 60 per second.

Appendix Table 2. Channels and Megacycles for the Major Television Systems

Ch	Mc	Ch	Mc	Ch	Mc
		United States of America: System M 525 Lines			
A-2	55.25/ 59.75	A-6	83.25/ 87.75	A-10	193.25/197.75
A-3	61.25/ 65.75	A-7	175.25/179.75	A-11	199.25/203.75
A-4	67.25/ 71.75	A-8	181.25/185.75	A-12	205.25/209.75
A-5	77.25/ 81.75	A-9	187.25/191.75	A-13	211.25/215.75
		United Kingdom: System A 405 Lines			
B-1	45.00/ 41.50	B-6	179.75/176.25	B-11	204.75/201.25
B-2	51.75/ 48.25	B-7	184.75/181.25	B-12	209.75/206.25
B-3	56.75/ 53.25	B-8	189.75/186.25	B-13	214.75/211.25
B-4	61.75/ 58.25	B-9	194.75/191.25	B-14	219.75/216.25
B-5	66.75/ 63.25	B-10	199.75/196.25		
		Ireland: System I 625 Lines and System A 405 Lines			
IB	53.75/ 59.75	IF	191.25/197.25	IJ	215.25/221.25
ID	175.25/181.25	IH	207.25/213.25		
		Continental Europe: System B 625 Lines*			
E-2	48.25/ 53.75	E-5	175.25/180.75	E-9	203.25/208.75
E-2A	49.75/ 55.25	E-6	182.25/187.75	E-10	210.25/215.75
E-3	55.25/ 60.75	E-7	189.25/194.75	E-11	217.25/222.75
E-4	62.25/ 67.75	E-8	196.25/201.75	E-12	224.75/229.75
		France and Monaco: System E 819 Lines			
F-2	52.40/ 41.25	F-7	177.15/188.30	F-10	199.70/188.55
F-4	65.55/ 54.40	F-8A	185.25/174.10	F-11	203.45/214.60
F-5	164.00/175.15	F-8	186.55/175.40	F-12	212.85/201.70
F-6	173.40/162.25	F-9	190.30/201.45		
		Italy: System B 625 Lines			
A	53.75/ 59.25	D	175.25/180.85	G	201.25/206.75
B	62.25/ 67.75	E	183.75/189.25	H	210.25/206.75
C	82.25/ 87.75	F	192.25/197.75	H1	217.25/222.75
		USSR and OIRT Members:† System D 625 Lines			
I	49.75/ 56.25	V	93.25/ 99.75	IX	199.25/205.75
II	59.25/ 65.75	VI	175.25/181.75	X	207.25/213.75
III	77.25/ 83.75	VII	183.25/189.75	XI	215.25/221.75
IV	85.25/ 91.75	VIII	191.25/197.75	XII	223.25/229.75
		Morocco: System B 625 Lines			
4	163.25/168.75	7	187.25/192.75	9	203.25/208.75
5	171.25/176.75	8	195.25/200.75	10	211.25/216.75
6	179.25/184.75				
		Australia: System B 625 Lines			
0	46.25/ 51.75	5	102.25/107.75	8	189.25/194.75
1	57.25/ 62.75	5A	138.25/143.75	9	196.25/201.75
2	64.25/ 69.75	6	175.25/180.75	10	209.25/214.75
3	86.25/ 91.75	7	182.25/187.75	11	216.25/221.75
4	95.25/100.75				

* Excluding France, Monaco, Italy and OIRT members.
† Excluding the German Democratic Republic.

Ch	Mc	Ch	Mc	Ch	Mc
		New Zealand: System B 625 Lines			
1	45.25/ 50.75	4	175.25/180.75	7	196.25/201.75
2	55.25/ 60.75	5	182.25/187.75	8	203.25/208.75
3	62.25/ 67.75	6	189.25/194.75	9	210.25/215.75
		Japan: System M 525 Lines			
J-1	91.25/ 95.75	J-5	177.25/181.75	J-9	199.25/203.75
J-2	97.25/101.75	J-6	183.25/187.75	J-10	205.25/209.75
J-3	103.25/107.75	J-7	189.25/193.75	J-11	211.25/215.75
J-4	171.25/175.75	J-8	193.25/197.75	J-12	217.25/221.75

Appendix Table 3. VHF/UHF Television Systems, Standards G to L, for
Band IV/V in Europe and Africa*

Standard	Video Band-width (Mc)	Picture/ Sound Sepa-ration (Mc)	Vestigial Side-band (Mc)	Picture Modu-lation	Sound Modu-lation	Frequency of Chromi-nance Subcarrier (Mc)	Power Ratio Picture/ Sound
G	5	5.5	0.75	Neg.	FM	4.43	5:1
H	5	5.5	1.25	Neg.	FM	4.43	5:1
I	5.5	6	1.25	Neg.	FM	4.43	5:1
K	6	6.5	0.75	Neg.	FM	4.43	5:1
L	6	6.5	1.25	Pos.	AM	4.43	8:1

* The systems were adopted by the European Broadcasting Conference in Stockholm in 1961, and by the African Broadcasting Conference in Geneva in 1963. They are 625-line systems only.

Appendix Table 4. Channels* and Vision Megacycles for
European Television Systems

Ch	Vision Mc	Ch	Vision Mc	Ch	Vision Mc	Ch	Vision Mc
21......	471.25	33......	567.25	45......	663.25	57......	759.25
22......	479.25	34......	575.25	46......	671.25	58......	767.25
23......	487.25	35......	583.25	47......	679.25	59......	775.25
24......	495.25	36......	591.25	48......	687.25	60......	783.25
25......	503.25	37......	599.25	49......	695.25	61......	791.25
26......	511.25	38......	607.25	50......	703.25	62......	799.25
27......	519.25	39......	615.25	51......	711.25	63......	807.25
28......	527.25	40......	623.25	52......	719.25	64......	815.25
29......	535.25	41......	631.25	53......	727.25	65......	823.25
30......	543.25	42......	639.25	54......	735.25	66......	831.25
31......	551.25	43......	647.25	55......	743.25	67......	839.25
32......	559.25	44......	655.25	56......	751.25	68......	847.25

* The sound carrier frequency for each channel can be determined by adding the appropriate figure to the vision carrier frequency given in Appendix Table 3 (5.5Mc for systems G and H; 6Mc for system I; and 6.5Mc for systems K and L). In West Germany Ch38 is reserved for aero-navigation.

Appendix Table 5. UHF Channels in the United States of America and Japan

Ch	Mc	Ch	Mc	Ch	Mc
UHF Channels: United States of America					
A-14	471.25/475.75	A-38	615.25/619.75	A-62	759.25/763.75
A-15	477.25/481.75	A-39	621.25/625.75	A-63	765.25/769.75
A-16	483.25/487.75	A-40	627.25/631.75	A-64	771.25/775.75
A-17	489.25/493.75	A-41	633.25/637.75	A-65	777.25/781.75
A-18	495.25/499.75	A-42	639.25/643.75	A-66	783.25/787.75
A-19	501.25/505.75	A-43	645.25/649.75	A-67	789.25/793.75
A-20	507.25/511.75	A-44	651.25/655.75	A-68	795.25/799.75
A-21	513.25/517.75	A-45	657.25/661.75	A-69	801.25/805.75
A-22	519.25/523.75	A-46	663.25/667.75	A-70	807.25/811.75
A-23	525.25/529.75	A-47	669.25/673.75	A-71	813.25/817.75
A-24	531.25/535.75	A-48	675.25/679.75	A-72	819.25/823.75
A-25	537.25/541.75	A-49	681.25/685.75	A-73	825.25/829.75
A-26	543.25/547.75	A-50	687.25/691.75	A-74	831.25/835.75
A-27	549.25/553.75	A-51	693.25/697.75	A-75	837.25/841.75
A-28	555.25/559.75	A-52	699.25/703.75	A-76	843.25/847.75
A-29	561.25/565.75	A-53	705.25/709.75	A-77	849.25/853.75
A-30	567.25/571.75	A-54	711.25/715.75	A-78	855.25/859.75
A-31	573.25/577.75	A-55	717.25/721.75	A-79	861.25/865.75
A-32	579.25/583.75	A-56	723.25/727.75	A-80	867.25/871.75
A-33	585.25/589.75	A-57	729.25/733.75	A-81	873.25/877.75
A-34	591.25/595.75	A-58	735.25/739.75	A-82	879.25/883.75
A-35	597.25/601.75	A-59	741.25/745.75	A-83	885.25/889.75
A-36	603.25/607.75	A-60	747.25/751.75		
A-37	609.25/613.75	A-61	753.25/757.75		
UHF Channels: Japan					
45	663.25/667.75	51	699.25/703.75	57	735.25/739.75
46	669.25/673.75	52	705.25/709.75	58	741.25/745.75
47	675.25/679.75	53	711.25/715.75	59	747.25/751.75
48	681.25/685.75	54	717.25/721.75	60	753.25/757.75
49	687.25/691.75	55	723.25/727.75	61	759.25/763.75
50	693.25/697.75	56	729.25/733.75	62	765.25/769.75

NOTES, BIBLIOGRAPHY, AND INDEX

Notes

Chapter II. The Facilities for Continental Broadcasting

1. *International Telecommunication Convention: Final Protocol to the Convention; Additional Protocols to the Convention; Resolutions, Recommendations and Opinion. Montreux, 1965.* Art. 4, paras. 17–19 (hereafter cited as *Montreux Convention 1965*).

2. *Montreux Convention 1965*, Art. 4, paras. 20–21.

3. *Ibid.*, Annex 2, para. 409.

4. *Ibid.*, Art. 22, paras. 260–261; Art. 48, paras. 303–305.

5. *Radio Regulations: Additional Radio Regulations; Additional Protocol; Resolutions and Recommendations. Geneva, 1959.* Art. 18, para. 725 (hereafter cited as *Radio Regulations*).

6. *Ibid.*, Art. 7, para. 422; Art. 28, para. 962.

7. *International Telecommunication Convention: Final Protocol to the Convention; Additional Protocols to the Convention; Resolutions, Recommendations, and Opinion. Geneva, 1959.* Final Protocol, Arts. VIII, XXIII, XXVI; *Montreux Convention 1965*, Final Protocol, Arts. VIII, X, XIII, XXVIII; *Final Protocol to the International Telecommunication Convention* (Buenos Aires, 1952), Sec. IV.

8. Material about the structure and organization of the ITU may be found in the *Montreux Convention 1965*; in an ITU brochure, *International Telecommunication —What It Is—What It Does—How It Works*; and in the illustrated centennial history of the organization, *From Semaphore to Satellite*. By far the most complete account of the ITU appearing before this publication was by George Arthur Codding, Jr., *The International Telecommunication Union: An Experiment in International Cooperation.* Much information about the ITU is given in a book by the same author, *Broadcasting without Barriers* (hereafter cited as Codding).

9. Its address is Place des Nations, 1211 Geneva 20, Switzerland.

10. *Radio Regulations*, Art. 5. A summary of the assignments is given in the *World Radio TV Handbook 1967*, 21st Ed., p. 274. Unless otherwise indicated, information about allocations, frequencies, and power is taken from this series (cited hereafter as *WRTH*). Although not so stated, references to kilocycles, megacycles, and other broadcast frequencies are on a *per second* basis; that is, the Washington 1927 allocation table referred to above extended from 10 kilocycles *per second* to 60 megacycles *per second*.

11. Codding, pp. 92–108.

12. *Ibid.*, pp. 94–95.

13. The composition and work of the International Frequency Registration Board are defined in the *Montreux Convention 1965*, Art. 12. See also Codding, pp. 88–92, 98–102; *From Semaphore to Satellite*, pp. 247–260.

14. *Montreux Convention 1965*, Art. 13; *From Semaphore to Satellite*, pp. 229–239.

15. United Nations, *General Assembly Resolution* 841 (IX), December 17, 1954.

16. Codding, pp. 70–75.

17. London *Times*, January 31, 1956, pp. 8, 12; London *Times*, March 14, 1956, p. 10; *New York Times*, January 31, 1956, pp. 1, 4; *New York Times*, March 7, 1956, p. 8; London *Times*, January 28, 1956, p. 6; London *Times*, January 16, 1959, p. 11; *Parliamentary Debates: Official Reports*, 5th Series, Commons 1955–1956, 548:587 (January 30).

18. London *Times*, July 26, 1966, p. 8.

19. United Nations General Assembly, *Official Records*: Fifth Session, Supplement No. 3 (A/1345), 1950, p. 67, and Supplement No. 20 (A/1775), Resolutions, p. 44; L. John Martin, *International Propaganda: Its Legal and Diplomatic Control*, contains various references to jamming and international law. See Index under "Radio," p. 276; also pp. 77–88.

20. United Nations General Assembly, *Official Records*: Fifth Session, 325 Plenary Meeting, December 14, 1950, pp. 666–667.

21. London *Times*, April 14, 1966, p. 6; London *Times*, June 24, 1966, p. 19; London *Times*, October 19, 1966, p. 12.

22. London *Times*, October 1, 1966, p. 6; London *Times*, October 24, 1966, p. 1.

23. London *Times*, June 7, 1966, p. 10; *EBU Review*, 85A:130 (June 1964); *EBU Review*, 87A:229–230 (October 1964); *EBU Review*, 89A:38–39 (February 1965); *New York Times*, November 28, 1965, p. 23L; *EBU Review*, 88A:285 (December 1964); Albert Namurois, "The Prevention of the Activities of 'Pirate' Broadcasting Stations," *EBU Review*, 90B:36–46 (March 1965).

24. Art. V.

25. Council of Europe, *European Agreement for the Prevention of Broadcasts Transmitted from Stations Outside National Territories*.

26. *A Bill to suppress broadcasting from ships, aircraft and certain marine structures*; London *Times*, July 29, 1966, p. 10; *New York Times*, July 29, 1966, p. 2; E. C. Robbins, "The Postmaster General and the Pirates," *EBU Review*, 102B:52–53 (March 1967).

27. Documentation Service I. F. J., VIII (42):1–2 (October 16, 1965); *New York Times*, June 23, 1966, p. 1; London *Times*, June 23, 1966, pp. 1, 12; London *Times*, October 13, 1966, p. 17; London *Times*, November 25, 1966, pp. 1–10; London *Times*, November 26, 1966, p. 8; London *Times*, November 30, 1966, p. 12; London *Times*, December 14, 1966, p. 6; London *Times*, January 2, 1967, p. 10; *Variety*, January 18, 1967, p. 39.

28. *New York Times*, November 28, 1965, p. 23.

29. British Broadcasting Corporation, "Why No Continuous Pop?" *BBC Record* 45, pp. 1–3.

30. *New York Times*, July 29, 1966, p. 2C; London *Times*, December 21, 1966, pp. 5–9; *Broadcasting. Presented to Parliament by the Post Master General by Command of Her Majesty December 1966*, pp. 6–7.

31. Karel Remes, "Prevention of Broadcasts Transmitted from Artificial Islands. Dutch Legislation on Installations on the High Seas," *EBU Review*, 90B:47–52 (March 1965).

32. *Ibid.*, pp. 49–50.

33. A. J. P. Tammes, "Freedom of the High Seas. Legitimacy of a 'Television Island,'" *EBU Review*, 86B:38–40 (July 1964).

34. The most convenient source of information about technical installations is a yearly publication, the *World Radio TV Handbook*.

35. *Annuario RAI 1966*, pp. 327–342. For program details on Italian broadcasting, see Chapter V.

36. "Germany and the Copenhagen Plan," *EBU Bulletin*, VI (No. 33):487–502 (September–October 1955); *EBU Review*, 84A:81–82 (April 1964). Maps showing

the locations of broadcasting stations in East and West Germany will be found in *Internationales Handbuch für Rundfunk und Fernsehen 1965/66,* pp. C27–36.

37. *WRTH 1967,* pp. 100–101.

38. Henning Wicht, "Sound Radio in the Federal Republic of Germany," *EBU Review,* 78B:27 (March 1963); *WRTH 1967,* pp. 94–100.

39. *BBC Handbook 1967,* pp. 106, 138.

40. *EBU Review,* 89A:32–33 (February 1965).

41. "The Development of Stereophonic Broadcasting," *EBU Review,* 85A:132–134 (June 1964); *Broadcasting,* June 8, 1966, p. 81; J. J. Geluk, "The Introduction of Stereophonic Broadcasting in the Netherlands," *EBU Review,* 97A:101–106 (June 1966); "BBC Stereophonic Broadcasting," *EBU Review,* 98A:173 (August 1966).

42. UNESCO, *Statistics on Radio and Television 1950–1960,* p. 60. See also "Radio and Television Licence Statistics, 1965," *EBU Review,* 96B:37 (March 1966).

43. *BBC Annual Report 1965–66,* p. 63; *BBC Handbook 1967,* p. 104; "Radio and Television Licence Statistics, 1966," *EBU Review,* 102B:36 (March 1967); Codding, pp. 28–30, 114–116, includes materials on the technical aspects of wired broadcasting.

44. UNESCO, *World Communications, Press, Radio, Television, Film,* p. 364. For a discussion of the technical aspects of wired broadcasting, including remote control of such networks, see "Wired Broadcasting Networks Automatization," *OIRT,* No. 4: 162–172 (1960). See also "Multiprogramme Wired Broadcasting in the USSR," *OIRT,* No. 6:27–31 (1962); Robert C. Sorensen and Leszek L. Meyer, "Local Uses of Wired Radio in Communist Ruled Poland," *Journalism Quarterly,* 32 (No. 3):343–348 (1955).

45. "Concert Hall of the Rumanian Radio," *OIRT,* No. 4:26–32 (1962).

46. Information supplied by RAI; *EBU Review,* 80B:48 (July 1963).

47. *L'Onde Electrique,* June 1965.

48. *France Actuelle,* March 15, 1964, p. 1.

49. *EBU Review,* 86A:168–173 (August 1964). Technical facilities are not the primary interest of this study and no further details are given here about equipment. Since equipment changes rapidly any detailed description would soon be outmoded anyway. An excellent source of information about the current design, construction, and operation of European radio and television equipment is the technical portion (Part A) of the European Broadcasting Union's *Review.* The *Review of the International Radio and Television Organization* does the same thing, though less well, for Eastern Europe.

50. All issues of *WRTH* contain charts comparing the various television systems. See, for example, *WRTH 1967,* p. 243. Details of the *OIRT* system are outlined in S. V. Novakovskij and D. I. Ermakov, "Consideration of Fundamental Characteristics of the OIRT Monochrome Television Standard," *OIRT,* No. 3:111–123 (1960).

51. The distinctions are detailed in *WRTH 1967,* p. 243.

52. For technical details of the three, see *EBU Review,* 87A:209–215 (October 1964).

53. *New York Times,* March 23, 1965, p. 1.

54. London *Times,* July 19, 1966, p. 1; London *Times,* July 23, 1966, p. 1; "Colour Television in Europe," *EBU Review,* 98A:138–141 (August 1966); Georges Hansen, "Colour Television Standards for Europe," *WRTH 1967,* pp. 28, 30. The assembly also was concerned with other matters pertaining to television as well as to FM radio and magnetic tape recording, although the discussion of television standards was the most important item.

55. "Meeting of CCIR Study Groups and XI in Vienna," *OIRT,* No. 4:41 (1965).

56. USIA, Research and Reference Service, *Overseas Television Developments in 1964,* p. 1; cf. *EBU Review,* 89A:46 (February 1965). It should be noted, however,

that the European figure includes many low power relay and satellite stations, so that the difference is much less than the figures suggest.

57. UNESCO, *Television: A World Survey*, pp. 12–14; *BBC Handbook 1967*, pp. 216–219.

58. *EBU Review*, 102A:86 (April 1967).

59. *WRTH 1967*, p. 244. Unless otherwise indicated, data on European television transmission facilities are based on *WRTH 1967*.

60. European Broadcasting Union, *This Is the EBU*, pp. 35–48; J. Treeby Dickinson, "Eurovision in 1964," *WRTH 1965*, pp. 20–22; Edgar T. Martin and George Jacobs, "Inter-Continental Television: Progress 1964—Future 1965," *WRTH 1965*, pp. 44–46; J. Treeby Dickinson, "Eurovision in 1965," *WRTH 1966*, pp. 30–32, 48; Ales Suchy, "Intervision in 1965," *WRTH 1966*, pp. 38–39; J. Treeby Dickinson, "Eurovision in 1966," *WRTH 1967*, pp. 22, 26; Marcel Bezençon, "Eurovision, or the Price of Fame," *EBU Review*, 85B:8–9 (May 1964); "Eurovision: Five More Years of Expansion," *EBU Review*, 85B:17–20 (May 1964); Jean D'Arcy, "Eurovision," *EBU Review*, 56B:6–12 (July 1959).

61. *BBC Handbook 1957*, pp. 215–216. Some other first-time European hookups are reviewed by Martin Pulling in "International Television," *EBU Review*, 79B:11–15 (May 1963).

62. For much more complete information about the earlier technical aspects of Eurovision, see Barber, *Eurovision as an Expression of International Cooperation in Western Europe*, pp. 190–200 (hereafter cited as Barber).

63. "Creation of the Intervision," *OIRT*, No. 2:70–74 (1960); "Intervision," *OIRT*, No. 2:3–5 (1962); "Experience in the Technical Operation of the Intervision Network," *OIRT*, No. 2:26–38 (1963).

64. Ales Suchy, "Intervision in 1965," *WRTH 1966*, pp. 38–39.

65. USIA, Research and Reference Service, *Overseas Television Developments in 1964*, p. 8; Frantisek Smolik, "Le Centre de Radiodiffusion de Prague," *OIRT*, No. 5:13–16 (1966).

66. G. Schadwinkel and G. Stump, "Das Modernisierte Tagesschau-Studio des NDR in Hamburg-Lokstedt," *Rundfunktechnische Mitteilungen*, No. 2:100–109 (1964).

67. Jerzy Rutkowski, "Central Radio and Television Station in Warsaw," *OIRT*, No. 4:14–16 (1961); Irena Kenska-Vyrozembska, "Construction of the Central Radio and Television House in Warsaw," *OIRT*, No. 5:23–30 (1964); "The Central Radio and TV House," *OIRT Information*, No. 5:14–15 (1965).

68. For data on new television production plans for West Germany's Zweites Deutsches Fernsehen in Mainz, see *EBU Review*, 97A:117–118 (June 1966); on a fifteen- to twenty-year radio and television project in Helsinki, *EBU Review*, 98A:168 (August 1966); on a new television center in Cologne, *EBU Review*, 98A:169–170 (August 1966).

69. V. I. Parkhomenko and A. G. Spirin, "Experience Gained with Practical Operation of KADR Video Tape Recorders at the Soviet Central Television," *OIRT*, No. 2:28–32 (1964); *OIRT Information*, No. 2:15 (1964).

70. "Broadcasting the IXth Winter Olympic Games: The Facilities Employed by the 'Osterreichischer Rundfunk at Innsbruck,'" *EBU Review*, 85A:96–109 (June 1964); Teiji Sahara, "Broadcasting the Olympic Games, Tokyo, 1964," *EBU Review*, 89A:3–12 (February 1965); Aldo Riccomi, "Eurovision and the Tokyo Olympic Games," *EBU Review*, 89A:13–19 (February 1965).

71. J. Treeby Dickinson, "Eurovision in 1964," *WRTH 1965*, pp. 20–22; Edgar T. Martin and George Jacobs, "Inter-Continental Television: Progress 1964—Future 1965," *WRTH 1965*, pp. 44–46; Edgar T. Martin and George Jacobs, "Inter-Continental Television Programs 1966—Future 1967," *WRTH 1967*, pp. 36, 38, 44; J. Treeby Dickinson, "Eurovision in 1965," *WRTH 1966*, pp. 30–32, 48. For a re-

view of the educational and cultural potentialities of satellite communication, see UNESCO, *Report of the Meeting of Experts on the Use of Space Communication by the Mass Media,* December 6–10, 1965.

72. *From Semaphore to Satellite,* pp. 283–304; George Jacobs, "Where to Listen for Satellite Signals," *WRTH 1966,* pp. 54, 58, 60.

73. Barber, pp. 285–286.

74. London *Times,* May 20, 1966, p. 16.

75. Leonard H. Marks, "The Role of Broadcasters in Space Communications," *EBU Review,* 84B:46–50 (March 1964); Leonard H. Marks, "Early Bird: A New Horizon for Broadcasts," *EBU Review,* 93B:41–44 (September 1965); Robert Lindsay, "What Will the Satellites Communicate?" *NAEB Journal,* July–August 1964, pp. 37–44; Robert Lindsay, "Forward in Space—Backward in Time," *Television Quarterly,* I (No. 4):50–54 (November 1962).

76. London *Times,* December 1, 1965, p. 9.

Chapter III. The Structure and Organization of Continental Broadcasting

1. For a thorough analysis of the Federal Communication Commission's legal powers over radio and television in the United States, see Joel Rosenbloom, "Authority of the Federal Communications Commission," in John E. Coons, ed., *Freedom and Responsibility in Broadcasting,* pp. 96–170.

2. *Radio Regulations,* Art. 18, para. 725.

3. *Communications Act of 1934,* Sec. 307 (a).

4. Paulu, *British Broadcasting,* p. 362.

5. Apparently Japan is the only country whose laws ever required the government to license stations without reference to program performance. (Namurois, *The Organization of Broadcasting,* pp. 50–57, hereafter cited as Namurois.)

6. Four points of view—authoritarian, libertarian, social responsibility, and Soviet Communist—are outlined in Fred S. Siebert, "The Role of Mass Communication in American Society," *Mass Media and Education: The Fifty-Third Yearbook of the National Society for the Study of Education,* Part 2, pp. 13–29. These are further treated in Fred S. Siebert, Theodore Peterson, and Wilbur Schramm, *Four Theories of the Press.*

7. John Milton, "Areopagitica: A Speech for the Liberty of Unlicensed Printing," *Areopagitica and Other Prose Writings,* pp. 58–59.

8. John Stuart Mill, "On Liberty," *Political Philosophers,* pp. 151–152.

9. Carl L. Becker, *Freedom and Responsibility in the American Way of Life,* p. 33.

10. *Schenck v. the United States,* 249 U.S. 47 (1919), p. 52.

11. Inkeles, *Public Opinion in Soviet Russia: A Study in Mass Persuasion,* p. 135. Chapter 9 of this book, "The Soviet Conception of the Press," is an excellent analysis of the Communist use of the information media.

12. G. Alexandrova, *Political Dictionary,* p. 422.

13. *Constitution of the USSR,* p. 26.

14. *Jugoslovenska Radiotelevizija Yearbook 1965,* Arts. 1, 2, 3, 6, 7, pp. 284–285. (Publications in this series are hereafter cited as *Yugoslav Yearbook,* followed by the year of publication.)

15. Namurois, pp. 61–62.

16. *Ibid.,* p. 78.

17. In earlier years, much of Europe's broadcasting was privately operated. (Jean Gantelme, "From Private Enterprise to the Idea of Public Service," *EBU Bulletin of Documentation and Information,* 1:41–54 (May 15, 1960). It will be noted that Gantelme's categorizations do not coincide with those of Namurois followed in this chapter.) Between 1920 and 1930, private enterprise was predominant in the systems

of eleven countries: Belgium, Bulgaria, Czechoslovakia, Denmark, Finland, the Netherlands, Poland, Spain, Sweden, the United Kingdom, and Yugoslavia. By 1950, however, only three such countries remained: Andorra, Monaco, and Spain. During this same decade, private operations administered as a concession from the state were the rule in seven countries: Estonia, France, Germany, Hungary, Italy, Luxembourg, and Portugal. On the other hand, whereas between 1920 and 1930 there were state-constituted corporations in only seven countries—France, Latvia, Lithuania, Sweden, Switzerland, the USSR, and Yugoslavia, by 1950 this was true of twenty: Albania, Belgium, Bulgaria, Czechoslovakia, Denmark, France, Germany, Greece, Latvia, Lithuania, Norway, Poland, Portugal, Rumania, Spain, Switzerland, Turkey, United Kingdom, USSR, and Yugoslavia.

The trend from private to public operation after World War II resulted from the general extension of government activities; increased recognition of the social and political value of broadcasting; and the necessity for large government grants to rebuild facilities devastated during the war. But this trend from private to public operation did not necessarily mean the elimination of commercial support; in fact, since the advent of television, there has been an increase in commercial broadcasting on the European continent, largely to meet higher program costs.

18. Unless otherwise indicated, material on broadcasting in the Soviet Union was secured in writing and from personal conferences with Soviet broadcasting authorities. Supplementary printed sources include Namurois, pp. 62–63; Inkeles, *Public Opinion in Soviet Russia*, pp. 226–233; E. W. Ziebarth, "Electronic Media in the Soviet Union," *Quarterly Journal of Speech*, 45 (No. 3):275–281 (October 1959); William S. Howell, "Program Production at Radio Moscow," *Journal of Broadcasting*, Fall 1960, pp. 327–338. E. W. Ziebarth and William S. Howell, "The Soviet Airwaves," in Robert T. Holt and John E. Turner, eds., *Soviet Union: Paradox and Change*, pp. 184–206.

19. Hugh Lunghi, "Shake-Up in Soviet Broadcasting," *The Listener*, March 31, 1960, pp. 565–567; "On the Further Development of Soviet Television: Decree of the CC CPSU January 29, 1960," *The Soviet Press in Translation*, II (No. 6): March 1962; "On Measures for the Further Improvement of the Work of Radio Broadcasting and Television," *The Soviet Press in Translation*, IV (No. 5): January 1964.

20. U.S. Foreign Broadcast Information Service, "The 23rd Congress of the Soviet Communist Party. Proceedings and Related Materials." *Daily Report: Supplement, USSR and East Europe*, 10:20 (April 8, 1966); *New York Times*, April 9, 1966, p. 2.

21. Namurois, p. 63. In all cases the sources cited for East European countries are supplemented by written and interview data received directly from the individual broadcasting administrations.

22. Namurois, p. 54, 63; Pigé, pp. 52–53; Aleksander Landau, "Organization and Finances in the Polish Radio and Television," *OIRT*, No. 5:5–9 (1962); "The Programme Council of the Radio and Television Committee," *OIRT Information*, No. 7: 11–12 (1964).

23. Terrou and Solal, *Legislation for Press, Film, and Radio*, pp. 199–200 (hereafter cited as Terrou and Solal); Pigé, pp. 53–54; Walter B. Emery, *Five European Broadcasting Systems*, pp. 52–61.

24. Namurois, pp. 63–64; Terrou and Solal, pp. 172–178.

25. Terrou and Solal, pp. 200–202.

26. The structure of Yugoslav broadcasting is outlined in *Yugoslav Yearbook 1965*, pp. 9–11. The same volume contains "The Basic Law on Radiobroadcasting Institutions," pp. 265–273; "Regulations on the Organization and Functioning of the Yugoslav Sound Broadcasting Service," pp. 278–283; "Law on the Press and Other Media of Information," pp. 284–287; and "Basic Law on Radio Communications," pp. 287–289.

27. The same pattern has been introduced for newspapers too (Carter R. Bryan,

NOTES

"The Press System of Yugoslavia: Communism with a Difference," *Journalism Quarterly*, 43 (No. 2):291–299 (Summer 1966).)

28. "Regulations on the Organization and Functioning of the Yugoslav Sound Broadcasting Service," *Yugoslav Yearbook 1965*, p. 281.

29. Pigé, p. 58; Terrou and Solal, pp. 179–186.

30. London *Times*, March 9, 1961, p. 11; London *Times*, February 23, 1962, p. 10; London *Times*, May 16, 1962, p. 10; *New York Times*, February 8, 1963, p. 1; London *Times*, February 8, 1963, p. 8; *New York Times*, February 21, 1963, p. 8; London *Times*, February 12, 1963, p. 10; London *Times*, July 11, 1963, p. 8; London *Times*, April 24, 1964, p. 10; *Variety*, May 13, 1964; *Listener*, February 20, 1958, p. 309; *Economist*, March 2, 1963, p. 785.

31. Wilson P. Dizard, *Television: A World View*, pp. 143, 145.

32. France. *National Assembly Debates*, May 26, 1964, pp. 1376–1379.

33. *Ibid.*, p. 1379.

34. London *Times*, May 22, 1964, p. 10.

35. France. *National Assembly Debates*, May 28, 1964, p. 1509.

36. *Office de Radiodiffusion-Télévision Française: Statuts, Régime Financier, Comités de Programmes* (hereafter cited as *Statuts*), Art. 1; "A New Statute for the French Broadcasting Organization," *EBU Review*, 87B:33–35 (September 1964).

37. *Statuts*, Art. 2.

38. *Ibid.*, Art. 3.

39. *Ibid.*, Art. 6.

40. *Ibid.*, Art. 8.

41. *Décret no. 64-740 du juillet 1964*; Namurois, pp. 101–102.

42. *Le Monde*, May 4, 1965, p. 6.

43. Henning Wicht, "Sound Radio in the Federal Republic of Germany," *EBU Review*, 78B:25–27 (March 1963); Hans Brack, "Broadcasting in the Federal Republic of Germany," *EBU Review*, 51B:2–3 (October 1958); *Internationales Handbuch für Rundfunk und Fernsehen 1965/66*, pp. C1–11 (hereafter cited as *Internationales Handbuch 1965/66*).

44. Namurois, pp. 93–94; Law on the "Hessischer Rundfunk" of 2nd October 1948.

45. Namurois, pp. 47–48; Hans Brack, "Organization of the Supra-Regional Responsibilities of Broadcasting in the Federal Republic of Germany," *EBU Review*, 62B:13–17 (July 1960); *Internationales Handbuch 1965/66*, pp. C24–26.

46. Hans Brack, "Organization of the Supra-Regional Responsibilities of Broadcasting in the Federal Republic of Germany," *EBU Review*, 62B:13–17 (July 1960); Egon Wagner, "Report from the Federal Republic of Germany," *EBU Review*, 67B:24 (May 1961).

47. London *Times*, October 15, 1959, p. 10; London *Times*, July 26, 1960, p. 8; *Television Today*, August 11, 1960, p. 20; London *Times*, August 26, 1960, p. 9; London *Times*, September 27, 1960, p. 8; London *Times*, August 20, 1960, p. 11; London *Times*, March 1, 1961, p. 10; London *Times*, March 2, 1961, p. 10; London *Times*, March 17, 1961, p. 13; Gerald Braunthal, "Federalism in Germany: The Broadcasting Controversy," *Journal of Politics*, 24:545–561, August 1962.

48. Namurois, pp. 76–77; Egon Wagner, "Report from the Federal Republic of Germany," *EBU Review*, 72B:48–51 (March 1962).

49. Egon Wagner, "Report from the Federal Republic of Germany," *EBU Review*, 84B:51–52 (March 1964); Egon Wagner, "Report from the Federal Republic of Germany," *EBU Review*, 91B:69–70 (May 1965); *New York Times*, March 20, 1965, p. 10; "Will the Press Octopus Grab TV?" quoted from *Der Spiegel*, *Atlas*, April 1965, pp. 218–221; "Press vs. Radio: A Problem of Competition in a German Context," *EBU Review*, 94B:77–80 (November 1965); Egon Wagner, "Report from the Federal Republic of Germany," *EBU Review*, 100B:70–73 (November 1966).

50. Albert Namurois, "The New Charter for Broadcasting in Belgium," *EBU*

Review, 63B:2–10 (September 1960); Namurois, pp. 48–49, 95–98, 104–105; Walter B. Emery, *Five European Broadcasting Systems,* pp. 1–20.

51. Albert Namurois, "The New Charter for Broadcasting in Belgium," *EBU Review,* 63B:10 (September 1960).

52. "The Origin, Development and Present Organization of Sound and Television Broadcasting in the Netherlands," *EBU Review,* 48B:9–11 (April 1958); Namurois, pp. 46–47, 54; Terrou and Solal, p. 199; NRU Press Service, *The Netherlands Radio Union in the Evolution of Dutch Broadcasting;* Walter B. Emery, *Five European Broadcasting Systems,* pp. 21–38. Information also was received from the Dutch broadcasting authorities.

53. *Televisie Nieuws,* No. 6:1(1962).

54. A. J. J. Van der Made, "The Netherlands: Proposals for Commercial Television," *EBU Review,* 78B:35–36 (March 1963); "The Second Television Programme in the Netherlands," *EBU Review,* 89B:14–16 (January 1965); John Tebbel, "How Europe Fights Commercial TV," *Saturday Review,* August 1965, pp. 46–47; Pigé, pp. 84–86; *Televisie Nieuws,* No. 2:4–5 (1962).

55. *New York Times,* February 27, 1965, p. 6; *New York Times,* March 3, 1965, p. 6; London *Times,* February 27, 1965, p. 8.

56. J. van Santbrink, "Legislation and the Broadcasting Institutions in the Netherlands. Part II: The Transitional System (1965) for Sound Broadcasting and Television in the Netherlands," *EBU Review,* 102B:53–59 (March 1967).

57. *Televisie Nieuws,* No. 4:1–4 (1967).

58. Information for this section was provided by the Dutch broadcasting authorities.

59. "RAI Monopoly Tested in the Constitutional Court," *EBU Review,* 63B:38–39 (September 1960); Paolo Greco, "Monopoly in Television Broadcasting Services and Freedom of Expression," *EBU Review,* 64B:29–34 (November 1960).

60. Cesare Mannucci, "Structure and Policy of the RAI-TV," *Gazette* 11 (No. 1): 57–67 (1965).

61. Namurois, pp. 54, 82, 93, 108; *EBU Review,* 60B:23–24 (March 1960); Olof Rydbeck, "Broadcasting in Sweden," *EBU Review,* 80B:6–10 (July 1963); Terrou and Solal, pp. 197–199; Sveriges Radio Aktiebolag (Articles of the Association).

62. Ingemar Lindblad, "The Future of Swedish Broadcasting," *EBU Review,* 92B: 15–18 (July 1965).

63. *EBU Bulletin,* VII (No. 39):681–682 (September–October 1956).

64. This was to be Article 36 *bis.* Namurois, p. 84.

65. *Concession pour l'usage des installations électriques et radioélectriques de l'entreprise des postes, téléphones et télégraphes suisses en vue de la diffusion publique de programmes de radiodiffusion sonore et de télévision* (hereafter cited as *License*); *EBU Review,* 89B:34–36 (January 1965); Namurois, pp. 53–54, 82–85.

66. *EBU Review,* 89B:35 (January 1965); *License,* Art. 13.

67. Arts. 6, 11.

68. Art. 14. See pp. 105–109 below for further details.

69. Pigé, pp. 95–98; Namurois, pp. 89–90; *Les Cahiers Luxembourgeois: Radio-Télé Luxembourg,* pp. 30–32, 46.

70. See pp. 14–15 above for information as to its technical installations and power.

71. *Le Monde,* May 29, 1965, p. 1.

72. Pigé, pp. 111–112; Egon Wagner, "Report from the Federal Republic of Germany," *EBU Review,* 91B:70–72 (May 1965).

73. Pigé, pp. 81–83; *New York Times,* January 14, 1965, p. 71; *Der Spiegel,* April 28, 1965, p. 94; "Un Troisième Poste Périphérique sur Ondes Longues: Radio Monte-Carlo," *Entreprise,* January 15, 1966, pp. 43, 47.

74. *Der Spiegel,* April 28, 1965, p. 94.

NOTES

Chapter IV. The Finances of Continental Broadcasting

1. Eugène Pons, *General Considerations on Licence Fees for Radio and Television Sets* (hereafter cited as Pons); "Radio and Television Licence Fees, European Broadcasting Zone, as of 31 December 1965," *EBU Review*, 98B:31–33 (July 1966); "Radio and Television Licence Statistics, 1965, European Broadcasting Zone," *EBU Review*, 96B:37 (March 1966).

2. "Radio and Television Licence Statistics, 1965, European Broadcasting Zone," *EBU Review*, 96B:37 (March 1966); "Radio and Television Licence Statistics, 1966, European Broadcasting Zone," *EBU Review*, 102B:36 (March 1967).

3. "Radio and Television Licence Fees, European Broadcasting Zone, as of 31 December 1965," *EBU Review*, 98B:31–33 (July 1966).

4. Pons, pp. 27, 40; *Variety*, January 5, 1966, p. 117.

5. *New York Times*, March 22, 1966, p. 83L; London *Times*, September 16, 1966, p. 9; London *Times*, November 9, 1966, p. 1. In Britain even long-term prisoners with radios in their cells must have licenses. (London *Times*, April 5, 1966, p. 6); *Annual Report and Accounts of the British Broadcasting Corporation 1965–66*, p. 102.

6. Pons, pp. 31–32, 33, 42.

7. Paulu, *British Broadcasting*, p. 414.

8. Paulu, *British Broadcasting in Transition*, p. 12.

9. "Bringing Christ to the Nations," in Polish, Slovene, German, and Russian.

10. *Internationales Handbuch für Rundfunk und Fernsehen 1965/66* (hereafter cited as *Internationales Handbuch 1965/66*), p. D3; Werbung im Rundfunk GmbH, *Werbefunk und Werbefernsehen in Hessen: Planungsunterlagen 1966*. All published sources are supplemented with information received from officials of West German broadcasting organizations.

11. "News of Commercial Television," *EBU Review*, 53B:27 (February 1959); "Germany (Federal Republic): Present Position of Commercial Television," *EBU Review*, 62B:26–27 (July 1960); Egon Wagner, "Report from the Federal Republic of Germany," *EBU Review*, 84B:52 (March 1964).

12. *Internationales Handbuch 1965/66*, pp. D3–4, 10–11.

13. *Ibid.*, p. D13.

14. "Draft Law on Radio-Televised Advertising in the German Federal Republic," Fédération Internationale des Editeurs de Journaux et Publications, *Bulletin d'Informations*, April 1965, pp. 8–9.

15. Bruno Vasari, *Financial Aspects of Broadcasting*, p. 43; *Broadcasting*, November 29, 1965, pp. 74–75.

16. Most of the material on broadcast advertising in Italy was provided by RAI Reference also was made to RAI, *This is RAI*, p. 15; Pigé, p. 248; Harry W. McMahan, "Dixan Proves Exciting Potentials of Carosello Format," *Advertising Age*, February 27, 1967, pp. 78, 80.

17. *EBU Review*, 47B:58 (February 1958).

18. Pigé, p. 225.

19. "Advertising on Swiss Television," *EBU Review*, 90B:33–34 (March 1965).

20. *EBU Review*, 90B:33 (March 1965); Jacques Bourquin, "A Year's Advertising on Swiss Television," *Bulletin d'Informations*, January 1966, pp. 4–8. The list is partly quoted and partly paraphrased from these two sources.

21. Jacques Bourquin, "A Year's Advertising on Swiss Television," *Bulletin d'Informations*, January 1966, pp. 6–8.

22. *Ibid.*, p. 8.

23. *Televisie Nieuws*, 6:1–2 (1966); *Televisie Nieuws*, 9:4 (1966); *Televisie Nieuws*, 3:1–3 (1967); *Televisie Nieuws*, 4:1–4 (1967); *EBU Review*, 93B:35 (September 1965); J. van Santbrink, "Legislation and the Broadcasting Institutions in the Netherlands. Part II: The Transitional System (1965) for Sound Broadcast-

ing and Television in the Netherlands," *EBU Review*, 102B:53–59 (March 1967). Information also was received from the Dutch broadcasting authorities.

24. London *Times*, September 2, 1966, p. 15.

25. "Radio in the Soviet Bloc," *East Europe*, November 1959, p. 15.

26. *Yugoslav Yearbook 1965*, pp. 142–144, 172–173.

27. *Yugoslav Yearbook 1964*, p. 179.

28. *Ibid.*, pp. 181, 183.

29. Bruno Vasari's *Financial Aspects of Broadcasting* is a study of *RAI* budget practices by the Director of Central Administration of Italian broadcasting. Although prepared as a guide for emerging nations, it does supply certain types of important information about broadcast finance.

Chapter V. Programs: Information

1. Carl L. Becker, *Freedom and Responsibility in the American Way of Life*, p. 33.

2. Quotation from Lenin cited by Alex Inkeles in *Public Opinion in Soviet Russia: A Study in Mass Persuasion*, p. 136.

3. Andrei Y. Vyshinsky, *The Law of the Soviet State*, pp. 617–618. Although at present Vyshinsky is no longer in favor in the USSR, the statement quoted seems entirely in line with current Soviet practice.

4. *Broadcasting. Copy of the Royal Charter for the Continuance of the British Broadcasting Corporation.* June 1964. (Cmd. 2385), 3 (a), Preamble; *Broadcasting. Copy of the Licence and Agreement dated 19th December 1963, between Her Majesty's Postmaster General and the British Broadcasting Corporation.* 1964. (Cmd. 2236), 14 (1, 2). These and further details are discussed in Paulu, *British Broadcasting in Transition*, pp. 22–23.

5. Statement by Sir Ian Jacob, *Ariel*, Autumn, 1954, p. 4.

6. *Television Act 1964*, Sec. 1 (4); *Television Act 1954*, Sec. 3 (1b).

7. "Denmark: Broadcasting Act, 1959," *EBU Review*, 60B:22 (March 1960).

8. *Statuts*, Art. 1.

9. Henning Wicht, "Sound Radio in the Federal Republic of Germany," *EBU Review*, 78B:27 (March 1963).

10. "Law on the 'Hessischer Rundfunk' of 2nd October 1948," II, para. 2.

11. Sedat Tolga, "Legislation Setting up the Radio-Television Association of Turkey," *EBU Review*, 88B:51 (November 1964).

12. *EBU Review*, 89B:35 (January 1965); *License*, Art. 13.

13. *Les Cahiers Luxembourgeois: Radio-Télé Luxembourg*, p. 32.

14. Wolfgang Kleinert, "Organizational Role of Broadcasting," *OIRT*, No. 4:148 (1960).

15. *OIRT*, No. 6:253 (1960), cf. Gerhard Eisler, "Twenty Years of the German Democratic Radio," *OIRT*, No. 2:6 (1965).

16. "Rubrics of Sofia Radio," *OIRT*, No. 2:56 (1960); "Bulgarian Radio," *OIRT*, No. 5:5 (1961).

17. Information on Czech, Hungarian, Polish, and Rumanian policies was derived from personal interviews with broadcasting officials in those countries.

18. *Yugoslav Yearbook 1964*, p. 117.

19. N. Sakontikov, "The Experience of the Central Television of the USSR in the Field of Political Broadcasts," *OIRT*, No. 6:3 (1962).

20. "Ukrainian Radio," *OIRT*, No. 5:27 (1961).

21. V. Nesterovitch, "The Way to Human Hearts," *OIRT*, No. 8:99 (1961).

22. *BBC Handbook 1967*, pp. 40–43. Information as to BBC schedules may be obtained from any week's issue of *The Radio Times*.

23. The yearly editions of the *World Radio TV Handbook* and of the *Internationales Handbuch für Rundfunk und Fernsehen* provide much current information

about the radio and television services of all countries. Another source is UNESCO's *World Communications: Press, Radio, Television, Film,* published in 1964, although it is out of date in view of the constant changes that take place.

24. Henning Wicht, "Sound Radio in the Federal Republic of Germany," *EBU Review,* 78B:25–29 (March 1963); "Germany (Federal Republic) NDR/SFB: Third Radio Programme's New Term," *EBU Review,* 95B:32 (January 1966); "Significance and Aims of *Norddeutscher Rundfunk's* Third Programme," *EBU Review,* 72B:30–31 (March 1962).

25. *Annuario RAI 1966,* pp. 13–22, 376, 320.

26. *Yugoslav Yearbook 1965,* pp. 11–12.

27. Rostislav Behal, "To Satisfy Listeners," *OIRT Information,* No. 8:1–2 (1965).

28. *OIRT Information,* No. 3:8–9 (1966); *OIRT Information,* No. 4:21–22 (1966); *OIRT Information,* No. 11:16 (1966).

29. *BBC Handbook 1967,* pp. 25–29, 217, 224.

30. Philippe Regueneau, "The Second French Television Programme," *EBU Review,* 86B:9–12 (July 1964).

31. "Third Programme Choice for Viewers: Accent on Education," *EBU Review,* 88B:43 (November 1964).

32. "Italy: Second Television Programme," *EBU Review,* 71B:26–27 (January 1962); RAI, *RAI,* p. 5.

33. Information about Russian television was obtained from the International Relations Department of the USSR State Committee for Broadcasting and Television.

34. *BBC Handbook 1967,* p. 45.

35. *Internationales Handbuch 1965/66,* pp. C40–41.

36. *Annuario RAI 1966,* p. 319.

37. *Yugoslav Yearbook 1965,* p. 68.

38. *BBC Handbook 1967,* p. 38.

39. *Annuario RAI 1966,* p. 325.

40. *Yugoslav Yearbook 1965,* pp. 148–149.

41. Jiri Hronek, "The Future of Radio in the Era of Television," *OIRT,* No. 3:21–23 (1963); F. K. Zeman, "The Future of Radio in the Era of Television," *OIRT,* No. 4:3–5 (1963); "Special Number, Sound Radio Today," *EBU Review,* 103B (May 1967).

42. Jean-Pierre Méroz, "The Community of French-Language Radio Programmes," *EBU Review,* 86B:30–31 (July 1964); Jean-Pierre Méroz, "Community of French-Language Radio Programmes," *EBU Review,* 92B:31–32 (July 1965).

43. Viktor Ergert, "Joint Production of Television Films by the German-Language Television Services," *EBU Review,* 65B:28–29 (January 1961); G. Gerhard, "Meeting of German-speaking Schools Broadcasting Services," *EBU Review,* 72B:23 (March 1963).

44. Henrik Hahr, "Scandinavia Pools Television Resources," *EBU Review,* 59B: 2–4 (January 1960); *EBU Review,* 83B:9 (January 1964).

45. *OIRT Information,* No. 4:10 (1964); *Variety,* February 22, 1967, p. 44.

46. M. Muller, "International Contacts of the GDR Radio," *OIRT,* No. 1:8–10 (1962); *OIRT Information,* No. 4:16–17 (1966). The OIRT publishes a bulletin in several languages, including English, that lists radio and television programs produced by its members that are available for foreign use.

47. *OIRT Information,* No. 3:16–18 (1964).

48. *Ibid.,* No. 4:1 (1964).

49. *Ibid.,* No. 9:5 (1964); USIA Research and Reference Service, *Overseas Television Developments in 1964,* p. 3.

50. *Statutes of the European Broadcasting Union,* Art. 2; *This Is the EBU.*

51. "International Radio Week 1965," *EBU Review,* 95B:28 (January 1966).

52. Paul Bellac, "Origin and First Steps of the EBU Programme Committee: Start of Eurovision," *EBU Review,* 85B:21–24 (May 1964); *This Is the EBU,* pp. 35–48.

53. "Eurovision Programme Statistics up to 31st December 1963," *EBU Review,* 85B: 25–27 (May 1964).

54. "News Overhauls Sport in the Eurovision Exchanges," *EBU Review,* 91B: 12–13 (May 1965).

55. *EBU Review,* 48B:30–31 (April 1958); Paul Gilson, "UNESCO Conference on Programme Exchanges: Exchanges in Prospect and Prospects of Exchanges," *EBU Review,* 53B:18–20 (February 1959); "European Agreement on Programme Exchanges by Means of Television Films," *EBU Review,* 53B:40–41 (February 1959); "Eurovision and Its Legal Problems," *EBU Review,* 55B:24–28 (June 1959); "Entry into Force of the Two European Agreements," *EBU Review,* 68B:26 (July 1961).

56. D. Schmotz and H. Seidowski, "Some Notes Concerning the Prospects of Programme Exchange in the Framework of Intervision," *OIRT,* No. 6:11–14 (1965); Nikolai Skatchko, "Five Years," *OIRT,* No. 2:3–5 (1965).

57. N. A. Skatchko, "Years of Development," *OIRT,* No. 2:3–6 (1966).

58. Rose Matuz, "TV News in the Framework of Television Political Programmes," *OIRT,* No. 2:3 (1963).

59. Zbygniew Lipinski, "Radio Commentary," *OIRT,* No. 4:151 (1960).

60. *Broadcasting. Copy of the Licence and Agreement dated 19th December 1964, between Her Majesty's Postmaster General and the British Broadcasting Corporation.* December 1964. (Cmd. 2236.) 14 (3); *Television Act 1964,* 18 (1–4).

It is interesting to notice the sequence by which the British Broadcasting Corporation gradually gained permission to publicly identify as such those materials broadcast at government request. In the first *Licence and Agreement,* effective January 1, 1927, it was stated that the BBC should "send from all or any of the said Stations any matter" which a government department might require, and that the Postmaster General could "require the Corporation to refrain from sending any broadcast matter." (*Licence and Agreement,* Cmd. 2756, Sec. 4 (2, 3).) The Ullswater Committee, acting upon the BBC's request, recommended in 1935 that the Corporation "should have discretionary power to announce that any given notice is broadcast at the request of a named Department." (*Report of the Broadcasting Committee 1935,* Cmd. 5091, Sec. 54.) The new *Licence,* which took effect in 1937 stated that when the Corporation was requested to broadcast any specified material, the notice from the Postmaster General "may specify whether or not the Corporation may at its discretion announce that the Notice has been given." (*Licence and Agreement,* Cmd. 5329, Sec. 4 (3).)

The ensuing license, while continuing authority for the government to request announcements or other material to be broadcast, said that the Corporation "when sending such matter may at its discretion announce that it is sent at the request of a named Department." And while continuing the authority of the Postmaster General to require the Corporation to "refrain from sending any broadcast matter," it went on to say that the notice should specify "whether or not the Corporation may at its discretion announce Notice has been given." (*Licence and Agreement,* Cmd. 5329, Sec. 4, (2, 3).) These provisions were continued in the *Licence* of 1946. (*Licence and Agreement,* Cmd. 5975, Sec. 4 (3, 4).)

By the time of the 1952 license, this had been altered so that the BBC was free to decide whether or not to announce, not only that it *had* been required to broadcast some particular material, but also if required to *refrain* from any type of broadcasting. (*Licence and Agreement,* Cmd. 8579, Sec. 15, (3, 4).) This authority has been continued in subsequent licenses, and its equivalent provided for the ITA. (*Television Act 1964,* #18 (1–4).)

61. *Statuts,* Article 5.

62. Albert Namurois, "The New Charter for Broadcasting in Belgium," *EBU Review*, 63B:9 (September 1960).

63. *EBU Review*, 89B:35 (January 1965); *License*, Art. 13.

64. "Law on the 'Hessischer Rundfunk' of 2nd October 1948," II, para. 3 (3, 5).

65. UNESCO, *News Agencies: Their Structure and Operation*, pp. 179–180.

66. UNESCO, *Statistics on Radio and Television 1950–1960*, pp. 61–69, 83–87. These figures must be used with care in view of the differences in classification from country to country.

67. *Internationales Handbuch 1965/66*, pp. C44, 94, 147, 190.

68. *Annuario RAI 1966*, pp. 319, 325.

69. UNESCO, *World Communications: Press, Radio, Television, Film*, p. 366.

70. Olof Rydbeck, "Coordinating the Two Services," *EBU Review*, 91B:40–42 (May 1965).

71. *License*, Art. 13 (3).

72. Kenneth Dick, "The Newsfilm Agency's Expanding Role in the Age of Speed," *EBU Review*, 91B:36–37 (May 1965).

73. Jacques Sallebert, "The Trials and Triumphs of an Overseas Representative," *EBU Review*, 91B:24–25 (May 1965).

74. Hans-Joachim Reiche, "The Daily Achievement in the Newsroom," *EBU Review*, 91B:15–17 (May 1965); Deutsches Fernsehen, *Tagesschau*.

75. *Televisie Nieuws*, No. 21:2 (1964).

76. For a critical view of German television news coverage, see Alphons Silbermann, *Bildschirm und Wirklichkeit*.

77. BBC, *The Year That Made the Day*.

78. "The Greatest TV Coverage in the History of Dutch Television," *Televisie Nieuws*, No. 3:1–2 (1966).

79. Luca di Schiena, "Television Expeditions Abroad," *EBU Review*, 91B:19–20 (May 1965).

80. "Live Eurovision Transmission of Matterhorn Centenary Ascent," *EBU Review*, 93B:30 (September 1965).

81. *BBC Handbook 1967*, pp. 65–70; *Annual Report and Accounts of the British Broadcasting Corporation 1965–66*, pp. 37–41.

82. Egon Wagner, "Report from the Federal Republic of Germany," *EBU Review*, 76B:45 (November 1962).

83. "Law on the 'Hessischer Rundfunk' of 2nd October 1948," II, para. 3 (6); material provided by Hessischer Rundfunk.

84. Material supplied by Radiodiffusion-Télévision Belge.

85. Information supplied by the Swiss Broadcasting Corporation.

86. Material supplied by Sveriges Radio.

87. *New York Times*, October 21, 1965, p. 2.

88. London *Times*, December 2, 1965, p. 10.

89. *Broadcasting*, December 20, 1965, p. 68.

90. *New York Times*, January 26, 1966, p. 5.

91. *New York Times*, November 17, 1966, p. C15; *New York Times*, March 5, 1967, pp. 1, 17; *New York Times*, March 6, 1967, p. 32.

92. *OIRT Information*, No. 7:1 (1964).

93. *New York Times*, December 15, 1966, pp. 1, 14, 19.

94. USIA, Research and Reference Service, *Overseas Television Developments in 1964*, p. 3.

95. "Law on the 'Hessischer Rundfunk' of 2nd October 1948," II, para. 3 (7); information supplied by Hessischer Rundfunk.

96. Information supplied by Radiodiffusion-Télévision Belge.

97. Information supplied by Nederlandse Radio Unie.

98. Information supplied by Sveriges Radio.

99. RAI, *Tribuna Politica: Regolamento*; RAI, *Special Political and Electoral Broadcasts.*

100. *OIRT Information*, No. 5:10 (1964).

101. The main sources for this section are the religious broadcasting issue of the *European Broadcasting Union Review*, 97B: May 1966, and information supplied directly by the broadcasting organizations.

102. *WRTH 1967*, pp. 122–124, 250. Jesús García Jiménez, "Spanish Religious Programmes on Radio and Television," *EBU Review*, 97B:40–42 (May 1966).

103. "Vatican Radio," *EBU Review*, 97B:12–15 (May 1966); *WRTH 1967*, p. 135.

104. Muhtar Korukou, "The Problems of Religious Broadcasting on Turkish Radio and Television," *EBU Review*, 97B:43–44 (May 1966).

105. Popy Rigopoulou, "A Brief Survey of Greek Religious Broadcasting," *EBU Review*, 97B:24–25 (May 1966).

106. Pierre Petit and Jacques Anjubault, "Full Range of Options in French Radio and Television Programming," *EBU Review*, 97B:16–19 (May 1966).

107. "Law on the 'Hessischer Rundfunk' of 2nd October 1948," II, para. 3 (2, 3).

108. See above, p. 74. *Televisie Nieuws*, No. 4:1–2 (1963); Bernard F. Takkenberg, "The Structure of Religious Broadcasting on Netherlands Radio and Television," *EBU Review*, 97B:29–31 (May 1966).

109. Gunnar Dahmen, "Popularity of Church Services in Scandinavia," *EBU Review*, 97B:36–37 (May 1966).

110. Bernard F. Takkenberg, "The Structure of Religious Broadcasting on Netherlands Radio and Television," *EBU Review*, 97B:30 (May 1966).

111. Jesús García Jiménez, "Spanish Religious Programmes on Radio and Television," *EBU Review*, 97B:41 (May 1966).

112. Kenneth Lamb, "Freedom and Responsibility in Religious Broadcasting," *EBU Review*, 97B:45–48 (May 1966); Henry Jones, "The Relationship between Broadcasters and the Churches," *EBU Review*, 97B:49–52 (May 1966).

113. Pierre Petit and Jacques Anjubault, "Full Range of Options in French Radio and Television Programming," *EBU Review*, 97B:18 (May 1966).

114. Information about in-school broadcasting in Europe may be obtained from the following sources: *Proceedings of the International Conference of Broadcasting Organizations on Sound and Television School Broadcasting*; European Broadcasting Union, *First Seminar for Producers and Directors of Schools Television* (1962), *Second Seminar for Producers and Directors of Schools Television* (1963), and *Third Seminar for Producers and Directors of Schools Television* (1965). Six *EBU Reviews* have been devoted almost entirely to educational broadcasting: 69B: September 1961; 70B: November 1961; 72B: March 1962; 75B: September 1962; 82B: November 1963; 88B: November 1964. The first 1966 issue of the *Review* of the OIRT also is devoted principally to broadcasts for children.

115. Antonio Carlos Leonidas, "School Broadcasting," *EBU Review*, 75B:20 (September 1962).

116. J. Gorus, "Flemish-Language Sound Broadcasts to Schools," *EBU Review*, 70B:8 (November 1961).

117. Valdemar Christensen, "School Broadcasting," *EBU Review*, 70B:10 (November 1961).

118. Maria Wisniewska, "School Television Programmes in Poland," *OIRT*, No. 1:10 (1965).

119. John Scupham, "New Trends in School Broadcasting: Some Reflections on the Tokyo Conference," *EBU Review*, 88B:9–15 (November 1964).

120. Henri Dieuzeide, "School Broadcasting: Its Fundamental Purposes and the Individual Characteristics of Sound and Television with Special Attention to Audi-

NOTES

ence Organization and the Assessment of Results," *EBU Review*, 88B:16 (November 1964); Henri Dieuzeide, *Teaching Through Television*, p. 25.

121. "School Broadcasting as a Substitute for Direct Teaching," UNESCO, *Broadcasting to Schools*, pp. 173–174.

122. Hrvoje Juracic, "Broadcasting and the Schools," *EBU Review*, 72B:6 (March 1962).

123. "Teaching by Television," *EBU Review*, 69B:4–7 (September 1961).

124. A. J. J. van der Made, "Sound and Television Programmes for Schools," *EBU Review*, 70B:34–35 (November 1961); Helmi Palmen, "The Use of Film-Strips and Slides in School Radio," *EBU Review*, 85B:32–33 (May 1964).

125. Henri Dieuzeide, "School Television in France," *Proceedings of the International Conference of Broadcasting Organizations on Sound and Television School Broadcasting*, pp. 105–112; "Educational Radio and Television: RTF Broadcasts to Schools," *EBU Review*, 70B:22–27 (November 1961); Henri Dieuzeide, "Notes for a Rational Theory on the Use of Radio and Television for Educational Purposes," *EBU Review*, 75B:45–57 (September 1962); Henry R. Cassirer, *Television Teaching Today*, pp. 197–216; "School Broadcasting," *EBU Review*, 75B:11–14 (September 1962).

126. Franz Reinholz, "School Sound Programmes in the Federal Republic of Germany," *Proceedings of the International Conference of Broadcasting Organizations on Sound and Television School Broadcasting*, pp. 88–92; Paul Gerhardt, "Broadcasting for Schools," *EBU Review*, 70B:28–31 (November 1961); G. Gerhard, "Meeting of German-Speaking Schools Broadcasting Services," *EBU Review*, 72B:23 (March 1962); Ursula Klamroth, "School Television Programmes," *EBU Review*, 73B:23–25 (May 1962).

127. Golina Jankovic, "Educational Sound Programmes in Yugoslavia," *Proceedings of the International Conference of Broadcasting Organizations on Sound and Television School Broadcasting*, pp. 74–78; Hrvoje Juracic, "The First Year of School Television," *EBU Review*, 69B:33–36 (September 1961); Hrvoje Juracic, "Broadcasting and the Schools," *EBU Review*, 72B:4–9 (March 1962); *Yugoslav Yearbook 1964*, pp. 82–84.

128. Felicia Wagrowska, "School Sound Programs in Poland," *Proceedings of the International Conference of Broadcasting Organizations on Sound and Television School Broadcasting*, pp. 141–144; "New Programme Forms, Experiences and Organization of Work: Polish Television," *OIRT*, No. 6:18 (1961); Maria Wisniewska, "Popular-Scientific and Educational Broadcasts of the Polish Television," *OIRT*, No. 4:10–11 (1964).

129. Zdenek Michalec, "Czechoslovak Television Programmes for Schools," *OIRT*, No. 4:151–153 (1960).

130. RAI, *School Broadcasting in Italy*, pp. 15–30.

131. RAI, *This Is Telescuola*; RAI, *School Broadcasting in Italy*; Italo Neri, "Educational Television," *EBU Review*, 69B:14–17 (September 1961); Maria Grazia Puglisi, "Telescuola Enters Its Second Year," *EBU Review*, 59B:12–13 (January 1960); Maria Grazia Puglisi, "Origin and Aims of School Television in Italy," *Proceedings of the International Conference of Broadcasting Organizations on Sound and Television School Broadcasting*, pp. 43–49; Henry R. Cassirer, *Television Teaching Today*, pp. 217–223.

132. Heinz von Plato, "Eurovision and Youth Programmes," *EBU Review*, 84B:6 (March 1964).

133. A. Menjshikova, "The Radio Broadcasting in the Out-of-School Education of Children," *OIRT*, No. 5:22 (1965).

134. S. Böhme, "Socialistic Programmes for Children on German GDR Television," *OIRT*, No. 2:53 (1960).

135. "Educational Broadcasts of the Rumanian Radio for Children and Youth," *OIRT*, No. 4:21 (1962).

136. A. Menjshikova, "The Radio Broadcasting in the Out-of-School Education of Children," *OIRT*, No. 5:16, 18 (1965).

137. "Educational Broadcasts of the Rumanian Radio for Children and Youth," *OIRT*, No. 4:20 (1962).

138. Zdenek Michalec, "Television and Children's Activity," *OIRT*, No. 4:6–8 (1961).

139. S. Böhme, "Socialistic Programmes for Children on German GDR Television," *OIRT*, No. 2:55–56 (1960).

140. Rik Vanden Abbeele, "A Trick of the Light . . . ," *EBU Review*, 84B:10–11 (March 1964).

141. "Emphasis on Audience Participation," *EBU Review*, 84B:12 (March 1964).

142. Adelino Feijoo Teikeira, "Marionettes Lead the Way," *EBU Review*, 84B: 21–22 (March 1964).

143. Heinz von Plato, "Eurovision and Youth Programmes," *EBU Review*, 84B:7 (March 1964).

144. A. Menjshikova, "The Radio Broadcasting in the Out-of-School Education of Children," *OIRT*, No. 5:15–22 (1965).

145. Victor Popa, "Broadcasts for Children of the Rumanian Radio and Television," *OIRT*, No. 1:11–15 (1966). I also had an interview with Mr. Popa which covered much of the same material in his article.

146. Inga Dahlsgaard, "Denmarks Radio and Adult Education," *EBU Review*, 70B: 12–14 (November 1961); H. Schaafsma, "TELEAC—an Educational Television Service in the Netherlands," *EBU Review*, 102B:15–17 (March 1967).

147. Tadeusz Kornecki, "The Role and Tasks of Popular Scientific Broadcasts: The Work of the Department of Educational Broadcasts of the Polish Radio," *OIRT*, No. 4:3–5 (1964); M. Wisznewska, "Popular-Scientific and Educational Broadcasts of the Polish Television," *OIRT*, No. 4:10–11 (1964).

148. Henry R. Cassirer, "Television Extends Higher Education: A Pilot Project in Poland," *UNESCO Chronicle*, September 1966, pp. 346–351.

149. "New Broadcasts of the Department of Political Broadcasts of the Rumanian Radio and Television," *OIRT*, No. 4:15–16 (1963).

150. Herman Verdin, "Complementing Basic Instruction," *EBU Review*, 94B:11–12 (November 1965).

151. Information supplied by Czechoslovak Radio. Ctibor Tahy, "Czechoslovakia," in Brian Groombridge, ed., *Adult Education and Television: A Comparative Study in Three Countries*, pp. 55–84.

152. Maria Gheorghieva, "Popularization of Scientific and Technical Knowledge on the Air," *OIRT*, No. 6:270 (1960).

153. N. Kartsov, "New Aspects in the Artistic Broadcasts of the Soviet Radio," *OIRT*, No. 5:192–194 (1960).

154. "Radio Cultural University," *OIRT*, No. 1:5–7 (1962).

155. Werner Zscheile, "Educational Programmes for Adults of the Television of the German Democratic Republic," *OIRT*, No. 2:16–21 (1965); "The Television Academy—Educational Programmes of the German Television Service," DDR Deutscher Fernsehen, *Press Information*; *OIRT Information*, No. 5:9–10 (1965); Alois Schardt, "Bayerischer Rundfunk's 'Telekolleg,'" *EBU Review*, 102B:40–41 (March 1967).

156. Jofre Dumazedier, *Television and Rural Adult Education: the Tele-Clubs in France.*

157. "School Broadcasting," *EBU Review*, 75B:12–14 (September 1962).

158. A. de Chambure, "An Educational Impulse for Viewers in France," *EBU Review*, 94B:15–17 (November 1965).

NOTES

159. Theo Fleischman, "International University of the Air: Services to Education," *EBU Review,* 70B:60–61 (November 1961); Armand Lanoux, "International University of the Air: the VIIth Session," *EBU Review,* 70B:61–64 (November 1961); Armand Lanoux, "The Largest University in the World: The International Radio-Television University (URI)," *EBU Review,* 83B:22–24 (January 1964).

160. "Modern Language Courses," *EBU Review,* 55B:4–6 (June 1959); 65B:10–25 (January 1961); 75B:59–62 (September 1962); 77B:12–17 (January 1963); Christopher Dilke, "English by Television," *EBU Review,* 89B:18–20 (January 1965); Christopher Dilke, *English by Radio and Television.*

161. RAI, *School Broadcasting in Italy,* pp. 66–82; Maria Grazia Puglisi, "Television and the Fight against Illiteracy," *EBU Review,* 82B:6–11 (November 1963); Italo Neri, "Educational Television," *EBU Review,* 75B:16 (September 1962); Italo Neri, "From Illiteracy to the Outposts of Scientific Research," *EBU Review,* 94B:27–29 (November 1965).

162. "Third Programme Choice for Viewers: Accent on Education," *EBU Review,* 88B:43 (November 1964); *OIRT Information,* No. 12:12–13 (1964); "Aims and Structure of Third Television Programme in Northwest Germany," *EBU Review,* 94B:65 (November 1965); Helmut Oeller, "The Outlook for Adult Education in the Society of Tomorrow," *EBU Review,* 94B:19–20 (November 1965); Helmut Oeller, "The Bayerischer Rundfunk Study Programme," *Television and Adult Education,* January 1965, pp. 5–16.

163. Joseph Rovan, "The Third Programme of the Bavarian Television," *Television and Adult Education,* January 1965, p. 2.

164. Henri Dieuzeide, *Teaching through Television,* pp. 49–62; "School Broadcasting," *EBU Review,* 75B:12 (September 1962).

165. M. R. Bataille, "Agricultural Broadcasting in France," *EBU Review,* 80B:21–22 (July 1963). Most of this issue of the *EBU Review* was devoted to agricultural broadcasting.

166. Olle Berglund, " 'Selling' Agriculture on Television," *EBU Review,* 80B:27–29 (July 1963).

167. Poul Jørgensen, "Agriculture as Television Material," *EBU Review,* 80B:17–20 (July 1963).

168. Jens Fr. Lawaetz, "Agrovision," *EBU Review,* 80B:11–12 (July 1963).

169. "The Bulgarian Radio," *OIRT,* No. 5:202–203 (1960).

170. Mihaly Kovacs, "The Hungarian Radio," *OIRT,* No. 5:204–206 (1960).

171. A. Sroga, "The Polish Radio," *OIRT,* No. 1:14–16 (1961).

172. "Rural Broadcasts," *OIRT,* No. 6:274–275 (1960).

173. " 'Foremost Agricultural Workers Compete': Broadcasts of the Rumanian Radio," *OIRT,* No. 4:24–25 (1962).

174. Heinz Stange, "Agricultural Broadcasts of the GDR Radio," *OIRT,* No. 1:17–19 (1964).

175. Alojzy Sroga, "Economic and Agricultural Broadcasts of the Polish Radio," *OIRT,* No. 2:17–20 (1964).

176. Lists of broadcast times and frequencies are given in all editions of the *World Radio and TV Handbook* as well as in the *Internationales Handbuch für Rundfunk und Fernsehen,* which lists the frequencies used in short-wave broadcasting from 2306 up to 29005 kilocycles. (See for example the *Handbuch for 1965/66,* pp. E108–188.) There also are periodic summaries by the USIA Research and Reference Service, such as *Developments in International Broadcasting by Communist Countries in 1965.*

177. *BBC Handbook 1967,* p. 103. For a review of current British activities in a world setting, see pp. 79–102. See also Don R. Browne, "The Limits of the Limitless Medium—International Broadcasting," *Journalism Quarterly,* 42 (No. 1):82–86, 164 (Winter 1965).

178. USIA Research and Reference Service, *Overseas Television Developments in 1963*, pp. 2–3.

179. *Internationales Handbuch 1965/66*, pp. C204–213; Don R. Browne, "RIAS Berlin: A Case Study of a Cold War Broadcast Operation," *Journal of Broadcasting*, X (No. 2):119–135 (Spring 1966).

180. "Television Wooing of West Germans," London *Times*, July 29, 1957, p. 6; "Germany's Radio War," *Economist*, January 20, 1962, pp. 234–235.

181. USIA Research and Reference Service, *Overseas Television Developments in 1964*, pp. 3–4; *East Europe*, 13 (No. 3):13 (March 1964); *OIRT Information*, No. 9:5–6 (1965). Some information was gathered from conversations with broadcasting executives in both Eastern and Western Europe.

182. *BBC Handbook 1966*, pictures between pp. 96–97.

Chapter VI. Programs: Entertainment

1. For a recent survey of both public and private patronage of the arts in Europe, see Frederick Dorian, *Commitment to Culture*.

2. *Internationales Handbuch 1965/66*, p. C83.

3. *Ibid.*, pp. C125–126, 147. Unless otherwise indicated all percentages are of total program times.

4. *Ibid.*, p. C190.

5. *Annuario RAI 1966*, p. 319. Some music on local services was not included in these figures.

6. *Ibid.*, p. 325.

7. *Yugoslav Yearbook 1965*, pp. 67, 70, 148.

8. Data received directly from the broadcasting organizations named.

9. Corneel Mertens, "Radio and Light Music," *EBU Review*, 90B:6–7 (March 1965); "Second International Festival of Light and Dance Music in Leipzig," *OIRT*, No. 2:54–64 (1961).

10. Henri Barraud, "The Twenty-Fifth Anniversary of the National Orchestra of the R. T. F.," *EBU Review*, 53B:2–3 (February 1959).

11. *Internationales Handbuch 1965/66*, p. C82, 121, 145, 205.

12. The RIAS Orchestra has now become a Radio Orchestra, serving also Sender Freies Berlin.

13. RAI, *RAI*, p. 8.

14. *Internationales Handbuch 1965/66*, pp. C214–215.

15. Jack Bornoff, "Broadcasting and the International Festivals," *EBU Review*, 57B:12–15 (September 1959). American educational stations carry a good deal of tape recorded music from European festivals.

16. *Yugoslav Yearbook 1965*, p. 215.

17. *EBU Review*, 98A:171–172 (August 1966).

18. *Variety*, December 28, 1966, p. 43.

19. See, for example, Radiodiffusion-Télévision Belge, *Reconnaissance des Musiques Modernes*, p. 4.

20. "Music on Television," *OIRT*, No. 1:1 (1960).

21. V. Merkulov, "Some Ideas Regarding Intervision Musical Broadcasts," *OIRT*, No. 2:21–22 (1964).

22. *Annuario RAI 1966*, pp. 213–219.

23. *Ibid.*, pp. 269–271. A list of premières and other significant musical broadcasts in Germany, both East and West, is given in *Internationales Handbuch 1965/66*, pp. C234–241. There is a detailed list of music on Yugoslav radio in *Yugoslav Yearbook 1965*, pp. 110–141. The weekly program magazines of all countries usually list details of the major light and serious music programs.

24. Radiodiffusion-Télévision Belge, *Reconnaissance des Musiques Modernes*.

NOTES

25. *OIRT Information*, No. 2:4–6 (1965).

26. V. S. Osravsky and I. D. Simonov, "Development of New Electromusical Instruments in the USSR," *OIRT*, No. 6:29–33 (1963).

27. *EBU Review*, 96A:74–75 (April 1966); *OIRT Information*, No. 5:11 (1964); G. Steinke, "On the Way to a New Sound Art?" *OIRT*, No. 6:19–21 (1965).

28. Allessandro Grassi, "Notes on the Subject of Electronic Music," *EBU Review*, 70B:66–73 (November 1961).

29. Marcel Lobet, *Dix Années de Ballets à la Télévision Belge*, pp. 73–78.

30. There is a summary of Italian television ballet in RAI, *Dieci Anni di Televisione in Italia*, pp. 142–143.

31. See, for example, an account of folk song compositions in Bulgaria: Gheorghi Boyddjiyev, "Competitions of Amateurs—Form of Finding New Radio Singers, Collecting Folk Songs, and Promoting Song Traditions of the Bulgarian People," *OIRT*, No. 4:11 (1961).

32. "Broadcasts Devoted to the Life and Work of Georg Enescu," *OIRT*, No. 1: 6–7 (1963); Juri Berkovac, "Symphony, Vocal and Chamber Music in the Broadcasts of the Czechoslovak Radio," *OIRT*, No. 4:20–21 (1963); Dietrich Brennecke, "An Hour of Music for Youth—a Series of the Berlin Radio," *OIRT*, No. 5:6–8 (1965).

33. Lionel Salter, "Orchestral Music on Television," *EBU Review*, 62B:8–12 (July 1960). On the televising of opera see Lionel Salter, "Opera at Home," *EBU Review*, 96B:12–18 (March 1966).

34. *Yugoslav Yearbook 1964*, pp. 79–82.

35. Briggs, *Birth of Broadcasting*, p. 281.

36. *Annuario RAI 1966*, pp. 220–223, 319; *Annuario RAI 1965*, p. 333.

37. Norddeutscher Rundfunk, *Hörspiel im Winter 1964/65*; Süddeutscher Rundfunk, *Das Hörspiel Oktober-Dezember 1964*. For a list of original radio plays broadcast in both West and East Germany in 1964, see *Internationales Handbuch 1965/66*, pp. C226–233.

38. Roger L. Cole, "European Radio Drama Still Lives," *NAEB Journal*, January–February 1965, pp. 3–9.

39. Horst Angermüller, "The Radio Play in the German Democratic Republic," *OIRT*, No. 4:12–15 (1965).

40. See also *OIRT Information*, No. 5:5–6 (1964); *OIRT Information*, No. 9:8 (1964); *OIRT Information*, No. 2:9–10 (1965).

41. Lájos Lorand, "The Theatre at the Microphone and Cultural-Educational Work," *OIRT*, No. 1:10–11 (1960).

42. Anna Major, "A Report on the 'Szabo Family' and Serial Broadcasts in General," *OIRT*, No. 6:15–18 (1965); *OIRT Information*, No. 4:12–13 (1964); *OIRT Information*, No. 3:13–14 (1966).

43. Wladyslaw Zeslawski, "The Radio Novel," *OIRT*, No. 2:11–15 (1965); *OIRT Information*, No. 10:11 (1965); Alexander Malachowski, "Literary Reportage," *OIRT*, No. 4:22–25 (1965); "Literary Artistic Reportage on the Rumanian Radio," *OIRT*, No. 4:23 (1962).

44. Veselin Nikolov, "New Literary Broadcasts of the Sophia Radio," *OIRT*, No. 4:9–10 (1961).

45. RAI, *RAI*, p. 5; *Annuario RAI 1966*, pp. 272–275, 325.

46. For a list of television plays broadcast in East and West Germany during 1964, see *Internationales Handbuch 1965/66*, pp. C242–247; Norddeutscher Rundfunk, *Fernsehspiele im Winter 1964/65*.

47. Werner Fehlig, "Development of Dramatic Art in the Television of the German Democratic Republic," *OIRT*, No. 2:17–19 (1962).

48. DDR Deutscher Fernsehfunk, *Fernseh Film Katalog*, introduction.

49. Jon Klossowicz, "The Television Theatre," *OIRT*, No. 1:17–18 (1965).

50. M. Radnev, "Theatrical Broadcasts of the Bucharest Television Studio," *OIRT*, No. 1:8–10 (1963).

51. *Yugoslav Yearbook 1964*, pp. 114, 123–124.

52. Barber, 174–175; *Televisie Nieuws*, No. 11:4 (1963).

53. The *EBU Review* devoted portions of five issues to television design: 62B: July 1960; 64B: November 1960; 66B: March 1961; 71B: January 1962; 76B: November 1962. These included impressive pictures of the sets described in the articles.

54. *OIRT Information*, No. 10:5 (1965); DDR Deutscher Fernsehfunk, *Press Information Bulletin*.

55. Descriptions of these and many other documentary programs on Dutch television may be found in the monthly publication of the Dutch television press department, *Televisie Nieuws*. The programs referred to above are described in the issues listed below: No. 3:8 (1963); No. 4:9 (1963); No. 5:9, 10 (1963); No. 6:9 (1963); No. 7:11 (1963); No. 8:5 (1963); No. 10:1–2, 10 (1963); No. 10:8 (1963); No. 12:6 (1964); No. 19:5 (1964); No. 20:6 (1964); No. 26:2 (1965); No. 27:2 (1965); No. 28:5 (1965); No. 31:5 (1965); No. 8:2, 4 (1966).

56. *Internationales Handbuch 1965/66*, pp. C40–41, 83.

57. UNESCO, *World Communications: Press, Radio, Television, Film*, p. 289.

58. *Annuario RAI 1966*, pp. 319, 325.

59. *New York Times*, April 17, 1966, p. 64L.

60. Barber, p. 169–171; *EBU Review*, 91B:78 (May 1965); *EBU Review*, 96B: 65 (March 1966).

61. Examples are taken from the monthly Netherlands Foundation press release, *Televisie Nieuws*.

62. *Minneapolis Tribune*, April 22, 1956, p. 7F; *New York Times*, March 30, 1956, p. 12.

63. T. R. Fyvel, "The Impact of Television in Europe," *London Calling*, March 14, 1957, pp. 8–9, 12.

64. *Variety*, December 2, 1959, p. 37.

65. *EBU Review*, 51B:13 (October 1958).

66. *OIRT Information*, No. 5:13 (1964).

67. *Televisie Nieuws*, No. 11:7 (1963); *Televisie Nieuws*, No. 13:1–2 (1964); *Televisie Nieuws*, No. 5:1–2 (1966).

68. Thomas Petry, "West German TV—The Way Ahead," *Television Quarterly*, II (No. 3):58–67 (Summer 1963).

69. Jack Gould, "TV: West German Sees More Satire Than We Do," *New York Times*, April 5, 1966, p. 87L.

70. Thomas J. Hamilton, "Censorship as the Germans Do It," *New York Times*, January 16, 1966, p. 4E.

71. *Annuario RAI 1966*, pp. 34, 276–278; *Annuario RAI 1965*, pp. 387–389.

72. For partial lists of the films broadcast on West and East German television see *Internationales Handbuch 1965/66*, pp. C243–249. Material on Yugoslavia's use of films is given in *Yugoslav Yearbook 1965*, pp. 167–172.

73. *Variety*, February 9, 1966, p. 24.

74. Serge Kuznetsov, "Films in the Moscow Television," *OIRT*, No. 3:7–8 (1964).

75. *Broadcasting*, May 16, 1966, pp. 27–29; Al Husted, "American Television Abroad," *Electronic Age*, Autumn 1966, pp. 31–34. Although most of this is entertainment, these figures also include such documentaries as CBS's "Twentieth Century" and NBC's "Victory at Sea." (Dizard, "U.S. Television's Overseas Markets," *Television: A World View*, pp. 155–178. See also the monthly magazine, *Telefilm International*.)

76. *New York Times*, May 23, 1966, p. 71M.

77. USIA Research and Reference Service, *Overseas Television Developments in 1964*, p. 18.

78. London *Times,* June 3, 1966, p. 12; *New York Times,* June 29, 1966, p. 75M; London *Times,* November 17, 1966, p. 20; *Annual Report and Accounts of the British Broadcasting Corporation 1965–66.* (Cmd. 3122.) pp. 25–28.

79. Société Suisse de Radiodiffusion et Télévision, *Annuaire 1964,* pp. 5, 53.

80. *Annuario RAI 1965,* pp. 37, 39, 40, 69.

81. *Ibid.,* pp. 366–367, 415–416.

82. *Internationales Handbuch 1965/66:* Bayerischer Rundfunk, p. C40; Radio Bremen, p. C94; Saarländischer Rundfunk, p. C104; Süddeutscher Rundfunk, pp. C124–125; Südwestfunk, p. C147; Zweites Deutsches Fernsehen, p. C190; Deutscher Fernsehfunk (East German Television), p. C221.

83. Karel Mikyska, "Relays of Sports Events in Television," *OIRT,* No. 5:8–15 (1963).

84. *EBU Review,* 68B:14 (July 1961).

85. *OIRT Information,* No. 6:5–6 (1964).

86. Werner Cassbaum, "Full Use of Productional Possibilities of Television in Sports Transmissions," *OIRT,* No. 2:12–13 (1963).

87. *Televisie Nieuws,* No. 7:1–2 (1963).

88. Joseph Virdis and Frank R. Tappolet, "La Retransmission des Jeux Olympiques de Tokyo," Société Suisse de Radiodiffusion et Télévision, *Annuaire 1964,* pp. 13–16; Ernst P. Braun, "The Tokyo Olympics: An EBU Operation," *EBU Review,* 89B:9–12 (January 1965).

89. "Intervision," *OIRT,* No. 2:3–5 (1962); Nikolai Skatchko, "Five Years," *OIRT,* No. 2:3–5 (1965).

90. N. A. Skatchko, "Years of Development," *OIRT,* No. 2:3–6 (1966).

91. "Eurovision Programme Statistics, January 1, 1964 Through December 31, 1964," *EBU Review,* 91B:51–53 (May 1965); "News Overhauls Sport in the Eurovision Exchanges," 91B:12–13 (May 1965).

92. *Televisie Nieuws,* No. 18:1–2 (1964); *Televisie Nieuws,* No. 27:1–2 (1965).

93. *Etudes de Radio-Télévision: Les Cahiers RTB,* No. 1:2 (1963).

94. Kurt Schulz, "Radio Information from the Cybernetic Point of View," *OIRT,* No. 6:22–24 (1965).

95. Andrzej Sitinski, "Public Polls in Radio and Television Broadcasting," *OIRT,* No. 4:3–7 (1965); "Relations and Cooperation of the Polish Radio with Listeners," *OIRT,* No. 6:262–266 (1960); Janina Zajac, "The Work of the Department of Programme Evaluation," *OIRT,* No. 3:19–20 (1965).

96. Jaroslav Kotouc, "Television Research in the Central Television Studio of Prague," *OIRT,* No. 2:23–25 (1964); Zdenka Kadlecova, "The Czechoslovak Radio and Its Listeners," *OIRT,* No. 1:21–23; Jiri Lederer, "Research of Listeners to the Czechoslovak Radio," *OIRT,* No. 5:3–5 (1963).

97. For example, there is nothing on the order of Leo Bogart's *The Age of Television.*

98. Data supplied by the broadcasting organizations cited except for the United Kingdom: *BBC Handbook 1967,* p. 198; Italy, *Annuario RAI 1966,* pp. 364–365.

99. RAI, *Ricerche nel Settore della Radio,* pp. 17, 18.

100. *Televisie Nieuws,* No. 4:6–8 (1963).

101. *Ibid.,* p. 6.

102. Jaroslav Kotouc, "Television Research in the Central Television Studio of Prague," *OIRT,* No. 2:23–25 (1964).

103. RAI, *Il pubblico della Radio nel 1963,* p. 106.

104. *Annuario RAI 1965,* p. 189.

105. *Televisie Nieuws,* No. 30:1 (1965); No. 2:1 (1966).

106. Radio-Télévision Belge, *Le Referendum du Xè Anniversaire de la Télévision,* 1963, p. 5.

107. "Le Programme Culturel de la Radio Belge: Indication sur son Public," *Etudes de Radio-Télévision: Les Cahiers RTB*, No. 2:48–50 (1963).

108. RAI, *Il Terzo Programma e il suo Pubblico*, pp. 9, 16.

109. *Annuario RAI 1965*, pp. 186–187; RAI, *Il Pubblico della Radio nel 1963*, pp. 25, 40.

110. Gabriel Thoveron, "L'Écoute Radio en Belgique: Caractèrs et Évolution," *Etudes de Radio-Télévision: Les Cahiers RTB*, No. 6:2 (1964).

111. "Notes sur Quelques Effets de l'Expansion de la TV sur les Loisirs en Belgique," *Etudes de Radio-Télévision: Les Cahiers RTB*, No. 3/4:107–120 (1963).

112. USIA, Research and Reference Service, *Overseas Television Developments in 1964*, p. 18.

113. *OIRT Information*, No. 10:11 (1965).

114. For further discussion of this topic see Paulu, *British Broadcasting in Transition*, pp. 183–188.

Chapter VII. Conclusions and Comments

1. USIA, Research and Reference Service, *The Impact of American Commercial Television in Western Europe*; Wilson P. Dizard, *Television: A World View*, pp. 283–292.

Bibliography

There has been relatively little systematic research and writing about continental broadcasting, compared to what has been published in the United States and what now is emerging in the United Kingdom. (A brief survey of continental research is given above on pp. 223–234.) Nevertheless, there is more material than most students—surely than most Americans—realize.

The best collection is in the library of the European Broadcasting Union in Geneva, which in addition to many books has reports from various European broadcasting organizations. The library of the International Telecommunication Union, also in Geneva, has much excellent technical material.

All broadcasting organizations publish some reports as well as many brochures and program guides, although these usually are available only on direct application. The Belgian, Italian, and German systems are among the leaders in research and publication. For current information the most convenient sources are the *Reviews* of the EBU in Geneva and the OIRT in Prague.

The publications cited in this book are classified below in three categories: Books and Pamphlets; Newspapers and Periodicals; and Government publications.

Books and Pamphlets

Alexandrova, G., V. Galianova, and N. Rubinsteina. *Political Dictionary*. Moscow: Department of Political Literature, 1940.

Barber, Russell. *Eurovision as an Expression of International Cooperation in Western Europe*. Unpublished Ph.D. dissertation, Northwestern University, 1965.

Becker, Carl. *Freedom and Responsibility in the American Way of Life*. New York: Alfred A. Knopf, 1945.

Bogart, Leo. *The Age of Television*. Second Ed. New York: F. Unger, 1958.

Briggs, Asa. *The History of Broadcasting in the United Kingdom*. Vol. I, *The Birth of Broadcasting*. Vol. II, *The Golden Age of Wireless*. London: Oxford University Press, 1965.

British Broadcasting Corporation. *BBC Handbook 1957*. London: British Broadcasting Corporation, 1957.

_____. *BBC Handbook 1966*. London: British Broadcasting Corporation, 1966.

_____. *BBC Handbook 1967*. London: British Broadcasting Corporation, 1967.

_____. "Why No Continuous Pop?" *BBC Record 45*. London: British Broadcasting Corporation, October 1966.

_____. *Listening to the World. A lecture by John Campbell . . . in the Concert Hall at Broadcasting House*. London: British Broadcasting Corporation, 1967.

_____. *The Year That Made the Day*. London: British Broadcasting Corporation [1954].

Les Cahiers Luxembourgeois: Radio Télé Luxembourg, 1961.

Cassirer, Henry R. *Television Teaching Today.* Paris: UNESCO, 1960.

Codding, George A., Jr. *Broadcasting Without Barriers.* Paris: UNESCO, 1959.

_____. *The International Telecommunication Union: An Experiment in International Cooperation.* Leiden: E. J. Brill, 1952.

Coons, John E., ed. *Freedom and Responsibility in Broadcasting.* Evanston, Ill.: Northwestern University Press, 1961.

Constitution of the Union of Soviet Socialist Republics. Washington, D.C.: Information Bulletin, Embassy of the USSR, 1945.

Council of Europe. *European Agreement for the Prevention of Broadcasts Transmitted from Stations Outside National Territories.* European Treaty Series No. 53. Strasbourg: 1965.

DDR Deutscher Fernsehfunk. *Fernseh Film Katalog.* Berlin: Presse-Abteilung des Deutschen Fernsehfunks, 1964.

_____. *Presseinformationen: TV.* Berlin: Presse-Abteilung des Deutschen Fernsehfunks, 1965.

Deutsches Fernsehen. *Tagesschau.* n.d.

Dieuzeide, Henri. *Teaching Through Television.* Paris: Organisation for Economic Co-operation and Development, 1953.

Dilke, Christopher. *English by Radio and Television.* London: British Broadcasting Corporation, 1966.

Dizard, Wilson P. *Television: A World View.* Syracuse: Syracuse University Press, 1966.

Dorian, Frederick. *Commitment to Culture.* Pittsburgh: University of Pittsburgh Press, 1964.

Dumazedier, Jofre. *Television and Rural Adult Education: the Tele-Clubs in France.* Paris: UNESCO, 1956.

Emery, Walter B. *Five European Broadcasting Systems.* Journalism Monographs No. 1. Austin, Texas: Association for Education in Journalism, 1966.

European Broadcasting Union. *Advertising on Radio and Television.* Geneva: European Broadcasting Union, 1966. Monograph No. 4.

_____. *First Seminar for Producers and Directors of Schools Television. Summary.* Geneva: European Broadcasting Union, 1963.

_____. *Second Seminar for Producers and Directors of Schools Television. Summary.* Geneva: European Broadcasting Union, 1964.

_____. *Statutes of the European Broadcasting Union (E.B.U.) 1961.* Geneva: European Broadcasting Union, 1961.

_____. *Third Seminar for Producers and Directors of Schools Television. Summary.* Geneva: European Broadcasting Union, 1966.

_____. *This Is the EBU.* Geneva: European Broadcasting Union, 1965.

Florinsky, Michael T., ed. *Encyclopedia of Russia and the Soviet Union.* New York: McGraw-Hill, 1961.

Groombridge, Brian, ed. *Adult Education and Television: A Comparative Study in Three Countries.* London: UNESCO, 1966.

Hessischer Rundfunk. *Presse-Information. Law on the 'Hessischer Rundfunk' of 2nd October 1948.* Frankfurt: Hessischer Rundfunk.

Holt, Robert, and John E. Turner, eds. *Soviet Union: Paradox and Change.* New York: Holt, Rinehart, and Winston, 1963.

Inkeles, Alex. *Public Opinion in Soviet Russia: A Study in Mass Persuasion.* Cambridge: Harvard University Press, 1950.

Internationales Handbuch für Rundfunk und Fernsehen 1965/66. Hamburg: Hans-Bredow-Instit für Rundfunk und Fernsehen, 1965.

International Telecommunication Union. *From Semaphore to Satellite.* Geneva: General Secretariat of the ITU, 1965.

_____. *International Telecommunication Convention. Final Protocol to the Con-*

BIBLIOGRAPHY

vention; Additional Protocols to the Convention, Resolutions, Recommendations and Opinions. Geneva, 1959. Geneva: General Secretariat of the ITU, 1959.

――――――. *International Telecommunication Convention. Final Protocol to the Convention. Additional Protocols to the Convention. Resolutions, Recommendations and Opinions. Montreux, 1965.* Geneva: General Secretariat of the ITU, 1965.

――――――. *Radio Regulations: Additional Radio Regulations; Additional Protocol; Resolutions and Recommendations.* Geneva: General Secretariat of the ITU, 1959.

――――――. *International Telecommunication Union: What It Is—What It Does— How It Works.* Geneva: General Secretariat of the ITU, n.d.

Jugoslovenska Radiotelevizija Yearbook 1965. Belgrade: Jugoslovenska Radiotelevizija and Yugoslav Institute of Journalism, 1965.

League of Nations. *Treaty Series.* Vol. 186, Nos. 4301–4327. [Geneva] 1938.

Lobet, Marcel. *Dix Années de Ballets à la Télévision Belge.* Brussels: Les Cahiers RTB [1964].

Martin, L. John. *International Propaganda: Its Legal and Diplomatic Control.* Minneapolis: University of Minnesota Press, 1958.

Mill, John Stuart. "On Liberty," in *Political Philosophers.* New York: Carlton House, 1947.

Milton, John. "Areopagitica: A Speech for the Liberty of Unlicensed Printing." *Areopagitica and Other Prose Writings.* New York: Book League of America, 1929.

Namurois, Albert. *Problems of Structure and Organization of Broadcasting in the Framework of Radiocommunications.* Geneva: European Broadcasting Union, 1964.

National Society for the Study of Education. *The Fifty-Third Yearbook. Mass Media and Education.* Chicago: University of Chicago Press, 1954.

Netherlands Radio Union in the Evolution of Dutch Broadcasting. Heuvellaan, the Netherlands: NRU Press Service, n.d.

Norddeutscher Rundfunk. *Fernsehspiele im Winter 1964/65.* Hamburg: Norddeutscher Rundfunk, 1965.

――――――. *Hörspiel im Winter 1964/65.* Hamburg: Norddeutscher Rundfunk, 1965.

――――――. *Sender Freies Berlin. Das Dritte Programm Frühjahr 1965.* Hamburg: 1965.

Paulu, Burton. *British Broadcasting in Transition.* Minneapolis: University of Minnesota Press, 1961.

――――――. *British Broadcasting: Radio and Television in the United Kingdom.* Minneapolis: University of Minnesota Press, 1956.

Pigé, François. *La Télévision dans le Monde—Organisation Administrative et Financière.* Paris: Société Nationale des Entreprises de Presse, 1962.

Pons, Eugène. *General Considerations on Licence Fees for Radio and Television Sets.* Geneva: European Broadcasting Union, 1964.

Pousseur, Henri. *Reconnaissance des Musiques Modernes.* Charleroi, Belgium: Radiodiffusion-Télévision Belge, n.d.

Radio-Télévision Belge. *Le Referendum du Xè Anniversaire de la Télévision.* Report No. 44. Brussels: Radiodiffusion-Télévision Belge, 1964.

RAI-Radiotelevisione Italiana. *Annuario RAI 1965.* Rome: Edizioni Radiotelevisione Italiana, 1965.

――――――. *Annuario RAI 1966.* Rome: Edizioni Radiotelevisione Italiana, 1966.

――――――. *Dieci Anni di Televisione in Italia.* Rome: Edizioni Radiotelevisione Italiana, 1964.

――――――. *Il Pubblico della Radio nel 1963.* No. 9. Turin: Edizioni Radiotelevisione Italiana, 1964.

――――――. *Il Terzo Programma e il Suo Pubblico.* No. 4. Turin: Edizioni Radio Italiana, 1959.

_____. *Proceedings of the International Conference of Broadcasting Organizations on Sound and Television School Broadcasting.* Rome: Edizioni Radio Italiana, 1961.

_____. *Ricerche nel Settore della Radio.* No. 8. Turin: Edizioni Radiotelevisione Italiana, 1963.

_____. *School Broadcasting in Italy.* Rome: Radiotelevisione Italiana, 1961.

_____. *Special Political and Electoral Broadcasts.* Rome: Edizioni Radio Italiana, 1966.

_____. *RAI.* New York: RAI Corporation, 1963.

_____. *This Is RAI.* Turin: Edizioni Radio Italiana, 1963.

_____. *This Is Telescuola.* Rome: Radiotelevisione Italiana, 1964.

_____. *Tribuna Politica: Regolamento.* Rome: Radiotelevisione Italiana, 1964.

Sender Freies Berlin. "Stereophony in Radio," in *Informations.* Berlin: Sender Freies Berlin, n.d.

Siebert, Fred S., Theodore Peterson, and Wilbur Schramm. *Four Theories of the Press: The Authoritarian, Libertarian, Social Responsibility and Soviet Communist Concepts of What the Press Should Be and Do.* Urbana, Ill.: University of Illinois Press, 1956.

Silbermann, Alphons. *Bildschirm und Wirklichkeit. Über Presse und Fernsehen in Gegenwart und Zukunft.* Frankfurt: Ullstein, 1966.

Société Suisse de Radiodiffusion et Télévision. *Annuaire 1964.* 33rd Report. Berne: Société Suisse de Radiodiffusion et Télévision, 1964.

Süddeutscher Rundfunk. *Das Hörspiel Oktober–Dezember 1964.* Stuttgart: Süddeutscher Rundfunk, 1964.

Sveriges Radio. *Sveriges Radio Aktiebolag (Articles of Association).* Stockholm: Sveriges Radio, n.d.

Terrou, Fernand, and Lucien Solal. *Legislation for Press, Film, and Radio.* Paris: UNESCO, 1951.

UNESCO. *Broadcasting to Schools.* Paris: UNESCO, 1949.

_____. *News Agencies: Their Structure and Operation.* Paris: UNESCO, 1953.

_____. *Report of the Meeting of Experts on the Use of Space Communications by the Mass Media.* Paris: UNESCO, 1966.

_____. *Statistics on Radio and Television 1950–60.* Paris: UNESCO, 1963.

_____. *Television: A World Survey.* Paris: UNESCO, 1953.

_____. *World Communications: Press, Radio, Television, Film.* New York: UNESCO, 1964.

United Nations General Assembly. *Official Records.* Fifth Session, Supplement No. 3 (a/1345), 1950. New York: United Nations, 1951.

_____. *Official Records.* Fifth Session, 325 Plenary Meeting, December 14, 1950. New York: United Nations, 1955.

_____. *General Assembly Resolution.* IX (No. 841): December 17, 1954.

United States Federal Communications Commission. *The Communications Act of 1934.* Washington, D.C.: U.S. Government Printing Office, 1961.

United States Information Agency. Research and Reference Service. *Developments in International Broadcasting by Communist Countries in 1965.* Washington, D.C.: 1966.

_____. *Impact of American Commercial Television in Western Europe.* Washington, D.C.: 1962.

_____. *Overseas Television Developments in 1963.* Washington, D.C.: 1964.

_____. *Overseas Television Developments in 1964.* Washington, D.C.: 1965.

United States Treaties and Other International Agreements. Treaty Series No. 962. *North American Regional Broadcasting Agreement. . . .* Washington, D.C.: U.S. Government Printing Office, 1941.

BIBLIOGRAPHY

————. *International Telecommunication Convention*. Buenos Aires: General Secretariat of the ITU, 1952.

Vasari, Bruno. *Financial Aspects of Broadcasting*. Geneva: European Broadcasting Union, 1965.

Vyshinsky, Andrei Y., ed. *The Law of the Soviet State*. New York: MacMillan, 1948.

Werbung im Rundfunk GmbH. *Werbefunk und Werbefernsehen in Hessen: Planungsunterlagen*. Frankfurt: Werbung im Rundfunk GmbH, 1966.

World Radio TV Handbook 1965. Nineteenth Ed. Hellerup, Denmark: World Radio-Television Handbook Company, Ltd., 1964.

World Radio TV Handbook 1966. Twentieth Ed. Hellerup, Denmark: World Radio-Television Handbook Company, Ltd., 1965.

World Radio TV Handbook 1967. Twenty-first Ed. Hellerup, Denmark: World Radio-Television Handbook Company, Ltd., 1966.

Yugoslav Radio and Television Yearbook 1964. Belgrade: Yugoslav Radio and Television and Yugoslav Institute of Journalism, 1965.

Newspapers and Periodicals

Ariel. London.

Atlas. Marion, Ohio.

Broadcasting. Washington, D.C.

Broadcasting Yearbook 1967. Washington, D.C.

Bulletin de la Radio Télévision Scolaire. Paris.

Daily Report. Supplement. USSR and East Europe. The 23rd Congress of the Soviet Communist Party. Proceedings and Related Materials. Washington, D.C.

East Europe. New York.

EBU Bulletin of Documentation and Information. Geneva.

EBU Review. Geneva.

Economist. London.

Electronic Age. New York.

L'Enseignement du Journalism. Strasbourg.

Entreprise. Paris.

Etudes de Radio-Télévision. Les Cahiers RTB. Brussels.

FIEJ-Bulletin d'Informations. Paris.

Financial Times. London.

France Actuelle. Paris.

Gazette. Leiden, the Netherlands.

I.F.J. Documentation Service. Brussels.

Journal of Broadcasting. Los Angeles.

Journal of Politics. Gainesville, Fla.

Journalism Quarterly. Iowa City, Iowa.

Listener. London.

London Calling. London.

Manchester Guardian Weekly. Manchester.

Minneapolis Sunday Tribune. Minneapolis, Minn.

Le Monde. Paris.

NAEB Journal. Urbana, Ill.

New York Times. New York.

OIRT Information. Prague.

L'Onde Electrique. Paris.

Quarterly of Film, Radio, and Television. Los Angeles.

Quarterly Journal of Speech. New York.

Radio and Television Review of the International Radio and Television Organization. Prague.

Radio Times. London.

Rundfunktechnische Mitteilungen. Hamburg.
Saturday Review. New York.
Soviet Press in Translation. Madison, Wis.
Der Spiegel. Hamburg.
Spot Radio Rates and Data. Skokie, Ill.
Spot Television Rates and Data. Skokie, Ill.
Telefilm International. Hollywood, Calif.
Televisie Nieuws. Hilversum, Holland.
Television and Adult Education. Paris.
Television Quarterly. New York.
Television Today. London.
Times. London.
Variety. New York.

Miscellaneous Government Publications

FRANCE

Assemblée Nationale. Chambre des Députés. *Annales. Débats Parlementaires.* 1964.
Office de Radiodiffusion-Télévision Française. *Statuts, Régime Financier, Comités de Programmes.* Paris: Journaux Officiels, July 1964.

SWITZERLAND

Concession pour l'usage des installations électriques et radio électriques de l'entreprise des postes, téléphones, et télégraphes (suisses) en vue de la diffusion publique de programmes de radiodiffusion sonore et de télévision. Berne, 1964.

UNITED KINGDOM

Annual Report and Accounts of the British Broadcasting Corporation 1965–66. London: Her Majesty's Stationery Office (Cmd. 3122.) 1966.
Broadcasting: Copy of the Licence and Agreement, dated the 29th day of November 1946 between Her Majesty's Postmaster General and the British Broadcasting Corporation. (Cmd. 6975.) 1946.
Broadcasting: Copy of the Licence and Agreement dated the 12th Day of June 1952 between Her Majesty's Postmaster General and the British Broadcasting Corporation. (Cmd. 8579.) 1952.
Broadcasting: Copy of the Licence and Agreement dated 19th December 1963, between Her Majesty's Postmaster General and the British Broadcasting Corporation. (Cmd. 2236.) 1963.
Broadcasting: Copy of the Royal Charter for the Continuance of the British Broadcasting Corporation. (Cmd. 8605.) 1962.
Broadcasting: Copy of the Royal Charter for the Continuance of the British Broadcasting Corporation. (Cmd. 2385.) 1964.
Broadcasting: Drafts of (1) Royal Charter . . . for the Continuance of the British Broadcasting Corporation; and (2) Licence and Agreement between His Majesty's Postmaster General and the British Broadcasting Corporation. (Cmd. 5329.) 1936.
Broadcasting: Presented to Parliament by the Postmaster General by Command of Her Majesty, December 1966. (Cmd. 3169.) 1966.
Marine, &c., Broadcasting (Offences): *A Bill to Suppress Broadcasting from Ships, Aircraft and Certain Marine Structures.* (Bill 94.) London: Her Majesty's Stationery Office, 1966.
Parliamentary Debates. House of Commons. *Official Reports.* Fifth Series. Vols. 528, 548, 621.

BIBLIOGRAPHY

Report of the Broadcasting Committee 1935. (Cmd. 5091.) 1936.

Television Act 1954. 2 and 3 Eliz. 2 Ch. 55. London: Her Majesty's Stationery Office, 1954.

Television Act 1964. Chapter 21. London: Her Majesty's Stationery Office, 1964.

Wireless broadcasting: Drafts of (1) Royal Charter . . . for the Incorporation of the British Broadcasting Corporation; and (2) Licence and Agreement . . . between H. M. Postmaster General and . . . the British Broadcasting Corporation. (Cmd. 2756.) 1926.

UNITED STATES

Schenck v. The United States. 249 U.S. 47. (1919).

Index

Adenauer, Konrad: influence on German television, 67

Advertising: 4, 7, 94–112, 239–240; in West Germany, 4, 67, 68, 98–102; in the Netherlands, 72–73, 75, 109; in Sweden, 81–82; on billboards in sports stadiums, 94n; pressures for and against, 95–96; early history of, 95, 259n17–260n17; on Europe 1 (Saar), 96–97; on private commercial stations, 96–98; in Luxembourg, 97–98; on state-chartered systems, 98–109; in Italy, 102–105; in Switzerland, 105–109; in USSR, 110, 110n; in Hungary, 110–111; in Rumania, 111; in Yugoslavia, 111–112; prohibited for political purposes, 155; American and European systems compared, 239–240

Albania: does not have broadcast advertising, 110; experimental television, 130

American Forces Network, 27, 208

Andorra: does not have television, 37; Radio des Vallées, 87; Radio Andorra, 87n; receiver license not required, 90

Ansagerinnen, 131–132

Areopagitica: A Speech for the Liberty of Unlicensed Printing to the Parliament of England, 48

Atlantic City Conference, 1947, 12, 16, 17n, 19

Audience research: for in-school broadcasting, 166, 168, 169, 171; for continental broadcasting, 223–234, 244–245; number and distribution of radio licenses, 226–228; number and distribution of television licenses, 228–230; program preferences, 230–232, 244–245

Austria: community television antennas, 44n; discussion programs in, 156

Becker, Carl: on freedom of speech, 49

Belgium: outlaws pirate stations, 23; radio facilities of, 26, 31, 197; television line standards, 33, 33n, 34, 34n; television facilities, 38, 41; community television antennas, 44n; legal structure and organization of broadcasting, 69–71; political broadcasting, 152–153; discussion programs, 156; in-school programs, 164; music programs, 192, 195; ballet telecasts, 195–196; audience research, 224, 231, 232–233

British Broadcasting Corporation (BBC): pirate broadcasters, 21–24 *passim*; FM radio, 28; radio studios, 32n; Coronation programs for Europe, 39; imaginary news bulletins cause riots, 47; absence of government control, 63n; Radio Luxembourg, 95n; program objectives, 120; radio networks, 124; Third Programme, 124, 125, 182; television networks, 129; radio program percentages, 132; television program percentages, 133; identification of materials broadcast at government request, 143, 266n60; political broadcasting, 151–152; religious programs, 161; English by radio and television, 180–181; television music, 198; documentary programs, 206. *See also* United Kingdom

INDEX

Speakerines, 131–132

Stalin, Joseph: use of radio, 3; on freedom of the press, 49

Stereophonic broadcasting, 28–29n

Stockholm, Sweden: conferences on broadcasting frequencies, 14, 14n

Sweden: outlaws pirate broadcasters, 21–23 *passim*; wired distribution of radio programs, 29; legal structure and organization of broadcasting, 79–82; operating expenses, 112, 113; radio program pattern, 126; news broadcasting, 145, 149n; political broadcasting, 153; discussion programs, 156–157; religious programs, 161; in-school programs, 164, 165; agricultural programs, 185; music programs, 192; radio drama, 200–201; American telefilms on Swedish television, 216n

Switzerland: radio facilities, 28; wired distribution of radio programs, 29, 30, 236; television line standards, 34–35; April fool radio program causes disturbance, 47; referendum on television, 82–83; legal structure and organization of broadcasting, 82–85; languages used, 82n; program objectives, 84, 121; television advertising, 105–109; television networks, 129n; radio news, 144, 145; television news, 148; sports programs, 151, 218; political broadcasting, 153; music programs, 197; television light entertainment, 212

Teleclubs (French adult education on television), 179, 184

Telescuola, 164, 166, 170–172

Television Acts of 1954 and 1964 (ITA), 120

Television broadcasting facilities: channels classified and assigned, 12–13, 14n; standards for black and white, 33–35; standards for color, 35–37, 236–237; first uses of, 37, 37n; countries with, 37–38, 128–129n; studios and equipment, 41–43; video tape recorders, 42–43; community antennas, 43–44n; for coverage in remote areas, 43, 151, 219–220; network patterns, 128–131; hours on the air, 131; use of closed circuits, 183–184, 220; world systems for, 249–252. *See also* Eurovision; International Telecommunication Union; Intervision

Third programs, in radio and television, 124, 125, 125n, 126, 182–183, 191, 231–232

Turkey: religious programs, 6, 159; program objectives, 121

Union of Soviet Socialist Republics: reservations to ITU conventions, 11; boycotts Copenhagen Convention of 1948, 14; jamming by, 18, 19; radio facilities, 26–27; wired distribution of radio programs, 29, 30–31, 236; color television standards, 35–37; television facilities, 37, 38–39, 42, 42n; community television antennas, 44n; Molnya satellites, 45, 146; freedom of speech in, 49–50, 51, 119n; legal structure and organization of broadcasting, 52–55; Communist party and broadcasting, 54–55; international broadcasts, 54, 186, 187; licenses not required for receivers, 90; advertising, 110; program objectives, 122–123, 194; radio program pattern, 127–128; television program pattern, 131; television program percentages, 133–134; radio news, 144, 145; television news, 146, 149; children's programs, 173, 174–175; adult education programs, 177–178; third television service, 183; agricultural programs, 185; music programs, 191, 192, 194, 195, 197, 198; ballet telecasts, 196; light entertainment on television, 210, 210n; film programs, 213, 214, 215; audience research, 226

United Kingdom: jams Greek broadcasts to Cyprus, 18–19, 20; pirate broadcasting stations for, 21–25 *passim*; wired distribution of radio programs, 30n; television line standards, 33, 34, 37, 129; television facilities, 37, 42; receiver licenses, 91, 93. *See also* British Broadcasting Corporation

United States: Communications Act of 1934, 10n, 116n, 245; reservations to ITU conventions, 11; disregards Copenhagen Convention of 1948, 14, 14n; financial support for pirate broadcasting, 21; uses European frequencies, 27–28; Federal Communications Commission, 28, 36n, 47, 245; television line standards, 33;

color television standards, 36n; cited during debates on commercial broadcasting, 96, 239; news about on European broadcasts, 150, 150n; American films on European television, 212–216 *passim*, 242–243; American and European broadcasting compared, 235–245 *passim*

Vatican City: does not have television stations, 37; receiver license not required, 90; religious programs, 159
Voice of America, 208

War of the Worlds (radio program), 47
Welles, Orson, 47
West Germany. *See* German Federal Republic
Wired distribution systems: description, 29–31, 236; licenses required, 91

Yugoslavia: press law, 50–51; legal structure and organization of broadcasting, 57–58; advertising, 111–112; operating expenses, 114–115; Mihajlo Mihajlov imprisoned, 117; program objectives, 122; radio program pattern, 126; radio program percentages, 133; television program percentages, 133; television documentaries, 149; discussion programs, 158; in-school programs, 164, 165, 169; music programs, 190–191; radio drama, 200; audience research, 225, 225n, 233